METHODS

OF LOGIC

METHODS

OF LOGIC

THIRD EDITION

W. V. QUINE
Edgar Pierce Professor of Philosophy
Harvard University

HOLT, RINEHART AND WINSTON, INC.
New York   Chicago   San Francisco
Atlanta   Dallas   Montreal
Toronto   London   Sydney

TO MARJORIE

PREFACE

This book is meant to engender a feeling for logical structure and validity and to develop convenient techniques of formal reasoning. In its previous editions it has been the textbook for twenty years in my basic logic course, a college course of one semester. The course is not Freshman Thought, but it is a course for the general student and it does not presuppose Freshman Thought or other special training. The course also serves as a prerequisite for specialized courses in logic; and it is hoped correspondingly that *Methods in Logic* may furnish a foundation for further building.

With a view to accommodating varied purposes, I have marked thirty percent of the book as dispensable. For a short course, or a course covering supplementary matters of some other sort, those portions may conveniently be omitted.

This third edition, which is a new book by half, exceeds previous editions in the variety of its methods. In the logic of truth functions I retain the methods of previous editions as central, but take up alternative methods too, partly for historical interest and partly for the sake of multiple perspectives on the subject matter. I take up truth tables, normal-form tests, and the method of axioms. Material is added on the problem of simplifying truth functions.

In the logic of one-place predicates the text departs again from previous editions, and matters become more intuitive in various ways. I postpone quantifiers for a while and work rather with a more algebraic logic of predicates. This and the Boolean algebra of classes are contrasted ontologically but equated algorithmically. The decision procedure is geared to validity, rather than to consistency as was the method of canonical schemata in previous editions. The decision procedure is extended to cover the monadic logic of quantification when quantification is introduced. We get much of the logic of quantification, including the rules of passage to prenex form, before ascending to polyadic predicates.

On ascending to these, I press another decision procedure for a while: a validity test for prenex schemata of the Bernays-Schönfinkel class, those whose universal quantifiers come first. Only after that do I retreat to a general proof procedure—and not even then to a method of natural deduction, such as dominated the general logic of quantification in previous editions. My main method at this point is rather the simple procedure of *reductio ad absurdum* by instantiation. It is the method that was used in the completeness proof in the appendix of the preceding edition. In this edition it is used again in the completeness proof but also, using it as basis, I introduce and justify a variety of alternative proof procedures. Some of them proceed by Skolem functions; some are axiomatic; and the last of the series is natural deduction. The title of the book becomes more appropriate than ever.

There is the drawback here of an *embarras de richesse*, leaving the reader in a quandary as to which method to try on the next problem. But this drawback is more than offset by the increased depth of understanding that comes of approaching logical structure from a plurality of angles. Anyway, a more nearly single-minded line can be recovered by skipping the material that is marked as omissible.

There is more text than before by a fifth. (Closer spacing and wider format hide this.) Questions of decidability and completeness are treated somewhat more fully than before. On the other hand the thin sections on set theory at the end of the book have been thinned yet a little more, because some of their coverage seemed arbitrary where so much else was passed over. I have preferred to shift the burden of these themes to *Set Theory and Its Logic*.

At the suggestion of the publisher I have extended the historical notes and the exercises and have answered exercises selectively in the back pages.

In the first edition, twenty years ago, I thanked the Harvard University Press for permission to borrow from Section 2 of my *Mathematical Logic* and Ginn and Company for permission to adapt some examples from *Elementary Logic*. The passages concerned are still here, and the appreciation remains. I also reiterate my thanks of twenty years ago to Professors George D. W. Berry, George B. Burch, Joseph L. Cobitz, Nelson Goodman, Robert F. McNaughton, and James W. Oliver, to Dr. Oliver Straus, and to my wife, for their helpful criticisms of the work in progress.

The second edition, much revised, should have come out in 1956, but was delayed three years by an inadvertent reprinting of the old version. In it I had Professor Burch to thank again for interim improvements; also Professors Alonzo Church, Marcus W. Dick, Richard S. Palais, William T. Parry, Samuel J. Todes, and Andrew P. Ushenko, and Mr. Donald P. Quimby.

In this third edition I am further indebted, for useful suggestions and corrections, to Professors George Boolos, Leigh S. Cauman, Burton Dreben, Dagfinn Føllesdal, Peter T. Geach, Hiram J. McLendon, Charles Parsons, Joseph L. Ullian, and, again as of old, James W. Oliver. To Ullian my debt is greatest, for a productive examination of most of the manuscript.

There is a correction due to Geach—one of his lesser ones, indeed—that I would report here for the purpose of sharing the pleasure of my surprise. I had cited '$(x)(\exists y)(y$ is mother of $x)$' as a platitude, but Geach pointed out that it is false, even when the variables are restricted to persons. Some value of 'y' would have to be impersonal, on pain of vicious regress.

W. V. Q.

Cambridge, Massachusetts

CONTENTS

PART IV. GLIMPSES BEYOND

INTRODUCTION

Logic, like any science, has as its business the pursuit of truth. What are true are certain statements; and the pursuit of truth is the endeavor to sort out the true statements from the others, which are false.

Truths are as plentiful as falsehoods, since each falsehood admits of a negation which is true. But scientific activity is not the indiscriminate amassing of truths; science is selective and seeks the truths that count for most, either in point of intrinsic interest or as instruments for coping with the world.

For truth ordinarily attaches to statements by virtue of the nature of the world. It is a commonplace, inaccurate but not unfounded, that a statement is true when it corresponds to reality, when it mirrors the world. A fundamental way of deciding whether a statement is true is by comparing it, in some sense or other, with the world—or, which is the nearest we can come, by comparing it with our experience of the world.

Strictly speaking, what admit of truth and falsity are not statements as repeatable patterns of utterance, but individual events of statement utterance. For, utterances that sound alike can vary in meaning with the occasion of the utterance. This is due not only to careless ambiguities, but to systematic ambiguities which are essential to the nature of language. The pronoun 'I' changes its reference with every change of speaker; 'here' changes its reference with every significant movement through space; and 'now' changes its reference every time it is uttered.

So the crucial point of contact between description and reality is to be sought in the utterance of a statement on the occasion of an experience which that statement utterance directly reports. The seeing of a green patch, and the simultaneous utterance 'Green patch now', constitute the sort of composite event which, in its rare occurrences, gladdens the heart of the epistemologist.

Such events, fundamental though they are epistemologically, are rare because of the social nature of language. Language is a social institution serving, within its limitations, the social end of communication; so it is not to be wondered that the objects of our first and commonest utterances are socially shared physical objects rather than private experiences. Physical objects, if they did not exist, would (to transplant Voltaire's epigram) have had to be invented. They are indispensable as the public common denominators of private sense experience.

But utterances about physical objects are not verifiable or refutable by direct comparison with experience. They purport to describe, not experience, but the external world. They can be compared with the external world only through the medium of our experience of that world, but the connection between our experience and the world already involves a step of hypothesis or inference which precludes any direct and conclusive confrontation of the utterance with its subject matter. There is many a slip betwixt objective cup and subjective lip.

So statements, apart from an occasional collectors' item for epistemologists, are connected only deviously with experience. The latest scientific pronouncement about positrons and the statement that my pen is in my hand are equally statements about physical objects; and physical objects are known to us only as parts of a systematic conceptual structure which, taken as a whole, impinges at its edges upon experience. As far as knowledge is concerned, no more can be claimed for our whole body of affirmations than that it is a devious but convenient system for relating experiences to experiences. The system as a whole is under-determined by experience, but implies, given certain experiences, that certain others should be forthcoming. When such predictions of experience turn out wrong, the system has to be changed somehow. But we retain a wide latitude of choice as to what statements of the system to preserve and what ones to revise; any one of many revisions will be sufficient to unmake the particular implication which brought the system to grief. Our statements about external reality face the tribunal of sense experience not individually but as a corporate body.

But such choice of what to revise is subject to a vague scheme of priorities. Some statements about physical objects, e.g., 'My pen is in my hand', 'The mercury is at 80', are in some sense closer to possible experience than others; and such statements must be guarded pretty jealously once the appropriate experiences have appeared. Should revision of the system become necessary, other statements than these are to suffer. It is only by such an allocation of priority that we can hope to claim any empirical content or objective reference for the system as a whole.

There is also, however, another and somewhat opposite priority: the more fundamental a law is to our conceptual scheme, the less likely we are to choose it for revision. When some revision of our system of statements is called for, we prefer, other things being equal, a revision which disturbs the system least. Actually, despite the apparent opposition between this priority and the one previously noted, the one involves the other. For, the connection between a statement such as 'My pen is in my hand' and the experiences which are said to verify it is itself a matter of general principles central to the system.

Where the two priorities come into conflict, either is capable of prevailing. Statements close to experience and seemingly verified by the appropriate experiences may occasionally be given up, even by pleading hallucination, in the extreme case where their retention would entail a cataclysmic revision of fundamental laws. But to overrule a multiplicity of such statements, if they reinforce one another and are sustained by different observers, would invite criticism.

The priority on law, considered now apart from any competition with the priority on statements verified by experience, admits of many gradations. Conjectures of history and economics will be revised more willingly than laws of physics, and these more willingly than laws of mathematics and logic. Our system of statements has such a thick cushion of indeterminacy, in relation to experience, that vast domains of law can easily be held immune to revision on principle. We can always turn to other quarters of the system when revisions are called for by unexpected experiences. Mathematics and logic, central as they are to the conceptual scheme, tend to be accorded such immunity, in view of our conservative preference for revisions which disturb the system least; and herein, perhaps, lies the "necessity" which the laws of mathematics and logic are felt to enjoy.

In the end it is perhaps the same to say, as one often does, that the laws of mathematics and logic are true simply by virtue of our conceptual scheme. For, it is certainly by virtue of that scheme that those laws are central to it; and it is by virtue of being thus central that the laws are preserved from revision at the expense of statements less strategically situated.

It is also often said that the laws of mathematics and logic are true by virtue of the meanings of the words '+', '=', 'if', 'and', etc., which they contain. This also I can accept, for I expect it differs only in wording from saying that the laws are true by virtue of our conceptual scheme.

But it must now be remarked that our conservative preference for those revisions which disturb the system least is opposed by a significant contrary force, a force for simplification. Far-reaching revision of the fundamental laws of physics was elected in recent decades, by considerations of simplicity, in preference to the welter of *ad hoc* subsidiary laws which would otherwise have been needed to accommodate the wayward experiences of Michelson and Morley and other experimenters. Continued experiment "confirmed" the fundamental revisions, in the sense of increasing the simplicity differential.

Mathematical and logical laws themselves are not immune to revision if it is found that essential simplifications of our whole conceptual scheme will ensue. There have been suggestions, stimulated largely by quandaries of modern physics, that we revise the true-false dichotomy of current logic in favor of some sort of tri- or *n*-chotomy. Logical laws are the most central and crucial statements of our conceptual scheme, and for this reason the most protected from revision by the force of conservatism; but, because again of their crucial position, they are the laws an apt revision of which might offer the most sweeping simplification of our whole system of knowledge.

Thus the laws of mathematics and logic may, despite all "necessity," be abrogated. But this is not to deny that such laws are true by virtue of the conceptual scheme, or by virtue of meanings. Because these laws are so central, any revision of them is felt to be the adoption of a new conceptual scheme, the imposition of new meanings on old words. No such revolution, by the way, is envisaged in this book; there will be novelties of approach and technique in these pages, but at bottom logic will remain unchanged.

For the most part, as has been stressed in the foregoing paragraphs, our statements relate only remotely to experience. The system of statements as a whole has its experiential implications; but the individual statements, apart from the peripheral few which directly describe experience as such, are relevant to experience only indirectly through their participation in the system. It is only by way of the relations of one statement to another that the statements in the interior of the system can figure at all in the prediction of experience, and can be found deserving of revision when prediction fails. Now of these relations of statements to statements, one of conspicuous importance is the relation of logical implication: the relation of any statement to any that follows logically from it. If one statement is to be held as true, each statement implied by it must also be held as true; and thus it is that statements internal to the system have their effects on statements at the periphery.

But for implication, our system of statements would for the most part be meaningless; nothing but the periphery would make sense. Yet implication is not really an added factor; for, to say that one statement logically implies a second is the same as saying that a third statement of the system, an 'if-then' compound formed from the other two, is logically true or "valid." Logical truths are statements on a par with the rest, but very centrally situated; they are statements of such forms as '$x = x$', 'p or not p', 'If p then p', 'If p and q then q', 'If everything is thus and so then something is thus and so', and others more complex and less quickly recognizable. Their characteristic is that they not only are true but stay true even when we make substitutions upon their component words and phrases as we please, provided merely that the so-called "logical" words '$=$', 'or', 'not', 'if-then', 'everything', 'something', etc., stay undisturbed. We may write any statements in the 'p' and 'q' positions and any terms in the 'thus and so' positions, in the forms cited above, without fear of falsity. All that counts, when a statement is logically true, is its structure in terms of logical words. Thus it is that logical truths are commonly said to be true by virtue merely of the meanings of the logical words.

The chief importance of logic lies in implication, which, therefore, will be the main theme of this book. Techniques are wanted for showing, given two statements, that the one implies the other; herein lies logical deduction. Such techniques will be developed, for increasingly inclusive portions of logic, as the book proceeds. The objects of deduction, the things related by implication, are statements; so statements will constitute not merely the medium of this book (as of most), but the primary subject matter.

Strictly speaking, as urged earlier, what admit of meaning and of truth and falsity are not the statements but the individual events of their utterance. However, it is a great source of simplification in logical theory to talk of statements in abstraction from the individual occasions of their utterance; and this abstraction, if made in full awareness and subject to a certain precaution, offers no difficulty. The precaution is merely that we must not apply our logical techniques to examples in which one and the same statement recurs several times with changed meanings, owing to variations in immediate context. But such examples are easily enough adjusted to the purposes of logic by some preliminary paraphrasing, by way of bringing the implicit shifts of meaning into explicit form. (Cf. Chapter 8.)

Logic and mathematics were coupled, in earlier remarks, as jointly enjoying a central position within the total system of discourse. Logic as commonly presented, and in particular as it will be presented in this book, seems to differ from mathematics in that in logic we talk about statements and their interrelationships, notably implication, whereas in mathematics we talk about abstract nonlinguistic things: numbers, functions, and the like. This contrast is in large part misleading. Logical truths, e.g., statements of the form 'If p and q then q', are not about statements; they may be about anything, depending on what statements we put in the blanks 'p' and 'q'. When we talk *about* such logical truths, and when we expound implications, we are indeed talking about statements; but so are we when we talk *about* mathematical truths.

But it is indeed the case that the truths of mathematics treat explicitly of abstract nonlinguistic things, e.g., numbers and functions, whereas the truths of logic, in a reasonably limited sense of the word 'logic', have no such entities as specific subject matter. This is an important difference. Despite this difference, however, logic in its higher reaches is found to bring us by natural stages into mathematics. For, it happens that certain unobtrusive extensions of logical theory carry us into a realm, sometimes also called 'logic' in a broad sense of the word, which does have abstract entities of a special kind as subject matter. These entities are classes; and the logical theory of classes, or set theory, proves to be the basic discipline of pure mathematics. From it, as first came to be known through the work of Frege, Dedekind, Weierstrass, and their successors in the late nineteenth century and after, the whole of classical mathematics can be generated. Before the end of the book we shall have ascended through four grades of logic in the narrower sense, and emerged into set theory; and here we shall see, as examples of the derivation of classical mathematics, how the concept of number and various related notions can be defined.

I
TRUTH FUNCTIONS

1

NEGATION, CONJUNCTION, AND ALTERNATION

The peculiarity of *statements* which sets them apart from other linguistic forms is that they admit of truth and falsity, and may hence be significantly affirmed and denied. To deny a statement is to affirm another statement, known as the *negation* or *contradictory* of the first. To deny 'The Taj Mahal is white' is to affirm 'The Taj Mahal is not white'. Note that this negation is opposed to the original not as black to white, but as nonwhite to white; it counts as true in every case except the case of whiteness.

The commonest method of forming the negation of statements in ordinary language is by attaching 'not' (or 'does not', etc.) to the main verb, as in the foregoing example. But if the verb is governed by 'sometimes' or 'always', the negation is formed rather by substituting 'never', or 'not always'. If the statement is compound and thus has no main verb, its negation has to be phrased more elaborately; e.g., 'It is not the case both that ... and that ...'. But, despite such irregularities of ordinary language, a little care suffices for constructing a clear negation of any given statement, the guiding consideration being simply this: the negation is to count as false if the given statement is true, and the negation is to count as true under any and all circumstances under which the given statement is false.

In logical studies it is convenient to adopt a single sign of negation, consisting of the prefix '$-$', applied to statements as wholes. Thus '$-$(Jones is away)' means 'Jones is not away'; the parentheses here serve to group, as a single whole, the statement to which '$-$' is applied. The sign '$-$' might be translated into words as 'it is not the case that'; briefly it may be pronounced 'not'. When a statement is represented as a single letter 'p', as is commonly done in logical discussion, the sign of negation will be placed above instead of in front; thus we shall write '$\bar{p}$' instead of '$-p$' for the negation of 'p'.

Instead of affirming each of several statements we can, equivalently, affirm a single statement which is known to logicians (in contrast to grammarians) as the *conjunction* of the given statements. The conjunction of two or more statements is commonly expressed in English by linking the statements by 'and', or commas, or a combination of the two: 'Some are born great, some achieve greatness, and some have greatness thrust upon them.' In logical studies it is convenient to express the conjunction simply by writing the component statements in juxtaposition; e.g., '(some are born great) (some achieve greatness) (some have greatness thrust upon them)'—where again the parentheses serve merely to mark off the component statements as wholes. If we think of 'p', 'q', and 'r' as statements, their conjunction is represented as 'pqr'.

9

The meanings of negation and conjunction are summed up in these laws: *The negation of a true statement is false; the negation of a false statement is true; a conjunction of statements all of which are true is true; and a conjunction of statements not all of which are true is false.*

We see immediately that '$\bar{\bar{p}}$', the negation of '$\bar{p}$', will be true if and only if '$\bar{p}$' is false, hence if and only if 'p' is true; so there is no point in writing a double negation '$\bar{\bar{p}}$', amounting as it does simply to 'p'. It is equally evident that the conjunction 'pp' amounts simply to 'p'.

Consider now '$p(qr)$'. This, being the conjunction of 'p' and 'qr', is to be true if and only if 'p' and 'qr' are both true: and 'qr' in turn is to be true if and only if 'q' and 'r' are both true. Hence '$p(qr)$' is true if and only if 'p', 'q', and 'r' are all true; in other words, '$p(qr)$' amounts simply to the three-way conjunction 'pqr'. In the same way it may be seen that '$(pq)r$' amounts simply to 'pqr'. We may therefore drop parentheses and always write 'pqr', viewing this at will as the conjunction of 'pq' and 'r', as the conjunction of 'p' and 'qr', and as the conjunction of 'p', 'q', and 'r'. Conjunction is, in mathematical jargon, *associative:* internal grouping is immaterial in 'pqr', just as in the sum '$x + y + z$' or product 'xyz' of arithmetic. Conjunction contrasts in this respect with the arithmetical operation of division; for note that the parentheses in '$12 \div (6 \div 2)$' and '$(12 \div 6) \div 2$' make all the difference between 4 and 1.

While the associative law for addition, multiplication, and conjunction justifies suppressing parentheses, their suppression should not make us forget that the law is still there and doing its work. We may best regard the notation 'pqr' of three-way conjunction as an abbreviation specifically and arbitrarily of (say) '$(pq)r$'; then, when in practice we treat 'pqr' also as '$p(qr)$', what is strictly afoot rather is a logical transformation of '$(pq)r$' into its equivalent '$p(qr)$'.

Another respect in which conjunction resembles addition and multiplication, and differs from division, is that it is *commutative;* i.e., order is immaterial, there being no need to distinguish between 'pq' and 'qp'.

But conjunction was lately observed to enjoy also a third convenient property, not shared by addition and multiplication; viz., 'pp' reduces to 'p'. Conjunction is *idempotent,* to persist in the jargon. Taken together, these three properties of conjunction come simply to this: once we have an inventory of all the distinct components of a continued conjunction, no further details of the constitution of the conjunction need concern us.

Having touched on negation and conjunction, which correspond to 'not' and 'and', we turn now to a third way of forming statements from statements. It is called *alternation,* and corresponds to the connective 'or', or 'either-or'. This connective is subject in ordinary discourse to conflicting usages. One sense is the *nonexclusive,*[1] according to which the compound is true so long as at least one of the components is true. Under this usage the statement:

---

[1] I follow Cooley in preferring this awkward term to the more usual but somewhat misleading 'inclusive'.

(Either) Jones is ill or Smith is away

is true if Jones is ill and Smith is away, true again if Jones is not ill but Smith is away, true again if Jones is ill but Smith is not away, and false only in case Jones is neither ill nor Smith away. The other sense in which 'or' is sometimes used, called the *exclusive,* construes the compound as true just in case *exactly* one of the components is true. In this sense of 'or', the compound becomes false not only when the components are both false (Jones neither ill nor Smith away) but also when the components are both true (Jones ill and Smith away).

The ambiguity of 'or' is commonly resolved, in ordinary usage, by adding the words 'or both' or 'but not both'. Thus the nonexclusive sense is expressible in the unambiguous fashion:

Jones is ill or Smith is away or both,

and the exclusive sense thus:

Jones is ill or Smith is away but not both.

When we are confronted with 'p or q' by itself, we do not in general know which interpretation to assign to it. Often the choice is immaterial, in that either sense would serve equally. For example, consider the expression '$x \leq y$', i.e., '$x < y$ or $x = y$'. It makes no difference whether 'or' here is understood in the nonexclusive or the exclusive sense. The only difference between the two senses occurs in the case where both components are true; but when the components concerned are '$x < y$' and '$x = y$', the case of joint truth does not arise either in fact or in the mind of the speaker.

It is a common error to believe that examples like '$x < y$ or $x = y$' are clear cases of the use of 'or' in the exclusive sense, and in consequence of this error there is a tendency to overestimate the role which the exclusive sense of 'or' plays in everyday language. The clauses '$x < y$' and '$x = y$' are, of themselves, mutually exclusive or incompatible clauses; but this incompatibility, far from establishing that the context '$x < y$ or $x = y$' uses 'or' in the exclusive sense, deprives us of the one case in which we might hope to distinguish between the exclusive and nonexclusive senses. Since the clauses '$x < y$' and '$x = y$' are already of such nature as to exclude each other, it is immaterial whether we understand 'or' as repeating this exclusion or not.

If we want to establish indisputable instances of the exclusive use of 'or', we must imagine circumstances in which the person who uses 'or' has a positive purpose of denying, explicitly within the given statement, the joint truth of the components. Such examples are rare, but they exist. In an example given by Tarski it is supposed that a child asks his father to take him to the beach and afterwards to the movie. The father replies, in a tone of refusal, "We will go either to the beach or to the movie." Here the exclusive use is clear; the father means simultaneously to promise and to refuse. But it is much easier to find cases in which the nonexclusive interpretation is obligatory. For example, when it is decreed that passports will be issued only to persons who were born in the country or who are married to natives of the country, this does not mean that passports will be refused to persons who were born in the country and are married to natives. Most use of 'or' in everyday language is either of this type which admits only of the nonexclusive interpretation, or of the type of '$x < y$ or $x = y$', which admits both interpretations indifferently.

Latin has distinct words for the two senses of 'or': *vel* for the nonexclusive and *aut* for the exclusive. In modern logic it is customary to write 'v', reminiscent of 'vel', for 'or' in the nonexclusive sense: '$p \lor q$'. It is this mode of compounding statements, and only this, that is called *alternation*. When the ambiguous 'or' of ordinary language appears hereafter in the book, let us agree to construe it in this nonexclusive sense. If occasions arise where the exclusive sense of 'or' is really wanted, it is easy enough to express it explicitly:

$$p \text{ or } q \text{ but not both,}$$

or equivalently:

$$\text{Either } p \text{ and not } q \text{ or } q \text{ and not } p,$$

i.e., in symbols:

$$p\bar{q} \lor \bar{p}q.^2$$

The meaning of alternation, then, is given by this rule: *An alternation is true if at least one of the components is true, and otherwise false.* Whereas a conjunction is true if and only if its components are all true, an alternation is false if and only if its components are all false. In a metaphor from genetics, conjunction and alternation may be contrasted thus: in conjunction, truth is recessive and falsity dominant; in alternation, truth is dominant and falsity recessive.

Because the explanation of alternation is just the same as that of conjunction except for interchanging the roles of truth and falsehood, it is evident that the formal properties of conjunction must reappear as properties of alternation; thus alternation, like conjunction, is associative, commutative, and idempotent. We can render '$(p \lor q) \lor r$' and '$p \lor (q \lor r)$' indifferently as '$p \lor q \lor r$'; we can interchange '$p \lor q$' with '$q \lor p$'; and we can reduce '$p \lor p$' to 'p'. All that matters in a continued alternation, as in a continued conjunction, is an inventory of the distinct components.

Though the grouping of components is irrelevant within a continued conjunction and within a continued alternation, it is important where conjunction and alternation are mixed; we must distinguish, e.g., between

---

² After Chapter 3, this may be also written '$p \equiv \bar{q}$'.

'*pq* ∨ *r*' and '*p*(*q* ∨ *r*)'. In Chapter 5 a systematic technique will appear whereby all complexes of conjunction, alternation, and negation can conveniently be analyzed; meanwhile, however, it is easy to see in advance that '*pq* ∨ *r*' and '*p*(*q* ∨ *r*)' are bound to behave in quite unlike ways. One clear point of divergence is this: '*p*(*q* ∨ *r*)', being a conjunction with '*p*' as a component, cannot be true unless '*p*' is true, whereas '*pq* ∨ *r*', being an alternation with '*r*' as one component, will be true so long as '*r*' is true, even if '*p*' be false.

Grouping is likewise important when negation occurs in combination with conjunction or alternation. We are not likely, indeed, to confuse '*p̄q*' with '− (*pq*)', nor '*p̄* ∨ *q*' with '− (*p* ∨ *q*)', for in the one case only '*p*' is negated while in the other case the whole compound is negated. But what is less evident is that we must distinguish also between '− (*pq*)' and '*p̄q̄*', and between '− (*p* ∨ *q*)' and '*p̄* ∨ *q̄*'. Let us see what these distinctions are, taking '*p*' as 'penicillin was flown in' and '*q*' as 'a quarantine was imposed'. There are four possible situations:

pq: Penicillin was flown in and a quarantine was imposed.
p̄q: Penicillin was not flown in but a quarantine was imposed.
pq̄: Penicillin was flown in and no quarantine was imposed.
p̄q̄: Penicillin was not flown in nor was a quarantine imposed.

Now '− (*pq*)' denies just the first of the four situations, and so comes out true in the second, third, and fourth. Thus '− (*pq*)' is quite different from '*p̄q̄*', which holds in the fourth case only. As for '*p̄* ∨ *q̄*', this holds whenever one or both of '*p̄*' and '*q̄*' hold; hence in the second, third, and fourth cases. We can therefore equate '*p̄* ∨ *q̄*' with '− (*pq*)'. Finally '− (*p* ∨ *q*)' holds in the one case where '*p* ∨ *q*' fails—hence in the fourth case alone; so we may equate '− (*p* ∨ *q*)' with '*p̄q̄*'.

So '− (*pq*)' does not amount to '*p̄q̄*', but to '*p̄* ∨ *q̄*'; and '− (*p* ∨ *q*)' does not amount to '*p̄* ∨ *q̄*', but to '*p̄q̄*'. We may distribute the negation sign of '− (*pq*)' and '− (*p* ∨ *q*)' over '*p*' and '*q*' individually only on pain of changing conjunction to alternation and vice versa.[3]

A little reflection reveals the same relationship in ordinary language. Clearly '*p̄q̄*', or 'Not *p* and not *q*', may be phrased 'Neither *p* nor *q*'; and it is scarcely surprising that 'Neither *p* nor *q*' should amount to '− (*p* ∨ *q*)', the negation of 'Either *p* or *q*'. Again '− (*pq*)' may be read 'Not both *p* and *q*', and from this it is no leap to 'Either not *p* or not *q*'.

If we read the negation sign as 'it is not the case that', the distinctions of grouping become automatic.

− (*pq*):   It is not the case that both *p* and *q*.
p̄q̄:   It is not the case that *p* and it is not the case that *q*.
− (*p* ∨ *q*):   It is not the case that either *p* or *q*.
p̄ ∨ *q̄*:   It is not the case that *p* or it is not the case that *q*.

---

[3] These equivalences are called DeMorgan's laws. See Chapter 10.

Of these four the first and last, we have seen, come to the same thing; and similarly for the second and third.

HISTORICAL NOTE: The use of the dash to express negation, and of juxtaposition to express conjunction, comes down from Peano (fl. 1886–1901) and earlier writers. The bar over the letter was used for negation by C. S. Peirce from 1870. The tilde '∼', a modified 'n', saw some use as a negation sign in the nineteenth century and was revived by Whitehead and Russell. It has considerable currency today, also in writings of my own. Because in the present book there is much negating of single letters, however, I have here favored Peirce's bar for its compactness and perspicuity; and, given that, the dash is more in keeping than the tilde as negation sign for longer expressions. The alternation sign 'v' dates from Whitehead and Russell and is now used by almost all logicians. But the term for alternation is less uniform; some writers, following Whitehead and Russell, use the less suggestive term 'disjunction'. Custom varies in the notation for conjunction; some invert the alternation sign for the purpose, and some, following Hilbert (1928), use '&'. For negation there is a deviant sign '⌐' that has gained some currency.

EXERCISES

1. Which of the four cases:

    Jones ill, Smith away,
    Jones not ill, Smith away,
    Jones ill, Smith not away,
    Jones not ill, Smith not away

    make the statement:

    Jones is not ill or Smith is not away

    come out true when 'or' is construed exclusively? nonexclusively?

2. Construing 'or' exclusively or nonexclusively is indifferent to the truth or falsity of the statement above in certain of the four cases. Which cases are those?

3. Construing 'p' as 'penicillin was flown in' and 'q' as 'the quarantine was lifted', distinguish in phrasing between '$-(p \lor q)$' and '$\bar{p} \lor q$'. Under what circumstances would one of these compounds come out true and the other false?

4. Are there circumstances in which '$\bar{p} \lor q$', '$p \lor \bar{q}$', '$\bar{p} \lor \bar{q}$', and '$-(p \lor q)$' all come out true?

2
TRUTH FUNCTIONS

All that is strictly needed for a precise understanding of negation, conjunction, and alternation is stated in these laws:

'$\bar{p}$' is true if and only if 'p' is false,
'$pq\ldots s$' is true if and only if all of 'p', 'q', $\ldots$, 's' are true,
'$p \vee q \vee \ldots \vee s$' is true if and only if 'p', 'q', $\ldots$, 's' are not all false.

Now it is evident from these laws that negation, conjunction, and alternation share the following important property: in order to be able to determine the truth or falsity of a negation, conjunction, or alternation, it is sufficient to know the truth or falsity of the component parts.

It is convenient to speak of truth and falsity as *truth values;* thus the truth value of a statement is said to be truth or falsity according as the statement is true or false. What we have just observed, then, is that the truth value of a negation, conjunction, or alternation is determined by the truth values of its components. This state of affairs is expressed by speaking of negation, conjunction, and alternation as *truth functions.* In general, a compound is called a *truth function of* its components if its truth value is determined in all cases by the truth values of the components. More precisely: a way of forming compound statements from component statements is *truth-functional* if the compounds thus formed always have matching truth values as long as their components have matching truth values.[4]

The property of truth-functionality which is thus enjoyed by negation, conjunction, and alternation may be better appreciated if for contrast we examine a non-truth-functional compound:

Jones died because he ate fish with ice cream.

Even agreeing that the components 'Jones died' and 'Jones ate fish with ice cream' are true, we may still dispute over the truth value of this compound. The truth value of the compound is not determined simply by the truth values of the component statements, but by these in company with further considerations; and very obscure those further considerations are. On the other hand the truth value of the conjunction:

Jones ate fish with ice cream and died

or of the alternation:

---

[4] I thank James A. Thomas for reporting an error in my old phrasing of this.

Jones ate fish with ice cream or died

or of the negation:

Jones did not die

admits of no dispute whatever once the truth values of 'Jones ate fish with ice cream' and 'Jones died' are known individually.

The compound 'p because q' is shown not to be a truth function of 'p' and 'q' by the fact that it comes out true when some truths are put for 'p' and 'q' and false when other truths are put for 'p' and 'q'. In the case of '$p \vee q$', 'pq', and '$\bar{p}$', on the other hand, one true component is as good as another and one false component is as bad as another so far as the truth or falsity of the compound is concerned.

Any particular truth function can be adequately described by presenting a schedule showing what truth values the compound will take on for each choice of truth values for the components. Our three basic truth functions themselves, indeed, were summarily so described in the opening lines of the present section. Any unfamiliar fourth truth-functional symbol could likewise be introduced and adequately explained simply by saying what truth values on the part of the components are to make the new compound true and what ones are to make it false. A symbol 'excl-or' for the exclusive 'or', e.g., would be fully explained by a stipulation that 'p excl-or q' is to be false when 'p' and 'q' are taken as both true or both false, and true in the remaining two cases ('p' true and 'q' false or vice versa).

This question now arises: do our negation, conjunction, and alternation constitute a sufficient language for *all* truth-functional purposes? Given an explanation of a new truth-functional symbol (e.g., 'excl-or'), can we always be sure that the new symbol will be translatable into our existing notation? The answer is that negation and conjunction are always sufficient, without even alternation!

E.g., consider again 'p excl-or q'. This has been explained as false in just the case (a) where 'p' and 'q' are both true and the case (b) where 'p' and 'q' are both false. Therefore 'p excl-or q' amounts simply to denying, simultaneously, 'pq' and '$\bar{p}\bar{q}$'; for 'pq' holds in case (a) and there alone, and '$\bar{p}\bar{q}$' holds in case (b) and there alone. Therefore 'p excl-or q' amounts to:

$$-(pq) - (\bar{p}\bar{q}),$$

the conjunction of '$-(pq)$' and '$-(\bar{p}\bar{q})$'; for this conjunction simultaneously denies 'pq' and '$\bar{p}\bar{q}$' and nothing more. The compound 'p excl-or q' is false in the two cases where '$-(pq) - (\bar{p}\bar{q})$' is false, and true in the two cases where '$-(pq) - (\bar{p}\bar{q})$' is true. So the symbol 'excl-or' is superfluous; conjunction and negation suffice.

In the same way the symbol '$\vee$' of alternation itself can be seen to be superfluous. The one case where '$p \vee q$' is to be false is the case where 'p' and 'q' are both false—i.e., the case where '$\bar{p}\bar{q}$' holds. So instead of writing '$p \vee q$' we may simply deny '$\bar{p}\bar{q}$', writing '$-(\bar{p}\bar{q})$'.

These two simple examples of translating truth functions into negation and conjunction illustrate a general method which works for almost any truth function. Given a description of a truth function—i.e., given simply a schedule showing what truth values the compound is to take on for each choice of truth values for the components—we can construct a truth function out of negation and conjunction which answers the description. The general method will become evident if illustrated once more, this time with a less simple and more arbitrary example than 'excl-or' and '$\vee$'. This time a certain truth function of 'p', 'q', and 'r' is described as follows, let us say. It is to come out true in the five cases:

'p' false, 'q' true, 'r' true,
'p' true, 'q' false, 'r' true,
'p' true, 'q' true, 'r' false,
'p' false, 'q' true, 'r' false,
'p' false, 'q' false, 'r' false

and false in the remaining three cases:

'p' true, 'q' true, 'r' true,
'p' false, 'q' false, 'r' true,
'p' true, 'q' false, 'r' false.

Now these three latter cases are the cases respectively where 'pqr' is true, where '$\bar{p}\bar{q}r$' is true, and where '$p\bar{q}\bar{r}$' is true; so the compound which we are seeking is obtained simply by simultaneously negating these three unwanted cases, in a conjunction thus:

$$-(pqr) \; -(\bar{p}\bar{q}r) \; -(p\bar{q}\bar{r}).$$

Our compound thus denies, explicitly, just those cases in which it was to come out false; in all other cases it comes out true.

Clearly this same method will work for any example so long as there are *some* cases, one or more, in which the desired compound is to come out false. We thus have a routine whereby *almost* any described truth function can be written out in terms of negation and conjunction. The only truth functions which our routine fails to take care of are the ones which are to be true in *all* cases, regardless of the truth values of the components. These trivial exceptions call, then, for separate treatment; and a treatment is straightway forthcoming which is correspondingly trivial. If our problem is to express a truth function of 'p', 'q', 'r', and 's' (say) which will come out true regardless of what truth values are assigned to 'p', 'q', 'r', and 's', we may solve it simply by writing:

$$- (p\bar{p}qrs).$$

Clearly '$p\bar{p}qrs$' will come out false in all cases, on account of '$p\bar{p}$'; therefore '$-(p\bar{p}qrs)$' will come out true in all cases.

So it is now clear that negation and conjunction constitute a sufficient language for all truth-functional purposes. Far from needing ever to add further notations for hitherto inexpressible truth functions, we can even drop the notation '∨' which is already at hand. But we shall not drop it, for it facilitates certain technical manipulations (cf. Chapters 10–12).

It should be remarked that conjunction is really no less superfluous than alternation; for the fact is that an adequate notation for truth functions is constituted not only by negation and conjunction, but equally by negation and alternation. To see this it is sufficient to observe that the conjunction 'pq' itself is translatable into terms of negation and alternation, as '$-(\bar{p} \lor \bar{q})$'. This expression is equivalent to 'pq', in the sense that it comes out true where 'p' and 'q' are both true, and otherwise false. For, '$-(\bar{p} \lor \bar{q})$' is true if and only if '$\bar{p} \lor \bar{q}$' is false, hence if and only if '$\bar{p}$' and '$\bar{q}$' are both false, and hence if and only if 'p' and 'q' are both true.

In lieu of negation and conjunction, or negation and alternation, a *single* connective can be made to suffice—viz., '$|$', construed as follows: '$p | q$' is to be true if and only if 'p' and 'q' are not both true. '$p | q$' amounts to what would be expressed in terms of conjunction and negation as '$-(pq)$'; but, if we start rather with '$|$' as basic, we can express '$\bar{p}$' in terms of '$|$' as '$p | p$', and 'pq' as '$(p | q) | (p | q)$'. Another connective which would suffice by itself is '$\downarrow$', or 'neither-nor'. '$p \downarrow q$' amounts to what would be expressed in terms of conjunction and negation as '$\bar{p}\bar{q}$'; but, if we start rather with '$\downarrow$' as basic, we can express '$\bar{p}$' as '$p \downarrow p$' and 'pq' as '$(p \downarrow p) \downarrow (q \downarrow q)$'.

HISTORICAL NOTE: The logic of alternation, conjunction, and negation was investigated systematically in ancient times by the Stoics,[5] in the Middle Ages by Petrus Hispanus, Duns Scotus, and others,[5] and in modern times mainly by Boole (1847 onward) and Schröder (1877 onward). The terms 'truth value' and 'truth function' are translated from Frege (1879). The reductions to '$|$' and '$\downarrow$' are due to Sheffer (1913).

EXERCISES

1. Obtain a compound of 'p', 'q', and 'r', using only conjunction and negation, which will come out true whenever exactly two of 'p', 'q', and 'r' are true, and otherwise false.

2. Do the same using only alternation and negation. One way would be to translate the previous answer.

[5] See Łukasiewicz, "Zur Geschichte," cited in the Bibliography.

3
THE CONDITIONAL

Besides 'and' and 'or', another connective of statements which plays an important part in everyday language is 'if-then'. A statement of the form 'if p then q' is called a *conditional*. The component in the position of 'p' here is called the *antecedent* of the conditional, and the component in the position of 'q' is called the *consequent*.

A conjunction of two statements is true, we know, just in case both components are true: and an alternation is true just in case one or both components are true. Now under what circumstances is a conditional true? Even to raise this question is to depart from everyday attitudes. An affirmation of the form 'if p then q' is commonly felt less as an affirmation of a conditional than as a conditional affirmation of the consequent.[6] If, after we have made such an affirmation, the antecedent turns out true, then we consider ourselves committed to the consequent, and are ready to acknowledge error it if proves false. If on the other hand the antecedent turns out to have been false, our conditional affirmation is as if it had never been made.

Departing from this usual attitude, however, let us think of conditionals simply as compound statements which, like conjunctions and alternations, admit as wholes of truth and falsity. Under what circumstances, then, should a conditional as a whole be regarded as true, and under what circumstances false? Where the antecedent is true, the above account of common attitudes suggests equating the truth value of the conditional with that of the consequent; thus a conditional with true antecedent and true consequent will count as true, and a conditional with true antecedent and false consequent will count as false. Where the antecedent is false, on the other hand, the adoption of a truth value for the conditional becomes rather more arbitrary; but the decision which proves most convenient is to regard all conditionals with false antecedents as true. The conditional 'if p then q', so construed, is written '$p \supset q$' and called the *material conditional*. It is construed as true where 'p' and 'q' are true, also where 'p' is false and 'q' true, and also where 'p' and 'q' are both false; and it is construed as false only in the remaining case, viz., where 'p' is true and 'q' false.

The sign '$\supset$', like '$\vee$', is superfluous. We know from Chapter 2 how to construct, by means of conjunction and negation alone, a compound which shall be false in just the one case where 'p' is true and 'q' false; viz., '$-(p\bar{q})$'. We could dispense with '$\supset$' altogether, always writing '$-(p\bar{q})$' instead of '$p \supset q$'. Yet another rendering, readily seen to come to the same thing, is

---

[6] I am indebted here to Dr. Philip Rhinelander. Elsewhere in this chapter I draw upon Section 2 of my *Mathematical Logic* by permission of the Harvard University Press.

'$\bar{p} \vee q$'. However, the superfluous sign '$\supset$' will prove eventually to facilitate technical manipulations.

Now consider the statement:

(1)   If anything is a vertebrate, it has a heart.

This, to begin with, is not a conditional in the sense with which we have been concerned above, for it is not really a compound of two statements 'anything is a vertebrate' and 'it has a heart'. The form of words 'it has a heart' is not a statement, true or false, which can be entertained in its own right, and be mooted to be true in case there are vertebrates. Rather, (1) must be viewed as affirming a bundle of individual conditionals: If a is a vertebrate, a has a heart; if b is a vertebrate, b has a heart; and so on. In short:

(2) No matter what x may be, if x is a vertebrate then x has a heart.

But it is important to note that, of the bundle of conditionals which (2) affirms, each individual conditional can quite suitably be interpreted as a material conditional. For, if we reflect that the material conditional '$p \supset q$' amounts to '$-(p\bar{q})$', and then rewrite (2) accordingly, we have:

No matter what x may be, it is not the case that x both is a vertebrate and does not have a heart.

or briefly:

(3)   Nothing is a vertebrate and yet does not have a heart

—which does full justice to the original (1). So a *generalized conditional*, such as (1), can in full accordance with common usage be construed as affirming a bundle of material conditionals. Taken as a whole, the generalized conditional is a topic for Part II; it lies beyond the present phase of analysis, which concerns only the compounding of statements explicitly from blocklike components which are self-contained statements in turn.

Another use of 'if-then' which is certainly not to be construed in the fashion of '$p \supset q$' is the *contrafactual conditional;* e.g.:

(4)   If Eisenhower had run, Truman would have lost.

Whoever affirms a conditional thus in the subjunctive mood is already prepared in advance to maintain also, unconditionally, the falsehood of the antecedent, but still he thinks the conditional adds some information. Surely, then, he does not consider that such a conditional is automatically verified (like '$p \supset q$') simply by the falsity of the antecedent. This kind of conditional is not subject to the earlier remark to the effect that in ordinary usage a conditional is dropped from consideration, as empty and uninteresting, once its antecedent proves false.

The contrafactual conditional is best dissociated from the ordinary conditional in the indicative mood. Whatever the proper analysis of the contrafactual conditional may be, we may be sure in advance that it cannot be truth-functional; for, obviously ordinary usage demands that some contrafactual conditionals with false antecedents and false consequents be true and that other contrafactual conditionals with false antecedents and false consequents be false. Any adequate analysis of the contrafactual conditional must go beyond mere truth values and consider causal connections, or kindred relationships, between matters spoken of in the antecedent of the conditional and matters spoken of in the consequent. It may be wondered, indeed, whether any really coherent theory of the contrafactual conditional of ordinary usage is possible at all, particularly when we imagine trying to adjudicate between such examples as these:

> If Bizet and Verdi had been compatriots, Bizet would have been Italian;
> If Bizet and Verdi had been compatriots, Verdi would have been French.

The problem of contrafactual conditionals is in any case a perplexing one,[7] and it belongs not to pure logic but to the theory of meaning or possibly the philosophy of science. We shall not recur to it here.

So the material conditional '$p \supset q$' is put forward not as an analysis of general conditionals such as (1), nor as an analysis of contrafactual conditionals such as (4), but, at most, as an analysis of the ordinary singular conditional in the indicative mood. Even as an analysis of such conditionals the version '$p \supset q$' (or '$-(p\bar{q})$') is sometimes felt to be unnatural, for it directs us to construe a conditional as true no matter how irrelevant its antecedent may be to its consequent, so long as it is not the case that the antecedent is true and the consequent false. The following conditionals, e.g., qualify as true:

(5)   If France is in Europe then the sea is salt,
(6)   If France is in Australia then the sea is salt,
(7)   If France is in Australia then the sea is sweet.

No doubt this result seems strange; but I do not think it would be any less strange to construe (5)–(7) as false. The strangeness is intrinsic rather to the statements (5)–(7) themselves, regardless of their truth or falsity; for it is not usual in practice to form conditionals out of component statements whose truth or falsity is already known unconditionally. The reason this is not usual is readily seen: Why affirm a long statement like (5) or (6)

---

[7] See Nelson Goodman, "The problem of counterfactual conditionals."

when we are in position to affirm the shorter and stronger statement 'The sea is salt'? And why affirm a long statement like (6) or (7) when we are in position to affirm the shorter and stronger statement 'France is not in Australia'?

In practice, one who affirms 'If p then q' is ordinarily uncertain as to the truth or falsehood individually of 'p' and of 'q' but has some reason merely for disbelieving the combination 'p and not q' as a whole. We say:

If Jones has malaria then he needs quinine,

because we know about malaria but are in doubt both of Jones' ailment and of his need of quinine. Only those conditionals are worth affirming which follow from some manner of relevance between antecedent and consequent —some law, perhaps, connecting the matters which these two component statements describe. But such connection underlies the useful application of the conditional without needing to participate in its meaning. Such connection underlies the useful application of the conditional even though the meaning of the conditional be understood precisely as '$-(p\bar{q})$'.

The situation is quite similar, indeed, in the case of the connective 'or'. The statement:

France is in Europe or the sea is sweet

is as little worth affirming as (5)–(7) and for the same reason: we can save breath and yet convey more information by affirming simply 'France is in Europe'. In practice one who affirms 'p or q' is ordinarily uncertain as to the truth or falsehood individually of 'p' and of 'q', but believes merely that at least one of the two is true because of a law or some other manner of relevance connecting the matters which the two component statements describe. Yet clearly no meaning need be imputed to 'or' itself beyond the purely truth-functional meaning "not both false".

The question how well '$p \supset q$' conforms to the ordinary indicative 'if-then' is in any case one of linguistic analysis, and of little consequence for our purposes. What is important to note is that '$p \supset q$', the so-called material conditional, is to have precisely the meaning '$-(p\bar{q})$' (or '$\bar{p} \lor q$'); and it will become evident enough, as we proceed, how well adapted this concept is to purposes for which the idiom 'if-then' naturally suggests itself. In particular, as already noted, the material conditional is precisely what is wanted for the individual instances covered by a general conditional of the type (1).

The idiom 'p if and only if q', called the *biconditional*, amounts obviously to the conjunction of two conditionals, 'if p then q' and 'if q then p'. All that has been said regarding the interpretation of the conditional applies *mutatis mutandis* to the biconditional; whatever use 'if-then' may be put to, and whatever meaning it may be conceived to have, a corresponding use and a corresponding meaning must accrue to 'if and only if'. When in particular the conditional is construed as the material conditional '$p \supset q$', the corresponding biconditional is called the *material biconditional* and written '$p \equiv q$'. Since '$p \equiv q$' may be regarded simply as an abbreviation of '$(p \supset q)$ $(q \supset p)$', or '$-(p\bar{q}) -(q\bar{p})$', it is evidently false in two and only two cases: in the case where 'p' is true and 'q' false, and in the case where 'q' is true and 'p' false. In other words, a material biconditional is true if the components are alike in truth value (both true or both false), and it is false if the components differ in truth value.

The sign '$\equiv$', like '$\supset$' and 'v', is dispensable; indeed, we have already seen that '$p \equiv q$' may be expressed in terms of conjunction and negation as '$-(p\bar{q}) -(q\bar{p})$'. But, as will appear in due course, each of these three dispensable signs plays a special part in facilitating the techniques of logic.

HISTORICAL NOTE: The material conditional goes back to Philo of Megara. It was revived in modern logic by Frege (1879) and Peirce (1885). The conditional sign '$\supset$' was used by Gergonne as early as 1816, though not in the material sense. In some current writing this sign gives way to '$\rightarrow$', and '$\equiv$' to '$\leftrightarrow$' or to '$\sim$'. The appropriateness of the material version was vigorously debated in ancient times (cf. Peirce, 3.441 ff; Łukasiewicz, "Zur Geschichte", p. 116), and has become a current topic of controversy as well. The issue has been clouded, however, by failure to distinguish clearly between the conditional and implication (cf. Chapter 7).

EXERCISES

1. It was said in a footnote in Chapter 1 that 'p or q' in the exclusive sense could be written '$p \equiv \bar{q}$'. Explain why.

2. Translate '$p \equiv q$' into terms purely of alternation and negation.

4

GROUPING

A conspicuous type of ambiguity in ordinary language is ambiguity of grouping. The statement:

> Rutgers will get the pennant and Hobart will be runner-up if
> Rzymski is disqualified,

e.g., is hopelessly ambiguous in point of grouping; there is no telling whether Rutgers' getting the pennant is supposed to be contingent upon Rzymski's being disqualified. If so the logical form is '$p \supset qr$', and otherwise it is '$q(p \supset r)$', where 'p' represents 'Rzymski is disqualified', 'q' represents 'Rutgers gets the pennant', and 'r' represents 'Hobart is runner-up'.

In complex statements of ordinary language the intended grouping sometimes has to be guessed, as above, and sometimes has to be inferred from unsystematic cues, as illustrated by the following example:

(1)   If the new mail-order campaign does not break the Dripsweet
        monopoly and restore freedom of competition then Jones will
        sell his car and mortgage his home.

The words 'if' and 'then' here are helpful in determining the grouping, for they frame the complex antecedent of the conditional just as clearly as if they were parentheses. But they do not show how much text is intended for the consequent of the conditional. Should we stop the consequent of the conditional at the last 'and', or construe it as running clear to the end? The proper answer is evident at a glance; however, let us note explicitly why. The clauses 'Jones will sell his car' and 'Jones will mortgage his home' have been telescoped by omitting the repetition of 'Jones will'; and this affords conclusive evidence that the 'and' here is intended to coördinate just these two clauses, rather than reaching farther back to include a whole conditional as one component of the conjunction. So we know that (1) is to be construed as a conditional, having as antecedent:

the new mail-order campaign does not break the Dripsweet
        monopoly and restore freedom of competition

and as consequent:

Jones will sell his car and mortgage his home.

But there remains a question of grouping within the antecedent: is the 'not' to govern the whole, or is it to govern just the part preceding 'and'? Obviously the whole. And note that the obviousness of this choice is due to much the same telescoping device as was observed before: the words 'restore freedom of competition' which follow the 'and' must, because of their fragmentary character, be construed as coördinate with 'break the Dripsweet monopoly'. So (1) is a conditional of the form '$-(pq) \supset rs$', where 'p' means 'the new mail-order campaign breaks the Dripsweet monopoly', 'q' means 'the new mail-order campaign restores freedom of competition', 'r' means 'Jones will sell his car', and 's' means 'Jones will mortgage his home'.

We all have an extraordinary finesse at ordinary language; and thus it is that the correctness of the above interpretation of (1) is bound to have been more immediately evident to all of us than the reasons why. But an examination of the reasons affords some notion of the sorts of unsystematic devices whereby ordinary language succeeds in its indications of grouping, such times as it succeeds at all.

We noted the effectiveness of 'if' and 'then' in marking the boundaries of the antecedent of a conditional. In similar fashion 'either' and 'or' may be used to mark the boundaries of the first component of an alternation; and similarly 'both' and 'and' may be used to mark the boundaries of the first component of a conjunction. Thus the ambiguity of:

> Jones came and Smith stayed or Robinson left

can, by inserting 'either' at the appropriate point, be resolved in favor of '$pq \vee r$' or '$p(q \vee r)$' at will:

> Either Jones came and Smith stayed or Robinson left,
> Jones came and either Smith stayed or Robinson left.

Grouping may also be indicated in ordinary language by inserting a vacuous phrase such as 'it is the case that', balanced with another 'that' to show coordination of clauses. A further device is the insertion of emphatic particles such as 'else' after 'or', or 'also' or 'furthermore' after 'and'; such reinforcement of a connective has the effect of suggesting that it is a major one.

It is evident by now that the artificial notations of logic and mathematics enjoy a great advantage over ordinary language, in their use of parentheses to indicate grouping. Parentheses show groupings unfailingly, and are simple to use. They have the further virtue of allowing complex clauses to be dropped mechanically into place without distortion of clause or of context. This particular virtue has been of incalculable importance; without it mathematics could never have developed beyond a rudimentary stage.

Even so, parentheses can be a nuisance. Unless conventions are adopted for omitting some of them, our longer formulas tend to bristle with them and we find ourselves having to count them in order to pair them off. Actually two conventions for minimizing parentheses have been tacitly in use now for some pages; it is time they were stated. One is this: the connectives '$\vee$', '$\supset$', and '$\equiv$' are treated as marking a greater break than conjunction. Thus '$pq \vee r$' is understood as having the grouping '$(pq) \vee r$', and not '$p(q \vee r)$'—as is well suggested by the typographical pattern itself. Similarly '$p \vee qr$' means '$p \vee (qr)$', '$pq \supset r$' means '$(pq) \supset r$', etc. The other convention to which we have been tacitly adhering is this: the negation sign is understood as governing as little as possible of what follows it. Thus '$-(pq)r$' means '$(-(pq))r$', not '$-((pq)r)$'; similarly '$-(p \vee q)r$' means '$(-(p \vee q))r$', not '$-((p \vee q)r)$'; and so on.

An auxiliary notation of dots will now be adopted which will have the effect of eliminating *all* parentheses, so far as Part I is concerned, except those directly connected with negation. Perhaps this expedient will seem to reduce parentheses beyond the point of diminishing returns; actually its main value lies in clearing the way for a new influx of parentheses in Part II and beyond.

Dots are reinforcements. They may be thought of as a systematic counterpart of the practice in ordinary language, noted above, of inserting 'else', 'also', etc. To begin with, if we want to convey the meaning '$p(q \vee r)$' and thus create a greater break at the point of conjunction than at the point of alternation, we shall insert a dot at the point of conjunction thus: '$p . q \vee r$'. For '$(p \vee q)r$' similarly we shall write '$p \vee q . r$', for '$p(q \supset r)$' we shall write '$p . q \supset r$', etc.

Next, if at some occurrence of '$\vee$' or '$\supset$' or '$\equiv$' we want to create a still greater break than is expressed by the dot of conjunction, we shall insert a dot alongside '$\vee$' or '$\supset$' or '$\equiv$'; thus '$(p . q \vee r) \equiv s$' becomes '$p . q \vee r . \equiv s$'. Just as the undotted '$\vee$' or '$\supset$' or '$\equiv$' marks a greater break than the undotted conjunction, so the dotted '$\vee$' or '$\supset$' or '$\equiv$' marks a greater break than the dot of conjunction. The dot which is thus added to reinforce '$\vee$' or '$\supset$' or '$\equiv$' goes on the side where the reinforcement is needed; thus '$(p \supset q . r) \vee s$' becomes '$p \supset q . r . \vee s$', but '$p \supset (q . r \equiv s)$' becomes '$p \supset . q . r \equiv s$'. Again '$(p . q \equiv r) \vee (p \supset q . r)$', calling for reinforcement on both sides of the central '$\vee$', becomes '$p . q \equiv r . \vee . p \supset q . r$'.

When we want to create a still greater break at some point of conjunction than is expressed by a dotted '$\vee$' or '$\supset$' or '$\equiv$' in the neighborhood, we shall put a double dot '$:$' for the conjunction. When we want to create a still greater break than this at '$\vee$' or '$\supset$' or '$\equiv$', we shall put a double dot alongside '$\vee$' or '$\supset$' or '$\equiv$'; and so on to larger groups of dots. What might be written fully in terms of parentheses as:

$$s \vee (p(q \supset r) \equiv (p \vee q)r)t,$$

e.g., is written with help of dots as follows:

(2) $\qquad\qquad s \vee : p . q \supset r . \equiv . p \vee q . r : t.$

In general thus the connectives '$\vee$', '$\supset$', and '$\equiv$' fare alike. Any group of dots alongside any of these connectives represents a greater break than is represented by the same number of dots standing alone as a sign of conjunction, but a lesser break than is represented by any larger group of dots.

Parentheses will continue to be used to enclose a compound governed by a negation sign; the notations '$-(pq)$', '$-(p \vee q)$', etc. thus persist unchanged. Dots have no power, of course, to transcend parentheses; in '$-(p \vee q . r)s$', e.g., the dot is powerless to group the 's' with the 'r'.

[8]

We need no parentheses or other indicators of grouping if, with

---

[8] Text marked off by the right angles may conveniently be omitted for purposes of a shorter course.

Łukasiewicz, we write each connective before the expressions that it connects instead of writing it between. His notations for 'pq', '$p \lor q$', '$p \supset q$', '$p \equiv q$', and '$\bar{p}$' were 'Kpq', 'Apq', 'Cpq', 'Epq', and 'Np'. The alternation (2) above becomes this in his notation:

(3)   AsKEKpCqrKApqrt.

The grouping is unique and inevitable. The initial 'A' shows that the whole is an alternation whose first component is 's' and whose second component is the rest. The ensuing 'K' shows that that rest is a conjunction. The first component of that conjunction is, in view of the ensuing 'E', a biconditional. Continuing thus, we elicit the intended structure in full.

We have been recognizing conjunctions of not just two components, but of any number; and alternations similarly. In the Łukasiewicz notation this freedom must be curtailed; 'pqr' may be rendered either 'KpKqr', that is, '$p . qr$', or 'KKpqr', that is, '$pq . r$', these being equivalent; but it must be rendered one way or the other, and not simply 'Kpqr'. Correspondingly for '$p \lor q \lor r$'; it must be rendered 'ApAqr' or 'AApqr'. To permit 'Kpqr' and 'Apqr' would open the way to ambiguity of the following sort: 'KA$pqrs$' could be taken either as 'K(Apqr)s', that is, '$p \lor q \lor r . s$', or as 'K(Apq)rs', that is, '$p \lor q . rs$'. This confusion would matter; the reader can find an assignment of truth values to 'p', 'q', 'r', and 's' that makes '$p \lor q \lor r . s$' true and '$p \lor q . rs$' false.

Łukasiewicz's notation enjoys an arrestingly simple grammar. What strings of letters constitute coherent formulas? 'Cpq' yes; 'ApNKpq' yes; (3) yes; 'pKpNq' no; 'ApKq' no. Here is a simple test, due also to Łukasiewicz. Counting from the beginning of the formula, keep score of the occurrences of statement letters ('p', 'q', etc.) and of two-place connectives ('C', 'A', 'K', 'E'). The occurrences of statement letters outnumber the occurrences of connectives when you reach the end of a proper formula, and not before. I leave the reader to satisfy himself of this rule by experiment.

This notation clearly commands theoretical interest. In practice, dots and parentheses seem more perspicuous.

Students are tempted to tinker with the dot conventions with a view to economy. They note, e.g., that '$p \lor . q \equiv . r \lor s$' would do in lieu of my '$p \lor : q \equiv . r \lor s$'; it admits of only the desired interpretation '$p \lor (q \equiv . r \lor s)$', since '$(p \lor . q \equiv) r \lor s$' makes no sense. Such economies are ill advised. If an extra dot speeds up the reading, it pays its way. When elegance is what we want, we can get it in full measure by switching to the Łukasiewicz notation.

HISTORICAL NOTE: During the fifteenth, sixteenth, and seventeenth centuries the *vinculum* was commonly used in mathematical writing to indicate grouping. It is an underline or overline. Thus '$p \lor : q \equiv . r \lor s$' might be rendered '$p \lor \underline{q \equiv \underline{r \lor s}}$'. The dots began with Peano and were taken up by Whitehead and Russell and later logicians, subject to varying conventions. The Łukasiewicz notation dates from 1929.[9]

EXERCISES

1. Show how the ambiguous statement:

    John will play or John will sing and Mary will sing

    could be rendered unambiguous, in each of two senses, by telescoping clauses.

2. Indicate and justify the appropriate grouping of:

    If they either drain the swamp and reopen the road or dredge the harbor, they will provide the uplanders with a market and themselves with a bustling trade.

3. Rewrite these using dots:

    $$(p(q \lor r) \supset s) \equiv (pq \supset s)(pr \supset s),$$
    $$-(p \lor q)(r \lor s) \supset -(p \lor q)s.$$

4. Rewrite this using parentheses:

    $$p \supset . \, q \lor r . \, p \lor qs :\equiv :. \, \bar{q}\bar{r} \lor. \, \bar{p} . \, \bar{q} \lor \bar{s} :\supset \bar{p}.$$

5. Rewrite the three above in Łukasiewicz's notation.

5
TRUTH-VALUE ANALYSIS

In Chapter 2 a compound was said to be a truth function of its components when its truth value is determined by those of the components; and it was then observed that conjunction and negation constitute an adequate notation for truth functions. In view of this latter circumstance it is natural

[9] See Tarski, *Logic, Semantics, Metamathematics*, p. 39.

and convenient hereafter to conceive the notion of truth function in a purely notational way: the *truth functions of* given components are all the compounds constructed from them by means exclusively of conjunction and negation (and the dispensable further connectives 'v', '⊃', '≡'). Thus '$\bar{p}$' is a truth function of 'p', and '$-(p \vee \bar{r} . \equiv pq) \supset r$' is a truth function of 'p', 'q', and 'r'. We also count 'p' itself a truth function of 'p'.

A truth function of letters 'p', 'q', etc., is strictly speaking not a statement, of course, since the letters are themselves not actual statements but mere dummies in place of which any desired statements may be imagined. Hereafter the letters 'p', 'q', etc., and all truth functions of them will be called *schemata* (singular: schema). More specifically they will be called *truth-functional schemata* when it becomes necessary to distinguish them from schemata involving logical devices of other than truth-functional kind. Schemata are logical diagrams of statements; the letters 'p', 'q', etc., by supplanting the component clauses of a statement, serve to blot out all the internal matter which is not germane to the broad outward structures with which our logical study is concerned.

By *interpretation* of the letter 'p' (or 'q', etc.) may be meant specification of an actual statement which is to be imagined in place of the letter. By interpretation of 'p' may also be meant simply specification of a truth value for 'p'. The two senses of 'interpretation' can be used pretty interchangeably because each actual statement S has a specific truth value (known or unknown) and that truth value is all that matters to the truth value of any truth function of S.

A convenient graphic method of imposing interpretations, of the second of the above varieties, is simply to supplant the letters in a schema by the mark 'T' for truths and '⊥' for falsehoods.[10] Computing then directly with these marks, we can quickly determine what truth value the whole schema takes on under the imposed interpretations. Thus, suppose our problem is to determine the truth value of the schema '$-(pq \vee \bar{p}\bar{q})$' for the case where '$p$' is interpreted as true and 'q' as false. We simply put 'T' for 'p' and '⊥' for 'q' in the schema, getting '$-(T{\perp} \vee \overline{T}\overline{\perp})$'. But, since '$\overline{T}$' reduces to '⊥' and '$\overline{\perp}$' to 'T', this becomes '$-(T{\perp} \vee {\perp}T)$'. Further, since a conjunction with false component is false, 'T⊥' reduces to '⊥' and so does '⊥T'. So the whole is now down to '$-({\perp} \vee {\perp})$'. But, an alternation of falsehoods being false, '⊥ v ⊥' reduces to '⊥'; the whole thus becomes '$\overline{\perp}$', or 'T'. This outcome means that our original schema '$-(pq \vee \bar{p}\bar{q})$' comes out true when '$p$' is interpreted as true and 'q' as false.

The process whereby '$-(T{\perp} \vee \overline{T}\overline{\perp})$' was reduced to 'T' will be called *resolution*. The simplest of the steps involved in resolution, viz. reduction of '$\overline{T}$' to '⊥' and of '$\overline{\perp}$' to 'T', will always be tacit hereafter; we shall never write '$\overline{T}$' nor '$\overline{\perp}$', but immediately '⊥' and 'T', as if the notation of negation

---

[10] We need not fumble for a pronunciation of '⊥' coördinate with the pronunciation 'tee' of 'T', for the words 'true' and 'false' themselves are short enough to serve conveniently as pronunciations of the two signs. Before deploring my preference of '⊥' to the initial 'F' of 'false', note the urgent need of 'F' for other purposes in Parts II–IV.

as applied to 'T' and '⊥' consisted simply in inverting. The other steps of
resolution illustrated in the above example were reduction of 'T⊥', '⊥T',
and '⊥ v ⊥' to '⊥'. These steps, and all further ones for which there might
be occasion in other examples, may conveniently be codified in the form of
nine *rules of resolution:*

(i) *Delete 'T' as component of conjunction.* (Thus 'TTT' reduces to
'TT' and thence to 'T'; '⊥T' reduces to '⊥'; etc. Reason: a conjunction
with a true component is true or false according as the rest of it is true
or false.)

(ii) *Delete '⊥' as component of alternation.* (Thus '⊥ v ⊥ v ⊥' reduces
to '⊥ v ⊥' and thence to '⊥'; '⊥ v T' reduces to 'T'; etc. Reason: an alternation with a false component is true or false according as the rest of
it is true or false.)

(iii) *Reduce a conjunction with '⊥' as component to '⊥'.*

(iv) *Reduce an alternation with 'T' as component to 'T'.*

(v) *Drop 'T' as antecedent of a conditional.* (Reason: a conditional
with true antecedent is true or false according as the consequent is true
or false.)

(vi) *Reduce a conditional with '⊥' as antecedent, or 'T' as consequent,
to 'T'.* (Thus 'T ⊃ T', '⊥ ⊃ T', and '⊥ ⊃ ⊥' reduce to 'T'.)

(vii) *If a conditional has '⊥' as consequent, reduce the whole to the
negation of the antecedent.*

(viii) *Drop 'T' as component of a biconditional.* (Thus 'T ≡ T' reduces
to 'T', and 'T ≡ ⊥' and '⊥ ≡ T' reduce to '⊥'.)

(ix) *Drop '⊥' as component of a biconditional and negate the other side.*
(Thus '⊥ ≡ ⊥' reduces to 'T', and 'T ≡ ⊥' and '⊥ ≡ T' reduce to '⊥'.)

Set up according to these rules, our original example of resolution
amounts to no more than this:

$$-(T⊥ v ⊥T)$$
$$-(⊥ v ⊥) \quad \text{(changing 'T⊥' and '⊥T' each to '⊥' by (i) or (iii))}$$
$$T \quad \text{(changing '⊥ v ⊥' to '⊥' by (ii))}$$

Turning to a more elaborate example, let us determine the truth value
of '*pq* v *p̄r̄* .⊃. *q* ≡ *r*' for the case where '*p*' and '*q*' are interpreted as false
and '*r*' as true.

$$⊥⊥ v T⊥ .⊃. ⊥ ≡ T$$
$$⊥⊥ v T⊥ .⊃ ⊥ \quad \text{(changing '⊥ ≡ T' to '⊥' by (viii) or (ix))}$$
$$-(⊥⊥ v T⊥) \quad \text{(by (vii))}$$
$$-(⊥ v ⊥) \quad \text{(by (iii) twice)}$$
$$T \quad \text{(changing '⊥ v ⊥' to '⊥' by (ii))}$$

Thus '*pq* v *p̄r̄* .⊃. *q* ≡ *r*' comes out true when false statements are put for
'*p*' and '*q*' and a true one for '*r*'.

Let us feign contact with reality by considering an actual statement of the form '$pq \lor \bar{p}\bar{r} . \supset . q \equiv r$':

(1)   If either the resident and the deputy resident both resign or the resident neither resigns nor exposes the *chargé d'affaires,* in either case the deputy resident will resign if and only if the resident exposes the *chargé d'affaires.*

What we have found is that (1) comes out true in the case where neither the resident nor the deputy resident resigns and the resident exposes the *chargé d'affaires.*

We have evaluated the schema '$pq \lor \bar{p}\bar{r} . \supset . q \equiv r$' for one interpretation: 'p' and 'q' as false and 'r' as true. There remain seven other interpretations that might be considered: 'p', 'q', and 'r' all true, 'p' and 'q' true and 'r' false, 'p' and 'r' true and 'q' false, and so on. The eight cases can be systematically explored, with evaluation of the schema for each case, by the following method. First we put 'T' for 'p', leaving 'q' and 'r' unchanged, and make all possible resolutions by (i)–(ix):

$$\mathsf{T}q \lor \bot\bar{r} . \supset . q \equiv r$$
$$q \lor \bot\bar{r} . \supset . q \equiv r \qquad \text{(changing '}\mathsf{T}q\text{' to '}q\text{' by (i))}$$
$$q \lor \bot . \supset . q \equiv r \qquad \text{(changing '}\bot\bar{r}\text{' to '}\bot\text{' by (iii))}$$
$$q \supset . q \equiv r \qquad \text{(changing '}q \lor \bot\text{' to '}q\text{' by (ii))}$$

Then we put 'T' for 'q' in this result and resolve further:

$$\mathsf{T} \supset . \mathsf{T} \equiv r$$
$$\mathsf{T} \equiv r \qquad \text{(by (v))}$$
$$r \qquad \text{(by (viii))}$$

We have now found that whenever 'p' and 'q' are both interpreted as true, our original schema resolves to 'r'—hence becomes true or false according as 'r' is true or false. This disposes of two of the eight cases. Next we return to our intermediate result '$q \supset . q \equiv r$' and put '$\bot$' for 'q':

$$\bot \supset . \bot \equiv r$$
$$\mathsf{T} \qquad \text{(by vi))}$$

This shows that our original schema comes out true whenever 'p' is interpreted as true and 'q' as false, regardless of 'r'. This disposes of two more of our eight cases. Now we go all the way back to our original schema and put '$\bot$' for 'p':

$$\bot q \lor \mathsf{T}\bar{r} . \supset . q \equiv r$$
$$\bot \lor \mathsf{T}\bar{r} . \supset . q \equiv r \qquad \text{(by (iii))}$$
$$\mathsf{T}\bar{r} \supset . q \equiv r \qquad \text{(by (ii))}$$
$$\bar{r} \supset . q \equiv r \qquad \text{(by (i))}$$

Putting 'T' for 'r' here and resolving further, we have:

$$\bot \supset. q \equiv \mathsf{T}$$
$$\mathsf{T} \qquad \text{(by (vi))}$$

This shows that our original schema comes out true whenever '*p*' is interpreted as false and '*r*' as true, regardless of '*q*'. Two more cases are disposed of. Finally we go back to '$\bar{r} \supset. q \equiv r$' and put '$\bot$' for '*r*':

$$\mathsf{T} \supset. q \equiv \bot$$
$$q \equiv \bot \qquad \text{(by (v))}$$
$$\bar{q} \qquad \text{(by (ix))}$$

So whenever '*p*' and '*r*' are both interpreted as false, our schema resolves to '$\bar{q}$'—hence becomes false or true according as '*q*' is interpreted as true or false.

The foregoing analysis might conveniently have been carried out in a single array as follows:

$$pq \vee \bar{p}\bar{r} .\supset. q \equiv r$$

$\mathsf{T}q \vee \bot\bar{r} .\supset. q \equiv r$	$\bot q \vee \mathsf{T}\bar{r} .\supset. q \equiv r$
$q \vee \bot\bar{r} .\supset. q \equiv r$	$\bot \vee \mathsf{T}\bar{r} .\supset. q \equiv r$
$q \vee \bot .\supset. q \equiv r$	$\mathsf{T}\bar{r} \supset. q \equiv r$
$q \supset. q \equiv r$	$\bar{r} \supset. q \equiv r$

$\mathsf{T} \supset. \mathsf{T} \equiv r \quad \bot \supset. \bot \equiv r \qquad \bot \supset. q \equiv \mathsf{T} \qquad \mathsf{T} \supset. q \equiv \bot$
$\mathsf{T} \equiv r \qquad\qquad \mathsf{T} \qquad\qquad\qquad \mathsf{T} \qquad\qquad q \equiv \bot$
$r \qquad\qquad\qquad\qquad\qquad\qquad\qquad\qquad\qquad \bar{q}$
$\mathsf{T} \quad \bot \qquad\qquad\qquad\qquad\qquad\qquad\qquad\qquad \bot \quad \mathsf{T}$

This is called a *truth-value analysis*. The general method may be summed up as follows. We make a grand dichotomy of cases by putting first 'T' and then '$\bot$' for some chosen letter, say '*p*'. The expressions thus formed are the respective headings of a bipartite analysis. Then we resolve both expressions, by (i)–(ix), until we end up with 'T' or '$\bot$' or some schema. If a schema results, we then proceed to develop, under that schema, a new bipartite analysis with respect to a chosen one of its letters. We continue thus until all end results are single marks—'T' or '$\bot$'. Each end result shows what truth value the original schema will take on when its letters are interpreted according to the marks which have there supplanted them.

Actually all intermediate steps of resolution are so obvious, and so readily reconstructed at will, that they may hereafter be left to the imagination. Thus the truth-value analysis above would in future be condensed as follows:

$$pq \vee \bar{p}\bar{r} .\supset. q \equiv r$$

$\mathsf{T}q \vee \bot\bar{r} .\supset. q \equiv r \qquad\qquad\qquad \bot q \vee \mathsf{T}\bar{r} .\supset. q \equiv r$
$q \supset. q \equiv r \qquad\qquad\qquad\qquad\qquad \bar{r} \supset. q \equiv r$
$\mathsf{T} \supset. \mathsf{T} \equiv r \quad \bot \supset. \bot \equiv r \qquad \bot \supset. q \equiv \mathsf{T} \qquad \mathsf{T} \supset. q \equiv \bot$
$r \qquad\qquad \mathsf{T} \qquad\qquad\qquad \mathsf{T} \qquad\qquad \bar{q}$
$\mathsf{T} \quad \bot \qquad\qquad\qquad\qquad\qquad\qquad\qquad \bot \quad \mathsf{T}$

There is no need always to choose '*p*' as the first letter for which to put 'T' and '⊥'. It is better to choose the letter which has the most repetitions, if repetitions there be, and to adhere to this plan also at each later stage. Thus it was, indeed, that whereas in the second stage on the left side of the above analysis '*q*' was chosen for replacement by 'T' and '⊥', on the other hand in the second stage on the right side '*r*' was chosen. This strategy tends to hasten the disappearance of letters, and thus to minimize work.

A method of truth-value analysis that has long been usual in the literature is that of *truth tables*. For the schema '*pq* ∨ *p̄r̄* .⊃. *q* ≡ *r*' last analyzed, the truth table is this:

p	q	r	pq	$\bar{p}$	$\bar{r}$	$\bar{p}\bar{r}$	$pq \vee \bar{p}\bar{r}$	$q \equiv r$	$pq \vee \bar{p}\bar{r} .\supset. q \equiv r$
T	T	T	T	⊥	⊥	⊥	T	T	T
⊥	T	T	⊥	T	⊥	⊥	⊥	T	T
T	⊥	T	⊥	⊥	⊥	⊥	⊥	⊥	T
⊥	⊥	T	⊥	T	⊥	⊥	⊥	⊥	T
T	T	⊥	T	⊥	T	⊥	T	⊥	⊥
⊥	T	⊥	⊥	T	T	T	T	⊥	⊥
T	⊥	⊥	⊥	⊥	T	⊥	⊥	T	T
⊥	⊥	⊥	⊥	T	T	T	T	T	T

The first three columns exhaust the assignments of truth values to the letters. The succeeding columns list the truth values of progressively more complex components of the schema for each assignment to the letters. Each of these succeeding columns is derived from earlier columns by reasoning tantamount to what I have called resolution.

The truth table can be constructed more compactly thus:

p q	$\vee$	$\bar{p}$ $\bar{r}$	$.\supset.$	$q \equiv r$
TTT	T	⊥⊥⊥	T	TTT
⊥⊥T	⊥	T⊥⊥	T	TTT
T⊥⊥	⊥	⊥⊥⊥	T	⊥⊥T
⊥⊥⊥	⊥	T⊥⊥	T	⊥⊥T
TTT	T	⊥⊥T	⊥	T⊥⊥
⊥⊥T	T	TTT	⊥	T⊥⊥
T⊥⊥	⊥	⊥⊥T	T	⊥T⊥
⊥⊥⊥	T	TTT	T	⊥T⊥

We begin this construction by writing out the schema and inscribing the appropriate columns under its single letters and their negations. Then we derive the column for '*pq*', building it under the middle of that conjunction. Similarly for '*p̄r̄*' and '*q ≡ r*'. Then we derive the column for the alternation, building it under the '∨'; and finally we build the column for the whole schema under its main connective, '⊃'.

But the branching notation of truth-value analysis that we just previously arrived at is, we see, briefer still than this compacted truth table. The saving increases markedly, moreover, when the number of distinct letters is increased, as the reader can verify by experiment. For four letters, after all, the truth table runs to sixteen lines; for five, thirty-two. The saving increases further when, as in the next section, the analysis specifically seeks consistency or validity; for these questions are answered by truth tables only when the tables are nearly finished, whereas under our branching procedure of truth-value analysis they often are answered early in the game.

HISTORICAL NOTE: The pattern of reasoning that the truth table tabulates was Frege's, Peirce's, and Schröder's by 1880. The tables have been prominent in the literature since 1920 (Łukasiewicz, Post, Wittgenstein). The compact style last displayed above is from my *Mathematical Logic*, 1940.

EXERCISES

1. Suppose they drain the swamp but neither reopen the road nor dredge the harbor nor provide the uplanders with a market; and suppose nevertheless they do provide themselves with a bustling trade. Determine, under these circumstances, the truth value of the statement in Exercise 2 of the preceding chapter. Method: represent the components as '*p*', '*q*', '*r*', '*s*', '*t*'; put 'T' and '⊥' appropriately for the letters; resolve.

2. Suppose they neither drain the swamp nor reopen the road but that they both dredge the harbor and provide the uplanders with a market, and still do not provide themselves with a bustling trade. What then is the truth value of the statement in Exercise 2 of the preceding chapter?

3. Make a truth-value analysis of each of the schemata:

    $$p \supset pq, \qquad p \supset . p \vee q, \qquad p \supset . p \supset q, \qquad p \supset . p \equiv q.$$

    Present your work in full, showing intermediate steps of resolution; afterward circle those intermediate lines for omission, to show how the work would look in the condensed style.

4.   For comparison perform two truth-value analyses of '$p \supset q \,.\, q \supset r$', first following and then flouting the strategy of choosing the most frequent letter.

6

CONSISTENCY
AND VALIDITY

A truth-functional schema is called *consistent* if it comes out true under some interpretation of its letters; otherwise *inconsistent*. A truth-functional schema is called *valid* if it comes out true under every interpretation of its letters. The schema '$p\bar{q}$', for example, is consistent, for it comes out true when 'p' is interpreted as true and 'q' as false; but it is not valid, since there are other interpretations of 'p' and 'q' which make it come out false.

The way to test a truth-functional schema for validity and consistency is obvious: we carry out a truth-value analysis and see whether we get 'T' in every case (showing validity) or '⊥' in every case (showing inconsistency) or neither. Two examples of validity and inconsistency are respectively '$p \supset p$' and '$p\bar{p}$':

$$p \supset p \qquad\qquad\qquad p\bar{p}$$

$$\text{T} \supset \text{T} \qquad ⊥ \supset ⊥ \qquad \text{T}⊥ \qquad ⊥\text{T}$$
$$\text{T} \qquad\qquad \text{T} \qquad\qquad ⊥ \qquad\qquad ⊥$$

Valid schemata were already exploited at one point in the argument of Chapter 2, where '$-(p\bar{p}qrs)$' was cited.

$$-(p\bar{p}qrs)$$

$$-(\text{T}⊥qrs) \qquad\qquad\qquad -(⊥\text{T}qrs)$$
$$\text{T} \qquad\qquad\qquad\qquad\qquad \text{T}$$

In general, obviously, a schema is valid if and only if its negation is inconsistent, and a schema is inconsistent if and only if its negation is valid. Thus the negations '$-(p\bar{p})$' and '$-(p\bar{p}qrs)$' of the inconsistent schemata '$p\bar{p}$' and '$p\bar{p}qrs$' are valid, and the negation '$-(p \supset p)$' of the valid schema '$p \supset p$' is inconsistent.

A test of validity may be stopped short, with negative outcome, as soon as we come to a case yielding '⊥'; and a test of consistency may be stopped, with affirmative outcome, as soon as we come to a case yielding 'T'. Thus the analysis of '$pq \lor \bar{p}\bar{r} . \supset . q \equiv r$' in Chapter 5 might, if we had been interested only in consistency and validity, have been discontinued in this fragmentary state:

$$pq \lor \bar{p}\bar{r} . \supset . q \equiv r$$

$$\mathsf{T}q \lor \bot\bar{r} . \supset . q \equiv r$$
$$q \supset . q \equiv r$$
$$\mathsf{T} \supset . \mathsf{T} \equiv r$$
$$r$$
$$\mathsf{T} \qquad \bot$$

This much already suffices to show both that '$pq \lor \bar{p}\bar{r} . \supset . q \equiv r$' is consistent and that it is not valid.

'Validity' is not to be thought of as a term of praise. When a schema is valid, any statement whose form that schema depicts is bound to be, in some sense, trivial. It will be trivial in the sense that it conveys no real information regarding the subject matter whereof its component clauses speak. The statement:

(1)   If the Bruins win then the Bruins win,

whose form is depicted in the valid schema '$p \supset p$', gives us no information about the outcome of the game; indeed, any other clause, on any other subject matter, could be used here in place of 'the Bruins win' with as much and as little effect. Valid schemata are important not as an end but as a means. We shall see in another page or two that simple cases of validity afford shortcuts in the truth-value analysis of other schemata; and we shall see in the next section that the determination of certain complex cases of validity is tantamount to determining relations of equivalence and implication between other schemata.

Though the statements illustrative of valid schemata are always trivial in the sense noted above, they are not always trivial in the sense of being, like (1), recognizable on sight. Valid schemata may run to any length and any degree of complexity; and some even of moderate length cannot be recognized as valid without substantial computation. The same is true of consistency. Below is a schema of quite moderate complexity which, though by no means recognizable as valid on sight, is found to be valid by truth-value analysis.

$$pq \lor p\bar{r} \lor \bar{p}r \lor \bar{p}s \lor \bar{q}r \lor \bar{r}\bar{s}$$

$\mathsf{T}q \lor \mathsf{T}\bar{r} \lor \bot r \lor \bot s \lor \bar{q}r \lor \bar{r}\bar{s}$ $\bot q \lor \bot\bar{r} \lor \mathsf{T}r \lor \mathsf{T}s \lor \bar{q}r \lor \bar{r}\bar{s}$

$q \lor \bar{r} \lor \bar{q}r \lor \bar{r}\bar{s}$ $r \lor s \lor \bar{q}r \lor \bar{r}\bar{s}$

$q \lor \bot \lor \bar{q}\mathsf{T} \lor \bot\bar{s}$ $q \lor \mathsf{T} \lor \bar{q}\bot \lor \mathsf{T}\bar{s}$ $\mathsf{T} \lor s \lor \bar{q}\mathsf{T} \lor \bot\bar{s}$ $\bot \lor s \lor \bar{q}\bot \lor \mathsf{T}\bar{s}$

$q \lor \bar{q}$ T T $s \lor \bar{s}$

$\mathsf{T} \lor \bot \quad \bot \lor \mathsf{T}$ $\mathsf{T} \lor \bot \quad \bot \lor \mathsf{T}$

$\mathsf{T} \qquad \mathsf{T}$ $\mathsf{T} \qquad \mathsf{T}$

The test shows validity, but unimplemented inspection would have availed little.

Taking advantage of the really evident cases of validity and inconsistency, however, we may speed up our truth-value analyses hereafter. Schemata like '$q \vee \bar{q}$' and '$s \vee \bar{s}$', which emerged in the course of the analysis above, are now known to be valid, and hence to reduce to 'T' in all cases; hereafter, therefore, we may as well agree to reduce any such result directly to 'T', without further ceremony. Thus, in place of the configurations:

$$q \vee \bar{q} \qquad\qquad\qquad\qquad s \vee \bar{s}$$

$$\mathsf{T} \vee \perp \qquad \perp \vee \mathsf{T} \qquad\qquad \mathsf{T} \vee \perp \qquad \perp \vee \mathsf{T}$$
$$\mathsf{T} \qquad\qquad \mathsf{T} \qquad\qquad\qquad \mathsf{T} \qquad\qquad \mathsf{T}$$

which appeared in the lower corners of the analysis above, we shall in future write simply:

$$q \vee \bar{q} \qquad\qquad\qquad\qquad s \vee \bar{s}$$
$$\mathsf{T} \qquad\qquad\qquad\qquad\qquad \mathsf{T}$$

In general, any such patently valid schema may be reduced immediately to 'T' whenever it occurs in a truth-value analysis, whether in isolation or as component of a longer formula. Similarly any patently inconsistent schema such as '$p\bar{p}$', '$p\bar{p}qrs$', '$\bar{q}pqr$', etc. may be reduced immediately to '$\perp$' whenever it turns up in an analysis.

With these shortcuts in mind, let us analyze a really complex schema:

$$p \vee q \,.\, p \vee \bar{q} \,.\vee\, \bar{p}q :\equiv q \,.:\supset.\, pr \vee p\bar{r}$$
$$\mathsf{T} \vee q \,.\, \mathsf{T} \vee \bar{q} \,.\vee\, \perp q :\equiv q \,.:\supset.\, \mathsf{T}r \vee \mathsf{T}\bar{r} \qquad \perp \vee q \,.\, \perp \vee \bar{q} \,.\vee\, \mathsf{T}q :\equiv q \,.:\supset.\, \perp r \vee \perp \bar{r}$$
$$q \supset .\, r \vee \bar{r} \qquad\qquad\qquad\qquad -(q\bar{q} \vee q \,.\equiv q)$$
$$q \supset \mathsf{T} \qquad\qquad\qquad\qquad\qquad -(\perp \vee q \,.\equiv q)$$
$$\mathsf{T} \qquad\qquad\qquad\qquad\qquad\qquad -(q \equiv q)$$
$$\perp$$

The reduction of the left side to '$q \supset .\, r \vee \bar{r}$' proceeded by various steps of resolution, as usual. But in the next step, using our new shortcut, we put 'T' for the patently valid '$r \vee \bar{r}$' and got '$q \supset \mathsf{T}$', which then resolved into 'T'. On the right-hand side of the analysis, the reduction to '$-(q\bar{q} \vee q \,.\equiv q)$' proceeded by resolution as usual; then, using our new shortcut, we put '$\perp$' for the patently inconsistent '$q\bar{q}$', and got '$-(\perp \vee q \,.\equiv q)$', which resolved in turn into '$-(q \equiv q)$'. Here, using our new shortcut again, we put 'T' for the patently valid '$q \equiv q$' and conclude our work.

Where to draw the line between what is patently valid or inconsistent and what is not patently so is quite arbitrary. The '$-(q\bar{q} \vee q \,.\equiv q)$' in the right-hand part of the analysis above is itself an inconsistent schema, and so might have been supplanted immediately by '$\perp$' if its inconsistency had been felt to be sufficiently obvious. Similarly the '$q \supset .\, r \vee \bar{r}$' in the left-hand part of the analysis might have been supplanted directly by 'T'. For uniformity of classroom work, we might limit the category of "patently inconsistent" schemata to these two kinds: (a) conjunctions such as '$\bar{q}pqr$', '$p \vee q . r . - (p \vee q)$', etc., in which some part appears both plain and negated as component of the conjunction, and (b) biconditionals like '$p \equiv \bar{p}$' or '$-(qr) \equiv qr$'. But beware of '$p \supset \bar{p}$'; it is consistent.

We might limit the category of "patently valid" schemata to these two kinds: (a) alternations such as '$\bar{q} \vee p \vee q \vee r$', '$pq \vee r \vee - (pq)$', etc., in which some part appears both plain and negated as component of the alternation; (b) conditionals or biconditionals whose two sides are alike, e.g., '$q \equiv q$', '$qr \equiv qr$', '$p \vee q .\supset. p \vee q$'.

It is only to such schemata, then that our shortcut is to be applied; these, and only these, will be reduced appropriately to '$\bot$' or 'T' on sight.

From the validity of a schema we may infer, without separate test, the validity of any schema which is formed from it by *substitution*. From the validity, e.g., of '$p \vee \bar{p}$' we may infer the validity of the schema '$qr \vee - (qr)$', which is formed from '$p \vee \bar{p}$' by substituting 'qr' for 'p'. This is apparent from the definition of validity. Validity of '$p \vee \bar{p}$' means that '$p \vee \bar{p}$' is bound to come out true no matter what statement be put for 'p'; so it follows, as a special case, that '$qr \vee - (qr)$' will come out true no matter what statement 'qr' be made to represent—hence no matter what statements be put for 'q' and 'r'. *Substitution of schemata for letters preserves validity.* But it is clearly essential that 'substitution for a letter' be construed as meaning uniform substitution for every occurrence of the letter. From the validity of '$p \vee \bar{p}$', e.g., we are not entitled to infer validity of '$qr \vee \bar{p}$', nor of '$qr \vee - (qs)$'. It is permissible to put the same or different schemata for different letters, but we must always put the same schema for recurrences of the same letter.

Since inconsistency of a schema is simply validity of its negation, we may conclude further that *substitution of schemata for letters preserves inconsistency*. But note on the other hand that substitution cannot be depended upon to preserve consistency. The mere fact that the more general schema has *some* true instances (which is what consistency means) gives us no reason to suppose that the special case will share any of the true instances. The schema '$p \vee pq$', e.g., is consistent (as may be verified by truth-value analysis), but substitution of '$r\bar{r}$' for 'p' therein yields an inconsistent schema '$r\bar{r} \vee r\bar{r}q$'. Similarly, substitution for a letter in a nonvalid schema cannot be depended upon to yield a nonvalid schema; it may yield a valid or nonvalid one.

EXERCISES

1.   Test each of these for validity by truth-value analysis, exploiting the new shortcut regarding patently valid and patently inconsistent clauses:

$$p \supset q .\text{v.} q \supset p, \qquad p \vee qr \text{ v. } \bar{p} . \bar{q} \vee \bar{r},$$
$$p \equiv q .\text{v.} p \equiv \bar{q}, \qquad p \equiv q .\text{v.} q \equiv r .\text{v.} p \equiv r.$$

2. In each of the four schemata above, substitute '$p \vee q$' for 'p'. This is chiefly an exercise in adjusting dots to preserve proper grouping.

3. "If a schema is consistent but not valid, then by one set of substitutions we can get a valid schema from it, and by another set of substitutions an inconsistent schema." Is this true? Justify your answer.

4. By negating a consistent schema can you get a valid one? a consistent one? an inconsistent one? Illustrate your affirmative answers.

7
IMPLICATION

The most conspicuous purpose of logic, in its applications to science and everyday discourse, is the justification and criticism of inference. Logic is largely concerned with devising techniques for showing that a given statement does, or does not, "follow logically" from another. The statement 'No dropped freshman is eligible for the Bowdoin Prize', e.g., follows logically from 'No freshman is eligible for the Bowdoin or Bechtel Prize'; and the statement 'Cassius is not both lean and hungry' follows logically from 'Cassius is not hungry'. Now the first of these two examples lies beyond the scope of the truth-functional part of logic with which we are concerned in Part I, but the second example can already be treated here.

From the point of view of logical theory, the fact that the statement 'Cassius is not both lean and hungry' follows from 'Cassius is not hungry' is conveniently analyzed into these two circumstances: (a) the two statements have the respective logical forms '$-(pq)$' and '$\bar{q}$' (with 'Cassius is lean' and 'Cassius is hungry' supplanting 'p' and 'q'); and (b) there are no two statements which, put respectively for 'p' and 'q', make '$\bar{q}$' true and '$-(pq)$' false. Circumstance (b) will hereafter be phrased in this way: '$\bar{q}$' *implies* '$-(pq)$'. In general, one truth-functional schema is said to *imply* another if there is no way of so interpreting the letters as to make the first schema true and the second false.

Whether a truth-functional schema S_1 implies another, S_2, can be decided always by taking S_1 as antecedent and S_2 as consequent of a conditional, and testing the conditional for validity. For, according to our definition, S_1

implies S_2 if and only if no interpretation makes S_1 true and S_2 false, hence if and only if no interpretation falsifies the material conditional whose antecedent is S_1 and whose consequent is S_2. In a word, *implication is validity of the conditional.* To determine that '$\bar{q}$' implies '$-(pq)$', e.g., we check the validity of the corresponding conditional:

$$\bar{q} \supset -(pq)$$

$$\underset{\top}{\bot \supset -(p\top)} \qquad\qquad \underset{\top}{\top \supset -(p\bot)}$$

Next let us note an example which turns out negatively. That '$p \vee q$' does *not* imply 'pq' is found thus:

$$p \vee q .\supset pq$$

$$\underset{\top \quad \bot}{\underset{q}{\top \vee q .\supset \top q}}$$

Once having come out with a '$\bot$', we discontinue our test in the knowledge that '$p \vee q .\supset pq$' is not valid; i.e., that '$p \vee q$' does not imply 'pq'. This result does not mean that '$p \vee q .\supset pq$' does not come out true under *some* interpretations of 'p' and 'q', nor does it mean that '$p \vee q$' and 'pq' themselves do not come out simultaneously true under some interpretations of 'p' and 'q'. The failure of implication means merely that *some* interpretations which make '$p \vee q$' true make 'pq' false; or, what comes to the same thing, that some interpretations make '$p \vee q .\supset pq$' false.

By reflecting briefly on our methods of testing for implication, validity, and inconsistency, one sees that these four general laws hold:

(i) Any schema implies itself.

(ii) If one schema implies a second and the second a third then the first implies the third.

(iii) An inconsistent schema implies every schema and is implied by inconsistent ones only.

(iv) A valid schema is implied by every schema and implies valid ones only.

An easy familiarity with simple cases of implication between truth-functional schemata will be found to facilitate construction of proofs at even as advanced a level of logic as Chapters 29 ff. At that stage it will not be enough to be able to answer raised questions of implication, which we can do by truth-value analysis as above; we must also be able to raise the questions. We must be able to think up schemata which imply or are implied by a given schema and promise well as links in a proposed chain of argument. Such products of imagination can be checked mechanically by truth-value analysis, but thinking them up is an unmechanical activity. Facility in it depends on grasping the sense of simple schemata clearly enough to be able, given a schema, to conjure up quite an array of fairly simple variants which imply or are implied by it. Given '$p \lor q$', it should occur to us immediately that 'p' and 'q' and 'pq' and '$\bar{p} \supset q$' imply it and that '$p \lor q \lor r$' and '$\bar{p} \supset q$' are implied by it. Given '$p \supset q$', it should occur to us immediately that each of:

$$\bar{p}, \quad q, \quad qr, \quad \bar{p} \lor q, \quad \bar{q} \supset \bar{p}, \quad p \supset qr, \quad p \lor r . \supset q$$

implies it and that each of:

$$\bar{p} \lor q, \quad \bar{q} \supset \bar{p}, \quad p \supset . q \lor r, \quad p \supset q . \lor r$$

is implied by it. Such flashes need not be highly accurate, for we can check each hunch afterward by truth-value analysis. What is important is that they be prolific, and accurate enough to spare excessive lost motion.

No doubt repertoire is an aid to virtuosity in contriving implications, but understanding is the principal thing. When simple schemata are sufficiently transparent to us, we can see through them by the light of pure reason to other schemata which must come out true if these do, or which can not come out true unless these do. It is well to reflect upon the above examples and succeeding ones until it becomes obvious from the sheer meanings of signs that the implications must hold.

Readiness with implications is aided also, no doubt, by ease of checking. Accordingly a quick implication test called the *fell swoop* will now be explained which, though not general, works for an important range of simple cases.

Some schemata are visibly verifiable by one and only one interpretation of their letters. E.g., '$p\bar{q}$' comes out true when and only when 'T' is put for 'p' and '⊥' for 'q'. Now when S is such a schema, the question whether S implies a schema S' can be settled simply by supplanting 'p', 'q', etc., in S' by the values which make for truth of S, and resolving. If we come out with 'T' or a valid schema, then S implies S'; otherwise not. E.g., to determine that '$p\bar{q}$' implies '$p \supset q . \supset r$' we put 'T' for 'p' and '⊥' for 'q' in '$p \supset q . \supset r$' and resolve the result 'T $\supset$ ⊥ . $\supset$ r', getting 'T'.

In particular a fell swoop will settle any question of implication on the part of 'p' or '$\bar{p}$'. To find that 'p' implies '$q \supset p$' we put 'T' for 'p' in '$q \supset p$' and resolve the result '$q \supset$ T' to 'T'. To find that 'p' implies '$p \supset q . \supset q$' we put 'T' for 'p' in '$p \supset q . \supset q$' and resolve the result 'T $\supset q . \supset q$', coming out with the valid schema '$q \supset q$'. To find that '$\bar{q}$' implies '$-(pq)$', which was the example of Cassius, we could have simply put '⊥' for 'q' in '$-(pq)$' and resolved the result '$-(p⊥)$' to 'T'.

Some schemata, on the other hand, are visibly falsifiable by one and only one interpretation of their letters. E.g., '$-(pr)$' comes out false when and only when 'T' is put for 'p' and 'r'; '$p \supset r$' comes out false when and only when 'T' is put for 'p' and '⊥' for 'r'; '$p \lor r$' comes out false when and only when '⊥' is put for 'p' and 'r'; '$pr \supset s$' comes out false when and only when 'T' is put for 'p' and 'r' and '$\bot$' for 's'; and '$p \supset . r \lor s$' comes out false when and only when 'T' is put for 'p' and '$\bot$' for 'r' and 's'. Now when S' is a schema thus falsifiable by one and only one interpretation, the question whether a schema S implies S' can be settled simply by supplanting 'p', 'q', etc. in S by the values which make for falsity of S', and resolving. If we come out with '$\bot$' or an inconsistent schema, then S implies S'; otherwise not. For, the implication can fail only through truth of S where S' is false.

E.g., to find that '$p \supset q . q \supset r$' implies '$p \supset r$' we put 'T' for '$p$' and '$\bot$' for '$r$' in '$p \supset q . q \supset r$' and resolve the result 'T $\supset q . q \supset \bot$', getting the inconsistent schema '$q\bar{q}$'. To find that '$p \lor q . q \supset r$' implies '$p \lor r$' we put '$\bot$' for 'p' and 'r' in '$p \lor q . q \supset r$' and resolve, getting '$q\bar{q}$' again. To find that '$p \supset q . qr \supset s$' implies '$pr \supset s$' we put 'T' for '$p$' and '$r$' and '$\bot$' for '$s$' in '$p \supset q . qr \supset s$' and resolve.

In particular this backward variety of the fell swoop is convenient when we want to know whether a schema S implies 'p', or '$\bar{p}$'. To find that '$pq \lor p\bar{q}$' implies 'p' we put '$\bot$' for 'p' in '$pq \lor p\bar{q}$' and resolve the result '$\bot q \lor \bot\bar{q}$', getting '$\bot$'. To find that '$p \lor q . p \lor \bar{q}$' implies '$p$' we put '$\bot$' for '$p$' in '$p \lor q . p \lor \bar{q}$' and resolve the result '$\bot \lor q . \bot \lor \bar{q}$', getting the inconsistent schema '$q\bar{q}$'.

Fell swoops are possible only where the schema which is to do the implying clearly comes out true under one and only one interpretation, or else the schema which is to be implied comes out false under one and only one interpretation. The general test of implication, applicable in every case, is truth-value analysis of the conditional; the *full sweep* as opposed to the fell swoop.

Implication may be made to relate statements as well as schemata. When one schema implies another, and a pair of statements are obtained from the schemata by interpretation, we may say by extension that the one statement implies the other. Thus, besides saying that '$\bar{q}$' implies '$-(pq)$', we may make interpretations and say that 'Cassius is not hungry' implies 'Cassius is not lean and hungry'. But it is well here to say more explicitly that the one statement implies the other *truth-functionally*, adding the adverb as a reminder that the schemata which brought the two statements into an implication relationship were truth-functional schemata rather than schemata of kinds which have yet to be taken up in Part II and beyond. Truth-functional implication is, in other words, the relation which one statement bears to another when the second follows from the first by logical considerations within the scope of the logic of truth functions. The terms 'truth-functionally valid' and 'truth-functionally inconsistent' may be applied to statements in similar fashion.

Implication, as we have seen, is intimately related to the conditional. Implication holds when and only when the conditional is valid. This important connection has engendered a tendency among writers on logic to adopt 'implies', confusingly, as a reading of the conditional sign '$\supset$' itself. Then, since '$p \supset q$' has been explained as coming out true whenever 'p' is interpreted as false or 'q' as true, it is concluded with an air of paradox that every falsehood implies every statement and that every truth is implied by every statement. It is not perceived that '$\supset$' is at best an approximation to 'if-then', not to 'implies'.

In order fully to appreciate the distinction which I intend between '$\supset$', or 'if-then', and 'implies', it is necessary to become clearly aware of the difference between use and mention. When we say that Cambridge adjoins Boston we mention Cambridge and Boston, but use the names 'Cambridge' and 'Boston'; we write the verb 'adjoins' not between Cambridge and Boston, but between their names. When the mentioned objects are cities, as here, use and mention are unlikely to be confused. But the same distinction holds when the mentioned objects are themselves linguistic expressions. When we write:

The fifth word of "The Raven" rhymes with the eleventh

we mention the words 'dreary' and 'weary', but what we use are names of them. We write 'rhymes with' not between the rhyming words but between their names. We may also write:

'dreary' rhymes with 'weary',

but here again we are using names of the rhyming words in question—the names being in this case formed by adding single quotation marks. It would be not merely untrue but ungrammatical and meaningless to write:

Dreary rhymes with weary.

Now when we say that one statement or schema implies another, similarly, we are not to write 'implies' between the statements or schemata concerned, but between their names. In this way we mention the schemata or statements, we talk *about* them, but use their names. These names are usually formed by adding single quotation marks.[11] Validity and consistency are in this respect on the same footing with implication; we say that a schema or statement is valid or consistent by appending 'is valid' or 'is consistent' not to the schema or statement in question but to a name of it.

When on the other hand we compound a statement or schema from two others by means of 'if-then', or '$\supset$', we use the statements or schemata themselves and not their names. Here we do not *mention* the statements or schemata. There is no reference to them; they merely occur as parts of a longer statement or schema. The conditional:

If Cassius is not hungry then he is not lean and hungry

---

[11] When the expression to be named is displayed in an isolated line or lines, I make a colon do the work of single quotation marks; see above.

mentions Cassius, and says something quite trivial about him, but it mentions no statements at all. The situation here is the same as with conjunction, alternation, and negation.

We have made a point of handling 'if-then' truth-functionally. Among our topics of logical analysis, indeed, no place has been made for non-truth-functional ways of compounding statements. But the fact remains that implication, as a relation between statements, imputes intimate structural connections; it involves far more than the mere truth values of the two statements. This fact conflicts in no way with a strict adherence to truth-functional ways of *compounding* statements and schemata, insofar as statements or schemata are to be compounded at all. The verbs 'implies', 'is longer than', 'is clearer than', and 'rhymes with' are all on a par so far as the present contrasts are concerned: they connect, not statements to form compound statements, but names of statements to form statements about statements.

HISTORICAL NOTE: The distinction that was stressed just now was woefully neglected by Whitehead and Russell, who accorded '$p \supset q$' the readings 'if p then q' and 'p implies q' indifferently. The old controversy over the material conditional (Chapter 3) was, in consequence, aggravated. The truth function '$-(p\bar{q})$' meets some opposition as a rendering of 'if-then'; it meets more, and rightly, as a rendering of 'implies'. Certainly implication must be preserved as a strong relation, dependent upon the structure of the related statements and not just the truth values.

The habit of pronouncing '$\supset$' as 'implies' still persists, and is to be deplored. Partly it is encouraged by the trivial circumstance that 'if' breaks the word order, while 'implies' falls into the position of '$\supset$'. Anyone thus tempted should observe that '$\supset$' can be read without change of position as 'only if'; see page 47.

EXERCISES

1. Determine by truth-value analysis whether '$p \equiv . q \equiv r$' implies '$r \equiv . q \supset p$' or vice versa.

2. Do the same for these:

$$p \equiv qr . \supset pq, \qquad p \supset qr . \equiv pq.$$

3. Determine which of the four schemata:

$$p . p \supset q, \qquad \bar{q} . p \supset q, \qquad p . \bar{p} \supset q, \qquad p \supset q\bar{q}$$

imply 'q' and which imply '$\bar{p}$'. This means eight fell swoops.

4. Determine what implications hold between these:

$$p \supset q, \qquad p \lor q . \supset r, \qquad p \supset . q \lor r.$$

Note that '$p \supset . q \lor r$', like '$p \supset q$', becomes false under just one interpretation of its letters.

5. Determine what implications hold between these:

$$p\bar{q}, \qquad \bar{p} \equiv q, \qquad p \lor q.$$

6. Find as many schemata as you can, containing one occurrence each of 'p' and 'q' and no further letters, such that each implies '$\bar{p}$'. Also find as many as you can which are implied by '$\bar{p}$'.

7. Determine whether either of these statements implies the other:

The company is responsible if and only if the unit was an Interplex and installed since January.

If the unit was an Interplex, then it was installed since January and the company is responsible; and if the unit was not an Interplex, then it was not installed since January and the company is not responsible.

Method: Obtain schemata representing the logical forms of these statements by using 'p', 'q', and 'r' for the component statements; then test the schemata for implication. Be sure to use 'p' for one and the same component throughout both compounds and similarly for 'q' and 'r'. Be sure also to keep the proper groupings.

8
WORDS
INTO SYMBOLS

Logical inference leads from *premises*—statements assumed or believed for whatever reason—to *conclusions* which can be shown on purely logical grounds to be true if the premises are true. Techniques to this end are a primary business of logic, and have already begun to occupy our attention.

But whereas the connection between premises and conclusions is thus grounded in logic, ordinarily the premises and conclusions themselves are not; and herein precisely lies the *application* of logic to fields other than itself.

The premises and conclusions may treat of any topics and are couched, to begin with, in ordinary language rather than in the technical ideography of modern logic. It is as an aid to establishing implications that we then proceed to mutilate and distort the statements, introducing schematic letters in order to bring out relevant skeletal structures, and translating varied words into a few fixed symbols such as '⊃' and 'v' in order to gain a manageable economy of structural elements. The task of thus suitably paraphrasing a statement and isolating the relevant structure is just as essential to the application of logic as is the test or proof of implication for which that preliminary task prepares the way.

An example of how such paraphrasing reduces varied idioms to uniformity has already been noted in the notation of negation (cf. Chapter 1). The notation of conjunction has a similar effect; for in ordinary language conjunction is expressed not only by 'and' but also by 'but', by 'although', by unspoken punctuation, and in various other ways. Consideration of 'but' and 'although' is instructive, for it brings out a distinction between what may be called the logical and the rhetorical aspects of language. We are likely to say:

<blockquote>Jones is here but Smith is away,</blockquote>

rather than:

<blockquote>Jones is here and Smith is away,</blockquote>

because of the contrast between being here and being away; or, if the contrast between 'Jones is here' and 'Smith is away' attains such proportions as to cause surprise, as it might, e.g., if Jones is not in the habit of coming except to see Smith, we are likely to say:

<blockquote>Jones is here although Smith is away.</blockquote>

But the circumstances which render the compound true are always the same, viz., joint truth of the two components, regardless of whether 'and', 'but', or 'although' is used. Use of one of these words rather than another may make a difference in naturalness of idiom and may also provide some incidental evidence as to what is going on in the speaker's mind, but it is incapable of making the difference between truth and falsehood of the compound. The difference in meaning between 'and', 'but', and 'although' is rhetorical, not logical. Logical notation, unconcerned with rhetorical distinctions, expresses conjunction uniformly.

For a further example of the reduction of manifold idioms of ordinary language to uniformity in logical notations, consider the idiomatic variants of 'if-then':

If p then q, p only if q, q if p, q provided that p, q in case p.

The notation '$p \supset q$', insofar as it may be admitted as a version of 'if p then q' at all, is a version at once of all those variant idioms.

Note that the antecedent of a conditional, corresponding to the 'p' of '$p \supset q$', is not always the part which comes first in the vernacular. It is the part rather that is governed by 'if' (or by 'in case', 'provided that', etc.), regardless of whether it comes early or late in the conditional. Thus it is that 'p if q' goes over into '$q \supset p$', not '$p \supset q$'. But whereas 'if' is thus ordinarily a sign of the antecedent, the attachment of 'only' reverses it; 'only if' is a sign of the consequent. Thus 'p only if q' means, not 'p if q', but 'if p then q'; not '$q \supset p$', but '$p \supset q$'. E.g., 'You will graduate only if your bills have been paid' does not mean 'If your bills have been paid you will graduate'; it means 'If you will graduate, your bills (will) have been paid'.

The reader may have found 'if p then q' awkward as a pronunciation of '$p \supset q$', because of the separation of 'if' from 'then'. If so, the above observation on 'only if' deserves special attention; '$\supset$' may be read 'only if'.

It is particularly to be noted that 'only if' does not have the sense of '$\equiv$', which is '*if and* only if'. As the words suggest, 'p if and only if q' is a conjunction of 'p if q' and 'p only if q'—hence of '$q \supset p$' and '$p \supset q$'.

Among the linguistic variants of 'if p then q' listed above, one more might have been included: 'not p unless q'. This variant leads to the following curious reflection: if 'not p unless q' means '$p \supset q$', and '$p \supset q$' means '$\bar{p} \vee q$', then 'not p unless q' must mean '$\bar{p} \vee q$', which makes 'unless' answer to '$\vee$' and hence to 'or'. Whatever strangeness there may be in equating 'unless' or 'or' is precisely the strangeness of equating 'if-then' to '$\supset$'. It is sometimes felt that 'if-then' suggests a causal connection, or the like; and, insofar as it does, so also does 'unless'. But when we distill a truth function out of 'if-then' we have '$\supset$', and when we distill a truth function out of 'unless' we have '$\vee$', 'or'.

The evident commutativity of 'or', i.e., the equivalence of 'p or q' with 'q or p', is less evident with 'unless'. The statements:

(1)   Smith will sell unless he hears from you,
(2)   Smith will hear from you unless he sells

seem divergent in meaning. However, this divergence may be attributed in part to a subtle tendency in 'unless' compounds to mention the earlier event last when time relationships are important. Because of this tendency, we are likely to construe the vague 'hears from you' in (1) as meaning 'hears from you that he should not sell', and in (2) as meaning 'hears from you that he should have sold'. But if we are to compare (1) and (2) as genuine compounds of statements, we must first render each component unambiguous and durable in its meaning—if not absolutely, at least sufficiently to exclude shifts of meaning within the space of the comparison. Thus we should perhaps revise (1) and (2) to read:

> Smith will sell unless you restrain him,
> Smith will be reprimanded by you unless he sells,

and so consider them to be related not as 'p unless q' and 'q unless p', but merely as 'p unless q' and 'r unless p'.

Thus far we have been surveying in a cursory way that aspect of paraphrasing which turns on mere vocabulary. We have been correlating connective words of ordinary language with the connective symbols of symbolic logic. The last example, however, has brought to light another and subtler aspect of the task of paraphrasing: on occasion we must not only translate connectives but also rephrase the component clauses themselves, to the extent anyway of insuring them against material shifts of meaning within the space of the argument in hand. The necessity of this operation is seen more simply and directly in the following example. The two conjunctions:

(3)   He went to Pawcatuck and I went along,
(4)   He went to Saugatuck but I did not go along

may both be true; yet if we represent them as of the forms 'pq' and '$r\bar{q}$', as seems superficially to fit the case, we come out with an inconsistent combination '$pqr\bar{q}$'. Actually of course the 'I went along' in (3) must be distinguished from the 'I went along' whose negation appears in (4); the one is 'I went along to Pawcatuck' and the other is 'I went along to Saugatuck'. When (3) and (4) are completed in this fashion they can no longer be represented as related in the manner of 'pq' and '$r\bar{q}$', but only in the manner of 'pq' and '$r\bar{s}$'; and the apparent inconsistency disappears. In general, the trustworthiness of logical analysis and inference depends on our not giving one and the same expression different interpretations in the course of the reasoning. Violation of this principle was known traditionally as the *fallacy of equivocation*.

Insofar as the interpretation of ambiguous expressions depends on circumstances of the argument as a whole—speaker, hearer, scene, date, and underlying problem and purpose—the fallacy of equivocation is not to be feared; for, those background circumstances may be expected to influence the interpretation of an ambiguous expression uniformly wherever the expression recurs in the course of the argument. This is why words of ambiguous reference such as 'I', 'you', 'here', 'Smith', and 'Elm Street' are ordinarily allowable in logical arguments without qualification; their interpretation is indifferent to the logical soundness of an argument, provided merely that it stays the same throughout the space of the argument.

The fallacy of equivocation arises rather when the interpretation of an ambiguous expression is influenced in varying ways by immediate contexts, as in (3) and (4), so that the expression undergoes changes of meaning within the limits of the argument. In such cases we have to rephrase before proceeding; not rephrase to the extent of resolving all ambiguity, but to the extent of resolving such part of the ambiguity as might, if left standing, end up by being resolved in dissimilar ways by different immediate contexts within the proposed logical argument. The logical connectives by which components are joined in compounds must be thought of as insulating each component from whatever influences its neighbors might have upon its meaning; each component is to be wholly on its own, except insofar as its meaning may depend on those broader circumstances which condition the meanings of words in the compound as a whole or in the logical argument as a whole.

It often becomes evident, when this warning is borne in mind, that a compound which superficially seems analyzable in terms merely of conjunction and negation really calls for logical devices of a more advanced nature. The statement:

(5)   We saw Stromboli and it was erupting

is not adequately analyzed as a simple conjunction, for the construction 'was . . .-ing' in the second clause involves an essential temporal reference back to the first clause. A more adequate analysis would construe (5) rather as:

Some moment of our seeing Stromboli was a moment of its erupting,

which involves logical structures taken up in Part II.

The general enterprise of paraphrasing statements so as to isolate their logical structures has, we have thus far seen, two aspects: the direct translating of appropriate words into logical symbols (comprising just truth-functional symbols at this level of logic), and the rephrasing of component clauses to circumvent the fallacy of equivocation. Now a third aspect, of equal importance with the other two when our examples are of any considerable complexity, is determination of how to organize paraphrased fragments properly into a structured whole. Here we face the problem of determining the intended grouping. A few clues to grouping in statements of ordinary language have been noted (Chapter 4), but in the main we must rely on our good sense of everyday idiom for a sympathetic understanding of the statement and then re-think the whole in logical symbols. When a statement is complex, it is a good plan to look for the outermost structure first and then *paraphrase inward*, step by step. This procedure has the double advantage of dividing the problem up into manageable parts, and of keeping the complexities of grouping under control. E.g., consider the statement:

(6)   If Jones is ill or Smith is away then neither will the Argus deal be concluded nor will the directors meet and declare a dividend unless Robinson comes to his senses and takes matters into his own hands.

First we seek the main connective of (6). Reasoning as in Chapter 4, we can narrow the choice down to 'if-then' and 'unless'; suppose we decide on 'if-then'. The outward structure of (6), then, is that of a conditional; so let us impose just this much structure explicitly upon (6), postponing minuter analysis. We have:

(7)   Jones is ill or Smith is away ⊃ neither will the Argus deal be concluded nor will the directors meet and declare a dividend unless Robinson comes to his senses and takes matters into his own hands.

Next we may consider, as if it were a separate problem removed from (7), just the long compound 'neither ... hands'. We decide, let us suppose, that its main connective is 'unless'. Treating 'unless' as 'v', we turn (7) as a whole into:

(8)   Jones is ill or Smith is away ⊃. neither will the Argus deal be concluded nor will the directors meet and declare a dividend v Robinson will come to his senses and take matters into his own hands.

Now we take up, as if it were a separate problem removed from (8), the longest component not yet analyzed; viz., 'neither ... dividend'. The main connective here is clearly 'neither-nor'. Reflecting then that 'neither r nor s' in general goes into symbols as '$\bar{r}\bar{s}$', we rewrite 'neither ... dividend' accordingly; (8) thus becomes:

(9)   Jones is ill or Smith is away ⊃. − (the Argus deal will be concluded) − (the directors will meet and declare a dividend) v Robinson will come to his senses and take matters into his own hands.

Directing our attention finally to the various short compounds which remain unanalyzed in (9), we turn the whole into:

(10)   Jones is ill v Smith is away .⊃: − (the Argus deal will be concluded) − (the directors will meet . the directors will declare a dividend) v. Robinson will come to his senses   Robinson will take matters into his own hands.

Put schematically, the total structure is:

(11) $p \vee q .\supset. \bar{r} - (st) \vee uv.$

EXERCISES

1. Justify inference of the conclusion:

    If Smith is away and Robinson does not come to his senses then the Argus deal will not be concluded

    from (6). *Method:* Find the schema which corresponds to this conclusion as (11) does to (6); then show that this schema is implied by (11).

2. Determine which of these statements implies which:

    Jones is not eligible unless he has resigned his commission and signed a waiver.
    Jones is eligible if he has resigned his commission or signed a waiver.
    Jones is eligible only if he has signed a waiver.

    Method: Paraphrase the statements, represent their structure schematically, and test the schemata. Show all steps.

3. Paraphrase inward, showing and justifying each step:

    If either the Giants or the Bruins win and the Jackals take second place, then I'll recover past losses and either buy a clavichord or fly to Barbuda.

4. Paraphrase inward, showing and justifying each step:

    If the tree rings have been correctly identified and the mace is indigenous, then the Ajo culture antedated the Tula if and only if the Tula culture was contemporary with or derivative from that of the present excavation.

9

EQUIVALENCE

Two truth-functional schemata are called *equivalent* if they agree with each other in point of truth value under every interpretation of their letters, or in other words if they agree case by case under truth-value analysis.

In anticipation, various cases of equivalence were noted in Chapters 1–3:

'*p*' to '$\bar{\bar{p}}$', '*pp*', and '*p* ∨ *p*',   '*pq . r*' to '*p . qr*',

'*pq*' to '*qp*' and '$-(\bar{p} \vee \bar{q})$',   '*p* ∨ *q . ∨ r*' to '*p* ∨. *q* ∨ *r*',

'*p* ∨ *q*' to '*q* ∨ *p*' and '$-(\bar{p}\bar{q})$',   '$-(pq)$' to '$\bar{p} \vee \bar{q}$',

'*p* ⊃ *q*' to '$-(p\bar{q})$' and '$\bar{p}$ ∨ *q*',   '$-(p \vee q)$' to '$\bar{p}\bar{q}$',

'*p* ≡ *q*' to '*p* ⊃ *q . q* ⊃ *p*' and '$-(p\bar{q}) - (q\bar{p})$'.

To test two schemata for equivalence, we might make truth-value analyses of the two schemata and see if they agree case by case. But there is another way which tends to be easier: we may form a biconditional of the two schemata, and test it for validity. For, according to our definition, two schemata S_1 and S_2 are equivalent if and only if no interpretation makes S_1 and S_2 unlike in truth value; hence if and only if no interpretation falsifies the biconditional whose sides are S_1 and S_2. Thus, just as implication is validity of the conditional, so equivalence is validity of the biconditional.

To determine the equivalence of '*p . q* ∨ *r*' to '*pq* ∨ *pr*', e.g., we check the validity of the corresponding biconditional:[12]

$$p . q \vee r . \equiv . pq \vee pr$$

T . *q* ∨ *r* . ≡ . T*q* ∨ T*r*   ⊥ . *q* ∨ *r* . ≡ . ⊥*q* ∨ ⊥*r*

q ∨ *r* . ≡ . *q* ∨ *r*   T

T

In similar fashion it may be checked that '*p*' is equivalent to each of:

(1) $\bar{p}$,   *pp*,   *p* ∨ *p*,   *p* ∨ *pq*,   *p . p* ∨ *q*,   *pq* ∨ *p*$\bar{q}$,   *p* ∨ *q . p* ∨ $\bar{q}$.

It has been said that the most conspicuous purpose of logic, in its application to ordinary discourse, is the justification and criticism of inference. But a second purpose, almost as important, is transformation of statements. It is often desirable to transform one statement into another which "says the same thing" in a different form—a form which is simpler, perhaps, or more convenient for the particular purposes in hand. Now insofar as such transformations are justifiable by considerations purely of truth-functional structure (rather than turning upon other sorts of logical structure which lie beyond the scope of Part I), a technique for their justification is at hand

---

[12] In pursuance of the policy announced in Chapter 5, all intermediate steps of resolution in this analysis are left to the reader to fill in. The reason an intermediate stage '*q* ∨ *r* . ≡ . *q* ∨ *r*' is shown in the left-hand part of the analysis is that the passage from this to 'T' is not by resolution but by the rule of patently valid clauses, Chapter 6.

in our test of equivalence of truth-functional schemata. Transformation, e.g., of:

(2) The admiral will speak and either the dean or the president will introduce him

into:

(3) Either the admiral will speak and the dean will introduce him or the admiral will speak and the president will introduce him,

or vice versa, is justified by the equivalence of '$p . q \lor r$' to '$pq \lor pr$', and this equivalence is verified by mechanical test as above. The statements (2) and (3) may, by an extension of terminology similar to that made in Chapter 7, be spoken of as truth-functionally equivalent.

It is evident from our definitions and testing techniques that

  (i) Equivalence is mutual implication.

From this law and (i)–(iv) of page 40 these clearly follow:

  (ii) Any schema is equivalent to itself.
  (iii) If one schema is equivalent to a second and the second is equivalent to a third then the first is equivalent to the third.
  (iv) If one schema is equivalent to a second then the second is equivalent to the first. (Not so for implication!)
  (v) Valid schemata are equivalent to one another and to no others; and similarly for inconsistent schemata.

Substitution was observed in Chapter 6 to preserve validity. Since implication and equivalence are merely validity of a conditional and a biconditional, it follows that substitution also preserves implication and equivalence. From the equivalence of 'p' to each of the schemata in (1), e.g., we may infer by substitution that '$\bar{r}$' is equivalent to each of '$\bar{\bar{\bar{r}}}$', '$\bar{r}\bar{r}$', $\bar{r} \lor \bar{r}$', '$\bar{r} \lor \bar{r}s$', etc.; also that '$\bar{q}r$' is equivalent to each of '$- - (\bar{q}r)$', '$\bar{q}r\bar{q}r$', '$\bar{q}r \lor \bar{q}r$', etc.; and correspondingly for any other substitution upon 'p' and 'q' in (1). The particular family of equivalences thus generated will be used later as a means of simplifying schemata.

Appeal to substitution is helpful incidentally in justifying these two convenient ways of describing implication in terms of equivalence:

  (vi) S_1 implies S_2 if and only if S_1 is equivalent to the conjunction of S_1 and S_2.
  (vii) S_1 implies S_2 if and only if S_2 is equivalent to the alternation of S_1 and S_2.

To justify (vi), observe to begin with that '$p \supset q$' and '$p \equiv pq$' are equivalent by truth-value analysis. It follows by substitution, then, that the conditional formed of S_1 and S_2 is equivalent to the biconditional formed of S_1

and the conjunction of S_1 and S_2. So, by (v), that conditional is valid if and only if this biconditional is valid. But validity of the conditional is implication, and validity of the biconditional is equivalence; so (vi) follows. The justification of (vii) proceeds similarly from the verifiable equivalence of '$p \supset q$' and '$q \equiv . p \vee q$'.

The following two laws have to do only with implication, but I have deferred them to here because they are obtained easily from (vi) and (vii).

> (viii) S implies each of S_1 and S_2 if and only if S implies the conjunction of S_1 and S_2.
>
> (ix) S_1 and S_2 each imply S if and only if the alternation of S_1 and S_2 implies S.

Justification of (viii): Suppose S implies S_1 and S_2. Then S is equivalent, by (vi), to the conjunction of S and S_1, and also to the conjunction of S and S_2. So S is equivalent to the conjunction of all three. But, by (vi), this is the same as saying that S implies the conjunction of S_1 and S_2. So we have seen that, if S implies S_1 and also S_2, it implies their conjunction. The converse is trivial.

A parallel argument for (ix), based on (vii), is left to the reader.

The laws (viii) and (ix) afford a convenient extension of the method of fell swoop. E.g., to see whether '$pq \vee \bar{p}r \vee q\bar{r}$' implies a given schema, we have only (thanks to (ix)) to see whether each of 'pq', '$\bar{p}r$', and '$q\bar{r}$' individually implies it; and this may be seen by three fell swoops. Again, to see whether a given schema implies '$p \vee q . p \supset r . q \vee \bar{r}$', we have only (thanks to (viii)) to see whether it implies each of '$p \vee q$', '$p \supset r$', and '$q \vee \bar{r}$'; and this again may be seen by three fell swoops.

We must not hope to build (viii) and (ix) out into a square by supposing that S implies one or the other of S_1 and S_2 whenever S implies their alternation; nor, again, that S_1 or S_2 implies S whenever their conjunction implies S. After all, 'p' implies '$pq \vee p\bar{q}$' without implying either 'pq' or '$p\bar{q}$'; and 'p' is implied by '$p \vee q . p \vee \bar{q}$' but neither by '$p \vee q$' nor by '$p \vee \bar{q}$'.

Substitution consists always in putting schemata for single letters, and for all recurrences of the letters. When these restrictions are not met, the putting of one schema for another will be called not substitution but *interchange*. Thus interchange consists in putting one schema for another which need not be a single letter, and which need not be supplanted in all its recurrences. What has been said of substitution, that it preserves implication, equivalence, and inconsistency, cannot of course be said in general of interchange. But there are useful laws of interchange, the least of which is this *first law of interchange:* Think of '$\ldots p \ldots$' as any schema containing 'p', and of '$\ldots q \ldots$' as formed from '$\ldots p \ldots$' by putting 'q' for one or more occurrences of 'p'; then

$$'p \equiv q' \quad \text{implies} \quad '\ldots p \ldots . \equiv . \ldots q \ldots'.$$

(Similarly for any other letters instead of 'p' and 'q'.) Let us see why the law holds. We want to show that any interpretation of letters which makes

'$p \equiv q$' come out true will make '$\ldots p \ldots . \equiv . \ldots q \ldots$' come out true. But to make '$p \equiv q$' come out true we must either put 'T' for both 'p' and 'q' or else '⊥' for both 'p' and 'q'; and in either case '$\ldots p \ldots$' and '$\ldots q \ldots$', which differed only in 'p' and 'q', become indistinguishable from each other, so that their biconditional reduces to 'T'.

Now we can establish a more important *second law of interchange:* If S_1 and S_2 are equivalent, and S_2' is formed from S_1' by putting S_2 for one or more occurrences of S_1, then S_1' and S_2' are equivalent. E.g., this law enables us to argue from the equivalence of '$p \supset q$' and '$-(p\bar{q})$' to the equivalence of '$p \supset q \,.\mathsf{v}\, r$' and '$-(p\bar{q}) \,\mathsf{v}\, r$'. The rough idea is, in school jargon, that putting equals for equals yields equals.

This second law of interchange is established as follows. Choose any two letters not appearing in S_1' nor in S_2'. They are, let us imagine, 'p' and 'q'. Then put 'p' for the occurrences of S_1 in question in S_1'; the result may be represented as '$\ldots p \ldots$', and the result of similarly using 'q' may be represented as '$\ldots q \ldots$'. By the first law of interchange, '$p \equiv q$' implies '$\ldots p \ldots . \equiv . \ldots q \ldots$'. By substitution of S_1 for 'p' and S_2 for 'q' in this implication, we may conclude that the biconditional of S_1 and S_2 implies the biconditional of S_1' and S_2'. But the biconditional of S_1 and S_2 is valid, since S_1 and S_2 are equivalent. Therefore the biconditional of S_1' and S_2' is valid; cf. (iv) of page 40. Therefore S_1' and S_2' are equivalent.

This second law assures us that we can interchange equivalents S_1 and S_2 in any schema S_1' without affecting the outcome of a truth-value analysis; for, S_1' and the result S_2' will be equivalent, and equivalent schemata are schemata that agree case by case under truth-value analysis. There thus follows this *third law of interchange:* Interchange of equivalents preserves validity, implication, equivalence, and inconsistency; and, unlike substitution for letters, it even preserves consistency, nonvalidity, nonimplication, and nonequivalence.

Substitution for letters must, we saw, be construed as uniform and exhaustive; but there is no such requirement in the case of interchanging equivalents. If in the valid schema '$p \,\mathsf{v}\, \bar{p}$' we substitute 'qr' for 'p', we may infer the validity of '$qr \,\mathsf{v}\, -(qr)$' and this only; but if in that same valid schema '$p \,\mathsf{v}\, \bar{p}$' we elect rather to put 'pp' for its *equivalent* 'p', we are entitled thereby to infer the validity not merely of '$pp \,\mathsf{v}\, -(pp)$', but equally of '$pp \,\mathsf{v}\, \bar{p}$' and '$p \,\mathsf{v}\, -(pp)$'.

Since interchange of equivalents does not affect the outcome of a truth-value analysis, it proves to be a convenient adjunct to the technique of truth-value analysis; for, if we supplant schemata by simpler equivalents in the course of such analyses, our computations are reduced. In particular, accordingly, whenever a configuration of any of the seven forms depicted in (1) makes its appearance in the course of a truth-value analysis, let us immediately simplify it before proceeding. We are not only to put 'p' for its equivalents 'p', 'pp', '$p \,\mathsf{v}\, p$', '$p \,\mathsf{v}\, pq$', etc., but correspondingly '$\bar{r}$' for '$\bar{r}$', '$\bar{r}\bar{r}$', '$\bar{r} \,\mathsf{v}\, \bar{r}$', '$\bar{r} \,\mathsf{v}\, \bar{r}s$', etc., and '$\bar{q}r$' for '$--(\bar{q}r)$', '$\bar{q}r\bar{q}r$', '$\bar{q}r \,\mathsf{v}\, \bar{q}r$', etc.

With our new policy in mind let us take another turn at the long schema which was analyzed in Chapter 6:

$$p \lor q . p \lor \bar{q} . \lor \bar{p}q := q . : \supset . pr \lor p\bar{r}$$
$$p \lor \bar{p}q . \equiv q : \supset p$$

$$\mathsf{T} \lor \bot q . \equiv q : \supset \mathsf{T} \qquad\qquad \bot \lor \mathsf{T}q . \equiv q : \supset \bot$$
$$\mathsf{T} \qquad\qquad\qquad\qquad\qquad -(q \equiv q)$$
$$\bot$$

Here the original schema is subjected to some simplifications before the substitution of signs for '*p*' is even begun. The simplifications consist in reducing both '*p* ∨ *q* . *p* ∨ *q̄*' and '*pr* ∨ *pr̄*' to '*p*'; for '*p* ∨ *q* . *p* ∨ *q̄*' is the last of the schemata in (1), and '*pr* ∨ *pr̄*' is the next to last with '*r*' substituted for '*q*'.

Next let us turn back to the first long truth-value analysis of Chapter 6. Under the new procedure it would run rather thus:

$$pq \lor p\bar{r} \lor \bar{p}r \lor \bar{p}s \lor \bar{q}r \lor \bar{r}\bar{s}$$

$$\mathsf{T}q \lor \mathsf{T}\bar{r} \lor \bot r \lor \bot s \lor \bar{q}r \lor \bar{r}\bar{s} \qquad\qquad \bot q \lor \bot\bar{r} \lor \mathsf{T}r \lor \mathsf{T}s \lor \bar{q}r \lor \bar{r}\bar{s}$$
$$q \lor \bar{r} \lor \bar{q}r \lor \bar{r}\bar{s} \qquad\qquad\qquad\qquad r \lor s \lor \bar{q}r \lor \bar{r}\bar{s}$$
$$q \lor \bar{r} \lor \bar{q}r \qquad\qquad\qquad\qquad\qquad r \lor s \lor \bar{r}\bar{s}$$

$$\mathsf{T} \lor \bar{r} \lor \bot r \qquad \bot \lor \bar{r} \lor \mathsf{T}r \qquad\qquad \mathsf{T} \lor s \lor \bot\bar{s} \qquad \bot \lor s \lor \mathsf{T}\bar{s}$$
$$\mathsf{T} \qquad\qquad \bar{r} \lor r \qquad\qquad\qquad \mathsf{T} \qquad\qquad s \lor \bar{s}$$
$$\mathsf{T} \qquad\qquad\qquad\qquad\qquad\qquad\qquad \mathsf{T}$$

In this case none of the seven forms listed in (1) is visible in the original schema as it stands, but some emerge as the analysis proceeds. On the left side, '*q* ∨ *r̄* ∨ *q̄r* ∨ *r̄s̄*' is reduced to '*q* ∨ *r̄* ∨ *q̄r*' by putting '*r̄*' for '*r̄* ∨ *r̄s̄*'. On the right side, similarly, '*r* ∨ *s* ∨ *q̄r* ∨ *r̄s̄*' is reduced to '*r* ∨ *s* ∨ *r̄s̄*' by putting '*r*' for '*r* ∨ *q̄r*'.

Both of the simplifications last noted are based on the equivalence of '*p* ∨ *pq*' to '*p*'; but they involve also a mental switching of conjunctions and alternations. The clause '*r̄* ∨ *r̄s̄*' which is to give way to '*r̄*' is not even visible in '*q* ∨ *r̄* ∨ *q̄r* ∨ *r̄s̄*' until we think of the part '*q̄r* ∨ *r̄s̄*' as switched to read '*r̄s̄* ∨ *q̄r*'; nor is the clause '*r* ∨ *q̄r*' visible in '*r* ∨ *s* ∨ *q̄r* ∨ *r̄s̄*' until we think of the part '*s* ∨ *q̄r*' as switched to read '*q̄r* ∨ *s*'. Even when this clause '*r* ∨ *q̄r*' has been isolated, moreover, its equivalence to '*r*' is not inferred from the equivalence of '*p* ∨ *pq*' to '*p*' *merely* by substitution; we have also, mentally, to reread '*r* ∨ *q̄r*' as '*r* ∨ *rq̄*' by switching the conjunction. Such preparatory switching of alternations and conjunctions involves a tacit appeal to further equivalences: the equivalence of '*p* ∨ *q*' to '*q* ∨ *p*' and of '*pq*' to '*qp*'. But these steps drop out of consciousness if we school ourselves, as we well may, to disregard typographical order among the components of a conjunction and of an alternation.

It is arbitrary to single out just these seven equivalences, viz., the equivalence of '*p*' to each of the seven schemata in (1), as a basis for simplifications auxiliary to truth-value analyses. A further convenient equivalence, which could in fact have been exploited in both of the truth-value analyses last set forth, is the equivalence of '*p* ∨ *p̄q*' to '*p* ∨ *q*'. Another convenient one is the equivalence of '$p . \bar{p} \lor q$' to 'pq'. The practical investigator will use any simplificatory equivalences that occur to him. For the standardizing of exercises, a convenient compromise might be to allow use of the seven equivalences singled out in (1) and the further ones assembled at the beginning of the present chapter.

HISTORICAL NOTE: The confusion between implication and the conditional, deplored at the end of Chapter 7, has carried with it a confusion between equivalence and the biconditional. The deplorable habit still persists of pronouncing '$\equiv$' as 'is equivalent to' instead of as 'if and only if'.

EXERCISES

1. Determine which of these are equivalent to '$pq \supset r$' and which to '$p \lor q .\supset r$':

$$p \supset. q \supset r, \quad q \supset. p \supset r, \quad p \supset r . q \supset r, \quad p \supset r .\lor. q \supset r.$$

2. Determine which of these is equivalent to '$p \supset qr$' and which to '$p \supset. q \lor r$':

$$p \supset q . p \supset r, \qquad p \supset q .\lor. p \supset r.$$

3. Determine any equivalent pairs from among these:

$$p \supset q, \quad \bar{p} \supset \bar{q}, \quad \bar{p} \supset q, \quad q \supset p, \quad \bar{q} \supset \bar{p}, \quad \bar{q} \supset p.$$

This means fifteen short tests.

4. Making full use of the new simplification procedure, test each of the following three pairs for equivalence by truth-value analysis of biconditionals:

$$pq \lor pr \lor qr, \qquad p \lor q . p \lor r . q \lor r;$$
$$pqr \lor pqs \lor prs \lor qrs, \qquad p \lor q \lor r . p \lor q \lor s . p \lor r \lor s . q \lor r \lor s;$$
$$pqr \lor pq\bar{r} \lor p\bar{q}r \lor p\bar{q}\bar{r}, \qquad p \lor q \lor r . p \lor q \lor \bar{r} . p \lor \bar{q} \lor r . p \lor \bar{q} \lor \bar{r}.$$

5. By the same method, check the schemata:

$$p \supset. q \equiv r, \qquad pq \equiv pr, \qquad p \lor q .\equiv. p \lor r$$

for equivalence each with each.

6. Check these for equivalence by the same method:

$$p \supset q \cdot q \supset r \cdot r \supset p, \qquad p \equiv r \cdot q \equiv r.$$

7. See if the biconditional is associative.

8. Justify (ix).

10

ALTERNATIONAL NORMAL SCHEMATA

The notations 'v', '$\supset$', and '$\equiv$' are superfluous, we know, in that all use of them can be paraphrased into terms of conjunction and negation. The sign '$\supset$', however, has been seen to have a special utility in the testing of implication; for, to test implication we form a conditional (with help of '$\supset$') and test its validity. The sign '$\equiv$' has been seen to be of similar use in the testing of equivalence. So there is good reason for having added the strictly superfluous signs '$\supset$' and '$\equiv$'. Now the advantages of retaining 'v' are of quite a different kind, and will become evident in the course of the present section and the next.

What are known as DeMorgan's laws affirm the equivalence of

(i)   '$-(p \vee q \vee \ldots \vee s)$'   to   '$\bar{p}\bar{q}\ldots\bar{s}$'

and

(ii)   '$-(pq\ldots s)$'   to   '$\bar{p} \vee \bar{q} \vee \ldots \vee \bar{s}$'.

For the case of just 'p' and 'q', these laws were already noted in Chapter 1. The further cases follow by substitution and interchange. E.g., from the equivalence of '$-(p \vee q)$' to '$\bar{p}\bar{q}$' we have, by substitution of '$p \vee q$' for 'p' and 'r' for 'q', the equivalence of '$-(p \vee q \vee r)$' to '$-(p \vee q)\bar{r}$'; and thence, putting '$\bar{p}\bar{q}$' for its equivalent '$-(p \vee q)$', we obtain the equivalence of '$-(p \vee q \vee r)$' to '$\bar{p}\bar{q}\bar{r}$'.

DeMorgan's laws are useful in enabling us to avoid negating conjunctions and alternations. We never need apply negation to the whole of an alternation, since '$-(p \vee q \vee \ldots \vee s)$' is equivalent to '$\bar{p}\bar{q}\ldots\bar{s}$'; and we never need apply negation to the whole of a conjunction, since '$-(pq\ldots s)$' is equivalent to '$\bar{p}$ v $\bar{q}$ v $\ldots$ v $\bar{s}$'. Also of course we never need apply negation to a negation, since '$\bar{\bar{p}}$' is equivalent to 'p'. For that matter, we also never need apply negation to a conditional or biconditional; for, by the method of the preceding section it is easy to verify the equivalence of

(iii)   '$-(p \supset q)$'   to   '$p\bar{q}$'

and of

(iv)   '$-(p \equiv q)$'   to   '$\bar{p} \equiv q$'   and to   '$p \equiv \bar{q}$'.

So any truth-functional schema can be put over into an equivalent in which negation never applies to anything but individual letters. Transformation of this kind is generally conducive to easy intelligibility.

E.g., consider the forbidding schema:

(1) $-\{p \supset \bar{s}q . \supset \, -(sq \supset p) : -[-(rp) - (p \supset \bar{s})]\}$.

(It is of some help to vary parentheses thus with brackets and braces when they are deeply nested.) Now since (1) has the outward form '$-(tu)$', it can be transformed by (ii) to read:

$$-[p \supset \bar{s}q . \supset \, -(sq \supset p)] \, \mathsf{v} - -[-(rp) - (p \supset \bar{s})].$$

Cancellation of '$- -$' reduces this to:

(2) $-[p \supset \bar{s}q . \supset \, -(sq \supset p)] \, \mathsf{v} - (rp) - (p \supset \bar{s})$.

Then by (iii) we transform the first half of (2) into:

$$p \supset \bar{s}q . - -(sq \supset p),$$

or

$$p \supset \bar{s}q . sq \supset p,$$

so that (2) becomes:

(3) $p \supset \bar{s}q . sq \supset p . \mathsf{v} - (rp) - (p \supset \bar{s})$.

By (ii) again, '$-(rp)$' here becomes '$\bar{r}$ v $\bar{p}$', and, by (iii) again, '$-(p \supset \bar{s})$' becomes '$p\bar{\bar{s}}$' or 'ps', so that (3) comes down to:

(4) $p \supset \bar{s}q . sq \supset p . \mathsf{v}. \bar{r}$ v $\bar{p} . ps$,

in which, finally, all negation signs are limited to single letters. (4) is far easier to grasp than (1).

Such is the advantage of confining negation to single letters. Now it will be found in general that still further perspicuity can be gained by confining conjunction to single letters and negations of letters; and it will be found also that such confinement of conjunction can, like the confinement of negation to single letters, always be accomplished. The law which makes this possible is known as the *law of distributivity of conjunction through alternation*, and runs as follows:

'$p . q \lor r \lor \ldots \lor t$' is equivalent to '$pq \lor pr \lor \ldots \lor pt$'.

Regardless of the number of letters involved, the equivalence is readily verified by the method of the preceding section:

$$p . q \lor r \lor \ldots \lor t . \equiv . pq \lor pr \lor \ldots \lor pt$$

$$\mathsf{T} . q \lor r \lor \ldots \lor t . \equiv . \mathsf{T}q \lor \mathsf{T}r \lor \ldots \lor \mathsf{T}t \qquad \bot . q \lor r \lor \ldots \lor t . \equiv . \bot q \lor \bot r \lor \ldots \lor \bot t$$

$$q \lor r \lor \ldots \lor t . \equiv . q \lor r \lor \ldots \lor t \qquad\qquad \bot \equiv \bot$$

$$\mathsf{T} \qquad\qquad\qquad\qquad\qquad\qquad \mathsf{T}$$

This law, like the familiar identity:

$$x(y + z + \ldots + w) = xy + xz + \ldots + xw$$

of algebra, authorizes the convenient operation of "multiplying out." Thanks to it, we need never acquiesce in a conjunction which has an alternation as component; we can always distribute the other part of the conjunction through the alternation, as above, so as to come out with an alternation of simpler conjunctions.

Since order is immaterial to conjunction, such distribution can be worked equally well in reverse: not only is '$p . q \lor r \lor \ldots \lor t$' equivalent to '$pq \lor pr \lor \ldots \lor pt$', but also '$q \lor r \lor \ldots \lor t . p$' is equivalent to '$qp \lor rp \lor \ldots \lor tp$'. These two sorts of distribution are indeed one and the same, once we learn to ignore order of conjunction.

When we have a conjunction of two alternations, distribution takes the form of the familiar "cross-multiplying" of algebra; e.g., '$p \lor t . q \lor r \lor s$' comes out '$pq \lor pr \lor ps \lor tq \lor tr \lor ts$'. For, we begin by handling '$q \lor r \lor s$' as we might a single letter 'u'; thus, just as '$p \lor t . u$' would become '$pu \lor tu$' by (reverse) distribution, so '$p \lor t . q \lor r \lor s$' becomes '$p . q \lor r \lor s . \lor . t . q \lor r \lor s$'. Afterward, distribution of 'p' turns the part '$p . q \lor r \lor s$' into '$pq \lor pr \lor ps$', and distribution of 't' turns the part '$t . q \lor r \lor s$' into '$tq \lor tr \lor ts$'.

Let us now go back to (4) and improve it by distributing. We thereby change the part '$\bar{r} \lor \bar{p} . ps$' of (4) to '$\bar{r}ps \lor \bar{p}ps$', so that (4) becomes:

(5) $$p \supset \bar{s}q \, . \, sq \supset p \, .\text{v} \, \bar{r}ps \, \text{v} \, \bar{p}ps.$$

We can open the way to further distribution if we get rid of '$\supset$', translating '$t \supset u$' in general as '$\bar{t} \, \text{v} \, u$'. Such translation turns (5) into:

$$\bar{p} \, \text{v} \, \bar{s}q \, . \, -(sq) \, \text{v} \, p \, .\text{v} \, \bar{r}ps \, \text{v} \, \bar{p}ps,$$

which, when '$-(sq)$' is changed to '$\bar{s} \, \text{v} \, \bar{q}$' by (ii), becomes:

$$\bar{p} \, \text{v} \, \bar{s}q \, . \, \bar{s} \, \text{v} \, \bar{q} \, \text{v} \, p \, .\text{v} \, \bar{r}ps \, \text{v} \, \bar{p}ps.$$

Now the part '$\bar{p} \, \text{v} \, \bar{s}q \, . \, \bar{s} \, \text{v} \, \bar{q} \, \text{v} \, p$' can be "cross-multiplied," so that the whole becomes:

(6) $$\bar{p}\bar{s} \, \text{v} \, \bar{p}\bar{q} \, \text{v} \, \bar{p}p \, \text{v} \, \bar{s}q\bar{s} \, \text{v} \, \bar{s}q\bar{q} \, \text{v} \, \bar{s}qp \, \text{v} \, \bar{r}ps \, \text{v} \, \bar{p}ps.$$

We can quickly shorten this result by deleting the patently inconsistent clauses '$\bar{p}p$', '$\bar{s}q\bar{q}$', and '$\bar{p}ps$'. We then have:

(7) $$\bar{p}\bar{s} \, \text{v} \, \bar{p}\bar{q} \, \text{v} \, \bar{s}q\bar{s} \, \text{v} \, \bar{s}qp \, \text{v} \, \bar{r}ps.$$

Such deletion is a case of the procedure explained in Chapter 6: each of the patently inconsistent clauses may be thought of as supplanted by '$\bot$', which afterward drops by resolution ((ii) of Chapter 5).

Also we may drop any duplications from conjunctions—thus reducing '$\bar{s}q\bar{s}$' to '$\bar{s}q$'. This was the second of the seven forms of simplification noted in (1) of the preceding chapter. So (7) becomes:

(8) $$\bar{p}\bar{s} \, \text{v} \, \bar{p}\bar{q} \, \text{v} \, \bar{s}q \, \text{v} \, \bar{s}qp \, \text{v} \, \bar{r}ps,$$

which wears its meaning on its sleeve. This its equivalents (1) and (4) could scarcely have been said to do.

The forms (6)–(8) share the following three noteworthy properties: '$\supset$' and '$\equiv$' do not occur; negation is confined to single letters; and conjunction is confined to letters and negations of letters. Schemata having these three properties will be called *alternational normal schemata.*

This essentially negative characterization may be reformulated in more positive terms as follows. Let us speak of single letters and negations of single letters collectively as *literals;* thus 'p', 'q', '$\bar{p}$', etc. are literals. The alternational normal schemata, then, are the literals, the conjunctions of literals, the alternations of literals, the alternations of conjunctions of literals, and the alternations of literals with conjunctions of literals. This characterization can be put much more compactly if we allow ourselves to speak of conjunctions and alternations not only of two or more components but also of one component—meaning thereby the component itself.

Under this usage, '$\bar{p}$', '$\bar{p}q$', and '$\bar{p}q\bar{r}$' are conjunctions respectively of one, two, and three literals; and correspondingly for alternation. An alternational normal schema, then, is describable simply as any *alternation of conjunctions of literals*—that is, any alternation of *one* or more conjunctions of *one* or more literals. These conjunctions, whereof the alternational normal schema is an alternation, are called its *clauses*.

The process whereby (1) was transformed into its alternational normal equivalent (6) can be reproduced for all schemata. Given any schema, we can rid it of '$\supset$' and '$\equiv$' by familiar translations: '$p \supset q$' becomes '$\bar{p} \vee q$' and '$p \equiv q$' becomes '$pq \vee \bar{p}\bar{q}$'. We can confine negation to single letters by (i)–(iv), or simply by (i)–(ii) having first got rid of '$\supset$' and '$\equiv$'. Finally we can confine conjunction to literals by persistent distribution. The reader will find by experiment that labor is generally saved, in these transformations, by working from the outside inward.

This is all there is, strictly speaking, to transformation into alternational normal form. Simplification, however, as in passing from (6) to (8), is always welcome too. This gets rid, we saw, of duplications of a literal within a clause, and it gets rid of any inconsistent clause—unless of course the whole schema has boiled down to a single inconsistent clause, say '$\bar{q}sq$', whose omission would leave us with nothing at all. Even in this extreme case a small simplification can still be made: we can write '$p\bar{p}$', since all inconsistent schemata are equivalent.

Thus in the alternational normal form we have an immediate test of inconsistency: just simplify by dropping inconsistent clauses, in the above fashion, and see if nothing but a visibly inconsistent clause remains.

Alternational normal schemata are generally convenient because their net import is so readily grasped: we can tell at a glance what interpretations will make them true. E.g., an interpretation will make (8) true if and only if it either interprets 'p' and 's' as false (making the first clause of (8) true), or interprets 'p' and 'q' as false (making the second clause true), or interprets 's' as false and 'q' as true, or etc.

One of the simplification laws that were collected in (1) of Chapter 9 reduced '$pq \vee p\bar{q}$' to 'p'. If perversely we apply this law backwards, as a complication law, we can expand one alternational normal schema into another which has certain bold traits worth noticing. This expansive transformation is called *development;* 'p' goes into '$pq \vee p\bar{q}$' by development with respect to 'q'. Now if we persistently develop each clause of an alternational normal schema with respect to each letter that is absent from the clause, we arrive at the *developed alternational normal form*. For instance, '$\bar{s}q \vee \bar{r}ps$' becomes first:

$$\bar{s}qp \vee \bar{s}q\bar{p} \vee \bar{r}psq \vee \bar{r}ps\bar{q}$$

and eventually:

$$\bar{s}qpr \vee \bar{s}qp\bar{r} \vee \bar{s}q\bar{p}r \vee \bar{s}q\bar{p}\bar{r} \vee \bar{r}psq \vee \bar{r}ps\bar{q},$$

or, alphabetized:

$$p q r \bar{s} \vee p q \bar{r} \bar{s} \vee \bar{p} q r \bar{s} \vee \bar{p} q \bar{r} \bar{s} \vee p q \bar{r} s \vee p \bar{q} \bar{r} s.$$

This form, when thus alphabetized and freed of repetitions, is in effect a truth table; each of its clauses depicts one of the ways of assigning truth values to letters that makes the schema come out true. Implication becomes recognizable on sight: if the letters of two developed alternational normal schemata are alike, then the one schema implies the other just in case all its clauses are among the clauses of the other. The mark of validity, in developed alternational normal form, is that all possible clauses are present: all 2^n of them, where n is the number of different letters. The mark of inconsistency is disappearance; no clauses.

HISTORICAL NOTE: DeMorgan's laws were named for Augustus DeMorgan, who flourished in 1846–64; but they were known to William of Ockham five centuries earlier. (Cf. Łukasiewicz, "Zur Geschichte.") The idea of *development* and its name go back to DeMorgan's contemporary George Boole. The alternational normal form was familiar to Ernst Schröder by 1877 and is doubtless older. This form is often called, less suggestively, the disjunctive normal form.

EXERCISES

1. By successive transformations, transform each of these schemata into an alternational normal schema.

$$- (p \vee - \{q \vee - [r \vee - (q \vee p)] \}),$$
$$p \supset q . q \supset r . \supset . p \supset r,$$
$$p \supset q . \supset p := \bar{p},$$
$$p \equiv q . q \equiv r,$$
$$p \equiv q . \equiv r,$$
$$p q \equiv r.$$

2. Develop each of the results of the preceding exercise into developed alternational normal form.

3. Judge whether this is a sound general method of testing alternational normal truth-functional schemata for equivalence: *decide by fell swoop whether each clause of each schema implies the other schema.* Justify your judgment.

4. Check the implications in Exercises 1–4 of Chapter 7 by the method of developed alternational normal forms.

11
SIMPLIFICATION

The perspicuity of the alternational normal form can be enhanced by pressing simplification. In passing from (7) to (8) in the preceding chapter we used one of the seven forms of simplification which were noted in connection with (1) of page 52, viz. 'pp' to 'p'. But others of the seven may likewise be used to advantage, e.g., that of '$p \vee pq$' to 'p'. Thus, reducing '$\bar{s}q \vee \bar{s}qp$' to '$\bar{s}q$' in (8), we get:

$$(1) \qquad\qquad \bar{p}\bar{s} \vee \bar{p}\bar{q} \vee \bar{s}q \vee \bar{r}ps.$$

The result (1) itself is susceptible to yet a further simplification, covered by none of the seven. The initial clause of (1) is in fact redundant; (1) is equivalent to:

$$(2) \qquad\qquad \bar{p}\bar{q} \vee \bar{s}q \vee \bar{r}ps.$$

There is a quick way of testing any clause of an alternational normal schema to see if it can be thus dropped as redundant. The law (vii) of page 53 tells us how: just check, by fell swoop, whether the clause implies the rest of the schema. The clause '$\bar{p}\bar{s}$' of (1) is found by fell swoop to imply the remainder of (1), and this marks '$\bar{p}\bar{s}$' as redundant in (1).

The schema (6) of the preceding chapter was already an alternational normal schema. (2) here is another, and, we see, equivalent to (6). Simplification can go a long way.

Sometimes an alternational normal schema can be simplified by dropping not a whole clause but just a literal. This happened already in the preceding chapter when we moved from (7) to (8) on the strength of (1) of page 52. It can happen also in cases untouched by (1) of page 52. An example is afforded by '$pq \vee p\bar{q}r \vee \bar{p}\bar{q}\bar{r}$', which proves equivalent to '$pq \vee pr \vee \bar{p}\bar{q}\bar{r}$'.

There is a quick way of testing a literal in a clause C of an alternational normal schema S to see if it can be dropped as redundant. Just see, by fell swoop, whether the rest of C implies S. Thus take '$pqr \vee p\bar{r} \vee \bar{q}\bar{r}$'. To check that the '$r$' of '$pqr$' is redundant here, we check that 'pq' implies '$pqr \vee p\bar{r} \vee \bar{q}\bar{r}$'.

The general correctness of this method of testing is seen as follows. The rest of C—call it C'—will imply S just in case S is equivalent to the alternation of C' and S; this we know from (vii) of page 53. But this alternation contains as a part the alternation of C and C', and this part is reducible simply to C' by (1) of page 52. We see therefore that C' implies S just in case C' can supplant C in S.

Sometimes the elimination of a redundant literal can reward us doubly, by engendering a clausal redundancy that we can drop as well. Thus consider again our last example, '$pqr \lor p\bar{r} \lor \bar{q}\bar{r}$'. We see by three fell swoops that none of its three clauses is redundant. After we drop the redundant 'r', however, the remainder '$pq \lor p\bar{r} \lor \bar{q}\bar{r}$' has a redundant clause. Find it.

Two good ways are now before us for simplifying alternational normal schemata. We can test a clause for redundancy, and we can test a literal for redundancy, in each case by fell swoop. An alternational normal schema can, however, resist both redundancy tests and still admit of simplification in more devious ways. An example is:

$$(3) \qquad\qquad p\bar{q} \lor \bar{p}q \lor q\bar{r} \lor \bar{q}r.$$

By twelve fell swoops the reader can test each clause and each literal of (3) for redundancy and draw a blank every time. Yet (3) has a simpler equivalent, '$p\bar{q} \lor \bar{p}r \lor q\bar{r}$'.

Simplifications by these fell-swoop techniques are always beneficial, even failing the assurance that we have found a shortest equivalent. We may forgo such further reductions as that of (3) to '$p\bar{q} \lor \bar{p}r \lor q\bar{r}$', or we may press on with the next paragraphs.

It is remarkable that no quick and general method is known for reducing an alternational normal schema to a shortest equivalent. We have to exhaust possibilities. An adequate range of possibilities can be staked out by the following considerations. An alternational normal schema is an alternation of clauses each of which *implies* the schema (since 'p' implies '$p \lor q$'). Further, if we have checked for redundant literals and deleted them, we may be sure that each clause is a *prime* implicant of the schema; that is, when you drop any literal from a clause, the remainder of the clause ceases to imply the schema. So, if we somehow assemble all the prime implicants of a given schema, we may be sure that we have caught all the clauses of any shortest alternational normal equivalent of our schema. At our clumsiest we may then simply try the various combinations of prime implicants and select a shortest alternation that comes out equivalent to the original schema.

There is a mechanical method, due to Samson and Mills, for generating all the prime implicants of a schema. We start with an alternational normal schema that has been freed of redundant literals. This schema is an alternation of some of its prime implicants. Now if two of these clauses are opposed in one and only one letter, say 'p' (so that one clause has 'p' and the other has '$\bar{p}$'), take the conjunction of the rest of their literals. This conjunction (minus any duplications) is what I call the *consensus* of the two clauses. For instance, the first and third clauses of (3) have the consensus '$p\bar{r}$'; the second and fourth have '$\bar{p}r$'. It can be proved that this process of consensus-taking will turn up every missing prime implicant.[13]

Thus, to find a shortest normal equivalent of (3), we begin by generating its two missing prime implicants as above. Annexing them to (3), we have:

(4) $p\bar{q}$ ∨ $\bar{p}q$ ∨ $q\bar{r}$ ∨ $\bar{q}r$ ∨ $p\bar{r}$ ∨ $\bar{p}r$.

This is equivalent still to (3), by virtue of (vii) of page 53; it is a redundant equivalent. We know that its last two clauses can be dropped; but if, instead, we keep one or both of them, perhaps we can drop others, and more. So we make various experimental fell swoops. In the course of them we find not only that '$\bar{p}q$' implies the rest of (4) and so can be dropped, but also that '$\bar{q}r$' implies the rest of what remains and so can be dropped in turn, and also that '$p\bar{r}$' implies the rest of that. We end up thus with '$p\bar{q}$ ∨ $\bar{p}r$ ∨ $q\bar{r}$', an improvement on (3). There is another equally short version that we could get too; the reader might like to search it out.

HISTORICAL NOTE: The problem of simplifying truth-functional schemata has interested industry, because of an application to electric circuits. Thus picture two terminals and two intervening switches. If the switches are connected in parallel, then the current is on just in case the one switch *or* the other is closed. If they are connected in series, then the current is on just in case the one switch *and* the other are closed. Such are the roles of alternation and conjunction; and as for negation, it answers to the throwing of a switch. There results, as Claude Shannon observed in 1938, a correspondence between circuits and schemata. A practical technique for reducing a schema to a shortest equivalent schema would enable the engineer to reduce a circuit to a simplest equivalent circuit. I was still unaware of the elusiveness of such a technique as late as 1948, when I was working at the present book and hoping to base my whole treatment of truth-function logic upon an easy simplification routine. My first article on the problem appeared in 1952. By then the computation laboratory at Harvard had found it worthwhile actually to tabulate and publish the simplest equivalents of the 65,536 truth functions of four distinct letters. (See Aiken.) Because automata require complicated circuits, many studies of the simplification problem have been published in engineering media. It was in one such in 1954 that Samson and Mills presented the consensus method, as I am calling it, for getting all the prime implicants as in (4). In another such paper, in 1957, Ghazala showed a way of expediting the rest of the job, that of selecting an adequate minimum of prime implicants as in '$p\bar{q}$ ∨ $\bar{p}r$ ∨ $q\bar{r}$'. Meanwhile another engineer, Rolf K. Müller, showed me in 1955 that the major technical trouble lies in the surprising multitude of prime implicants, in the case of schemata with six or a dozen different

---

[13] See my *Selected Logic Papers*, pp. 166 f.

letters. Fridshal cites a nine-letter schema which, he claims, has 1698 prime implicants. Engineers have been programming computers to find simplifications of such schemata, but even so the task can be forbidding. A simplification technique that did not depend on any exhaustive survey of the prime implicants would be a boon.

EXERCISES

1. Check the equivalence of (1) to (2) by truth-value analysis.

2. Similarly for (3) and '$p\bar{q} \vee \bar{p}r \vee q\bar{r}$'.

3. Investigate these schemata for redundant clauses and redundant literals:

$$p\bar{q}\bar{r} \vee \bar{p}q \vee pr \vee qr, \qquad pq \vee p\bar{q}r \vee \bar{p}\bar{q}\bar{r}.$$

4. Do the same for the six alternational normal schemata obtained in Exercise 1 of Chapter 10.

5. Find another equivalent of (4), as short as '$p\bar{q} \vee \bar{p}r \vee q\bar{r}$'. Show steps.

6. Find all prime implicants of each of the six alternational normal schemata obtained in Exercise 1 of Chapter 10. (First drop any redundancies that were revealed just now by Exercise 4.)

7. Find a shortest alternational normal equivalent of each of the six.

12
DUALITY

All logical computation at the truth-functional level is essentially computation with 'T' and '⊥'. Hence it is to be expected that two schemata will be quite parallel in their behavior if they are just alike under truth-value analysis except for a thoroughgoing interchange of 'T' and '⊥'. Schemata so related are called *duals* of each other. They behave in relation to each other according to laws which, for their theoretical interest and occasional convenience, warrant some notice.

Though duals are opposed somewhat in the manner of 'T' to '⊥', they are not to be confused with mere contradictories or mutual negations. The prime example of duality, rather, is conjunction versus alternation. Conjunction and alternation are alike except for a *thoroughgoing* interchange of 'T' and '⊥', in the following sense. Conjunction, to begin with, is describable thus:

1st component	2nd component	result
T	T	T
⊥	T	⊥
T	⊥	⊥
⊥	⊥	⊥

Now to interchange 'T' and '⊥' merely in the last column would indeed produce a truth function which is the negation of conjunction. Interchange 'T' and '⊥' throughout all three columns, however, and what you get is precisely a description of alternation:

1st component	2nd component	result
⊥	⊥	⊥
T	⊥	T
⊥	T	T
T	T	T

Such is the sense in which '*pq*' and '*p* ∨ *q*' are said to be duals. In general the relationship between dual schemata S and S' is this: whenever each of '*p*', '*q*', etc. is interpreted oppositely for S and S', the truth values of S and S' turn out oppositely to each other.

Trivially, by this standard, '*p̄*' is dual not to '*p*' but to '*p̄*' itself; for, give opposite values to '*p*' and you get values for '*p̄*' which are opposite to each other.

The duality of '*pq*' to '*p* ∨ *q*' is evident without resort to the above tabulation if we simply compare the original descriptions of conjunction and alternation. A conjunction is true when its components are all true, and otherwise false; whereas an alternation is false when its components are all false, and otherwise true. These two descriptions are alike except for interchange of 'true' and 'false'; hence '*pq*' and '*p* ∨ *q*' are bound to behave alike except for a thoroughgoing interchange of the rôles of 'T' and '⊥'— which is what duality means. The self-duality of '*p̄*' is evident similarly from the general description of a negation as "true or false according as its component is false or true"; for, switch the words 'true' and 'false' in this description and you simply have the description of negation over again.

More generally now, consider any schema S built up of letters by means exclusively of negation, conjunction, and alternation (hence devoid of '⊃' and '≡'). Suppose a second schema S' is like S except that it has alternation wherever S has conjunction and vice versa. Then truth-value analyses of S and S' are bound to match except for interchange of 'T' and '⊥' throughout; for, we just saw that the explanations of conjunction and alternation are alike except for switching 'true' with 'false', and that the explanation of negation is unchanged by switching 'true' with 'false'. So S and S' are duals.

What has just been established will be called the *first law of duality:* Where S is any truth-functional schema devoid of '$\supset$' and '$\equiv$', the result of changing alternation to conjunction and vice versa throughout S is dual to S. This law affirms immediately the duality of 'pq' to '$p \vee q$', and the self-duality of '$\bar{p}$' and of 'p'. It affirms also the duality of '$\bar{p} \cdot q \vee \bar{r}$' to '$\bar{p} \vee q\bar{r}$', the duality of '$p\bar{q} \vee \bar{p}r$' to '$p \vee \bar{q} \cdot \bar{p} \vee r$', the duality of '$pq \vee qr \vee pr$' to '$p \vee q \cdot q \vee r \cdot p \vee r$', etc.

So we now have a quick and graphic way of forming a dual of a schema: interchange conjunction and alternation. This procedure depends, be it noted, on absence of '$\supset$' and '$\equiv$'; but we can get rid of '$\supset$' and '$\equiv$' in advance, since '$p \supset q$' may be rendered as '$\bar{p} \vee q$' and '$p \equiv q$' as '$\bar{p} \vee q \cdot \bar{q} \vee p$' or '$pq \vee \bar{p}\bar{q}$'.

In interchanging conjunction and alternation to get duals, special care must be taken to preserve grouping. In case of doubt, think of full parentheses as restored in lieu of the dot conventions. Thus '$p \cdot q \vee r$' has as dual not '$p \vee q \cdot r$' but '$p \vee qr$'. For, '$p \cdot q \vee r$' means '$p(q \vee r)$', and '$p \vee qr$' means '$p \vee (qr)$', in which the same pattern of grouping is preserved; '$p \vee q \cdot r$', on the other hand, means '$(p \vee q)r$', and is dual rather to '$pq \vee r$'.

Given any schemata S and S', now, we can test whether S' is a dual of S by forming an explicit dual of S according to the above method and then checking it for equivalence to S'. In particular we can thus determine whether a given schema S is a dual of itself; we have merely to form the explicit dual of S by switching conjunction with alternation, as explained, and then to test this result for equivalence to S. Apart from trivial cases, such as '$\bar{p}$', self-duality is rather rare; but it does occur. E.g., '$pq \vee pr \vee qr$' is dual to itself, since it is equivalent to its own explicit dual '$p \vee q \cdot p \vee r \cdot q \vee r$'. (Cf. Chapter 9, Exercise 4.)

Switching alternation with conjunction is not the only convenient way of forming a dual. Another way, which does not even require a preparatory elimination of '$\supset$' and '$\equiv$', is provided by the *second law of duality:* If in any schema you negate all letters and also the whole, you get a dual. This law is evident from the original definition of duality; for negating the letters has the same effect as reversing all interpretations of letters, and negating the whole reverses the truth value of the outcome.

DeMorgan's laws themselves (Chapter 10) are essentially duality principles, as may be seen by rearguing them in the present context. As dual of '$pq \ldots s$' the first law of duality cites '$p \vee q \vee \ldots \vee s$', whereas the second cites rather '$-(\bar{p}\bar{q}\ldots\bar{s})$'; these two must then be equivalent to each other, and thus DeMorgan's first law, (i) of Chapter 10, holds. (ii) admits of a parallel argument.

A *third law of duality* is this: A schema is valid if and only if its dual is inconsistent. For, if two truth-value analyses differ to the extent of a thoroughgoing interchange of 'T' and '$\perp$', clearly the one will show validity if and only if the other shows inconsistency.

Fourth law of duality: A schema S_1 implies a schema S_2 if and only if the dual of S_2 implies the dual of S_1. This is seen as follows. The duals of S_1 and S_2 behave like S_1 and S_2, under truth-value analysis, except for a switching of 'true' with 'false' throughout. Hence to say that no interpretation of letters makes S_1 true and S_2 false is the same as saying that no interpretation makes the dual of S_1 false and the dual of S_2 true.

Fifth law of duality: Schemata are equivalent if and only if their duals are equivalent. This follows from the fourth law, since equivalence is mutual implication.

The third, fourth, and fifth laws enable us, having established one validity or inconsistency or implication or equivalence by truth-value analysis or otherwise, to infer an additional inconsistency or validity or implication or equivalence without further analysis. E.g., having verified that '$p \lor \bar{q} \,.\, q \lor \bar{r} \,.\, r \lor s$' implies '$p \lor s$' (as may be done by the method of the fell swoop, Chapter 7), we may conclude by the fourth law of duality that 'ps' implies '$p\bar{q} \lor q\bar{r} \lor rs$'. This operation may, in contradistinction to the first, be spoken of as the *full swap*.

Either of DeMorgan's laws, (i)–(ii) of Chapter 10, follows from the other by the fifth law of duality. Again, from the law of distributivity of conjunction through alternation (Chapter 10) we can, by the fifth law of duality, infer a *law of distributivity of alternation through conjunction:*

$$\text{'}p \lor qr\ldots t\text{'} \text{ is equivalent to '}p \lor q \,.\, p \lor r \,.\,\ldots\,.\, p \lor t\text{'}.$$

This law shows that conjunction and alternation are in still more congenial relations to each other than are multiplication and addition. In arithmetic we can multiply out, thus:

$$x(y + z + \ldots + w) = xy + xz + \ldots + xw,$$

but we cannot "add out" thus:

$$x + yz\ldots w = (x + y)(x + z)\ldots(x + w).$$

In the case of alternation and conjunction, on the other hand, distribution works both ways.

Indeed, since by the fifth law of duality all equivalences continue to hold when conjunction and alternation are switched, we may conclude at once that the technique of reducing a truth-functional schema to a normal schema may be reproduced entire with alternation and conjunction switched. This switched procedure issues in *conjunctional* normal schemata such as:

$$p \lor \bar{q} \lor r \,.\, \bar{p} \lor s \,.\, q \lor \bar{r} \lor s$$

—i.e., in conjunctions of alternations of literals. The *clauses* of a conjunctional normal schema are alternations, not conjunctions; and the schema is a conjunction of its clauses.

Because of duality, any procedure for simplifying alternational normal schemata has an exact parallel for conjunctional normal schemata. In particular, just as any inconsistent clause such as '$\bar{q}sq$' drops from an alternational normal schema (as long as some clause remains), so any valid clause such as '$\bar{q} \vee s \vee q$' drops from a conjunctional normal schema.

It was noted in Chapter 10 that the alternational normal form affords an immediate test of inconsistency. The conjunctional normal form affords a corresponding test of validity: just simplify by dropping valid clauses in the above fashion and see if nothing but a visibly valid clause remains.

Along with the developed alternational normal form that confronted us in Chapter 10, a developed conjunctional normal form is assured by duality. Here the appropriate operation of development is the one that carries 'p' into '$p \vee q . p \vee \bar{q}$'. The conjunctional normal form '$\bar{s} \vee q . \bar{r} \vee p \vee s$' has the developed conjunctional normal form:

$$p \vee q \vee r \vee \bar{s} . p \vee q \vee \bar{r} \vee \bar{s} . \bar{p} \vee q \vee r \vee \bar{s}$$
$$. \bar{p} \vee q \vee \bar{r} \vee \bar{s} . p \vee q \vee \bar{r} \vee s . p \vee \bar{q} \vee \bar{r} \vee s,$$

the dual of what we saw at the end of Chapter 10. For two developed conjunctional normal forms having the same letters, the test of implication is the reverse of what it was for developed alternational normal forms; all the clauses of the implied schema are among those of the implying schema. The mark of inconsistency in developed conjunctional normal form is presence of all the 2^n possible clauses, and the mark of validity is disappearance.

HISTORICAL NOTE: The essence of duality is DeMorgan's laws, which, as noted, go back six centuries to William of Ockham. The full and deliberate treatment of duality dates from Schröder (1877).

EXERCISES

1. Which of the schemata:

$$p \equiv q, \qquad p \equiv \bar{q}, \qquad \bar{p} \equiv q, \qquad -(p \equiv q)$$

   are dual to which? Justify.

2. Write the duals of these:

$$p \supset q, \qquad q \supset p, \qquad -(p \supset q), \qquad -(q \supset p).$$

3. We saw in Chapter 11 a test of redundancy for a clause or a literal of an

alternational normal schema. What, by considerations of duality, should be the tests of redundancy for a clause or a literal of a conjunctional normal schema?

4. By successive transformations, transform each of the schemata of Exercise 1 of Chapter 10 into a conjunctional normal schema. Simplify where you can.

5. Expand the results of Exercise 4 into developed conjunctional normal form.

6. Test the four schemata of Exercise 1 of Chapter 6 for validity by putting them into conjunctional normal form.

13
AXIOMS

The application of logic to one or another scientific theory, such as arithmetic or some branch of physics, is sometimes made explicit by setting up what is called an axiom system. Certain statements of the theory are chosen as a starting point under the name of axioms, and then further statements, called theorems, are generated by showing that they are logically implied by the axioms. The implication concerned here goes beyond the kind of implication that we have thus far considered, namely truth-functional implication, and exploits also the further resources of logic that we shall turn to in later parts of the book.

A variant of the axiomatic method has often been used within logic itself, and even within truth-function logic, to generate valid schemata. Here the generating relation can no longer be cited simply as implication, since implication here is ubiquitous; any valid schema is implied by any and every schema. Instead, specific formal rules of inference are given. A usual one is *modus ponens:* if a theorem (or axiom; axioms count as theorems) is a conditional whose antecedent is also a theorem, then put down the consequent as a theorem. Another usual one is *substitution:* substitute any schema for all occurrences of a letter in a theorem. If we start with valid axioms, obviously these two rules will lead only to valid theorems.

One interesting choice of axioms, due to Łukasiewicz, comprises these three:

(1) $p \supset q .\supset: q \supset r .\supset. p \supset r,$

(2) $\qquad\qquad\qquad p \supset . \bar{p} \supset q,$

(3) $\qquad\qquad\qquad \bar{p} \supset p . \supset p.$

Let us generate some theorems by the two rules. Substitution of 'p' for 'q' in (2) gives:

(4) $\qquad\qquad\qquad\qquad p \supset . \bar{p} \supset p.$

Substitution of 'p' for 'r' in (1) gives:

(5) $\qquad\qquad\qquad p \supset q . \supset : q \supset p . \supset . p \supset p.$

Substitution of '$\bar{p} \supset p$' for 'q' in (5) gives:

(6) $\qquad\quad p \supset . \bar{p} \supset p : \supset :. \bar{p} \supset p . \supset p : \supset . p \supset p.$

Modus ponens, applied to (6) and (4), gives:

(7) $\qquad\qquad\quad \bar{p} \supset p . \supset p : \supset . p \supset p.$

Modus ponens, applied to (7) and (3), gives:

(8) $\qquad\qquad\qquad\qquad\quad p \supset p.$

This sequence of steps is called a *proof* of '$p \supset p$'. In a condensed notation the whole proof can be put thus:

$$\text{By (1),} \qquad [2\ (q/p) \supset : 3 \supset .]\ p \supset p.$$

The numeral '3' here stands as an abbreviation of the schema (3), hence '$\bar{p} \supset p . \supset p$'. The expression '2 ($q/p$)' stands for the schema (4), this being what (2) becomes when 'q' is supplanted by 'p'. Thus the whole string of symbols amounts to (6). The mention of (1) means that this whole schema (6) can be got from (1) by certain substitutions. A reader presented merely with this condensed proof would recover (6), compare its structure with that of (1), and discover for himself that '$\bar{p} \supset p$' and 'p' were the required substitutes for 'q' and 'r' in (1). The square brackets, finally, indicate excision by modus ponens—twice over, in this case.

This system visibly treats only of negation and the conditional. However, any truth-functional schema can be translated into those terms, since '$p \vee q$' and 'pq' are equivalent to '$\bar{p} \supset q$' and '$-(p \supset \bar{q})$'. There is a proof that every valid truth-functional schema, or its translation, can be got from the axioms (1)–(3) by the two rules. The system is in this sense *complete*.

Axiomatists are naturally concerned that their axioms be *independent*:

that none be derivable as a theorem from the rest, and hence dispensable. The independence of an axiom is neatly established if we can so reinterpret the symbols as to falsify that axiom while still preserving the validity of the other axioms and the soundness of the rules of inference. For instance, we can show that the axiom (3) is independent, in this system, by reinterpreting the negation sign as simply yielding a falsehood wherever applied. We keep the interpretation of '⊃'. Hence the rules of modus ponens and substitution remain sound and (1) remains valid. Also (2) comes out valid; for if '$\bar{p}$' comes out always false, '$\bar{p} \supset q$' comes out always true. But (3), thus reinterpreted, comes out false for false 'p'.

Again, to show (2) independent, reinterpret the negation sign as yielding a truth wherever applied.

Various other complete systems of independent axioms have been contrived for truth-function logic. Not all of them are based on negation and the conditional. Some use negation and alternation. One, due to Nicod and improved by Łukasiewicz, uses only the truth-functional connective '|', which, we saw (Chapter 2), suffices for expressing all the truth functions. This system has just one axiom:

$$p \mid . q \mid r : \mid :: s \mid . s \mid s : \mid :. s \mid q . \mid : p \mid s . \mid . p \mid s.$$

Its rules of inference are substitution and a variant of modus ponens which says that if a theorem has the form '$A \mid . B \mid C$' and has a theorem in the 'A' place, then the schema in the 'C' place is a theorem. If we define '$p \supset q$' as '$p \mid . q \mid q$', the axiom above becomes less bewildering:

$$p \mid . q \mid r : \mid :. s \supset s . \mid : s \mid q . \supset . p \mid s.$$

Axiomatic logic is one thing; the application of full-blown logic to extralogical axioms is another. The contrast between them is the contrast between what Sheffer called *foundational* and *postfoundational* systems. Foundational systems have their autonomous rules of inference; postfoundational systems just infer their theorems from their axioms by logical implication, deferring to logic for the analysis and the technology of that relation.

Still, foundational systems can be fashioned also for extralogical subject matter. An example is the following axiomatic algebra of subtraction.[14] There are two axioms:

$$x = x - (y - y), \qquad x - (y - z) = z - (y - x).$$

Substitution is again one of the rules of inference, and a second rule of inference allows us to put the left side of a theorem for the right in any theorem. Substitution in the second axiom, e.g., gives the theorem:

[14] From my *Selected Logic Papers*, pp. 54–60.

$$z - (x - (y - y)) = (y - y) - (x - z),$$

and from this and the first axiom by means of the second rule of inference we get the theorem:

$$z - x = (y - y) - (x - z).$$

A queerer example: the second rule of inference allows us to put the left side 'x' of the first axiom for the right side in that axiom itself; we get the theorem '$x = x$'.

We can get more. The system can be proved complete, in this sense: every equation that is constructed of this subtraction notation and is valid, or true for all values of its variables, is derivable from the two axioms by the two rules. Moreover, the notation is stronger than it looks; $x + y$ can be expressed in it, as $x - ((y - y) - y)$.

Usually, however, axiomatizations of extralogical subjects are post-foundational. There is a good reason: mass production. Once for all we develop logical techniques for establishing implication; afterward we can use these for deriving theorems from axioms in postfoundational systems on any subject.

On the other hand an axiom system for logic is necessarily foundational, and I would in conclusion remark further that it is of dubious value—especially in the logic of truth functions. This domain, after all, enjoys the luxury of a *decision procedure* for validity—that is, a mechanical test. Truth-value analysis affords one such test of validity; truth tables afford another; transformation into conjunctional normal form affords a third. Thus blessed, we should be unwise to make practical use of the axiomatic method in this domain. It is inferior in that it affords no general way of reaching a verdict of invalidity; failure to discover a proof for a schema can mean either invalidity or mere bad luck.

Lukasiewicz swore by axiomatic truth-function logic as a training ground for axiomatic method in more demanding domains. I swear rather by the sufficiency, unto the day, of the evil thereof. Axiomatic logic, with its schemata and its specific rules of inference, is very unlike postfoundational axiom systems. Training in the latter, if wanted, is best sought as such. Its main component is training in the recognition or proof of implication, since implication is what relates postfoundational axioms to the theorems; and such training is a pervading purpose of this book. There will be some specific notice of postfoundational axioms in Chapters 40 and 46. Meanwhile I have included this brief account of axiomatic truth-function logic partly for contrast and partly because of the prominence of the subject in earlier literature.

HISTORICAL NOTE: Frege, in 1879, was the first to axiomatize the logic of truth functions and to state formal rules of inference. Frege's system, like the Łukasiewicz system (1)–(3), was couched in negation and the conditional and proceeded by modus ponens and substitution; but the axioms were more cumbersome, and the rule of substitution was not made explicit. Whitehead and Russell couched their system, 1910, in negation and alternation. The Łukasiewicz system dates from 1929.[15] The Nicod-Łukasiewicz axiom dates from 1917 and 1931. The axiomatic approach continued to dominate truth-function logic through the thirties, and a score of systems are in print. The first proof of completeness of such a system is due to Post, 1921.[16]

EXERCISES

1. Prove '$\bar{p} \supset p .\supset. \bar{p} \supset q$' from (1)–(3) using the condensed proof notation.

2. Show the independence of (2) in detail.

3. In the Nicod-Łukasiewicz system, prove:

$$t \mid: s \mid. s \mid s .: \mid :: p \mid. q \mid r :\mid t .:\mid :. p \mid. q \mid r :\mid t$$

(which says '$t \mid. s \supset s :\supset:. p \mid. q \mid r :\mid t$' if we define '$\supset$' as before).

---

[15] See Tarski's *Logic, Semantics, Metamathematics*, p. 43.
[16] For a completeness proof shorter than most, see my *Selected Logic Papers*, pp. 159–163.

II
GENERAL TERMS
AND QUANTIFIERS

14

CATEGORICAL STATEMENTS

There are many simple and logically sound inferences for which the fore-going techniques are inadequate. An example is this:

No philosophers are wicked, *Schematically:* No G are H,
Some Greeks are philosophers; Some F are G;
Therefore some Greeks are not wicked. ∴ Some F are not H.

Note that 'F', 'G', and 'H' here stand not for statements, after the manner of 'p' and 'q' in Part I, but for common nouns—or, in logical parlance, for *terms*.[1] Whether these nouns be thought of as substantive or adjective is an insignificant question of phrasing. 'G' appears as a substantive in the above example, viz. 'philosophers', and 'H' as an adjective, 'wicked'; but we could rewrite the adjective as a substantive, 'wicked individuals', if we liked. In the same spirit we can even treat intransitive verbs as terms, in effect, thus reckoning 'Some fishes fly' as a case of 'Some F are G'; for the difference between 'Some fishes fly' and 'Some fishes are flying things' is purely notational. The nouns or verbs which figure as terms may also, of course, be complex phrases such as 'employed for ten years by Sunny-rinse', 'wear brass rings in their noses', etc. Whether terms be thought of as in the singular or the plural is also a logically insignificant question of phrasing; thus there is no need to distinguish between 'No philosopher is wicked' and 'No philosophers are wicked', nor between 'All philosophers are wise' and 'Every philosopher is wise'. There is no need even to distinguish between 'Some Greek is a philosopher' and 'Some Greeks are philosophers', provided that, as will be our practice here, we understand 'some' always to mean simply 'at least one'.

But, for all the latitude accorded to the concept of term, it remains clear that terms are never statements; and this is why the techniques of Part I are inadequate to the inference exhibited above. Part I dealt with the structures of compound statements relative only to their component statements; statements remained the smallest units of analysis. It is only now, in Part II, that we embark upon the analysis of those component statements in turn into the still smaller parts, not statements at all but terms,

---

[1] What are spoken of simply as terms in the present pages may, in view of developments in Parts III–IV, be designated more accurately as *general absolute terms*. Actually they will come to be known in Part III, though with a certain shift of emphasis, as *monadic predicates*. But this use of the word 'predicate' is not to be confused, if one can help it, with the mediaeval use explained in Chapter 16.

of which they are composed. Logically sound inferences depend for their soundness on the structures of the statements concerned, but the relevant structures may be either the broad outward structures studied in Part I or the finer substructures to which we are now turning. The example above is one which depends on structures of the latter kind.

It is the peculiarity of a statement to be true or false. It is the peculiarity of a term, on the other hand, to be *true of* many objects, or one, or none, and false of the rest. The term 'Greek' is true of each Greek, and the term 'wicked' is true of each wicked individual, and nothing else. The term 'natural satellite of the earth' is true of each natural satellite of the earth and nothing else, hence true of but one object, the moon. The term 'centaur' is true of each centaur and nothing else, hence true of nothing at all, there being no centaurs.

In place of the clumsy phrase 'is true of' we may also say 'denotes', in the best sense of this rapidly deteriorating word. But I prefer here to resist the temptation of good usage. 'Denotes' is so current in the sense of 'designates', or 'names', that its use in connection, say, with the word 'wicked' would cause readers to look beyond the wicked people to some unique entity, a quality of wickedness or a class of the wicked, as named object. The phrase 'is true of' is less open to misunderstanding; clearly 'wicked' is true not of the quality of wickedness, nor of the class of wicked persons, but of each wicked person individually.

When we are minded to speak of classes, the class of all the objects of which a term is true may, in keeping with a long tradition, be called the *extension* of the term. The extension of 'wicked' is thus the class of wicked persons; that of 'natural satellite of the earth' is the class whose sole member is the moon; and the extension of 'centaur' is the empty class. Terms may be said to *have* extensions, just as statements have truth values; but there is no need to think of a term as somehow a name *of* its extension, any more than there is to think of a statement as a name of its truth value.[2] Far better not, since the use of terms proceeds smoothly on the whole without assumption of any special category of abstract objects called classes. It is ordinarily sufficient to know that a given term is *true of* this and that individual and false of the other, without positing any single collective entity called the term's extension. Reason to appeal to extensions arises only in certain theoretical connections such as the general theory of validity, Chapters 18 ff.

Four ways of joining terms pairwise into statements have been treated as fundamental throughout the logical tradition stemming from Aristotle: 'All *F* are *G*', 'No *F* are *G*', 'Some *F* are *G*', and 'Some *F* are not *G*'. Statements of these four forms were called *categorical*. The four forms were distinguished by special nomenclature and by code letters '**A**', '**E**', '**I**', and '**O**', as follows.

A (Universal affirmative):   All *F* are *G*

---

[2] Cf. Carnap, *Meaning and Necessity*, pp. 23–32, 96–111.

E (Universal negative):   No *F* are *G*
I (Particular affirmative):   Some *F* are *G*
O (Particular negative):   Some *F* are not *G*

The form **A**, 'All *F* are *G*', may also be phrased 'If anything is an *F*, it is a *G*'; thus it is recognizable as the "generalized conditional" which was touched on in (1)–(3) of Chapter 3. Many other phrasings of **A** also come readily to mind: '*F* are *G*', 'Each (Every, Any) *F* is a *G*', 'Whatever is an *F* is a *G*', '*F* are exclusively *G*', 'Only *G* are *F*'.

E likewise has many phrasings: 'No *F* is (are) *G*', 'Nothing is both an *F* and a *G*', 'Nothing that is an *F* is a *G*', and even 'There is (are) no *FG*' (e.g., 'There is no black swan'), '*FG* do not exist'.

Correspondingly for **I**: 'Some *F* is (are) *G*', 'Something is both an *F* and a *G*', 'Something that is an *F* is a *G*', 'There is an *FG*', 'There are *FG*', '*FG* exist'. **O**, of course, has similar variants.

Often the terms properly answering to '*F*' and '*G*' are not directly visible at all in ordinary phrasing of statements. They may be partially covered up by such usages as 'nowhere', 'anywhere', 'always', 'everyone', 'whoever', 'whenever', etc. Thus the statement 'I go nowhere by train that I can get to by plane' is properly analyzable as of the form **E**, 'No *F* are *G*', but here we must understand '*F*' as representing 'places I go to by train' and '*G*' as representing 'places I can get to by plane'. The statement 'Everyone in the room speaks English' has the form **A**, 'All *F* are *G*', where '*F*' represents 'persons in this room' and '*G*' represents 'speakers of English'.

In this last example the restrictions to persons implicit in 'everyone' is essential, since there will be nonpersons in the room which do not speak English. In such an example as 'Everyone who pays his dues receives the Bulletin', on the other hand, 'everyone' is used instead of 'everything' only because of a habit of language, and not because the speaker feels any need of hedging his statement against such absurd objects as sub-human payers of dues. It would be pedantic to construe '*F*' for this example as 'persons who pay their dues', and quite proper to construe it as 'payers of dues'.

In putting statements of ordinary language over into the forms **A**, **E**, **I**, and **O** we must be on the alert for irregularities of idiom, and look beneath them to the intended sense. One such irregularity is omission of '-ever', as in 'Who hesitates is lost', 'I want to go where you go', 'When it rains it pours', 'She gets what she goes after'. Another irregularity is the nontemporal use of 'always', 'whenever', 'sometimes', 'never'. E.g., the statement:

The sum of the angles of a triangle is always equal to two right angles

really means:

The sum of the angles of any triangle is equal to two right angles, and may be rendered 'All *F* are *G*' where '*F*' represents 'sums of angles of triangles' and '*G*' represents 'equal to two right angles'.

Frequently an **I** construction having to do with time is implicit in the inflection of a verb; witness 'We saw Stromboli and it was erupting', which comes out as 'Some *F* are *G*' with '*F*' construed as 'times we saw Stromboli' and '*G*' as 'times Stromboli was erupting'. (Cf. Chapter 8, (5).) Further examples of temporal idioms which call for a little reflection, if the logical structure is to be properly extracted, are:

> I knew him before he lost his fortune,
> I knew him while he was with Sunnyrinse.

'Before' and 'while' here appear in the guise of statement connectives, like 'and' or 'or' or '⊃'. But the statements are better analyzed as of the form **I**, 'Some *F* are *G*', where '*F*' represents 'moments in which I knew him' and '*G*' represents in the one case 'moments before he lost his fortune' and in the other case 'moments in which he was with Sunnyrinse'.

Reflection, indeed, should be the rule. Proper interpretation is not generally to be achieved through slavish dependence upon a check-list of idioms. 'Always' usually means 'at all moments', but it would be unjust to construe 'Tai always eats with chopsticks' as 'Tai eats with chopsticks at all moments'. The proper interpretation of this example is 'All *F* are *G*' where '*F*' represents 'moments at which Tai eats' (not simply 'moments') and '*G*' represents 'moments at which Tai eats with chopsticks'.

The importance of reflecting upon context and the common sense of the concrete situation, rather than looking to any mere glossary, is manifest even in so basic a construction as 'An *F* is *G*'. 'A lady is present' is surely of the form **I**, but 'A Scout is reverent' is more likely to be intended in the form **A**. Caution is similarly needed in equating 'any' with 'every'; for, whereas the statements:

> John can outrun every man on the team,
> John can outrun any man on the team

need no distinguishing, a divergence appears as soon as 'not' is applied:

> John cannot outrun every man on the team,
> John cannot outrun any man on the team.

The first two statements are indistinguishably 'All *F* are *G*' (where '*F*' is 'man on the team' and '*G*' is 'whom John can outrun'); the third, however, is 'Some *F* are not *G*', while the fourth is 'No *F* are *G*'.

EXERCISES

Classify the following statements as between **A**, **E**, **I**, and **O**, and specify in each case what terms answer to '*F*' and '*G*'.

Blessed are the meek. We should all be as happy as kings.
All that glisters is not gold. A policeman's lot is not an 'appy one.
There is no god but Allah. There are smiles that make you blue.
Hope springs eternal. I journeyed hither a Boeotian road.
The rule applies to everyone. I was stopped by the door of a tomb.

15
VENN'S DIAGRAMS

In Venn's diagrammatic method (1880), overlapping circles are used to represent the two terms of a categorical statement. The region in which the two circles overlap represents the objects which are both F and G. This region, called a *lens* in geometry, is shaded in Diagram 2. Where 'F' is taken as 'French' and 'G' as 'generals', this region represents the French generals. Correspondingly the part of the F-circle which lies outside the G-circle represents the objects which are F but not G: the French non-generals, in the example. This region, called a *lune* in geometry, is shaded in Diagram 1. The significance of shading is emptiness; thus Diagram 2 affirms that no F are G, while Diagram 1 affirms that no F are other than G, or in other words that all F are G.

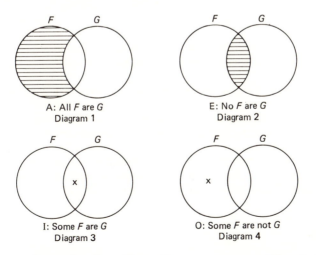

A: All *F* are *G*
Diagram 1

E: No *F* are *G*
Diagram 2

I: Some *F* are *G*
Diagram 3

O: Some *F* are not *G*
Diagram 4

Whiteness of a region in a Venn diagram means nothing but lack of information. In Diagram 2 the two lunes are left unshaded not because we think there are *F* which are not *G* and *G* which are not *F*, but because 'No *F* are *G*' gives us no information on the subject. All that 'No *F* are *G*' says is that the lens is empty, and this is all the information that Diagram 2 records. Similarly the lens and the right-hand lune in Diagram 1 are left unshaded merely because 'All *F* are *G*' gives us no information concerning these further regions.

The great region outside both circles represents the objects, if any, which are neither *F* nor *G*. It is left blank in Diagrams 1 and 2 because 'All *F* are *G*' throws no light on such objects, and neither does 'No *F* are *G*'.

So, whereas shading means emptiness, nonshading does not assure nonemptiness. For nonemptiness another symbol is used, viz., a cross. Thus 'Some *F* are *G*', which affirms nonemptiness of the lens, is expressed by putting a cross in the lens as in Diagram 3. Here again the blankness of the other areas implies neither emptiness nor nonemptiness, but represents mere lack of information.

'Some *F* are not *G*', finally, affirms no more nor less than that the part of the *F*-circle which lies outside the *G*-circle has something in it; so it is represented by putting a cross in that lune as in Diagram 4.

Certain simple laws of categorical statements are graphically reflected in the diagrams. The symmetry of Diagram 2, and of Diagram 3, reflects the fact that in **E** and **I** the order of terms is inessential: 'No *F* are *G*' amounts to 'No *G* are *F*', and 'Some *F* are *G*' to 'Some *G* are *F*'. Such switching of terms was known traditionally as *simple conversion*. The lopsidedness of Diagrams 1 and 4 reflects the fact that simple conversion is not in general applicable to **A** or **O**: 'All Greeks are men' is not to be confused with 'All men are Greeks', nor 'Some men are not Greeks' with 'Some Greeks are not men'.

A and **O** are mutual *contradictories*, or negations: **A** is true if and only if **O** is false. This relationship is reflected in the diagrams by the fact that Diagram 1 shows shading where, and only where, Diagram 4 shows a cross. With respect to blankness, or lack of information, Diagrams 1 and 4 are alike; with respect to information they simply and directly deny each other. Similarly **E** and **I** are mutual contradictories: **E** is true if and only if **I** is false.

A and **E**, 'All *F* are *G*' and 'No *F* are *G*', may also be felt to be somehow opposite to each other; however, their opposition is no matter of mutual negation, for we cannot say in general that **A** is true if and only if **E** is false. On the contrary, examples chosen at random are as likely as not to cause **A** and **E** to come out *both* false; this happens in particular when '*F*' is taken as 'French' and '*G*' as 'generals'. Similarly **I** and **O** are quite commonly both true, of course, as in this same example. But **A** and **O** are never both true nor both false, and similarly for **E** and **I**; here are the pairs of contradictories, or mutual negations.

Whereas **A** and **E** are very commonly both false and **I** and **O** are very commonly both true, it is less common for **I** and **O** to come out both false, or for **A** and **E** to come out both true; but these things will happen where there are no *F*. Clearly, where there are no *F*, 'Some *F* are *G*' and 'Some

F are not *G'* will both be false. Also, where there are no *F*, 'No *F* are *G'* will obviously be true; and yet 'All *F* are *G'* will likewise be true, in that there will be no *F* which is not *G*. These points are brought out diagrammatically by shading the *F*-circle in its entirety, as in Diagram 5, to mean that there are no *F*. This diagram verifies both **A** and **E**, for it shows both of the areas shaded which are shaded in Diagrams 1 and 2; and it falsifies both **I** and **O**, for it shows shading in place of both crosses of Diagrams 3 and 4.

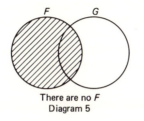

There are no *F*
Diagram 5

A, 'All *F* are *G'*, would seem at first glance to be stronger than **I**, 'Some *F* are *G'*, and to imply it; but it does not, because of the possibility of there being no *F*. Diagram 5 depicts the very situation where, though **A** holds, **I** fails. It may happen that all my dimes are shiny (in that I have no dime to the contrary), and yet be false that some of my dimes are shiny, simply because I have no dimes at all. The most we can say is that if all *F* are *G and there are F* then some *F* are *G*.

If the reader thinks it odd to say that all of one's dimes are shiny when one has no dimes, he is perhaps interpreting 'All *F* are *G'* to mean, not simply 'There is no *F* that is not *G'*, but 'There are *F* and each of them is *G'*. This, however, even if it be one of several defensible interpretations of an ambiguous idiom, is clearly not the interpretation which would make **A** the simple contradictory, or negation, of **O**: 'Some *F* are not *G'*. It is the general logical practice, and a convenient one, to understand 'All *F* are *G'* simply as the contradictory of **O**.

Diagram 5 as it stands was seen to reflect the fact that **I** does not follow from **A**. But Venn diagrams can also be used for constructive ends, as in showing that **I** follows from **A** supplemented with 'There are *F'*. To show this we set down the diagram for **A**, viz. Diagram 1, and then enter 'There are *F'* into the diagram by putting a cross in the *F*-circle. The cross must go in the unshaded part of the *F*-circle, since the shaded part is known to be empty. So the result, showing a cross in the lens as it does, verifies **I**.

What has been said of the relationship between **A** and **I** applies equally to **E** and **O**: from **E**, 'No *F* are *G'*, we may infer **O**, 'Some *F* are not *G'*, only if we make the further assumption that there are *F*. Diagram 5 shows the situation where, though **E** holds, **O** fails. But we can show that **O** follows from **E** and 'There are *F'*, by putting a cross in the *F*-circle of Diagram 2 and observing that we have verified **O**.

Finally let us observe a couple of simple inferences in which a conclusion is drawn from just a single premise, or assumption, instead of from two:

Some *F* are *G*,   There are no *F*,
∴ There are *G*.   ∴ No *F* are *G*.

These inferences are justified respectively by Diagrams 3 and 5; for Diagram 3 shows a cross in the *G*-circle in support of the conclusion 'There are *G*', and Diagram 5 shows a shaded lens in support of the conclusion 'No *F* are *G*'.

EXERCISES

1. Does **A, E, I** or **O** follow from 'There are no *G*'? Does **A, E, I,** or **O** conflict with 'There are no *G*'? Appeal to diagrams.

2. Make a diagram for 'All *F* are *G* and all *G* are *F*'. Is this compatible with 'No *F* are *G*'? Explain.

16
SYLLOGISMS

What are spoken of traditionally as *syllogisms*[3] are arguments wherein a categorical statement is derived as conclusion from two categorical statements as premises, the three statements being so related that there are altogether just three terms, each of which appears in two of the statements. Six examples follow; one of them was already noted in Chapter 14.

All men are mortal,   All *G* are *H*,
All Greeks are men;   All *F* are *G*;
∴ All Greeks are mortal.   ∴ All *F* are *H*.

No men are perfect,   No *G* are *H*,
All Greeks are men;   All *F* are *G*;
∴ No Greeks are perfect.   ∴ No *F* are *H*.

All philosophers are wise,   All *G* are *H*,
Some Greeks are philosophers;   Some *F* are *G*;
∴ Some Greeks are wise.   ∴ Some *F* are *H*.

[3] *Categorical* syllogisms, more specifically, to distinguish them from *hypothetical* syllogisms, which are certain truth-functional arguments manageable by the methods of Part I.

No philosophers are wicked,   No *G* are *H*,
Some Greeks are philosophers;   Some *F* are *G*;
∴ Some Greeks are not wicked.   ∴ Some *F* are not *H*.

All Greeks are men,   All *H* are *G*,
Some mortals are not men;   Some *F* are not *G*;
∴ Some mortals are not Greeks.   ∴ Some *F* are not *H*.

Some men are not Greeks,   Some *G* are not *H*,
All men are mortal;   All *G* are *F*;
∴ Some mortals are not Greeks.   ∴ Some *F* are not *H*.

A "valid" syllogism, ordinarily so-called, is a syllogism of such form as to be incapable of leading from true premises to a false conclusion. An easy test of validity of syllogisms is afforded by Venn's diagrams. Three overlapping circles are used, as in Diagrams 6 and 7, to represent the three terms '*F*',

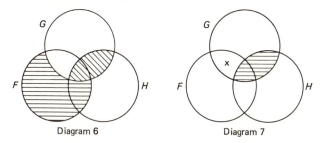

Diagram 6   Diagram 7

'*G*', and '*H*' of the syllogism. We inscribe the content of the two premises into the diagram by the method explained in connection with Diagrams 1–4, and then we inspect the diagram to see whether the content of the conclusion has automatically appeared in the diagram as a result. Thus, let us test the second syllogism of the list above. We record its first premise, 'No *G* are *H*', by shading the lens common to the *G*-circle and the *H*-circle; then we record the second premise, 'All *F* are *G*', by shading the lune which lies in the *F*-circle outside the *G*-circle. The result is Diagram 6. It bears out the desired conclusion 'No *F* are *H*', since the lens common to the *F*-circle and the *H*-circle is fully shaded.

Let us next test the fourth of our six examples. We record the first premise, 'No *G* are *H*', as before, and then we record the second premise, 'Some *F* are *G*', by putting a cross in what remains of the lens common to the *F*-circle and the *G*-circle; the result is Diagram 7. It bears out the conclusion 'Some *F* are not *H*', there being a cross in the *F*-circle outside the *H*-circle.

It is left to the reader to construct diagrams verifying the remaining four of the above six syllogisms. (In the last of them, the second premise should be handled first; note why.)

The diagrammatic method can be used to determine not merely whether a given conclusion follows from given premises, but whether any conclusion at all (of a syllogistic kind) is capable of following from given premises. For, the conclusion—in order to be the conclusion of a so-called syllogism at all—must be 'All *F* are *H*', 'No *F* are *H*', 'Some *F* are *H*', or 'Some *F* are not *H*'; hence, unless the two bottom circles of the finished diagram exhibit one of the four patterns shown in Diagrams 1–4, there is no conclusion. In Diagram 8, e.g., the bottom circles exhibit none of the four patterns of Diagrams 1–4; and this shows that the premises 'All *H* are *G*' and 'All *F* are *G*' cannot be the premises of any valid syllogism at all.

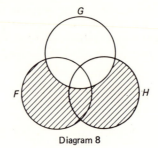

Diagram 8

As a further example consider the premises 'All *G* are *H*' and 'All *G* are *F*'. These are recorded in Diagram 9; and we see that the diagram justifies no

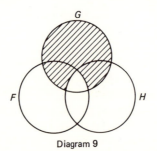

Diagram 9

categorical conclusion in '*F*' and '*H*'. But this pair of premises is interesting in that it *almost* justifies a categorical conclusion in '*F*' and '*H*', viz., 'Some *F* are *H*'. If we add just the further premise 'There are *G*', to allow us to put a cross in the one part of the *G*-circle that remains unshaded, we then find the conclusion 'Some *F* are *H*' justified by a cross common to the *F*-circle and the *H*-circle. Thus the reinforced syllogism:

All Spartans are brave,	All *G* are *H*,
All Spartans are Greeks,	All *G* are *F*,
There are Spartans;	There are *G*;
∴ Some Greeks are brave	∴ Some *F* are *H*

is valid.

In the traditional terminology the term which plays the rôle of '*F*' in 'All *F* are *G*', 'No *F* are *G*', 'Some *F* are *G*', or 'Some *F* are not *G*' is called the *subject* of the statement. The other term, playing the role of '*G*', is called the *predicate*.[4] The predicate of the conclusion is called the *major term* of the syllogism, and the subject of the conclusion is called the *minor term* of the syllogism. The remaining term, occurring in both premises but not in the conclusion, is called the *middle term* of the syllogism. Thus all the foregoing examples have been lettered in such a way as to make '*F*' the minor term, '*G*' the middle term, and '*H*' the major term.

The premise which contains the middle and major terms is called the *major premise* of the syllogism. The other premise, containing the middle and minor terms, is called the *minor premise*. Thus all the foregoing examples have been stated with the major premise first and the minor premise second.

Medieval logicians had a scheme for coding the various forms of syllogisms. They stipulated the respective forms of the premises and conclusion (as among **A**, **E**, **I**, and **O**) by a triple of letters; thus '**EAO**' meant that the major premise was of form **E**, the minor premise **A**, and the conclusion **O**. This much was said to indicate the *mood* of a syllogism. But, even given the mood of a syllogism, there remains the question whether the major premise has the major term as subject and the middle term as predicate, or vice versa; and correspondingly for the minor premise. The four possibilities of arrangement which thus arise are called *figures*, and referred to by number as follows:

	1st	2nd	3rd	4th
Major premise:	*GH*	*HG*	*GH*	*HG*
Minor premise:	*FG*	*FG*	*GF*	*GF*
Conclusion:	*FH*	*FH*	*FH*	*FH*

Specification of mood and figure determines the form of a syllogism completely. Thus the six examples at the beginning of the present chapter are respectively **AAA** in the first figure, **EAE** in the first figure, **AII** in the first figure, **EIO** in the first figure, **AOO** in the second figure, and **OAO** in the third figure.

The fourth of the six above, viz. **EIO** in the first figure, can be given variant forms by simple conversion (cf. preceding chapter) of one or both premises. We thus get:

No *H* are *G*,	No *G* are *H*,	No *H* are *G*,
Some *F* are *G*;	Some *G* are *F*;	Some *G* are *F*;
∴ Some *F* are not *H*.	∴ Some *F* are not *H*.	∴ Some *F* are not *H*.

These are **EIO** in the second, third, and fourth figures. Similarly **EAE** and **AII** in the first figure (the second and third of the examples at the beginning of the chapter) are carried by simple conversion into **EAE** in the second figure and **AII** in the third.

---

[4] The word 'predicate' will receive a different and more important meaning in Chapter 26.

The four syllogisms last mentioned, viz. **EAE** in the first and second figures and **AII** in the first and third, can be carried over into four further syllogisms by simple conversion of each of their conclusions. If we do this, though, we must afterward reletter '*F*' as '*H*' and '*H*' as '*F*' throughout the results in order that '*F*' may continue to represent the minor term and '*H*' the major term; also we must switch the order of the premises, so that the major premise may continue to appear first. The results, which the reader will do well to reproduce, are **AEE** in the fourth and second figures and **IAI** in the fourth and third.

Altogether, then, we have found fifteen valid forms:

FIRST FIGURE	SECOND FIGURE
AAA, EAE, AII, EIO	**EAE, AEE, EIO, AOO**

THIRD FIGURE	FOURTH FIGURE
IAI, AII, OAO, EIO	**AEE, IAI, EIO**

Note that no two of these fifteen have the same premises, when differences of figure are taken into account. We have here fifteen different pairs of premises, each with its appropriate conclusion. And it is readily verified by inspection of diagrams that none of these fifteen pairs of premises justifies any further syllogistic conclusion in addition to the one here indicated for it.

Viewed in terms merely of combinations and without regard to the existence of a valid conclusion, there are sixty-four possibilities for the premises of a syllogism. They may be **AA**, or **AE**, or **AI**, or **AO**, or **EA**, or **EE**, etc., to sixteen possibilities, and each of these sixteen may occur in any of four figures. In addition to the fifteen pairs of premises which have been found to yield valid syllogisms, therefore, there are forty-nine further pairs to consider. Now we saw in connection with Diagrams 8 and 9 how to check whether a given pair of premises justifies any syllogistic conclusion at all. If the reader so tests these forty-nine pairs (an hour's pastime), he will find that none of them justifies a syllogistic conclusion. The fifteen forms of syllogism listed above are the only valid ones.

In addition, however, nine forms come in for honorable mention. These nine are forms which, like the above example of the Spartans, need a small reinforcing premise. 'There are *F*' fills the bill for five of them, 'There are *G*' for three, and 'There are *H*' for one. Let me simply record the nine in tabular fashion:

1st FIGURE	2nd FIGURE	3rd FIGURE	4th FIGURE	ADDED PREMISE
AAI, EAO	**AEO, EAO**		**AEO**	There are *F*
		AAI, EAO	**EAO**	There are *G*
			AAI	There are *H*

Inferences involving so-called singular statements such as 'Socrates is a man', e.g.:

All men are mortal, Socrates is a man; ∴ Socrates is mortal,

were traditionally fitted into the syllogistic mold by treating the singular statements as of the form **A**. This procedure is artificial but not incorrect; we can construe 'Socrates is a man' as 'All *G* are *H'* where '*G'* represents 'things identical with Socrates'. The above inference thus was classified as **AAA** in the first figure. But we shall end up, in Part IV, with a different treatment of singular inference.

In traditional logic it was customary to propound various rules whereby to test the validity of a syllogism. Examples: every valid syllogism has a universal premise (**A** or **E**); every valid syllogism has an affirmative premise (**A** or **I**); every valid syllogism with a particular premise (**I** or **O**) has a particular conclusion; every valid syllogism with a negative premise (**E** or **O**) has a negative conclusion. There are further rules whose formulation depends on a concept of "distribution" which has been omitted from the present exposition. As a practical method of appraising syllogisms, rules are less convenient than the method of diagrams. Indeed, the very notions of syllogism and mood and figure need never have been touched on in these pages, except out of consideration for their prominence in logic during two thousand years; for we can apply the diagram test to a given argument out of hand, without pausing to consider where the argument may fit in the taxonomy of syllogisms. The diagram test is equally available for many arguments which do not fit any of the arbitrarily delimited set of forms known as syllogisms.

HISTORICAL **NOTE:** The terms 'categorical' and 'syllogism' derive from Aristotle. So do the fourfold classification of categorical statements, and the nomenclature of the parts of a syllogism, and the classification into moods and figures, except that the fourth figure is attributed rather to his pupil Theophrastus. The notion of distribution and the rules that involve it are medieval.

EXERCISES

1. Construct diagrams verifying the remaining four of the six syllogisms at the beginning of the chapter.

2. Determine by diagrams what syllogistic conclusion, if any, follows from each of the following pairs of premises.

    All who blaspheme are wicked; No saint blasphemes.
    No snakes fly; Some snakes lay eggs.
    Nothing that lays eggs has feathers; Some fishes have feathers.

Whatever interests me bores George; Whatever interests Mabel bores
George.
Whatever interests me bores George; Whatever interests George bores
Mabel.

3.   For each of the pairs in Exercise 2 which failed to yield a syllogistic
     conclusion, determine by diagram whether a supplementary premise
     of the form 'There are *F*', or 'There are *G*', or 'There are *H*', would
     suffice to bring forth a syllogistic conclusion.

17
LIMITS
OF THESE METHODS

The inferences to which we have thus far been applying Venn's diagrams
have all been made up of categoricals **A**, **E**, **I**, or **O** plus an occasional
auxiliary of the type 'There are *F*'. Actually the diagrams can be used
somewhat more widely; e.g., in arguing from the

PREMISES: Everyone east of the tracks is either slovenly or poor,
               Not everyone east of the tracks is poor

to the

CONCLUSION: Some slovenly persons are not poor.

We set up a three-circle diagram as usual, wherein '*F*' means 'slovenly
persons', '*G*' means 'persons east of the tracks', and '*H*' means 'poor persons'. Then the first premise is entered in the diagram by shading as empty
just that compartment of the circle *G* which lies outside both *F* and *H*; see
Diagram 10. The compartment thus shaded is neither a lune nor a lens,

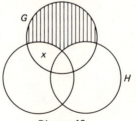

Diagram 10

but a third shape. It represents persons east of the tracks who are neither slovenly nor poor; and just such persons are denied existence by the first premise. Now the second premise, which says in effect 'Some *G* are not *H*', is recorded as usual by putting a cross in what remains of *G* outside *H*. The result is seen to substantiate the conclusion 'Some *F* are not *H*', since there is a cross in *F* outside *H*.

An innovation due to C. I. Lewis (1918) is the use of a long bar instead of the cross in Venn's diagrams. The advantage of the bar is that it can be made to lie across a boundary and thus indicate nonemptiness of a compound region. This innovation is useful in reasoning, e.g., from the

PREMISES: All of the witnesses who hold stock in the firm are
             employees,
           Some of the witnesses are employees or hold stock in
             the firm

to the

CONCLUSION: Some of the witnesses are employees.

We set up a three-circle diagram in which '*F*' means 'witnesses', '*G*' means 'stockholders in the firm', and '*H*' means 'employees'. The lens common to *F* and *G*, then, stands for the witnesses who hold stock in the firm; so, on the basis of the first premise, we shade the part of that lens which lies outside *H*. (See Diagram 11.) Next, on the basis of the other premise, we

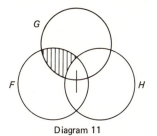

Diagram 11

run a bar through as much of the unshaded *F* as lies within *H* or *G*. The meaning of the bar is that one or another part of the total region marked by the bar has something in it. But the bar lies wholly within *F* and *H*; so the conclusion is sustained.

The utility and versatility of Venn's diagrams are particularly evident from these last two examples. A shortcoming of the diagrams, however, is that they lend themselves less readily to arguments involving four or more terms. A diagram of overlapping ellipses can be constructed for four-term arguments, but it calls for careful drawing; and there is no way whatever of constructing a diagram which will exhibit *five* or more ellipses or other simple regions in all combinations of overlapping. Where many terms are involved we may, however, try to break the argument down into parts involving manageably few terms. The following example is from Lewis Carroll:

PREMISES: "(1) The only animals in this house are cats;
"(2) Every animal is suitable for a pet, that loves to gaze at the moon;
"(3) When I detest an animal, I avoid it;
"(4) No animals are carnivorous, unless they prowl at night;
"(5) No cat fails to kill mice;
"(6) No animals ever take to me, except what are in this house;
"(7) Kangaroos are not suitable for pets;
"(8) None but carnivora kill mice;
"(9) I detest animals that do not take to me;
"(10) Animals that prowl at night always love to gaze at the moon."
CONCLUSION: "I always avoid a kangaroo."

This argument can be broken down as follows. From (1) and (5) we get the *lemma* or intermediate conclusion:

(11)   All animals in this house kill mice;

this is the sort of step to which a simple three-term diagram is adequate. From (8) and (11), similarly, we get:

(12)   All animals in this house are carnivora.

From (4) and (12) we get:

(13)   All animals in this house prowl at night.

From (6) and (13) we get:

(14)   All animals that take to me prowl at night.

Step by step in this fashion we can proceed to our desired conclusion, never using more than a three-term diagram for any one step. (If the reader cares to carry this through in detail, he should think of the universe as limited for purposes of the argument to animals—thus never bothering with 'animals' itself as a term.)

So we see that the purely mechanical method of diagrams proves inadequate when an argument turns on a *large number of terms;* a supplementary technique has to be invoked, such as that of resolving the argument into parts. Now another place where the unaided method of diagrams bogs down is where there is an *admixture of truth functions,* as in the following example:

PREMISES: If all applicants who received the second announcement are of the class of '00, then some applicants did not receive the second announcement.

Either all applicants received the second announcement or all applicants are of the class of '00.

CONCLUSION: If all applicants of the class of '00 received the second announcement then some applicants not of the class of '00 received the second announcement.

If we assign 'F', 'G', and 'H' in obvious fashion, the inference takes on the form:

All F who are G are $H \supset$ some F are not G,
All F are G v all F are H,
∴ All F who are H are $G \supset$ some F who are not H are G.

Diagrams are suited to handling the components 'All F who are G are H', 'Some F are not G', etc., and the methods of Part I are suited to '$\supset$' and 'v'; but just how may we splice the two techniques in order to handle a combined inference of the above kind?

So it is time to address ourselves to a more comprehensive theory. The three formulas last set forth, containing 'F', 'G', and 'H', are *schemata* of a sort, but differ from the schemata of Part I in containing 'F', 'G', etc. and such words as 'all', 'some', 'who are', etc., to the exclusion of 'p', 'q', etc. In the ensuing chapters such schemata will be reduced to a logical notation subject to a "decision procedure"—i.e., a mechanical routine for deciding validity, implication, consistency, etc. Such a decision procedure exists for truth-functional schemata in truth-value analysis; for the new class of schemata, however, the procedure will have to be more elaborate. Once it is at hand, all inferences of the sort we have been considering in the present Part—including the stubborn last example—can be adjudged mechanically by an implication test on premises and conclusion.

EXERCISES

1.   Check the soundness of each of these inferences by diagram:

All of the witnesses who hold stock in the firm are employees,
All of the witnesses are employees or hold stock in the firm;
∴ All of the witnesses are employees.

Everyone who knows both George and Mabel admires Mabel.
Some who know Mabel do not admire her.
∴ Some who know Mabel do not know George.

No European swans are black.
All black swans are European.
∴ No swans are black.

Only high-school graduates who can read French are eligible.
Some can read French who are not high-school graduates.
∴ Some who are not eligible can read French.

Everything is either a substance or an attribute.
Modes are not substances.
∴ Modes are attributes.

Hint: Be prepared to shade the limitless region outside all circles.

2. Finish the kangaroo argument and supply a three-term diagram to justify each step.

3. Using '*F*', '*G*', and '*H*' in the obvious way, make a Venn diagram for each of the following two statements (Ullian):

A thing is flexible if and only if it is either granulated or heavy.
If nothing flexible is heavy then not everything granulated is heavy.

18

BOOLEAN SCHEMATA

To say of an object x that it is an F, we write 'Fx'. Here then is a new sort of sentence schema: 'Fx', 'Gx', etc. These may be compounded by truth functions; e.g.

(1) $Fx \ . -Gx \ .\text{v.} \ Gx \supset Hx.$

We may conveniently abbreviate such compounds by extracting the 'x' everywhere and putting it at the end, thus:

$$[F\bar{G} \vee (G \supset H)]x.$$

We arrive in this way at schematic representations of certain complex terms: schemata such as '$\bar{G}$', '$F\bar{G}$', '$G \supset H$', '$F\bar{G} \vee (G \supset H)$', etc. They will be called *Boolean term schemata* because of a close kinship to Boolean algebra (Chapter 20).

Where 'F' is interpreted as 'black' and 'G' as 'swan', '$\bar{G}$' is 'nonswan'; 'FG' is 'black swan'; '$F\bar{G}$' is true of just the other black things; and '$F \lor G$' is true of swans and black things generally.

The concepts of validity, consistency, and implication carry over naturally to Boolean term schemata from the old truth-functional schemata. A term schema is called valid if, when the 'x' is restored, the resulting sentence schema is truth-functionally valid in the old sense. E.g., since '$Fx \lor -Fx$' or '$(F \lor \bar{F})x$' is valid, we call '$F \lor \bar{F}$' itself valid. Correspondingly for consistency and implication; thus '$F\bar{F}$' is called inconsistent and 'FG' is said to imply '$F \lor G$'.

The significance of such validity on the part of a term schema is that every interpretation of its letters turns it into a term that is true of every object x. But interpretation in what sense? In talking of interpretations of term letters, we do best to allow freedom in choosing the *universe of discourse*—the range of objects x relevant to the logical argument we are planning to carry through. Such freedom will commonly diminish by one the required number of terms, as we saw a few pages back in the kangaroo example. We interpret a term letter 'F', then, by settling which ones of those objects 'F' is to be construed as true of. A valid term schema, then, is one that will come out true of *all* objects of *any* chosen universe under *all* interpretations, within that universe, of its term letters.

A consistent term schema is true of *some* objects of *some* universes under *some* interpretations of its term letters. One term schema implies another when, in every universe of discourse, every interpretation makes the second schema come out true of everything that the first comes out true of.

Since Boolean term schemata have just the structure of the old truth-functional schemata, we can test them for validity, consistency, and implication by truth-value analysis as if the 'F', 'G', etc. were 'p', 'q', etc. We can even use fell swoop where appropriate. If it seems odd to substitute 'T' and '⊥' thus for term letters, then think of these tests as applying in reality not to the term schemata themselves but to the sentence schemata that would be got from the term schemata by restoring 'x' as in (1).

We shall make good use of the following law.

(i) If $A_1, \ldots, A_n$ are Boolean term schemata, and if each of them individually is consistent, and if $x_1, \ldots, x_n$ are any distinct objects, then in the universe consisting of $x_1, \ldots, x_n$ there is an interpretation of 'F', 'G', etc. that simultaneously makes A_1 true of x_1, and A_2 true of x_2, and so on.

This is almost as easily seen as stated. Since A_1 is consistent, there is a substitution of 'T' and '⊥' for 'F', 'G', etc. that makes A_1 resolve to 'T'. Similarly there is a perhaps different substitution of 'T' and '⊥' for 'F', 'G', etc. that makes A_2 resolve to 'T'. Similarly for $A_3, \ldots, A_n$. Now interpret 'F' as true of x_1 unless '⊥' was substituted for 'F' when A_1 resolved to 'T'; also interpret 'F' as true of x_2 unless '⊥' was substituted for 'F' when A_2 resolved to 'T'; and so on to x_n. Similarly for 'G', 'H', etc.

Example: Take A_1, A_2, and A_3 as '$F\bar{G}$', '$G\bar{H}$', and '$\bar{F}H$', and take x_1, x_2, and x_3 as Tom, Dick, and Harry. Substitution of 'T' for 'F' and '⊥' for 'G' makes '$F\bar{G}$' resolve to 'T'; so interpret 'F' and 'H' as true of Tom, and 'G' not. Similarly, in view of '$G\bar{H}$', interpret 'F' and 'G' as true of Dick, and 'H' not. Similarly, in view of '$\bar{F}H$', interpret 'G' and 'H' as true of Harry, and 'F' not. So 'F' is interpreted in the universe of Tom, Dick, and Harry as true of just Tom and Dick; 'G' is interpreted as true of just Dick and Harry; and 'H' is interpreted as true of just Tom and Harry.

When n is taken as 1, we get the following special case of (i).

(ii) If a Boolean term schema is consistent, then in a universe consisting of any one object there is an interpretation of 'F', 'G', etc. that makes the schema come out true of that object.

Since validity is inconsistency of the negation, (ii) can also be put thus:

(iii) If a Boolean term schema is not valid, then in a universe consisting of any one object there is an interpretation of 'F', 'G', etc. that makes the schema come out false of that object.

There is this further corollary.

(iv) If one Boolean term schema fails to imply another, then in a universe consisting of any one object there is an interpretation of 'F', 'G', etc. that makes the one schema true of that object and the other false of it.

This follows from (ii), since the failure of implication means consistency of the conjunction of the one schema with the negation of the other.

We write '∃' for 'there are', in the sense 'there is at least one'. It is a prefix which, applied to a general term, produces a statement; thus 'There are black swans', schematically '∃FG'. A schema consisting, like '∃FG', of '∃' followed by a Boolean term schema, will be called a *Boolean existence schema.*

The schematism of the example about the class of '00, at the end of the preceding chapter, goes over now into this:

(2) $-∃FG\bar{H} \supset ∃F\bar{G}$, $-∃F\bar{G} \vee -∃F\bar{H}$, $\therefore -∃FH\bar{G} \supset ∃F\bar{H}G$.

Schemata such as these three, which are truth functions of Boolean existence schemata, will be called *Boolean statement schemata.*

Such schemata are counted *valid* when they come out true under all interpretations in all *nonempty* universes. It is convenient now to make this exception of the empty universe because there are among the Boolean statement schemata, unlike the term schemata, certain ones such as '∃F ∨ ∃$\bar{F}$' which fail for the empty universe but are valid and useful otherwise. Usually the universe relative to which an argument is being carried out is already known or confidently believed not to be empty, so that the failure of a schema in the sole case of the empty universe is usually nothing against it from a practical point of view.

Usually, indeed, the universe wanted in arguments worthy of Boolean schemata is known or believed to have not merely some members, but many. In the definition of validity, then, instead of saying 'every nonempty choice of universe' why not say 'every choice of universe of more than eleven members'? The reason for not doing so is that *no* new schemata would be added to the category of valid schemata by such a liberalization of the definition. If a schema can be falsified by some interpretation of 'F', 'G', etc. in some small but not empty universe, it can be falsified also in bigger universes without end.

The reasoning is as follows. We are supposing a small but not empty universe; let x be an object in it. We are supposing, further, an interpretation of 'F', 'G', etc. in that universe that falsifies a given schema. Add, then, as many new objects to the universe as you like, and interpret 'F', 'G', etc. in the enlarged universe by letting all the new objects go along with x. That is, take 'F' as true of all or none of the new objects according as 'F' was interpreted as true or false of x; and similarly for 'G' and further letters. Then the new objects will be indistinguishable from x so far as the interpretation of our schema is concerned; the schema will be falsified now as before.

Happily, thus, the only exception that there is any occasion to make in defining validity is that of the empty universe. But we must not underestimate this exception. Occasionally an argument may most conveniently be carried through under a choice of universe whose nonemptiness is open to question. Still there is no need to cover the empty universe in our general theory of validity, because the question whether a schema holds for the empty universe is easily handled as a separate question. To decide whether a schema comes out true for the empty universe we have merely to put '⊥' for the existential clauses and resolve.

Just as a Boolean statement schema counts as valid when true under all interpretations in all nonempty universes, so it counts as *consistent* when true under some interpretation in some nonempty universe. One schema implies another if, in every nonempty universe, every interpretation that makes the one true makes the other true. As before, thus, inconsistency is validity of the negation and implication is validity of the conditional. Equivalence is, as before, mutual implication; also validity of the biconditional.

We proceed with a few laws about Boolean existence schemata.

(v) A Boolean existence schema is valid if and only if its term schema is valid.

For, if the term schema is valid, then every interpretation makes it true of everything, in any chosen universe, and therefore true of something in any nonempty universe. If on the other hand the term schema is not valid, then by (iii) there is an interpretation that makes the term schema come out false of the sole object in some universe, and the existence schema under that interpretation comes out false.

(vi) A Boolean existence schema is consistent if and only if its term schema is consistent.

For, if the term schema is consistent, then by (ii) there is an interpretation that makes the term schema come out true of something, and thus makes the existence schema come out true. If on the other hand the term schema is inconsistent, every interpretation makes it false of all objects and thus falsifies the existence schema.

(vii) One Boolean existence schema implies another if and only if the one term schema implies the other.

For, suppose the one term schema implies the other. Then any interpretation that makes the one term schema true of something will make the other true of the same thing. Then any interpretation that makes the one existence schema true will make the other true; so the one existence schema implies the other. Next suppose that the one term schema does not imply the other. Then, by (iv), there is an interpretation that makes the one term schema come out true of the sole member of some universe and makes the other come out false of it. This interpretation makes the one existence schema come out true and the other false. So the one existence schema does not imply the other.

Another remarkable thing about Boolean existence schemata is that they cannot conflict with one another. The conjunction '$\exists F\bar{G}$. $\exists G\bar{H}$. $\exists \bar{F}H$' is consistent despite the conflicts among '$F\bar{G}$', '$G\bar{H}$', and '$\bar{F}H$'. We have this:

(viii) A conjunction of Boolean existence schemata is consistent so long as each of them separately is consistent.

For, let $E_1, E_2, \ldots, E_n$ be any separately consistent existence schemata, and let the Boolean term schemata standing after '$\exists$' in these be respectively $A_1, A_2, \ldots, A_n$. By (vi), each of $A_1, A_2, \ldots, A_n$ is consistent. So, by (i), there is an interpretation that makes each of these come out true of a distinct object in an n-member universe. This interpretation makes E_1, $E_2, \ldots, E_n$ all come out true.

Arguing similarly but more complexly, we get also this similar but somewhat more complex law:

(ix) A Boolean existence schema is implied by a conjunction of Boolean existence schemata only if it is implied by one of them in isolation.

For, let E and $E_1, E_2, \ldots, E_n$ be Boolean existence schemata and suppose that none of $E_1, E_2, \ldots, E_n$ implies E; to show that their conjunction does not imply E. Let $A, A_1, A_2, \ldots, A_n$ be the term schemata standing in $E, E_1, E_2, \ldots, E_n$. By (vii), since E_1 does not imply E, A_1 does not imply A. So the conjunction of A_1 with the negation of A is consistent. Similarly for the conjunction of A_2 with the negation of A; and so on. So, by (i), there is an interpretation that makes each of these n conjunctions come out true of a distinct object in an n-member universe. But A is negated in each of these n conjunctions. So the interpretation makes A come out false of all n objects, while making $A_1, A_2, \ldots, A_n$ each true of at least one. So, on this interpretation, $E_1, E_2, \ldots, E_n$ all become true and E false. So the conjunction of $E_1, E_2, \ldots, E_n$ does not imply E.

We turn finally to an obvious but important law to the effect that the existence prefix is distributive over alternation.

| (x)   '$\exists (F \vee G)$' is equivalent to '$\exists F \vee \exists G$'.

Clearly, some persons are either saints or geniuses if and only if some are saints or some are geniuses. It is not excluded, of course, that there be both saints and geniuses, nor is it excluded that some of the saints be geniuses.

The obviousness of (x) must not be allowed to encourage the thought that '$\exists$' is distributive also over conjunction. (vii) assures us rightly enough that '$\exists FG$' implies '$\exists F . \exists G$', but the converse fails. There are round things and square, after all, but no round squares.

If this warning is unneeded, perhaps the next is more to the purpose: the combination '$-\exists$' is not distributive even over alternation. Thus take 'F' as 'horse' and 'G' as 'unicorn'. Then '$\exists G$' is false and therefore '$-\exists F \vee -\exists G$' is true; on the other hand '$-\exists (F \vee G)$' is false, since '$F \vee G$' is true of the horses.

Certainly (x) allows us to do some distribution in '$-\exists (F \vee G)$'. It allows us to change the part '$\exists (F \vee G)$' of '$-\exists (F \vee G)$' to '$\exists F \vee \exists G$', keeping the negation sign as a fixed context. '$-\exists (F \vee G)$' is the negation of '$\exists (F \vee G)$', and hence equivalent to the negation '$-(\exists F \vee \exists G)$' of '$\exists F \vee \exists G$'.

HISTORICAL NOTE: The idea of changeable universes goes back to DeMorgan (1846), as does the phrase 'universe of discourse'. Exclusion of the empty universe was implicit already in Frege's logic of 1879. The argument that was set forth above, for excluding the empty universe, is in Hilbert and Ackermann (1938, p. 92) and no doubt in earlier works. The sign '$\exists$' and its distribution law (x) are from Peano, 1895.

EXERCISES

1.   Schematize, in the style of (2), the five examples in Exercise 1 of Chapter 17.

2.   In view of (ix) and (vii), you can decide whether the schema:

$$\exists (F \equiv G) . \exists F\bar{G} . \exists (\bar{F} \vee \bar{G})$$

implies '$\exists \bar{F}G$'. How? Do so.

19

TESTS
OF VALIDITY

We are now in a position to test any Boolean statement schema for validity. I shall state and justify the tests case by case, according to the form of the schema. In all cases the tests reduce to truth-value analyses of Boolean term schemata.

(i) A Boolean existence schema is valid if and only if its term schema is valid. (This was (v) of the preceding chapter.)

(ii) The negation of a Boolean existence schema is valid if and only if the term schema is inconsistent.

For, the negation is valid if and only if the existence schema itself is inconsistent, and so, by (vi) of the preceding chapter, if and only if the term schema is inconsistent.

(iii) An alternation of negations of Boolean existence schemata is valid if and only if one of those negations meets the above validity test.

For, the alternation of negations amounts to the negation of the conjunction of the existence schemata; and this is valid just in case the conjunction is inconsistent. But, by (viii) of the preceding chapter, this conjunction is inconsistent just in case some one of the existence schemata is inconsistent, and hence just in case some one of the negations of existence schemata is valid.

The next test concerns the *existential conditional*, by which I mean a conditional whose antecedent is a Boolean existence schema or a conjunction of such and whose consequent is a Boolean existence schema.

(iv) An existential conditional is valid if and only if the Boolean term schema in one of the existence schemata in the antecedent implies the Boolean term schema in the consequent.

For, the existential conditional is valid if and only if the antecedent implies the consequent. By (ix) of the preceding chapter, this will happen if and only if one of the existence schemata in the antecedent implies the consequent. By (vii) of the preceding chapter, this will happen if and only if the one term schema implies the other.

The next one goes without saying.

(v) A conjunction of Boolean statement schemata of any of the forms covered in (i)–(iv) is valid if and only if each of them comes out valid under the tests (i)–(iv).

For completeness of our test of validity of Boolean statement schemata it now remains only to show that every Boolean statement schema can be got over into one of the five forms covered in (i)–(v), by performing equivalence transformations upon its parts. This recourse to interchangeable parts depends upon a law of interchange similar to what we saw in Chapter 9. We saw there that any component of a truth-functional schema can be supplanted by any equivalent without disturbing the validity or consistency of the whole and without affecting its relations of implication and equivalence to other schemata. Such interchange works equally for Boolean statement schemata, and for much the same reason. It worked for pure truth functions because the truth value of the compound statement depends on no features of the component statements except their truth values. And it works now for truth functions and '∃' because the truth value of the compound statement depends on no features of the component statements and terms except their truth values and their extensions.

To transform any given Boolean statement schema S into one of the five forms, we begin by transforming S into conjunctional normal form as of Chapter 12. For this purpose we treat each existence schema in S as if it were a single statement letter 'p', 'q', etc. This brings S into the form of a conjunction of alternations. Each of these alternations is an alternation of existence schemata or of negations of existence schemata or both. However, there is never any need to rest with an alternation of existence schemata, thanks to the distributivity law, (x) of the preceding chapter. Transformed by this law, each of our alternations will be an alternation of (one or more) negations of existence schemata and at most one existence schema. If it is an alternation of one such negation, it falls under (ii); if of several, (iii). If it is an alternation of no negations and one affirmative existence schema, it falls under (i). If finally it is an alternation of one or more negations of existence schemata and one existence schema, it amounts to an existential conditional and falls under (iv); for, '$\bar{p}_1 \vee \bar{p}_2 \vee \ldots \vee \bar{p}_n \vee q$' is equivalent to '$p_1 p_2 \ldots p_n \supset q$'.

For a simple illustration let us apply the test to the syllogism AII ·in the first figure. Rendered as Boolean statement schemata, the premises of this syllogism are '$-\exists G\bar{H}$' and '$\exists FG$' and the conclusion is '$\exists FH$'. So the inclusive Boolean statement schema to test for validity is:

$$-\exists G\bar{H} . \exists FG . \supset \exists FH.$$

Toward converting this to conjunctional normal form, we translate the conditional into alternation and negation.

$$-(-\exists G\bar{H} . \exists FG) \vee \exists FH.$$

Conversion into conjunctional normal form takes one more step:

$$\exists G\bar{H} \vee -\exists FG \vee \exists FH.$$

Then we fuse the two affirmative existence schemata.

$$-\exists FG \lor \exists (G\bar{H} \lor FH).$$

Rendered as an existential conditional, this becomes:

$$\exists FG \supset \exists (G\bar{H} \lor FH).$$

By the criterion (iv), finally, this is valid; for a fell swoop shows that 'FG' implies '$G\bar{H} \lor FH$'.

Let us apply the test to the argument regarding the class of '00. It got as far as the formulation (2) midway in the preceding chapter. To establish this implication we want to show the validity of the conditional:

$$-\exists FG\bar{H} \supset \exists F\bar{G} . -\exists F\bar{G} \lor -\exists F\bar{H} .\supset. -\exists FH\bar{G} \supset \exists F\bar{H}G.$$

Appreciable labor can commonly be saved if, to begin with, we permute the letters of each term into alphabetical order. This enhances the matching of terms and, therewith, the chances of simplification. We get this:

$$-\exists FG\bar{H} \supset \exists F\bar{G} . -\exists F\bar{G} \lor -\exists F\bar{H} .\supset. -\exists F\bar{G}H \supset \exists FG\bar{H}.$$

The stages of conversion into conjunctional normal form are left to the reader. If patently valid clauses of the type '$\bar{p} \lor q \lor p$' are deleted as they arise, this is what the reader is apt to end up with:

$$-\exists F\bar{G} \lor \exists F\bar{H} \lor \exists F\bar{G}H \lor \exists FG\bar{H}.$$

When we fuse the three affirmative existence schemata, this becomes:

$$-\exists F\bar{G} \lor \exists (F\bar{H} \lor F\bar{G}H \lor FG\bar{H}).$$

Rendered as an existential conditional, this becomes:

$$\exists F\bar{G} \supset \exists (F\bar{H} \lor F\bar{G}H \lor FG\bar{H}).$$

By the criterion (iv), finally, this is valid; for a fell swoop shows that '$F\bar{G}$' implies '$F\bar{H} \lor F\bar{G}H \lor FG\bar{H}$'.

Now one more example:

(1) $$\exists FG \lor \exists FH .\supset \exists [F(G \lor H)].$$

Paraphrasing the conditional into alternation and negation, we get:

$$-\exists FG . -\exists FH .\lor \exists [F(G \lor H)],$$

which distributes to conjunctional normal form thus:

$$-\exists FG \lor \exists[F(G \lor H)] . -\exists FH \lor \exists[F(G \lor H)].$$

Rendering this as a conjunction of existential conditionals, we have:

$$\exists FG \supset \exists[F(G \lor H)] . \exists FH \supset \exists[F(G \lor H)].$$

Here (v) is applicable; we have to see that both conditionals are valid, if the whole is to qualify as valid. Both conditionals do, by (iv), prove valid; for we find by fell swoop that '*FG*' implies '*F*(*G* ∨ *H*)' and so does '*FH*'.

A decision procedure for validity is of course a decision procedure at the same time for consistency, implication, and equivalence, since inconsistency, implication, and equivalence are validity of the negation, the conditional, and the biconditional.

The test of validity which is now before us always proceeds, we might say, by transforming a Boolean statement schema into a conjunction of genuine or defective existential conditionals; for the schemata covered in (i), (ii), and (iii) amount to defective existential conditionals, lacking antecedent or consequent. So the method may be called the *method of existential conditionals*.

A different validity test for Boolean statement schemata, due to Herbrand, I shall call the *cellular* method. In practice it tends to be more laborious than that of existential conditionals, but it is worth noting because it is so simply formulated. It operates with *cellular* existence schemata. A cellular existence schema in n given letters '*F*', '*G*', etc. has as its term schema just a conjunction of n literals in alphabetical order, each being one of those letters or its negation. Thus the cellular existence schemata in '*F*' are '$\exists F$' and '$\exists \bar{F}$'; those in '*F*' and '*G*' are '$\exists FG$', '$\exists F\bar{G}$', '$\exists \bar{F}G$', and '$\exists \bar{F}\bar{G}$'; those in '*F*', '*G*', and '*H*' are '$\exists FGH$', '$\exists FG\bar{H}$', and six more; and so on. Each corresponds thus to an uncut cell of the Venn diagram and says there is something in it.

Note next that any Boolean existence schema, say in n letters, can be transformed into an alternation of cellular existence schemata in those n letters. The method is as follows. Given an existence schema, put its term into developed alternational normal form (cf. Chapter 10) and then distribute '$\exists$' through the alternation. For instance, given '$\exists[\bar{F}(G \lor H)]$', we first put its term into alternational normal form, getting '$\exists(\bar{F}G \lor \bar{F}H)$', and then we develop it, getting:

$$\exists(\bar{F}GH \lor \bar{F}G\bar{H} \lor \bar{F}GH \lor \bar{F}\bar{G}H),$$

or, dropping the duplication,

$$\exists(\bar{F}GH \lor \bar{F}G\bar{H} \lor \bar{F}\bar{G}H).$$

Finally, distributing '$\exists$', we have:

$$\exists \bar{F}GH \vee \exists \bar{F}G\bar{H} \vee \exists \bar{F}\bar{G}H.$$

It follows that any Boolean statement schema S, say in n letters, can be rendered as a truth function of cellular existence schemata in those n letters. First, by a trivial move, each existence schema appearing in S can be made to contain all n letters. For, if an existence schema lacks 'H', we can just append '$H \vee \bar{H}$' to its term schema by conjunction. Thereupon, by the method of the preceding paragraph, we proceed to render each existence schema as an alternation of cellular existence schemata in the n letters.

Now the validity test that was going to be so simply formulable is just this:

> (vi) A truth function of cellular existence schemata in n given letters is a valid Boolean statement schema if and only if it resolves to 'T' under all assignments of 'T' and '$\perp$' to those cellular schemata (disregarding the assignment of '$\perp$' to all 2^n cellular schemata).

I shall not pause for a full proof of (vi), for it can quickly be made plausible by the following reflection upon Venn diagrams. When we undertake to interpret a Boolean statement schema, the only information that is going to matter to its truth or falsity is information as to which cells of the diagram are occupied and which are empty. Moreover, interpretation of any one cell as occupied or empty is independent of interpretation of other cells as occupied or empty. So the only thing that can make for validity of a Boolean statement schema, once the schema is resolved into the cellular existence schemata, is the external truth-functional structure by which it is built of those cellular existence schemata. (Exception: since we chose to define validity without responsibility for the empty universe, the parenthetical exemption is appended to (vi).)

As illustration let us test (1) again. First we supply missing letters to the existence schemata in (1).

$$\exists [FG(H \vee \bar{H})] \vee \exists [FH(G \vee \bar{G})] . \supset \exists [F(G \vee H].$$

Then we expand the terms into normal form, holding to alphabetical order.

$$\exists (FGH \vee FG\bar{H}) \vee \exists (FGH \vee F\bar{G}H) . \supset \exists (FG \vee FH).$$

Then we develop the terms, holding to alphabetical order and dropping a duplicate.

$$\exists (FGH \vee FG\bar{H}) \vee \exists (FGH \vee F\bar{G}H) . \supset \exists (FGH \vee FG\bar{H} \vee F\bar{G}H).$$

Then we distribute '$\exists$'.

$$\exists FGH \vee \exists FG\bar{H} \vee \exists FGH \vee \exists F\bar{G}H . \supset \exists FGH \vee \exists FG\bar{H} \vee \exists F\bar{G}H.$$

The truth-functional validity is visible.

The stipulation of alphabetical order in the definition of cellular existence schema is no mere labor saver now; it is essential to the soundness of (vi). If in this example we had written '$\exists FGH$' at some points and '$\exists FHG$' at others, the truth-functional validity of the outward structure would have been lost; the parts '$\exists FGH$' and '$\exists FHG$' would have fared like independent sentence letters 'p' and 'q'.

HISTORICAL NOTE: The first decision procedure for this much of logic was Löwenheim's (1915), but the first reasonably manageable one was Behmann's (1922). The method of existential conditionals is somewhat reminiscent of Behmann's. The cellular method stems rather from Herbrand (1930).

EXERCISES

1. Test each of the following schemata for validity by the method of existential conditionals.

$$\exists JF \supset . \exists (F\bar{G} \lor JG \lor GH),$$

$$\exists GJ . \exists GK . \supset . \exists (FGH \lor \bar{F}J \lor \bar{H}K).$$

2. Schematize the following statement and test for consistency (by testing the negation for validity) according to the method of existential conditionals.

    Some who take logic and Latin take neither physics nor Greek, but all who take either Latin or chemistry take both logic and Greek.

3. Five inferences were schematized in Exercise 1 of Chapter 18. Check them all, by testing the appropriate conditionals for validity according to the method of existential conditionals.

4. Check this inference by the same method.

    Nobody attended but parents of the cast.
    If no parents of the cast enjoyed the play, then no parents of the cast have a taste for high-class entertainment.
    ∴ If any attended who have a taste for high-class entertainment, then some parents of the cast enjoyed the play.

5. Repeat all four exercises using the cellular method.

20

BOOLEAN ALGEBRA

The letters '*F*', '*G*', etc. have been figuring in the present pages as schematic representations of general terms. If instead we view them as schematic names of classes, we are in a fair way to reinterpreting our Boolean schemata as formulas of the Boolean algebra of classes. *FG* is the *intersection* of the classes *F* and *G*, that is, the class of their common members; *F* v *G* is the *union*, got by pooling their members; $\bar{F}$ is the *complement* of *F*. Once we consign our Boolean term schemata thus to the grammatical category of names, it is natural to join them in equations, or identities—writing '*F* = *G*' to mean that *F* and *G* are the same class. Valid equations such as these emerge:

$$FG = GF, \qquad F \vee G = G \vee F, \qquad -(FG) = \bar{F} \vee \bar{G},$$
$$F(G \vee H) = FG \vee FH, \qquad F \vee GH = (F \vee G)(F \vee H).$$

An equation comes out valid just in case its two sides are equivalent in the sense of Chapter 18: equivalent by truth-value analysis.

Two extreme classes are the empty class Λ and the universe class V. Clearly

$$\Lambda = \bar{V}, \qquad F \vee \bar{F} = V. \qquad F\bar{F} = \Lambda.$$

In the ordinary algebra of numbers, it will be recalled, any equation can be converted to a form in which one side is '0'. Now it happens likewise that in Boolean algebra any equation can be converted to a form in which one side is 'Λ'. For, '*F* = *G*' means that the classes *F* and *G* have the same members; hence that there is nothing in $F\bar{G}$ nor in $\bar{F}G$; and hence that $F\bar{G} \vee \bar{F}G = \Lambda$.

Equally, if we prefer, we can always make one side 'V'; for '*F* = *G*' is equivalent also to '$FG \vee \bar{F}\bar{G} = V$'.

It has long been evident how to test a Boolean equation for validity, since it is just a matter of truth tables, or truth-value analysis. An equation with 'Λ' on one side is valid just in case its other side is truth-functionally inconsistent. An equation with 'V' on one side is valid just in case its other side is truth-functionally valid. And an equation of two Boolean term schemata, as we have been calling them, is valid (we noted) just in case the two are truth-functionally equivalent.

The formulas that belong to the notation of Boolean algebra comprise not only the Boolean equations but all the formulas that can be built up of them by truth functions. A test of validity for Boolean formulas in this inclusive sense is a more complicated matter. Such a test is afforded, however, by either of our validity tests of the preceding chapter, as follows.

To test the validity of a truth function of Boolean equations we first transform each equation so that the left side is 'Λ'; then we rewrite 'Λ =' as '−∃'. If there are any lingering occurrences of 'Λ' or 'V' elsewhere, we rewrite them as '$F\bar{F}$' and '$F \vee \bar{F}$'. Now our truth function of Boolean equations has become a Boolean sentence schema in the sense of Chapter 18, and can be tested for validity by either of the methods of Chapter 19. Or, if we prefer, we can easily rephrase the methods of Chapter 19 to render them applicable directly to truth functions of Boolean equations as they stand.

Is there more than a notational difference between a Boolean logic of terms, as in Chapters 18 f, and this algebra of classes? Nominally there is the difference between 'F' as depicting a general term and 'F' as depicting a class name. There is the difference between the general term 'man', or 'is a man', and the class name 'mankind'. (Cf. Chapter 14.) The general term is true of each of various individuals, men. The class name is a name of one abstract object, the class of men. By means of the general term we may speak generally of men and never raise the philosophical question whether, besides those various men, there is an additional object which is the class of them. The class name does raise that question, and it hints an affirmative answer.

The question is not an empty one. In Chapters 43 ff. we shall see that the assumption of classes can add materially to what can be formulated in a theory, even when what we are formulating is not itself about classes. Where we are interested in economy of means, and of keeping account of the assumptions needed in proving or defining something, we must take note of whether classes figure in the apparatus; sometimes they do and sometimes not.

In the case of Boolean algebra, still, we are free to disavow the assumption of classes, representing it as a mere manner of speaking; for we have seen how to translate Boolean algebra into the more innocent idiom of a Boolean logic of general terms. When the assumption of classes materially contributes to a theory, and cannot be thus facilely disavowed, the classes are assumed among the very objects that the general terms themselves are true of. They are assumed as values of the variables of quantification— to anticipate a notion which we shall take up in the next chapter. Meanwhile we may best look upon the Boolean algebra of classes as only a simulated little theory of classes and a figurative rendering of what is really nothing more than the Boolean logic of general terms.

HISTORICAL NOTE: The Boolean algebra of classes was founded by Boole in 1847 and improved by DeMorgan and Jevons in 1858 and 1864. It was anticipated in some measure by Leibniz in the seventeenth century. Between this logic and the logic of truth functions, whose antecedents are more ancient (cf. Chapter 2), there are of course conspicuous parallels; and they were noted already by Leibniz and Boole. But the full relationship between the logic of truth functions and the Boolean algebra of classes was not then as clear as it now becomes. The relationship is best reflected by the logic of Boolean schemata, Chapters 18 and 19.

Classes are also called sets. A speculative branch of mathematics called set theory stems from Cantor (fl. 1890). It is occupied largely with problems of infinity, and it treats of classes in substantial ways that are by no means to be dismissed like the Boolean class algebra as mere manners of speaking. We shall glimpse a little of it in Chapters 43–46. In that rarified air the term 'set' tends to be preferred to 'class', except in a certain technical context (see last pages of book) where the double terminology has been put to use to mark a special distinction.

In the current "new math" of the elementary schools, the exalted name of set theory is confusingly applied to the other end of the scale: to the Boolean algebra of classes, hence really the simple logic of general terms.

EXERCISES

1. Translate the following formulas into Boolean schemata in the sense of Chapters 18 and 19 and test them for validity by the method of existential conditionals.

$$F = F \vee G \vee H . \supset . F = F \vee G,$$
$$F \vee \bar{G} = G . \supset . F = G,$$
$$F = F \vee G . \equiv . FG = G,$$
$$FG = F \vee G . \equiv . F = G.$$

2. Reformulate the method of existential conditionals as a decision procedure applicable directly to truth functions of Boolean equations. (A serious exercise.)

21

QUANTIFICATION

A general term may, as remarked in Chapter 14, be thought of indifferently as singular or plural and as substantive, adjective, or verb. This latitude is all very well, but we could do with more. We would like to be able to

handle any statement about an object as predicating some general term of
that object, even when the sentence is complex and shows no neatly segregated term to the purpose. Already in the little exercise of Chapter 14
we saw that verbal contortions were needed to segregate the appropriate
terms. In many examples, e.g.:

(1) x used to work for the man who murdered the second husband of
     x's youngest sister,

it can be rather a challenge to find a term which, predicated of x, has the
same effect. We come out with:

(2)   former employee of own youngest sister's second husband's
        murderer.

This inconvenience can be eliminated by cleaving to the combination
'Fx' and letting the whole stand for any desired sentence with an 'x' in it,
e.g., (1). We no longer have to say what 'F' stands for by itself.
    On this approach the existence schema '$\exists F$' takes the form rather of an
existential quantification '$(\exists x)Fx$'. The 'x' that appeared so briefly in (1) of
Chapter 18 comes back to stay. Boolean statement schemata like those in
(2) of Chapter 18 now get spelled out:

$$-(\exists x)(Fx . Gx . -Hx) \supset (\exists x)(Fx . -Gx),$$
$$-(\exists x)(Fx . -Gx) \lor -(\exists x)(Fx . -Hx),$$
$$-(\exists x)(Fx . Hx . -Gx) \supset (\exists x)(Fx . -Hx . Gx).$$

Truth-functional connectives cease to apply to terms and term letters and
become restricted again to sentences and to schemata for sentences.
    The convenience of this move is that sentences like (1) can be substituted
bodily for 'Fx', 'Gx', etc. in schemata of the sort above. The inconvenience
is loss of brevity. But we may avail ourselves of the best of both worlds.
When our interest is in testing schemata for validity, rather than in substituting sentences in them, we are well advised to drop 'x' everywhere and
test the short Boolean statement schemata as before.
    There is good reason to accustom ourselves to the more cumbersome
notation of quantification, however, also apart from the convenience of
substitution. For we shall find in Part III that it extends naturally to
problems involving *relative* or polyadic general terms, in combinations like
'Fxy'. When we come to that, no convenient general condensation of notation comparable to the Boolean will be available.
    The so-called *existential quantifier* '$(\exists x)$' corresponds to the words 'there
is something x such that'. Application of '$(\exists x)$' to the expression:

(3) x is a book . x is boring

in the fashion:

(4) $(\exists x)(x$ is a book . x is boring$)$

is as much as to say that there is at least one object in the universe such
that, when 'x' in (3) is thought of as naming it, (3) becomes true. Thus (4)
goes into words fairly literally as:

(5)   There is something such that it is a book and it is boring;

more briefly as:

(6)   Something is a book and is boring;

more briefly still as:

Some books are boring.

Version (6) suggests that instead of adopting the queer and elaborate
notation (4) we might have invented a simpler symbolism:

(7) s is a book . s is boring,

where 's' is short for 'something'. However, this suggestion is wrong; for,
given (7), we would have no way of deciding whether to interpret it in the
manner of (6) or in the quite different manner:

(8)   Something is a book and something is boring.

The particular statements (6) and (8) are by chance both true, but we get
contrasting truth values if we shift our example from 'book' and 'boring'
to 'square' and 'round':

(9)   Something is a square and is round,   (false)
(10)   Something is a square and something is round.   (true)

One of the misleading things about ordinary language is that the word
'something' masquerades as a name but deviates in its behavior at crucial
points. When a genuine name is used, the distinction noted between (9)
and (10) and between (6) and (8) evaporates; the statements:

Maud is a book and is boring,
Maud is a book and *Maud* is boring,

e.g., are quite interchangeable. When 'something' is used, on the other hand, *scope* becomes important: we must distinguish visibly in one way or another between the case where the scope of 'something' is 'is a book and is boring', as in (6), and the case where 'something' recurs with two scopes, 'is a book' and 'is boring', as in (8). Ordinary language effects this distinction, in the case of (6) and (8), by using a compound predicate in (6) and not in (8). In more complex cases, ordinary language has to resort to various circumlocutions to maintain the distinction. In a notation adapted to purposes of logical analysis, however, uniformity is wanted. Thus it is that the notation of quantification exemplified in (4) is adopted, wherein the scope of 'something' is indicated explicitly by parentheses. The difference between (6) and (8) is maintained by writing (4) for (6) and, for (8), the following:

(11) $\qquad (\exists x)(x$ is a book$)$. $(\exists x)(x$ is boring$)$.

What (4) says is that at least one thing x fulfills the simultaneous conditions 'x is a book' and 'x is boring'; what (11) says, on the other hand, is that at least one thing fulfills 'x is a book' and at least one thing, same or different, fulfills 'x is boring'.

The existential quantifier has a companion-piece in the *universal quantifier* '(x)', which corresponds to the words 'each thing x (in the universe) is such that'. Application of '(x)' to the expression:

(12) $\qquad\qquad\qquad x$ is identical with x

in the fashion:

(13) $\qquad\qquad\qquad (x)(x$ is identical with $x)$

is called *universal quantification* of (12); and the result (13) is also spoken of as the universal quantification of (12). To say that (13) is true is to say that, no matter what object in the universe be imagined named by 'x' in (12), (12) becomes true. Thus (13) goes into words fairly literally as:

(14) $\qquad$ Each thing is such that it is identical with itself,

or more briefly:

$\qquad\qquad\qquad$ Everything is identical with itself.

Similarly the quantification:

(15) $\qquad\qquad\qquad (x)(x$ is a man $\supset x$ is mortal$)$

goes into words fairly literally as:

Each thing is such that if it is a man then it is mortal,

or more briefly:

All men are mortal.

We saw in (9)–(11) the necessity of indicating just how large a portion of a statement is to be comprised within the scope of a given occurrence of the word 'something'. The corresponding necessity in the case of 'everything' can be seen by contrasting the truth:

(16)   Everything is red or not red

with the falsehood:

(17)   Everything is red or everything is not-red.

In the notation of quantification, (16) becomes:

(18) $(x)[x$ is red $\lor -(x$ is red$)]$

while (17) becomes:

(19) $(x)(x$ is red$) \lor (x)-(x$ is red$).$

The distributivity noted in (x) of Chapter 18 is, in terms of quantification, the equivalence of the schemata:

(20) $(\exists x)(Fx \lor Gx),$ $(\exists x)Fx \lor (\exists x)Gx.$

The universal quantifier is similarly distributive over conjunction; the schemata:

(21) $(x)(Fx \cdot Gx),$ $(x)Fx \cdot (x)Gx$

are obviously equivalent.

Statements of ordinary language which at first glance seem to be conjunctions or conditionals often demand interpretation as quantifications of conjunctions or conditionals. Examples are:

(22)   Sadie stole something at the Emporium and exchanged it for a blouse,
(23)   If Sadie wants anything she manages to get it.

These must be interpretated as quantifications:

(24)   ($\exists x$)(Sadie stole x at the Emporium . Sadie exchanged x for a blouse),
(25)   (x)(Sadie wants x $\supset$ Sadie manages to get x),

rather than as a conjunction and conditional:

(26)   ($\exists x$)(Sadie stole x at the Emporium) . Sadie exchanged it for a blouse,
(27)   ($\exists x$)(Sadie wants x) $\supset$ Sadie manages to get it.

For, the 'it' of (22) clearly refers back across 'and' to 'something', and correspondingly the 'it' of (23) refers back to 'anything'. The quantifiers must be made to cover the whole compound as in (24) and (25), rather than just the first clause as in (26) and (27), so as to reach out to a lagging recurrence of 'x' in the position of 'it'.

Universal and existential quantification are intimately connected in meaning, through negation. If again we read 'Fx' as 'x is an F', then '($\exists x$)Fx' may be read:

There are F,   Some things are F, F exist;

hence its negation '$-(\exists x)Fx$' means:

There are no F,   Nothing is an F, F do not exist.

But to say that there are no F is the same as saying that everything is non-F: '(x)$-Fx$'. We thus have two ways of saying that there are no F: '$-(\exists x)Fx$' and '(x)$-Fx$'.

Again, since '(x)Fx' may be read:

All is F,   Everything is an F,
Each thing is an F,   There is nothing but F,

its negation '$-(x)Fx$' means:

Not everything is an F,   There are non-F,

which may equally well be rendered '($\exists x$)$-Fx$'. Thus the combination of signs '$-(\exists x)$' has the same effect as '(x)$-$', and the combination '$-(x)$' has the same effect as '($\exists x$)$-$'. It follows that we could get along without universal quantifiers altogether, adhering to existential ones; for, instead of writing '(x)Fx' we could always write the negation '$-(\exists x)-Fx$'. Equally we could get along without existential quantifiers, adhering to universal ones; for, instead of writing '($\exists x$)Fx' we could always write '$-(x)-Fx$'. Retention of the two kinds of quantifiers is dictated only by convenience.

Next let us survey the categorical forms **A**, **E**, **I**, and **O** (Chapter 14) in terms of quantification. **A**, to begin with, is expressed as '(x)(Fx $\supset$ Gx)', as already seen in the example (15) above. (This formulation, by the way, follows precisely the lines of what was called a "generalized conditional" in Chapter 3; cf. especially (2) of Chapter 3.) This being the case, beginners commonly make the mistake of concluding that **I** must become '$(\exists x)(Fx \supset Gx)$'. Since 'All F are G' and 'Some F are G' are alike verbally except for 'All' and 'Some', it is expected that their formulations in terms of quantification will be alike except for '(x)' and '$(\exists x)$'. Actually the proper formulation of **I** is rather '$(\exists x)(Fx . Gx)$'—as seen in (4) above. The words 'Some F are G' and 'All F are G', insofar as they suggest parallelism of structure, are misleading; the proper contrast of structure is better brought out by the expanded phrasings 'Some things are *both F and G*', 'Everything is, *if* an F, a G'.

To discourage the erroneous rendering '$(\exists x)(Fx \supset Gx)$' of **I** once and for all, let us stop to see what '$(\exists x)(Fx \supset Gx)$' really says. '$Fx \supset Gx$', to begin with, holds for any object x for which '$Fx . -Gx$' fails; thus it holds for every object x which is non-F, and it holds also for every object x which is G. Hence '$(\exists x)(Fx \supset Gx)$' says only that there is at least one object which is non-F or G; and this is bound to be true, regardless of how 'F' and 'G' are interpreted, except in the one extreme case where 'F' is true of everything in the universe and 'G' is true of nothing. The form '$(\exists x)(Fx \supset Gx)$' is so trivial, so rarely false, as to be seldom worth affirming.

Correct versions of **E** and **O** are straightway discoverable from those of **A** and **I**. **E**, 'No F are G', amounts to 'All F are non-G' and thus becomes '$(x)(Fx \supset -Gx)$'; whereas **O**, paralleling **I**, becomes '$(\exists x)(Fx . -Gx)$'. Thus, to sum up:

A: All F are G **E**: No F are G
    $(x)(Fx \supset Gx)$ $(x)(Fx \supset -Gx)$

I: Some F are G **O**: Some F are not G
    $(\exists x)(Fx . Gx)$ $(\exists x)(Fx . -Gx)$

If we think of the universe as limited to a finite set of objects $a, b, \ldots, h$, we can expand existential quantifications into alternations and universal quantifications into conjunctions; '$(\exists x)Fx$' and '$(x)Fx$' become respectively:

$$Fa \lor Fb \lor \ldots \lor Fh, \qquad Fa . Fb \ldots . . Fh.$$

The distinction between (4) and (11) then comes out quite clearly; '$(\exists x)(Fx . Gx)$' becomes:

$$Fa . Ga . \lor . Fb . Gb . \lor . \ldots . \lor . Fh . Gh,$$

whereas '$(\exists x)Fx . (\exists x)Gx$' becomes:

$$Fa \lor Fb \lor \ldots \lor Fh . Ga \lor Gb \lor \ldots \lor Gh.$$

The distinction between (18) and (19) comes out equally clearly. Furthermore the interchangeability of '$-(x)$' with '$(\exists x)-$' and of '$-(\exists x)$' with '$(x)-$' turns out to be a mere application of DeMorgan's laws (Chapter 10); for, '$-(x)Fx$' and '$(\exists x)-Fx$' become respectively:

$$-(Fa \cdot Fb \ldots \ldots Fh), \qquad -Fa \vee -Fb \vee \ldots \vee -Fh,$$

and '$-(\exists x)Fx$' and '$(x)-Fx$' become respectively:

$$-(Fa \vee Fb \vee \ldots \vee Fh), \qquad -Fa \cdot -Fb \ldots \ldots -Fh.$$

It thus appears that quantification could be dispensed with altogether in favor of truth functions if we were willing to agree for all purposes on a fixed and finite and listed universe $a, b, \ldots, h$. However, we are unwilling; it is convenient to allow for variations in the choice of universe. This is convenient not only because philosophers disagree regarding the limits of reality, but also because—as already noted—some logical arguments can be simplified by deliberately limiting the universe of discourse to animals or to persons or to the employees of a given firm for the space of the problem in hand. For most problems, moreover, the relevant universe comprises objects which we are in no position to list in the manner of $a, b, \ldots, h$. For many problems the universe even comprises infinitely many objects; e.g., the integers. Thus it is that quantification is here to stay.

HISTORICAL NOTE: Quantification, in a notation structurally equivalent to what we have here, was first introduced in 1879 by Frege. The notation used here dates from Whitehead and Russell. Some later writers have preferred '$(\forall x)$' as universal quantifier, for its analogy to '$(\exists x)$'. Others, wishing to stress the analogy of the two quantifiers to conjunction and alternation, have used enlarged variants '$\bigwedge$' and '$\bigvee$' of their conjunction and alternation signs instead of '$\forall$' and '$\exists$'.

EXERCISES

1. Rewrite these with help of quantifiers:

    John cannot outrun any man on the team,
    John cannot outrun every man on the team.

2. Rewrite the premises and conclusion about the slovenly and the poor (Chapter 17) with help of quantifiers. Similarly for the other examples in Chapter 17 and in Exercise 1 of Chapter 17 and Exercises 2 and 4 of Chapter 19.

3. Supposing the universe to comprise just *a, b, . . ., h,* express these truth-functionally:

$(\exists x)(Fx \vee Gx),$ $(x)(Fx \vee Gx),$ $(x)(Fx . Gx),$

$(\exists x)Fx \vee (\exists x)Gx,$ $(x)Fx \vee (x)Gx,$ $(x)Fx . (x)Gx.$

Which come out equivalent to one another?

22

RULES OF PASSAGE. MONADIC SCHEMATA

In the schemata in which we have illustrated quantification thus far, the scope of each occurrence of a quantifier has been a truth function of '*Fx*', '*Gx*', etc. But we can be more liberal, allowing some components of the scope to be devoid of '*x*' and represented simply as '*p*' or '*q*'.

It makes good sense, e.g., to write '$(\exists x)(p . Fx)$'. This should come out true under just those interpretations of '*p*' and '*F*' that make '*p . Fx*' true of at least one thing *x*. Those, of course, are just the interpretations that make '*p*' true and '*F*' true of something; so the two schemata:

(1) $(\exists x)(p . Fx), \qquad p . (\exists x)Fx$

are equivalent. By similar reasoning, so are the two schemata:

(2) $(x)(p . Fx), \qquad p . (x)Fx.$

The same may be expected of the pair:

(3) $(\exists x)(p \vee Fx), \qquad p \vee (\exists x)Fx$

and again of the pair:

(4) $\qquad$ $(x)(p \lor Fx),\qquad p \lor (x)Fx.$

These expectations can be confirmed by direct reasoning rather like what led to (1) and (2). But also, and perhaps more instructively, we can derive these equivalences from the others. Take (3). '$(\exists x)(p \lor Fx)$' amounts to '$-(x)-(p \lor Fx)$' and hence, by DeMorgan's law, to '$-(x)(\bar{p} . -Fx)$'. But the '$(x)(\bar{p} . -Fx)$' in this is equivalent by (2) to '$\bar{p} . (x)-Fx$'; so the whole '$-(x)(\bar{p} . -Fx)$' becomes '$-(\bar{p} . (x)-Fx)$', or, by DeMorgan's law, '$p \lor -(x)-Fx$', which is to say, '$p \lor (\exists x)Fx$'. Precisely parallel steps carry us from (1) to (4).

The equivalences:

(5) $\qquad$ $(\exists x)(p \supset Fx),\qquad p \supset (\exists x)Fx,$

(6) $\qquad$ $(x)(p \supset Fx),\qquad p \supset (x)Fx$

proceed immediately from (3) and (4), respectively, since '$p \supset$' amounts to '$\bar{p} \lor$'. But the two further equivalences that the reader is now perhaps on the point of expecting are not forthcoming. What are right are rather the following two; note the curious twist.

(7) $\qquad$ $(\exists x)(Fx \supset p),\qquad (x)Fx \supset p.$

(8) $\qquad$ $(x)(Fx \supset p),\qquad (\exists x)Fx \supset p.$

For all its oddity, (7) is easily got from (3). '$(\exists x)(Fx \supset p)$' amounts to '$(\exists x)(-Fx \lor p)$', hence to '$(\exists x)-Fx \lor p$', hence to '$-(x)Fx \lor p$', hence to '$(x)Fx \supset p$'. (8) proceeds similarly from (4).

In future applications of (1)–(4) a habit already acquired in Part I should be kept: that of ignoring order in conjunctions and in alternations. Thus, in the argument above I equated '$(\exists x)(-Fx \lor p)$' to '$(\exists x)-Fx \lor p$' on the strength of (3), ignoring the fact that (3) shows 'p' rather to the left of '$\lor$' and 'Fx' to the right.

Quantifiers are subject, in point of grouping, to the same convention which governs the negation sign (Chapter 4): a quantifier applies to the shortest possible ensuing sentence or schema. In '$(\exists x)(Fx \supset p)$' the quantifier is required by the parentheses to apply to the whole conditional; in '$(\exists x)Fx \supset p$', on the other hand, the quantifier is understood as lying within the antecedent and applying only to it. The distinction between '$(\exists x)(Fx \supset p)$' and '$(\exists x)Fx \supset p$' can be reproduced in words thus:

> There is something x such that if Fx then p,
> If there is something x such that Fx then p.

Similarly for '$(x)(Fx \supset p)$' and '$(x)Fx \supset p$':

Everything x is such that if Fx then p,
If everything x is such that Fx then p.

To appreciate the difference of meaning in this latter pair, take 'Fx' as 'x contributes' and 'p' as 'I'll be surprised'. Then '$(x)(Fx \supset p)$' says of each person, even the most generous, that if he contributes I'll be surprised. It says that I foresee no contribution at all. On the other hand '$(x)Fx \supset p$' reflects no such cynicism; it says only that I'll be surprised (as who wouldn't?) in the extraordinary event that they all contribute. In ordinary language the difference is drawn by opposing 'any' to 'every'; '$(x)(Fx \supset p)$' says that if anyone contributes I'll be surprised, while '$(x)Fx \supset p$' says only that if everyone contributes I'll be surprised.

In general the difference in English usage between 'any' and 'every' may have struck many of us as unsystematic and even mysterious. Scope of the universal quantifier is the key to it. Where distinction is needed between broader and narrower scope, as between '$(x)(Fx \supset p)$' and '$(x)Fx \supset p$', the English speaker's unconscious understanding is that 'any' calls for the broader scope and 'every' for the narrower. This rule works not only in connection with the conditional but also elsewhere, notably in connection with negation. Thus take the universe of discourse as consisting of all poems. 'I do not know any poem', then, and 'I do not know every poem', call respectively for the broader and the narrower scope:

$$(x) - (\text{I know } x), \qquad - (x)(\text{I know } x).$$

The equivalences (1)–(8) are *rules of passage*. They show how to move a quantifier across a conjunction sign, an alternation sign, or a conditional sign. Rules of passage for moving quantifiers across a negation sign were noted in the preceding chapter, in these two equivalences:

(9) $(x) - Fx, \qquad - (\exists x)Fx.$

(10) $(\exists x) - Fx, \qquad - (x)Fx.$

The 'p' in the rules of passage schematizes a sentence devoid of 'x', such as 'I'll be surprised'. But also the sentence in this position could be something like 'y will be surprised', such as to invite the eventual superimposition of an outside quantifier '(y)' or '$(\exists y)$'. To see how such a situation could arise, suppose we are given this example for analysis:

There is someone [some cynic] who, if anyone contributes,
    will be surprised.

Using the letter 'y' in our quantifier this time instead of 'x' (just for a change), we can transcribe our example thus as a first step:

$(\exists y)$(if anyone contributes, y will be surprised).

But the part 'if anyone contributes, y will be surprised' has the form '$(x)(Fx \supset p)$', or '$(x)(Fx \supset Gy)$. The whole thus becomes:

(11) $(\exists y)(x)(x$ contributes $\supset y$ will be surprised),

an instance of the schema '$(\exists y)(x)(Fx \supset Gy)$'.

The alphabetical choice of the letter of quantification is obviously arbitrary; '$(\exists x)Hx$' and $(\exists y)Hy$' both say simply that something is an H. The above example of nested quantification shows, however, why we want a variety of letters to choose from; we need to keep our cross-references straight. We want it to be clear in '$(\exists y)(x)(Fx \supset Gy)$' that the first quantifier relates to the consequent 'Gy' while the second relates to the antecedent 'Fx'.

Expressions such as 'x contributes', 'y will be surprised', and 'x contributes $\supset y$ will be surprised', which are like statements except for containing 'x' or 'y' without a quantifier, are called *open sentences*. They are fragmentary clauses, neither true nor false as they stand, and of interest only as potential parts of *closed sentences* such as (11). Closed sentences are what we have been calling statements; it is just these that have truth values. Open sentences are not statements. The analogue of an unquantified 'x' in ordinary language is a pronoun for which no grammatical antecedent is expressed or understood; and the analogue of an open sentence is a clause containing such a dangling pronoun. Open sentences may, as notational forms, be described as differing from various closed sentences only in lacking a quantifier; or they may be described equally well as differing from various other closed sentences only in containing 'x' in place of a name of a specific object.

Open sentences are neither true nor false, but they may, like terms, be said to be *true of* and *false of* various objects. The open sentence 'x is a book' may, like the term 'book' itself, be said to be true of each book and false of everything else; and 'x is a book . x is boring' may be said to be true of each boring book and false of everything else. '$x = x$' and 'x is a man $\supset$ x is mortal' are true of everything. In general, to say that an open sentence is true of a given object is to say that the open sentence becomes a true statement when 'x' is reinterpreted as a name of that object. The notion of the *extension* of a term (Chapter 14) likewise carries over to open sentences: the extension of an open sentence is the class of all the objects of which the open sentence is true.

Since the schematic letters 'p', 'q', etc. have come now to stand as well for open sentences, e.g. 'y will be surprised', as for statements, I shall take to calling them *sentence letters*. Note that these and the schematic term letters 'F', 'G', etc. differ basically in function from 'x', 'y', etc. Whereas 'x' can appear in sentences—even in closed sentences, with help of a quantifier—on the other hand 'p', 'q', etc. and 'F', 'G', etc. cannot appear in sentences at all;[5] they are merely dummy sentences and dummy terms, used in schemata which depict outward forms of sentences.

The letters 'x', 'y', 'z', and others, so used, are called *variables*. Care must be taken, however, to divorce this traditional word of mathematics from its archaic connotations. The variable is not best thought of as somehow varying through time, and causing the sentence in which it occurs to vary with it. Neither is it to be thought of as an unknown quantity, discoverable by solving equations. The variables remain mere pronouns for cross-reference to quantifiers; just as 'x' in its recurrences can usually be rendered 'it' in verbal translations, so the distinctive variables 'x', 'y', 'z', etc., correspond to the distinctive pronouns 'former' and 'latter', or 'first', 'second', and 'third', etc. The statement:

$$(\exists x)[\text{Sadie stole } x \text{ at the Emporium} . (\exists y)(\text{Sadie exchanged } x \text{ for } y)]$$

corresponds fairly literally to the words:

There is something such that Sadie stole it at the Emporium and such that there is something such that Sadie exchanged the former for the latter.

An occurrence of a variable in a sentence is called *free* in that sentence when it is unquantified; i.e., when it neither stands in, nor refers back to, any quantifier within the limits of the given sentence. Thus the occurrences of 'x' in:

(12) x is a man $\supset$ x is mortal, x is a book . x is boring

are free therein, but the occurrences of 'x' in:

$(x)(x$ is a man $\supset$ x is mortal), $(\exists x)(x$ is a book . x is boring)

are *bound*, i.e. not free, in these sentences. In the sentence:

(13) $(\exists x)(y$ is uncle of $x)$

the occurrence of 'y' is free, there being no '(y)' or '$(\exists y)$' present; but the occurrences of 'x' are bound, because of '$(\exists x)$'. One and the same occurrence of 'x' may be bound in a whole sentence and free in a part; the final occurrence of 'x' in (13), e.g., is bound in (13) but free in the part 'y is uncle of x'. In one and the same sentence, moreover, one occurrence of 'x' may be free and others bound; this happens in the conjunction:

(14) x is red . $(x)(x$ has mass),

---

[5] Exception: they may appear within quotation marks in sentences. But even a meaningless mark may appear within quotation marks in a sentence. The quotation as a whole is a meaningful name of the meaningless mark.

in which the quantifier has to do only with the second clause. (14) means '*x* is red and everything has mass', and could just as well be written with distinct variables:

(15)   *x* is red . $(y)(y$ has mass).

By starting with '*p*', '*q*', '*Fx*', '*Gx*', '*Fy*', etc., and applying quantifiers and the truth-functional notations, we obtain the *monadic quantificational schemata*. The restriction 'monadic' is due to the fact that we have not yet admitted elements like '*Fxy*'. Quantificational schemata, like sentences, will be called *open* if they contain one or' more free variables, and otherwise *closed*. Thus the schema:

$$(x)[Fx \supset (\exists y)(Gy . Hx)]$$

is closed, but its parts:

$$Fx \supset (\exists y)(Gy . Hx), \quad\quad (\exists y)(Gy . Hx), \quad\quad Gy . Hx$$

are all open. Truth-functional schemata, e.g. '$p \supset q$', count as closed quantificational schemata.

HISTORICAL **NOTE:** The rules of passage were explicit in Whitehead and Russell, 1910. The term is from Herbrand. The term 'open sentence' has been used by Carnap and others. The older term for the purpose is 'propositional function', but this can be misleading, since a function in the mathematical sense is best seen as a certain type of relation rather than as a notation.

EXERCISES

1. Supposing the universe limited to *a, b, . . . , h*, expand (7) and (8) by expanding the quantifications into alternation and conjunction.

2. There are no rules of passage for '$\equiv$'. Show, on the contrary, that no two of the schemata:

$$(x)(p \equiv Fx), \quad\quad p \equiv (x)Fx, \quad\quad p \equiv (\exists x)Fx, \quad\quad (\exists x)(p \equiv Fx)$$

are equivalent. Method: see what comes of resolution when 'T' is put for '*p*' throughout, and again when '⊥' is put for it.

3. What implications hold between the four schemata in Exercise 2? Method: same.

23

PRENEXITY
AND PURITY

The rules of passage work in either of two directions: to widen the scope of a quantifier or to narrow it. The one direction ends by bringing the formula into *prenex* form, where all quantifiers stand in an initial row governing all the rest of the formula. The other direction ends by *purifying* the formula, by causing the scope of each quantifier to be a truth function only of components each of which shows free occurrences of the variable of the quantifier.

Both of these uses of the rules of passage depend on preparatory transformations of other kinds. If the chosen direction is the one that leads to prenex form, then certainly we must paraphrase away any occurrence of '≡' that joins formulas having quantifiers in either of them. For we saw in an exercise that there are no rules of passage for '≡'. Any quantifier that is trapped in either of the formulas joined by '≡' will remain trapped and incapable of being brought into prenex position until we get rid of '≡' by paraphrase.

Another transformation preparatory to applying the rules of passage in a prenexing way is the relettering of bound variables. '$Fx . (\exists x)Gx$' is all right as it stands, simply as a conjunction of the open schema 'Fx' and the closed schema 'there are G' (which could as well be written '$(\exists y)Gy$'). The whole says that x is an F and there are G. But it will not do to apply the rule of passage (1) of the preceding chapter to '$Fx . (\exists x)Gx$' to obtain '$(\exists x)(Fx . Gx)$'. This last could mean that something is round and square, which is false, while the former means that x is round and something is square, which is true of any baseball x. The thing to do before applying the rule of passage (1) to '$Fx . (\exists x)Gx$' is to rewrite this as '$Fx . (\exists y)Gy$'; then we can proceed to '$(\exists y)(Fx . Gy)$'. We must remember that (1) simply does not directly apply to '$Fx . (\exists x)Gx$'; the 'p' in (1) stands necessarily for a formula without free 'x'.

Once these preparations are made, we convert a schema into prenex form simply by a succession of transformations according to the rules of passage (1)–(10). Example:

$$p \equiv (x)[Fx \supset (\exists y)(Fy . Gx)].$$

Paraphrasing the '≡' into a conjunction of conditionals, we get:

$$p \supset (x)[Fx \supset (\exists y)(Fy . Gx)] . (x)[Fx \supset (\exists y)(Fy . Gx)] \supset p.$$

Relettering,

$$p \supset (x)[Fx \supset (\exists y)(Fy . Gx)] . (z)[Fz \supset (\exists w)(Fw . Gz)] \supset p.$$

The remaining transformations are by the rules of passage (6), (7), (2), (1), (5), and (8), two steps at a time.

$$(x)[p \supset. Fx \supset (\exists y)(Fy . Gx)] . (\exists z)[Fz \supset (\exists w)(Fw . Gz) . \supset p].$$

$$(x)(\exists z)[p \supset. Fx \supset (\exists y)(Fy . Gx) : Fz \supset (\exists w)(Fw . Gz) . \supset p].$$

$$(x)(\exists z)[p \supset (\exists y)(Fx \supset. Fy . Gx) . (\exists w)(Fz \supset. Fw . Gz) \supset p].$$

$$(x)(\exists z)[(\exists y)(p \supset: Fx \supset. Fy . Gx) . (w)(Fz \supset. Fw . Gz :\supset p)].$$

$$(x)(\exists z)(\exists y)(w)(p \supset: Fx \supset. Fy . Gx :. Fz \supset. Fw . Gz :\supset p).$$

Note that at almost every stage there is some freedom of choice as to which quantifier to bring forward next.

The distributivity laws (20) and (21) of page 114 can conduce to speed in prenexing and to brevity in the result. Consider the example:

(1) $$(x)[(\exists y)(Fx \equiv Gy) \vee (\exists y)Fy] . (x)(Fx \vee Gx).$$

According to the plan just now laid, we would begin to prenex this example by relettering thus:

(2) $$(x)[(\exists y)(Fx \equiv Gy) \vee (\exists z)Fz] . (w)(Fw \vee Gw).$$

From this result, by six applications of the rules of passage (1)–(3) of the preceding chapter, we would move finally to the prenex schema:

(3) $$(x)(\exists y)(\exists z)(w)(Fx \equiv Gy .\vee Fz : Fw \vee Gw).$$

But if, instead of relettering (1) as (2), we simply apply the distributivity law (21) of page 114 to (1), we get this:

$$(x)[(\exists y)(Fx \equiv Gy) \vee (\exists y)Fy . Fx \vee Gx].$$

Then, applying the distributivity law (20) of page 114 to the portion '$(\exists y)(Fx \equiv Gy) \vee (\exists y)Fy$', we turn the whole into this:

$$(x)[(\exists y)(Fx \equiv Gy .\vee Fy) . Fx \vee Gx].$$

A single application of the rule of passage (1) of Chapter 22 turns this into the prenex schema:

(4) $$(x)(\exists y)(Fx \equiv Gy \;.\lor Fy : Fx \lor Gx),$$

which is simpler than the previous prenex result (3) and more quickly reached as well. For the sake of such benefits we can be well advised even to reletter quantifications to create duplications rather than to eliminate them. If we had been given (2) to begin with, we would have gained by relettering it as (1) and then proceeding as just now observed. Note, however, that this strategy of distributivity is the counsel only of efficiency; schemata *can* always be prenexed without it. What we strictly need to do is just para- phrase any biconditionals that contain quantifications, diversify all vari- ables of quantification, and apply the rules of passage.

In relettering it is important always to avoid collisions of variables. It is all right to change '$(\exists y)(Fx \lor Gy)$' to '$(\exists z)(Fx \lor Gz)$', but decidedly wrong to change it to '$(\exists x)(Fx \lor Gx)$'; for this, far from being a superficial alphabetical change of notation, is a crucial change of structure. When a quantification is relettered, the schema that stands as the scope of the quantifier must come to exhibit free occurrences of the new variable at all *and only* the places where it had exhibited free occurrences of the old vari- able. The '$Fx \lor Gz$' of the example above has free 'z' where and only where '$Fx \lor Gy$' had free 'y'; the '$Fx \lor Gx$', on the other hand, has free 'x' where but *not* only where '$Fx \lor Gy$' had free 'y'.

Whereas prenexing brings quantifiers out, purification drives them in. Purification, like prenexing, rests on preparatory transformations. Thus consider the impure quantification '$(\exists x)(Fx \;.\; p \lor Gx)$', whose impurity is '$p$', lacking '$x$'. As a preparatory transformation we convert the scope '$Fx \;.\; p \lor Gx$' of the quantifier into alternational normal form and then dis- tribute the quantifier through the alternation, thus:

$$(\exists x)(Fx \;.\; p \;.\lor. \; Fx \;.\; Gx),$$
$$(\exists x)(Fx \;.\; p) \lor (\exists x)(Fx \;.\; Gx).$$

Now we can apply the rule of passage (1) of Chapter 22, completing the purification.

$$(\exists x)Fx \;.\; p \;.\lor (\exists x)(Fx \;.\; Gx).$$

To purify a universal quantification whose impurity was similarly buried, we would begin by converting the scope of the quantifier to con- junctional normal form; for a universal quantifier distributes through conjunction. E.g., by steps dual to those above, the impure quantification '$(x)(Fx \lor. \; p \;.\; Gx)$' fares as follows:

$$(x)(Fx \lor p \;.\; Fx \lor Gx),$$
$$(x)(Fx \lor p) \;.\; (x)(Fx \lor Gx),$$
$$(x)Fx \lor p \;.\; (x)(Fx \lor Gx).$$

By a combination of these methods we can rid any quantificational schema of all impurities. The general routine is as follows. Wherever there is an impure quantification, put the scope of the quantifier into alternational or conjunctional normal form (according as the quantifier was existential or universal). However, prior to this and at every stage of the process, apply any applicable one of the rules of passage (1)–(8) of Chapter 22 on sight— always so as to drive quantifiers inward. Continue until all impurities are gone.

E.g., let us purify (1). By the rule of passage (4) of Chapter 22, (1) becomes:

(5) $\qquad (x)(\exists y)(Fx \equiv Gy) \vee (\exists y)Fy \,.\, (x)(Fx \vee Gx).$

Next we turn the '$Fx \equiv Gy$' of the impure quantification '$(\exists y)(Fx \equiv Gy)$' into alternational normal form, and distribute the '$(\exists y)$' through it. The whole of (5) becomes:

$$(x)[(\exists y)(Fx \,.\, Gy) \vee (\exists y)(-Fx \,.\, -Gy)] \vee (\exists y)Fy \,.\, (x)(Fx \vee Gx).$$

Now we can apply the rule of passage (1) of Chapter 22 twice, getting:

$$(x)[Fx \,.\, (\exists y)Gy \,.\text{v}.\, -Fx \,.\, (\exists y)-Gy] \vee (\exists y)Fy \,.\, (x)(Fx \vee Gx).$$

Next we turn the scope of the initial '(x)' into conjunctional normal form. The whole becomes:

$$(x)[Fx \vee (\exists y)-Gy \,.\, (\exists y)Gy \vee -Fx \,.\, (\exists y)Gy \vee (\exists y)-Gy] \vee (\exists y)Fy \\ .\, (x)(Fx \vee Gx).$$

Now we can apply the rule of passage (2) of Chapter 22.

$$(x)[Fx \vee (\exists y)-Gy \,.\, (\exists y)Gy \vee -Fx] \,.\, (\exists y)Gy \vee (\exists y)-Gy \\ .\text{v}\, (\exists y)Fy : (x)(Fx \vee Gx).$$

Next we distribute the '(x)'.

$$(x)[Fx \vee (\exists y)-Gy] \,.\, (x)[(\exists y)Gy \vee -Fx] \,.\, (\exists y)Gy \vee (\exists y)-Gy \\ .\text{v}\, (\exists y)Fy : (x)(Fx \vee Gx).$$

Now we can apply the rule of passage (4) of Chapter 22 twice.

(6) $\quad (x)Fx \vee (\exists y)-Gy \,.\, (\exists y)Gy \vee (x)-Fx \,.\, (\exists y)Gy \vee (\exists y)-Gy \\ .\text{v}\, (\exists y)Fy : (x)(Fx \vee Gx).$

This at last is pure. If we transcribe '(x)' as '$-(\exists x)-$' and then drop all variables, we can condense the whole into the Boolean schema:

(7) $-\exists \bar{F} \vee \exists \bar{G} . \exists G \vee -\exists F . \exists G \vee \exists \bar{G} . \vee \exists F : -\exists - (F \vee G).$

Thus the original schema (1), the prenex schemata (3) and (4), the pure schema (6), and the Boolean schema (7) all are equivalent.

A monadic quantificational schema has impurities as long as it has stacked quantifiers, i.e., as long as any quantifier has a quantifier in its scope. For, if a schema has any stacked quantifiers, then it will have at least two innermost stacked quantifiers—say '$(\exists x)$' and '(y)'. By this I mean that the scope of '$(\exists x)$' is a truth function of schemata one of which is the '(y)' quantification, and the '(y)' quantification contains no further quantifiers. But then either the '$(\exists x)$' quantification or the '(y)' quantification is bound to be impure. For, if the '(y)' quantification lacks free 'x', it renders the '$(\exists x)$' quantification impure. If on the other hand it has free 'x', then the scope of '(y)' is a truth function of schemata one of which is 'Fx' or 'Gx' or the like; and this renders the '(y)' quantification impure.

We have seen how to purify any monadic quantificational schema, and now we have seen further that the result will be devoid of stacked quantifiers. Each quantification will have as its scope a truth function merely of 'Fx', 'Gx', etc., if 'x' is the variable of the quantifier; 'Fy', 'p', etc. are driven out by the purification, and so are stacked quantifiers. Then, if we transcribe '(x)' again as '$-(\exists x)-$' and then drop the variables, as we did in passing from (6) to (7), all quantifications will disappear in favor of Boolean existence schemata.

We cannot quite say that every monadic quantificational schema is thus reducible to a Boolean schema, such as (7). (6) was thus reducible because it contained no sentence letters 'p', 'q', etc., and no unquantified 'Fz' or the like. But we can say that every Boolean schema that is *closed* (and hence devoid of unquantified 'Fz' and the like) is reducible in the observed fashion to a truth function of Boolean existence schemata and sentence letters. The method consists in purifying and finally transcribing universal quantifiers and dropping variables.

It thus emerges that the notational apparatus of monadic quantificational schemata, with its variables of quantification and all its stacked quantifiers and impurities, is needlessly inflated. The letters and truth functions of Part I and the Boolean existence schemata would have been apparatus enough. Still, there is an important reason for taking up the inflated apparatus: it prepares us for the advent in Part III of polyadic schemata, containing 'Fxy' and the like. At that point the kind of reducibility here observed will lapse.

HISTORICAL NOTE: The rules for prenexing and purifying are essentially just the rules of passage, which were known in 1910. But two later names are particularly associated respectively with prenexing and purifying: those of Skolem and Behmann. Skolem depended heavily on the prenex form for his proof procedure in polyadic quantification theory, much as we shall do. On the other hand Behmann's decision procedure of 1922 (see end of Chapter 19 above) depended on driving quantifiers in.

EXERCISES

1. Put the schema '$(x)Fx \supset . (x)Gx \equiv (x)Hx$' into prenex form.

2. Likewise '$(\exists x)Fx \equiv (\exists x)Gx . \supset (\exists x)Hx$'.

3. Purify '$(\exists x)(y)(Fx \equiv Gy . \supset Hy)$'.

4. Likewise '$(x)(\exists y)(Fx \supset Gy . \equiv Hy)$'.

24

VALIDITY AGAIN

A quantificational schema is valid if it comes out true under all interpretations in all nonempty universes. A term letter is interpreted, as before, by fixing its extension, i.e., settling what things in the universe it is to be true of. A sentence letter is interpreted, as before, by assigning it a truth value. A free variable is interpreted by assigning it some object in the universe.

The concepts of consistency, implication, and equivalence extend to quantificational schemata in similar fashion, and they are related to one another as usual: inconsistency is validity of the negation, implication is validity of the conditional, and equivalence is mutual implication, or validity of the biconditional.

The question of the validity of an open schema reduces to the question of the validity of a closed schema, its *universal closure*. This is a closed schema that we get from the open one by prefixing a universal quantifier for each free variable. Validity of '$(x)Fx \supset Fy$', e.g., is validity of '$(y)[(x)Fx \supset Fy]$'. This is evident from the meaning of the universal quantifier. To say that '$(x)Fx \supset Fy$' comes out true under all assignments of extensions to 'F' and objects to 'y', in a given universe, is to say that '$(y)[(x)Fx \supset Fy]$' comes out true simply under all assignments of extensions to 'F' in that universe.

Since an initial universal quantifier is indifferent to validity, it follows that an initial existential quantifier is indifferent to consistency. For, a schema '$....$' is inconsistent if and only if '$-(....)$' is valid, hence if and only if '$(x)-(\ldots)$' is valid, hence if and only if '$-(\exists x)(\ldots)$' is valid, hence if and only if '$(\exists x)(\ldots)$' is inconsistent.

We can test a closed monadic quantificational schema for validity, if it is devoid of sentence letters, by reducing it to a Boolean schema and then testing this by the method of existential conditionals or by the cellular method (Chapter 19) as we please. The method of reduction to a Boolean schema was illustrated in Chapter 23 in the transformation of (1) progressively into (5), (6), and finally (7).

Let us test the open schemata:

$$(x)Fx \supset Fy, \qquad Fy \supset (\exists x)Fx$$

for validity. As remarked, this means testing the closed schemata:

$$(y)[(x)Fx \supset Fy], \qquad (y)[Fy \supset (\exists x)Fx].$$

Purifying them by means of the rules of passage (6) and (8) of Chapter 22, we get:

$$(x)Fx \supset (y)Fy, \qquad (\exists y)Fy \supset (\exists x)Fx.$$

If despite their patent validity we persist in reducing these to Boolean schemata, we get:

$$-\exists \bar{F} \supset -\exists \bar{F}, \qquad \exists F \supset \exists F.$$

For a less trivial example, consider the inference:

$$Fz, \qquad (x)[(\exists y)Fy \supset Gx], \qquad \therefore (\exists y)(Fy . Gy).$$

To check the implication we test the open conditional:

$$Fz . (x)[(\exists y)Fy \supset Gx] . \supset (\exists y)(Fy . Gy)$$

for validity. This means testing the closed schema:

$$(z)\{Fz . (x)[(\exists y)Fy \supset Gx] . \supset (\exists y)(Fy . Gy)\}.$$

Proceeding to purify it, we apply the rule of passage (8).

$$(\exists z)\{Fz . (x)[(\exists y)Fy \supset Gx]\} \supset (\exists y)(Fy . Gy).$$

Next we apply the rule of passage (1).

$$(\exists z)Fz . (x)[(\exists y)Fy \supset Gx] . \supset (\exists y)(Fy . Gy).$$

Finally we apply the rule of passage (6).

$$(\exists z)Fz \,.\, (\exists y)Fy \supset (x)Gx \,.\supset\, (\exists y)(Fy \,.\, Gy).$$

Then we transcribe the universal quantifier and drop the variables.

$$\exists F \,.\, \exists F \supset -\exists\bar{G} \,.\supset\, \exists FG.$$

Choosing now the method of existential conditionals, we turn this into conjunctional normal form and simplify. It boils down to:

$$-\exists F \vee \exists\bar{G} \vee \exists FG.$$

Collecting the affirmative existential schemata as '$\exists(\bar{G} \vee FG)$', we end up with the existential conditional:

$$\exists F \supset \exists(\bar{G} \vee FG).$$

We check its validity by criterion (iv) of Chapter 19. That is, we check by fell swoop that 'F' implies '$\bar{G} \vee FG$'.

Note that this technique, again, depends for its soundness on a law of interchange of equivalents. Again, however, as in the case of truth-functional schemata (Chapter 9) and Boolean schemata (Chapter 19), all is in order; for it is evident here again that the truth value of a compound statement depends on no features of the component sentences and terms except their truth values and their extensions.

We turn finally to the question of a validity test for closed monadic quantificational schemata containing sentence letters. Such a schema will be valid, clearly, just in case it resolves to 'T' or to a valid schema under each substitution of 'T' and '⊥' for its sentence letters. So the test is truth-value analysis. If the analysis issues in '⊥' at any point, of course the schema was not valid. Otherwise we follow up with validity tests of any quantificational schemata issuing from the truth-value analysis.

Example:

$$(x)(Fx \equiv p) \,.\, (\exists x)Fx \equiv q \,.\supset\, p \equiv q$$

$(x)(Fx\equiv \mathsf{T}).(\exists x)Fx\equiv q.\supset.\mathsf{T}\equiv q$ $(x)(Fx\equiv \bot).(\exists x)Fx\equiv q.\supset.\bot\equiv q$

$(x)Fx.(\exists x)Fx\equiv q.\supset q$ $(x)-Fx.(\exists x)Fx\equiv q.\supset \bar{q}$

$(x)Fx.(\exists x)Fx\equiv \mathsf{T}.\supset \mathsf{T}$ $(x)Fx.(\exists x)Fx\equiv \bot.\supset \bot$ $(x)-Fx.(\exists x)Fx\equiv \mathsf{T}.\supset \bot$ $(x)-Fx.(\exists x)Fx\equiv \bot.\supset \mathsf{T}$

T $-[(x)Fx.-(\exists x)Fx]$ $-[(x)-Fx.(\exists x)Fx]$ T

The question of validity here reduces to the question of validity of '$-[(x)Fx \,.\, -(\exists x)Fx]$' and '$-[(x)-Fx \,.\, (\exists x)Fx]$'. These go over into Boolean schemata as '$-(-\exists\bar{F} \,.\, -\exists F)$' and '$-(-\exists F \,.\, \exists F)$'. The latter has the valid form '$-(\bar{p}p)$'. The other goes into conjunctional normal form as '$\exists \bar{F} \vee \exists F$', and so, by collection of affirmative existence schemata, '$\exists (\bar{F} \vee F)$'. This is valid by criterion (i) of Chapter 19.

Dismissal of '$-(-\exists F \cdot \exists F)$' as of the form '$-(\bar{p}p)$' was an obvious shortcut, falling outside the mechanical routine thus far set down. That routine would prescribe converting '$-(-\exists F \cdot \exists F)$' to conjunctional normal form as '$\exists F \vee -\exists F$', then rendering this as an existential conditional '$\exists F \supset \exists F$', and finally observing that the term schema in the antecedent implies the one in the consequent by fell swoop. It is worth noting that the mechanical routine covers such cases, but it would be silly to follow it.

When truth-value analysis is applied to quantificational schemata, as above, four supplementary rules of resolution are sometimes needed in addition to those in Chapter 5. Namely, '$(x)\mathsf{T}$', '$(\exists x)\mathsf{T}$', '$(x)\perp$', and '$(\exists x)\perp$' resolve to 'T', 'T', '$\perp$', and '$\perp$'. One of these is used when we test the following biconditional (which is reminiscent of the rule of passage (8) of Chapter 22).

$$
\begin{array}{cc}
 & (x)(Fx \supset p) \equiv. (\exists x)Fx \supset p \\
(x)(Fx \supset \mathsf{T}) \equiv. (\exists x)Fx \supset \mathsf{T} \quad & (x)(Fx \equiv \perp) \equiv. (\exists x)Fx \supset \perp \\
(x)\mathsf{T} \quad\quad\quad & (x)-Fx \equiv -(\exists x)Fx \\
\mathsf{T} \quad\quad\quad\quad &
\end{array}
$$

The remainder of this test consists in testing the remainder '$(x)-Fx \equiv -(\exists x)Fx$' for validity. This biconditional, which recalls (9) of Chapter 22, goes over into the Boolean schema '$-\exists F \equiv -\exists F$' and is thus seen to have the truth-functionally valid form '$p \equiv p$'.

We conclude with a full-dress example, starting in words.

PREMISES: If the Bissagos report is to be trusted then the *chargé d'affaires* is a mere tool of the sisal interests and none of the natives really favored the coupon plan.

If the *chargé d'affaires* is a mere tool of the sisal interests then some of the natives either really favored the coupon plan or were actuated by a personal animosity against the deputy resident.

CONCLUSION: If the Bissagos report is to be trusted then some who were actuated by a personal animosity against the deputy resident did not really favor the coupon plan.

Putting 'p' for 'the Bissagos report is to be trusted', 'q' for 'the *chargé d'affaires* is a mere tool of the sisal interests', 'Fx' for 'x is a native', 'Gx' for 'x really favored the coupon plan', and 'Hx' for 'x was actuated by a personal animosity against the deputy resident', we can represent the premises and conclusion by the mixed schemata:

$$p \supset. q . (x)(Fx \supset -Gx),$$
$$q \supset (\exists x)(Fx . Gx \vee Hx),$$
$$p \supset (\exists x)(Hx . -Gx).$$

Accordingly we submit the conditional:

$$p \supset. q . (x)(Fx \supset -Gx) : q \supset (\exists x)(Fx . Gx \vee Hx) : \supset. p \supset (\exists x)(Hx . -Gx)$$

to truth-value analysis. In so doing let us save space by temporarily abbreviating the three quantifications as '*A*', '*B*', and '*C*'.

$$p \supset qA . q \supset B . \supset. p \supset C$$
$$\mathsf{T} \supset qA . q \supset B . \supset. \mathsf{T} \supset C \qquad \bot \supset qA . q \supset B . \supset. \bot \supset C$$
$$qA . q \supset B . \supset C \qquad\qquad \mathsf{T}$$
$$\mathsf{T}A . \mathsf{T} \supset B . \supset C \qquad \bot A . \bot \supset B . \supset C$$
$$AB \supset C \qquad\qquad \mathsf{T}$$

So our problem reduces to a validity test of '*AB* ⊃ *C*', which is:

$$(x)(Fx \supset -Gx) . (\exists x)(Fx . Gx \vee Hx) . \supset (\exists x)(Hx . -Gx).$$

Transcribed as a Boolean schema, this becomes:

$$-\exists -(F \supset \bar{G}) . \exists[F(G \vee H)] . \supset \exists H\bar{G},$$

or, in conjunctional normal form,

$$\exists -(F \supset \bar{G}) \vee -\exists[F(G \vee H)] \vee \exists H\bar{G}.$$

When we collect the affirmative existence schemata, this becomes:

$$-\exists[F(G \vee H)] \vee \exists[-(F \supset \bar{G}) \vee H\bar{G}]$$

and so the existential conditional:

$$\exists[F(G \vee H)] \supset \exists[-(F \supset \bar{G}) \vee H\bar{G}].$$

Finally we check the validity of this, according to the criterion (iv) of Chapter 19, by verifying that '*F*(*G* ∨ *H*)' implies '−(*F* ⊃ $\bar{G}$) ∨ *H*$\bar{G}$). This again is done by truth-value analysis.

$$[F(G \vee H)] \supset [-(F \supset \bar{G}) \vee H\bar{G}]$$
$$[F(\mathsf{T} \vee H)] \supset [-(F \supset \bot) \vee H\bot] \qquad [F(\bot \vee H)] \supset [-(F \supset \mathsf{T}) \vee H\mathsf{T}]$$
$$F \supset F \qquad\qquad\qquad FH \supset H$$
$$\mathsf{T} \qquad\qquad\qquad\qquad \mathsf{T}$$

EXERCISES

1. Test these eight schemata for validity.

$$(y)[(x)Fx \supset Fy], \qquad (\exists y)[(x)Fx \supset Fy],$$
$$(y)[Fy \supset (x)Fx], \qquad (\exists y)[Fy \supset (x)Fx],$$
$$(y)[(\exists x)Fx \supset Fy], \qquad (\exists y)[(\exists x)Fx \supset Fy],$$
$$(y)[Fy \supset (\exists x)Fx], \qquad (\exists y)[Fy \supset (\exists x)Fx].$$

2. Check the biconditionals corresponding to (1)–(7) of Chapter 22.

3. Test each of these pairs for equivalence, by testing the biconditional.

$$(x)Fx, \qquad (x)(Fx \vee Gx) . (x)(Fx \vee - Gx);$$
$$(x)Fx, \qquad (x)(Fx . Gx) \vee (x)(Fx . - Gx);$$
$$(\exists x)Fx, \qquad (\exists x)(Fx \vee Gx) . (\exists x)(Fx \vee - Gx);$$
$$(\exists x)Fx, \qquad (\exists x)(Fx . Gx) \vee (\exists x)(Fx . - Gx).$$

4. Check the following argument.

PREMISES: The persons responsible for the recent kidnappings are experimental psychologists.
            If no experimental psychologists are known to the police, then none of the former bosses of the bootleg ring are experimental psychologists.

CONCLUSION: If any of the former bosses of the bootleg ring are responsible for the recent kidnappings then some experimental psychologists are known to the police.

III
GENERAL THEORY
OF QUANTIFICATION

25

SCHEMATA
EXTENDED

In the logical tradition terms are distinguished into two kinds, *relative* and *absolute*. The characteristic of a relative term is that it describes things only relatively to further things which have afterward to be specified in turn. Thus 'father' as in 'father of Isaac', and 'north' as in 'north of Boston', are relative terms. What were spoken of as terms in Chapter 14, on the other hand, are absolute terms. Words capable of behaving as relative terms can regularly be used *also* as absolute terms, through what amounts to a tacit existential quantification in the context; thus we may say absolutely that Abraham is a father, meaning that there is something of which Abraham is a father.

In English a convenient earmark of the relative use of a term is the adjoining of an 'of'-phrase or possessive modifier whose sense is not that of ownership. Thus 'father of Isaac', or 'Isaac's father', has nothing to do with proprietorship on Isaac's part, but means merely 'that which bears the father-relation to Isaac'. We can appreciate the distinction between the possessive 'my' and the relative 'my' by recalling what Dionysodorus said to Ctesippus with reference to the latter's dog: '. . . he is a father, and he is yours; therefore he is your father' (Plato, *Euthydemus*).

A relative term, like an absolute one, may occur indifferently as substantive, adjective, or verb. In 'x is a helper of y' we use the substantive, in 'x is helpful toward y' the adjective, and in 'x helps y' the verb; but logically there is no need to distinguish the three. Logically the important thing about relative terms is that they are true of objects pairwise. Whereas 'man', 'walks', etc., are true of Caesar, Socrates, etc., one by one, on the other hand the relative term 'helps' is true of Jesus and Lazarus as a pair (or, true of Jesus with respect to Lazarus), and true of Farley and Roosevelt as a pair (or, true of Farley with respect to Roosevelt), and so on. If as in the foregoing pages we write 'Fx' for 'x is an F', then the analogous notation in connection with relative terms should be 'Fxy', 'x is F to y'.

The order of 'x' and 'y' in 'x helps y' is in one respect accidental: 'x helps y' can as well be phrased 'y is helped by x'. But in another respect the order is essential: 'x helps y', e.g., 'Jesus helps Lazarus', is not equivalent to 'y helps x'. So the sentence 'x helps y' may be described equally as of the form 'Fxy' and as of the form 'Fyx', but the interpretations thus successively imposed on 'F' are then distinct from each other—as distinct as 'helps' and 'is helped by'. 'Fxy' cannot in general be equated with 'Fyx'.

Besides relative terms in the sense just now touched upon, which are *dyadic*, we may recognize also *triadic* ones, *tetradic* ones, and so on; e.g.,

'*Gxyz*' may mean '*x* gives *y* to *z*', and '*Hxyzw*' may mean '*x* pays *y* to *z* for *w*'.

There are forms of inference, logically no less sound than those dealt with in Part II, which are insusceptible to the methods of Part II simply because their analysis calls for recognition of relative terms. An example from Jungius (fl. 1640) is:

All circles are figures;   ∴ All who draw circles draw figures.

The premise can be represented in our previous notation as '$(x)(Fx \supset Gx)$', but the conclusion presents difficulties. We can indeed represent the conclusion as '$(x)(Hx \supset Jx)$', interpreting '*Hx*' as '*x* draws a circle' and '*Jx*' as '*x* draws a figure', but then the schemata '$(x)(Fx \supset Gx)$' and '$(x)(Hx \supset Jx)$' bear no visible interconnection which could justify inference of the one from the other. What we must do is extend our category of quantificational schemata to admit such forms as '*Hyx*' for '*y* draws *x*'. Then '*y* draws a circle' can be represented as '$(\exists x)(Fx \,.\, Hyx)$', and '*y* draws a figure' as '$(\exists x)(Gx \,.\, Hyx)$'; thereupon our conclusion as a whole, 'All who draw circles draw figures', becomes:

(1) $$(y)[(\exists x)(Fx \,.\, Hyx) \supset (\exists x)(Gx \,.\, Hyx)].$$

Quantification theory needs to be extended in such a way as to enable us to show, among other things, that '$(x)(Fx \supset Gx)$' implies (1).

Another example of the need of thus extending quantification theory is this:

PREMISE: There is a painting that all critics admire;
CONCLUSION: Every critic admires some painting or other.

With '*Gx*' interpreted as '*x* is a critic', and '*Hxy*' as '*x* admires *y*', we may represent 'all critics admire *y*' as '$(x)(Gx \supset Hxy)$'. So, interpreting '*Fy*' as '*y* is a painting', we may represent the above premise as:

(2) $$(\exists y)[Fy \,.\, (x)(Gx \supset Hxy)].$$

Further, since '*x* admires some painting or other' becomes '$(\exists y)(Fy \,.\, Hxy)$', the conclusion as a whole takes on the form:

(3) $$(x)[Gx \supset (\exists y)(Fy \,.\, Hxy)].$$

One more example:

PREMISE: There is a philosopher whom all philosophers contradict,
CONCLUSION: There is a philosopher who contradicts himself.

The premise here has a form closely similar to (2).

(4) $\qquad\qquad (\exists y)[Fy \, . \, (x)(Fx \supset Gxy)]$.

The conclusion is simply '$(\exists x)(Fx \, . \, Gxx)$'.

We saw in Chapter 21 how differences in grouping could affect the meaning of a quantification; '$(x)(Fx \lor Gx)$' had to be distinguished from '$(x)Fx \lor (x)Gx$', and '$(\exists x)(Fx \, . \, Gx)$' from '$(\exists x)Fx \, . \, (\exists x)Gx$'. Considerations of this kind come to loom larger now that we need quantifications within quantifications. Thus, let us reflect next on the expression:

(5) $\qquad\qquad (x)[Fx \supset (\exists y)(Fy \, . \, Gxy)]$.

If we interpret 'Fx' as 'x is a number' and 'Gxy' as 'x is less than y', then (5) comes to mean:

$\qquad$ Every number is such that some number exceeds it,

or briefly 'Every number is exceeded by some number'. This might carelessly be rephrased 'Some number exceeds every number' and then be put back into symbols as:

$\qquad (\exists y)(y$ is a number . y exceeds every number),

i.e., (4). But actually there is all the difference between (5) and (4) that there is between truth and falsity. (5) says that for every number there is a larger, which is true, whereas (4) says there is some great number which, at once, exceeds every number. This last is false on two counts: for there is no greatest number, and even if there were it would not exceed itself.

The distinction in form between (3) and (2) is the same as just now stressed between (5) and (4). The wording of the premise and conclusion about paintings illustrates again the awkwardness of ordinary language in keeping the distinction clear. The notation of quantification is handier in this respect.

The mathematical concept of limit provides, for readers familiar with it, an apt further illustration of the above distinction. A function $f(x)$ is said to approach a limit h, as x approaches k, if for every positive number ϵ there is a positive number δ such that $f(x)$ is within ϵ of h for every x ($\neq k$) within δ of k. In terms of quantifiers this condition appears as follows:

$$(\epsilon)\{\epsilon > 0 \, . \supset (\exists \delta)[\delta > 0 \, . \, (x)(0 < |x - k| < \delta \, . \supset . \, |f(x) - h| < \epsilon)]\}.$$

As textbooks rightly emphasize, we must think of ϵ as chosen first; for each choice of ϵ a suitable δ can be chosen. This warning is, in effect, a warning against confusing the above formula with the essentially different one:

$$(\exists \delta)\{\delta > 0 \,.\, (\epsilon)[\epsilon > 0 \,.\!\supset\, (x)(0 < |x - k| < \delta \,.\!\supset.\, |f(x) - h| < \epsilon)]\}.$$

The distinction between these two formulas will be recognized as identical with that between (5) and (4), and between (3) and (2).

The essential contrast between (5) and (4), and between (3) and (2), becomes simpler and more striking when we compare:

(6) $(x)(\exists y)Fxy, \quad (\exists y)(x)Fxy.$

Suppose we interpret 'Fxy' as 'x and y are the same thing', so that the schemata (6) become:

(7) $(x)(\exists y)(x$ and y are the same thing),
(8) $(\exists y)(x)(x$ and y are the same thing).

For each chosen object x, clearly there will be an object which is the same (viz., the chosen object x itself). Of each object x, therefore, the sentence:

$$(\exists y)(x \text{ and } y \text{ are the same thing})$$

is true. So (7) is true. On the other hand, as long as there are more objects than one in the universe, no one object can be the same as each; i.e., no one object y can be such that

$$(x)(x \text{ and } y \text{ are the same thing}).$$

So (8) is false.

In general '$(x)(\exists y)Fxy$' says that once any object whatever x is fixed upon, an object y is forthcoming such that Fxy. Different choices of x may bring forth different choices of y. On the other hand '$(\exists y)(x)Fxy$' says that some object y can be fixed upon such that, for this same fixed y, 'Fxy' will hold for all comers x.

Supposing a limited universe of objects a, b, ..., h, let us see how '$(x)(\exists y)Fxy$' and '$(\exists y)(x)Fxy$' compare when the quantifications are expanded into conjunctions and alternations (cf. end of Chapter 21). '$(x)(\exists y)Fxy$' becomes first:

$$(\exists y)Fay \,.\, (\exists y)Fby \,.\, \ldots \,.\, (\exists y)Fhy$$

and then:

$$Faa \lor Fab \lor \ldots \lor Fah \,.\, Fba \lor Fbb \lor \ldots \lor Fbh \,.\, \ldots$$
$$Fha \lor Fhb \lor \ldots \lor Fhh.$$

On the other hand '$(\exists y)(x)Fxy$' becomes first:

$$(x)Fxa \lor (x)Fxb \lor \ldots \lor (x)Fxh$$

and then:

$Faa \, . \, Fba \, . \, . \, . \, . \, Fha \, .\lor. \, Fab \, . \, Fbb \, . \, . \, . \, . \, Fhb \, .\lor. \, . \, . \, .\lor.$
$$Fah \, . \, Fbh \, . \, . \, . \, . \, Fhh.$$

It was remarked in Chapter 21 that though in ordinary language the words 'something' and 'everything' masquerade as substantives, their behavior deviates from that of genuine substantives. Further examples of such deviation are provided by (7) and (8). For, (7) might be put into words as 'Everything is identical with something', and (8) as 'Something is identical with everything'. If 'everything' and 'something' really behaved like names, we should expect these two statements to be equivalent—and in fact we should expect both to be false. But actually, as seen, (7) is true and (8) false. Further, if 'nothing' and 'everything' were genuine names we should certainly expect 'Nothing is identical with everything' to be false; actually, however, this statement simply denies (8) and hence is true. Also we might expect 'Everything is identical with everything' to be equivalent to the truth 'Everything is identical with itself', whereas actually it expresses the falsehood:

(9) $\qquad\qquad (x)(y)(x$ is identical with $y).$

One reason why quantificational analysis aids clear thinking is simply that the spurious substantives 'something', 'everything', and 'nothing' (and their variants 'somebody', 'nobody', 'everybody') give way to a less deceptive idiom.

The combination '$(x)(y)$' in (9) is not to be thought of as somehow a double quantifier; '$(x)(y)Fxy$' is simply a quantification of '$(y)Fxy$' as a whole. Whereas (1)–(8) show existential quantifications within universal ones and vice versa, (9) shows universal within universal.

Part III brings no new logical symbols for use in sentences. Already toward the end of Chapter 22 we had an example about Sadie's shoplifting that was the equal of any sentence formulable in Part III. Our new gains are not in sentences but in schemata. The schemata now before us are the *quantificational schemata* generally, not just the monadic ones. They comprise 'p', 'q', 'Fx', 'Fy', 'Gx', 'Hxy', 'Hyx', 'Hxx', '$Fxyz$', etc., and everything thence constructible by truth-function notations and quantifiers. The polyadic ingredients—'Hxy' and its suite—are what are new. (It is customary not to use the same term letter with different numbers of variables—thus 'Fx' and '$Fxyz$'—within one schema or within the schemata of one problem. Conventions could be devised to accommodate such use.)

Though the enrichment touches only the schemata, it is a crucial one. As remarked, it enables us to establish new implications between sentences. The broadened domain of schemata sustains a broadened concept of validity, and hence of implication, which so exceeds the bounds of Part II as to resist any comparable treatment. For validity of quantificational schemata in general it is impossible to devise a decision procedure. (Cf. Chapter 33.) The same applies of course to consistency, implication, and equivalence.

The definition of validity is as before: truth under all interpretations in all nonempty universes. The definitions of consistency, implication, and equivalence follow suit. Interpretation of a polyadic term letter, like that of a monadic term letter, consists in fixing its extension. In the monadic case this means settling what things in the universe the letter is to be true of. In polyadic cases it means settling what pairs of things in the universe, or what triples, etc., it is to be true of.

The impossibility of a decision procedure for validity will not deter us from developing procedures for proving validity. As noted in Chapter 13, the difference is that a decision procedure assures an affirmative or negative answer every time, while a proof procedure assures at best an eventual affirmative answer where an affirmative answer is in order. Proof procedures for general quantification theory will occupy most of Part III.

HISTORICAL NOTE: An algebra of relations was propounded by DeMorgan in 1864 and much improved in 1870 by Peirce. It is related to polyadic quantification theory much as the Boolean algebra of classes is related to monadic quantification theory, though, as Korselt showed in about 1914,[1] its scope is not quite so broad. By 1879, thanks to Frege, full quantification theory was at hand.

EXERCISES

1. Supposing the universe limited to a, b, ..., h, expand the quantifications into alternation and conjunction in each of the following examples:

    $$(x)(y)Fxy, \quad (\exists x)(\exists y)Fxy, \quad (y)(x)Fxy, \quad (\exists y)(\exists x)Fxy.$$

    Do each in two stages.

2. Rewrite these with help of quantification:

    > Every solid is soluble in some liquid or other,
    > There is a liquid in which every solid is soluble.

3. Rewrite this example (DeMorgan's) with help of quantification:

---

[1] See van Heijenoort, pp. 229, 233.

If all horses are animals then all heads of horses are heads of animals.

4. Express, with help of quantification, the likeliest interpretation of the statement:

    She had a ring on every finger.

5. Where '*F*' means 'harms', and the universe is mankind, put these unambiguously and idiomatically into words:

    $(\exists x)(y)Fyx,$
    $(x)[(\exists y)Fxy \supset Fxx],$
    $(x)[(y)(Fyx \supset Fxy) \supset Fxx].$

6. Supposing the universe to comprise just the points on an endless line, judge each of these statements as to truth value and explain your reasoning.

    $(\exists x)(y)(\exists z)(x$ is between y and $z),$
    $(y)(\exists x)(\exists z)(x$ is between y and $z),$
    $(\exists x)(\exists z)(y)(x$ is between y and $z).$

7. Express each of these statements with help of quantification and indicate its truth value.

    Nothing is identical with nothing,
    Something is identical with something,
    Everything is identical with nothing,
    Nothing is identical with anything.

26

PREDICATES
AND SUBSTITUTION

It was remarked at the end of Chapter 7 that validity may be attributed not only to truth-functional schemata but also, by extension, to the sentences whose forms those sentences depict; but that it is well then to add the qualifier 'truth-functional'. Correspondingly a sentence obtainable by substitution in a valid quantificational schema is *quantificationally* valid. Such a sentence is true, or true for all values of its free variables. But it may or may not be truth-functionally valid; its truth may depend solely on its truth-functional structure, or it may depend partly on how the quantifiers are arranged.

We may also note an intermediate grade, *monadic* validity. A sentence is quantificationally valid if it can be got by substitution in a valid quantificational schema; it is monadically valid, more particularly, if it can be got by substitution in a valid quantificational schema which is monadic; and it is truth-functionally valid if it can be got by substitution in a valid truth-functional schema.

Similar remarks apply to implication on the part of sentences: it can be quantificational, and more particularly monadic, and still more particularly truth-functional. Similarly for inconsistency.

In logical theory the schema is what is in focus, but still it is the sentence finally that matters. The purpose of schemata is simply to facilitate the logical study of sentences by depicting their logical forms. What relates the schemata to the sentences that they schematize is substitution. We get the sentence by substituting in the schema. It is time to examine this connection.

For truth-functional schemata the relevant notion of substitution was clear and simple: just substitute sentences for sentence letters, and always the same sentence for the same letter. For Boolean schemata the notion was equally simple: just substitute absolute general terms for term letters, and the same term for the same letter.

The move to quantificational schemata, even to monadic ones, complicates matters. Our first reason for the move, in Chapter 21, was to allow 'Fx' as a whole to stand for a sentence, without the fuss of isolating a term corresponding to 'F' by itself; so at this point we want no longer to speak of substitution of terms for term letters. But neither can we speak simply of substitution of arbitrary sentences for 'Fx', 'Fy', etc.; a certain correspondence must be preserved between the substitutes for 'Fx' and 'Fy'. What correspondence?

First approximation: the substitutes must be sentences that are alike except that the one has free occurrences of 'x' in all and only the places where the other has free occurrences of 'y'. Examples:

	Fx	Fy
(1)	x is proud of the team,	y is proud of the team.
(2)	x is proud of z,	y is proud of z.
(3)	x is proud of x,	y is proud of y.
(4)	$(\exists z)(x$ is proud of $z)$,	$(\exists z)(y$ is proud of $z)$.

In each pair the one sentence says of x what the other says of y: that he is proud of the team, proud of z, proud of himself, proud of something. Still, the requirement that the free occurrences of 'x' wholly match those of 'y' is too restrictive. For, along with pride of self, pride of something, pride of the team, pride of z, another alternative that needs to be allowed is pride of x:

(5) x is proud of x, y is proud of x.

This is not to disallow the pair (3); it is additional. Both pairs need to be recognized as legitimate and different pairs of substitutions for 'Fx' and 'Fy'.

Thus the desired requirement, vaguely speaking, is that the sentences substituted for 'Fx' and 'Fy' be sentences that say respectively of x and y *some* one same thing—be it pride of self or pride of x. To leave matters thus would be to resume the fuss of always isolating a term to correspond to 'F'— the fuss noted in (1) and (2) of Chapter 21. But there is an easy way out. We supplant the notion of term by that of *predicate*,[2] conceiving predicates artificially in the image of sentences as follows: a predicate is like a sentence except that it contains the arbitrary sign '①', or '①' and '②', or '①', '②', and '③', etc., in some places appropriate to free variables. Then, where 'Fx' is to mean 'x is red', we explain 'F' not as the term 'red' but as the predicate '① is red'. Where 'Fx' is to mean (1) of Chapter 21, we explain 'F' as the predicate:

(6)   ① used to work for the man who murdered the second husband of ①'s youngest sister.

Where 'Gxy' is to mean:

> x used to work for the man who murdered y and y was the second husband of x's youngest sister

we explain 'G' as the predicate:

> ① used to work for the man who murdered ② and ② was the second husband of ①'s youngest sister.

The circled numerals are merely numbered blanks showing where the variables are to be put in passing from 'F' to 'Fx', or 'Fxy', etc.: the leftmost of the variables is to be put for '①', the next for '②', and so on.

If a meaning for these strange expressions called predicates be demanded, e.g., for (6), an answer is 'former employee of own youngest sister's second husband's murderer'; for circled numerals may be viewed simply as a supplementary device, more convenient and systematic than those existing in ordinary language, for abstracting complex terms out of complex sentences.

---

[2] If the reader has not yet forgotten the medieval sense of 'predicate' explained in Chapter 16, let him do so now.

Thus the shift which we have made from terms to predicates can be viewed as a case merely of improving and renaming the idea of term.

So far as our work is concerned, however, we can as well view these predicates merely as auxiliary diagrams useful in specifying what open sentences are to be put for 'Fx', 'Fy', etc., or for 'Fxy', 'Fyz', etc., in a schema. We shall not use predicates themselves as actual parts of sentences, since the variables to which the predicates are applied take the place of the circled numerals. Where 'F' is interpreted, e.g., as:

(7)   ② amuses ① more than y amuses ②,

the schema:

(8) $(\exists x)Fxy \lor (\exists x)Fyx \mathbin{.\supset} (\exists x)Fxx$

becomes:

(9) $(\exists x)(y$ amuses x more than y amuses $y)$
      $\lor (\exists x)(x$ amuses y more than y amuses $x)$
                    $.\supset (\exists x)(x$ amuses x more than y amuses $x).$

The importance of the predicate (7) is as an intermediary diagram, or so to speak a template or stencil, helpful in determining just what combinations of sentences *can* legitimately be put, e.g., for 'Fxy', 'Fyx', and 'Fxx' in (8). It would be harder, without appeal to (7), to detect the essential relationship between the arrangement of variables in (9) and that in (8).

Our schematic letters 'F', 'G', etc., called term letters up to now, may be seen hereafter as standing schematically for predicates. I shall hereafter call them *predicate letters*. A similar shift in nomenclature took place in Chapter 22 when 'p', 'q', etc. came to be called sentence letters. These small terminological meanders are a convenient way of accommodating the growing theory. Note that 'F', 'G', etc. could retroactively be regarded as standing for predicates from the beginning, back in Chapter 14. It is just that the term account was simpler.

What we substitute for predicate letters, then, are predicates? Yes, in a suitably complicated sense of substitution. Substitution of a given predicate for a given predicate letter, say 'F', in a given schema consists in supplanting each occurrence of 'F' *and* the attached variables by a sentence which we prepare from the predicate by putting those successive attached variables respectively for '①', '②', etc. Here, pending two restrictions that will presently appear, is the definition of predicate substitution.

The question regarding 'Fx' and 'Fy' that was raised early in this chapter is now answered to a second approximation. The pairs (1)–(5) of substitutes for 'Fx' and 'Fy' are accounted for now by these five predicates as substitutes for 'F': '① is proud of the team', '① is proud of z', '① is proud of ①', '$(\exists z)($① is proud of $z)$', and '① is proud of x'.

Consider, however, this predicate '$(\exists z)(①$ is proud of $z)$' and its variant '$(\exists x)(①$ is proud of $x)$'. Taken in isolation as they stand, these two predicates are on an equal footing; they come to the same thing—'proud of something'—and the alphabetical difference in their bound variables is purely notational. Any special contextual considerations aside, they are equally good substitutes for 'F'. But note now what a difference environment can make. The two are by no means equally good substitutes for 'F' when 'F' has the context 'Fx'. Substitution of the predicate '$(\exists x)(①$ is proud of $x)$' for 'F' in 'Fx' and 'Fy' would give the pair of sentences:

(10) $(\exists x)(x$ is proud of $x)$, $(\exists x)(y$ is proud of $x)$.

This pair, unlike (1)–(5), is ill mated. There is no one 'same thing' that the left sentence says about x and the right about y. The sentence at the right says that y is proud of something, but the one at the left says nothing at all about x; it says only that someone is proud of himself, and it could as well be rendered '$(\exists z)(z$ is proud of $z)$'. It has no free 'x'.

Consequently we must hedge our definition of predicate substitution with this *first restriction:* Variables entering the predicate in place of the circled numerals must not be such as to be captured by quantifiers within the predicate.

The original question regarding 'Fx' and 'Fy' now has its full and precise answer—as long as we abstract from any particulars having to do with special contexts in turn of 'Fx' and 'Fy'. But when, as in the above definition of predicate substitution, we speak of substitution for 'F' throughout some schema, further questions of context arise. Thus suppose we are substituting for 'F' not just in 'Fx' and 'Fy' as heads of two columns (1)–(5), but in the valid schema '$(x)Fx \supset Fy$'. Substitution of the predicate '$①$ is proud of x' for 'F' in 'Fx' and 'Fy' had been legitimate, yielding the pair of sentences (5); but it is not legitimate in the context '$(x)Fx \supset Fy$', for it would yield:

(11) $(x)(x$ is proud of $x) \supset. y$ is proud of x,

which by no means inherits the logical structure to which '$(x)Fx \supset Fy$' owed its validity. This last says that if everything is F then y is; (11) says only that if everyone is proud of himself then, irrelevantly, this fellow is proud of that one.

Broadly speaking, the trouble in (11) is the same as in (10): an occurrence of 'x' has been captured by a quantifier. While the substitution carries 'Fy' into a sentence that says a certain thing about y, it carries 'Fx' into a sentence that does not say the corresponding thing, nor indeed anything, about x. Insofar the troubles in (10) and (11) are alike, but in detail their causes are opposite. In (10) a quantifier that had been lurking in the substituted predicate '$(\exists x)(①$ is proud of $x)$' captured the free 'x' that was waiting in 'Fx'. In (11), conversely, a quantifier lurking in the context of '*Fx*' captured the free '*x*' of the substituted predicate '① is proud of *x*'. So the notion of substitution must be subjected still to this *second restriction:* Variables free in the predicate must not be such as to be captured by quantifiers in the schema into which the predicate is substituted.

We may sum up the two restrictions symmetrically thus: Quantifiers of the substituted predicate must not capture variables of the schema in which the substitution takes place, and variables of the substituted predicate must not be captured by quantifiers of the schema in which the substitution takes place. These restrictions simply ward off confusions of variables which, if allowed, would cause substitution to deviate from its intended purpose of interpreting predicate letters.

In turning quantificational schemata into sentences we have not only predicate letters but also sentence letters to reckon with. For sentences the appropriate operation of substitution is simpler, there being no question of putting variables for circled numerals. Substitution of a sentence for a sentence letter in a schema consists as usual in putting the sentence for all occurrences of the letter. The first of the two restrictions set forth above, moreover, no longer has a place, there being no circled numerals. But the *second restriction carries over:* Variables free in the substituted sentence must not be such as to be captured by quantifiers in the schema into which the sentence is substituted. This restriction merely makes explicit the understanding that governed '*p*' in Chapter 22: '*p*' represented, in those contexts, a sentence devoid of free '*x*'.

HISTORICAL **NOTE:** What I am calling predicates are what Peirce (1892 and after) called *rhemes*, except that, where he left blanks, I write circled numerals to keep the blanks in order. Whitehead and Russell, in their notation for what they called propositional functions, used circumflexed variables '*ŵ*', '*x̂*', etc. in the sense of my circled numerals; and I have reluctantly departed from their precedent only because the circled numerals are less confusing. (Using '*ŵ*' and '*x̂*' instead of '①' and '②' in (7), we would have had to say that the *positionally* first and second variables after each occurrence of '*F*' in (8) are to supplant the *alphabetically* first and second circumflexed variables of the predicate.) My rejection of their phrase 'propositional function' is motivated by a grave ambiguity in their use of it; sometimes it referred not just to certain expressions, which predicates are meant to be, but to the corresponding properties or attributes.

The point of the predicates and their circled numerals is to keep substitution under control. For we see that substitution, central to logic though it is, becomes a rather subtle matter when we get to polyadic quantification theory. I know of no full and correct formulation of substitution for polyadic predicate letters prior to that of 1934 by Hilbert and Bernays. Mine in these pages dates from *Elementary Logic*, 1941. It differs from theirs not just in the detail of circled numerals but also in its two restrictions having to do with the capturing of variables; Hilbert and Bernays countered those contingencies by the more drastic expedient of using different parts of the alphabet for their bound and free variables.

EXERCISES

1. Substitute each of the predicates:

   ① is ashamed of x, x is ashamed of ①,   ① is ashamed of ①

   for 'F' in 'Fx'. Compatibly with the restrictions on substitution, which of these predicates can be substituted for 'F' in '$(\exists x)Fx$'? What does the resulting statement mean?

2. Find a predicate which, substituted for 'F' in '$Fxy \supset Fyx$', will yield:

$$y^x = xy + y \;.\supset. \; x^x = yy + x.$$

3. Decide which of the following predicates may, compatibly with the restrictions on substitution, be substituted for 'F' in '$(\exists x)Fxy$':

   ② praised ② to ①,   ② praised y to ①,
   ② praised ① to ①, $(\exists y)$(② praised y to ①),
   ② praised x to ①, $(\exists z)$(② praised z to ①).

   Put the results of those legitimate substitutions into words, supposing the universe limited to mankind.

27
SUBSTITUTION OF SCHEMATA

Substitution of sentences and predicates for sentence letters and predicate letters in schemata gives us sentences that illustrate the logical forms that those schemata depict. But substitution also takes another direction and serves another purpose: substitution of schemata in schemata to produce more schemata. A notable feature of such substitution was remarked upon at the truth-functional level in Chapters 6 and 13: substitution in valid schemata gives valid schemata.

Early in the preceding chapter we noted that a quantificationally valid sentence might or might not be, more particularly, monadically valid or even truth-functionally valid. Now similar distinctions apply to quantificational schemata themselves. A valid polyadic schema may be *monadically valid*, in the sense of issuing by substitution from a valid monadic one. An example is '$(x)Gxy \supset Gyy$', which issues from '$(x)Fx \supset Fy$'. And of course a quantificational schema may be truth-functionally valid; this trait was appealed to already in Chapter 19.

When we were getting sentences by substitution, what we substituted were sentences and predicates. To get schemata by substitution, what we substitute for sentence letters are ordinary quantificational schemata— call them for the moment *sentence schemata*—and what we substitute for predicate letters are *predicate-schemata*, e.g., '$G① \lor (\exists z)Hz①$'. Predicate-schemata are doubly artificial expressions conceived in the image of sentence schemata but containing circled numerals. Just as a predicate is like a sentence except for containing '①', or '①' and '②', etc., in some places appropriate to free variables, so a predicate-schema is like a sentence schema except for containing '①', or '①' and '②', etc., in some places appropriate to free variables.[3]

When we substitute a predicate-schema for a predicate letter in a sentence schema, the sentence schema resulting from the substitution does not actually contain the predicate-schema with its circled numerals, any more than a sentence contains a predicate with its circled numerals. Substitution of a predicate-schema for a predicate letter in a sentence schema, e.g., '$G① \lor (\exists z)Hz①$' for 'F' in '$(x)Fx \supset Fy$', proceeds precisely according to the rules and restrictions of predicate substitution laid down in the preceding chapter. The result is:

(1) $(x)[Gx \lor (\exists z)Hzx] \supset . Gy \lor (\exists z)Hzy.$

Another example, viz., substitution of '$G① \lor -H①$' for 'F' and 'Gy' for 'p', leads from:

(2) $(x)(Fx \supset p) \equiv . (\exists x)Fx \supset p$

---

[3] There will be no occasion to speak of predicate-schemata beyond the limits of the present chapter. On the other hand sentence schemata, such as have been known up to now as "quantificational schemata" and commonly just as "schemata," will continue to be the focus of attention. The precaution will be taken of never referring to predicate-schemata simply as schemata, but always by full title, and of hyphenating the title as a reminder of its indissolubility. The word 'schema' without modifier will therefore continue to mean sentence schema as heretofore. Such time as predicate-schemata continue to be in the air, however, the contrasting phrase "sentence schema" will be held to for emphasis.

to:

$$(3) \qquad (x)(Gx \lor -Hx \,.\supset Gy) \equiv. \; (\exists x)(Gx \lor -Hx) \supset Gy.$$

In general the utility of substitution, here as in Part I, is as a means of generating valid schemata from valid schemata. E.g., since (1) and (3) were got by substitution in schemata which were seen in Chapter 24 to be valid, we conclude that (1) and (3) are valid.

Substitution can be depended upon to transmit validity for essentially the reasons already noted in Chapter 6. But it will be well to review the matter now in the new setting. To begin with let us see why it is that the above substitution in (2) yields a valid result. Validity of the result (3) means truth under all interpretations of 'G' and 'H' and the free variable 'y', within any nonempty universe. Suppose the universe fixed, then, and consider any particular choice $\mathfrak{J}$ of such interpretations; what we want to see is that (3) comes out true under $\mathfrak{J}$. To see this we derive from $\mathfrak{J}$ the following interpretations for the schematic letters of (2): we interpret 'F' as having the extension which '$G① \lor -H①$' comes to have under $\mathfrak{J}$, and we interpret 'p' as having the truth value which 'Gy' comes to have under $\mathfrak{J}$. Being valid, (2) must come out true under these interpretations; hence (3), which simply repeats (2) under these interpretations, comes out true too.

More generally, suppose a sentence schema S' obtained by substitution in S. Each free variable and each schematic letter in S has a correspondent among the materials of S'; this correspondent is in each case either the same letter over again, or else a substituted sentence schema or predicate-schema. Now given any choice $\mathfrak{J}$ of interpretations for the free variables and schematic letters of S', let us adopt as interpretation of each free variable or schematic letter of S the same object or truth value or extension which has already accrued to its correspondent through $\mathfrak{J}$. S, so interpreted, matches S' as interpreted by $\mathfrak{J}$. Since this works for each choice of $\mathfrak{J}$, we see that S' is valid (or true for all interpretations) if S is.

The function of the two restrictions on substitution in Chapter 26 is to assure that the correspondents just now spoken of really correspond. Let us now have some examples showing how substitution can fail to transmit validity when the restrictions are violated.

Substitution of '$(\exists y)G①y$' for 'F' in '$(x)Fx \supset Fy$', in violation of the first restriction, would yield:

$$(4) \qquad (x)(\exists y)Gxy \supset (\exists y)Gyy. \qquad \text{(invalid)}$$

That this is not valid, despite the validity of '$(x)Fx \supset Fy$', is seen by confining the universe to numbers and interpreting 'G' as '② exceeds ①'; thereupon the antecedent of (4) becomes true ('for every number there is a greater') and the consequent false.

Substitution of '$Gx①$' for 'F' in '$(x)Fx \supset Fy$', in violation of the second restriction, would yield:

(5) $(x)Gxx \supset Gxy.$ (invalid)

That this is not valid may be seen by taking 'G' as 'identical with'; then (5) says 'If everything is identical with itself then x is identical with y', and this is clearly not true for every choice of x and y. Or, to restate this refutation in more explicit relation to the definition of validity: when we adopt a universe of two or more objects, and take one of these objects as interpretation of the free 'x' of (5) and a different one as interpretation of 'y', and interpret 'G' as having the extension of '① is identical with ②', thereupon (5) becomes false.

In (1), the expressions 'Gx v $(\exists z)Hzx$' and 'Gy v $(\exists z)Hzy$' which supplanted the 'Fx' and 'Fy' of '$(x)Fx \supset Fy$' are symmetrical in 'x' and 'y': the one expression has 'x' where, and only where, the other has 'y'. In the invalid substitution which led to (5), on the other hand, the expressions 'Gxx' and 'Gxy' which supplanted 'Fx' and 'Fy' fail to show this symmetry; 'Gxy' does not have 'y' everywhere that 'Gxx' has 'x'. The reader must be warned that this asymmetry has nothing to do with the invalidity of (5). It is unnecessary, in general, for the expression supplanting 'Fx' to have 'x' where and only where the expression supplanting 'Fy' has 'y'. It is quite proper, e.g., to substitute '$G①y$' for 'F' in '$(x)Fx \supset Fy$' and infer the validity of:

(6) $(x)Gxy \supset Gyy$

(e.g., 'If everyone hates y then y hates himself'). Despite the asymmetry of 'Gxy' and 'Gyy' with respect to 'x' and 'y', (6) is a genuine special case of '$(x)Fx \supset Fy$', as a verbal comparison immediately reflects: 'If everything is an F then y is an F'; 'If everything is a G of y then y is a G of y'; 'If everyone is a Herbert-hater then Herbert is a Herbert-hater'.

To be assured of the correctness of a substitution, we need look only to these points: we must be able, on demand, to specify the actual sentence schema or n-place predicate-schema which is substituted for the sentence letter or n-adically occurring predicate letter; we must be sure that the sentence schema or predicate-schema has been introduced at each occurrence of the letter; we must be sure that at each point of introducing the predicate-schema the particular variables there appended to the predicate letter have been put for the circled numerals; and finally we must be sure that the substitution has not led to new capturing of variables by quantifiers, in violation of the two restrictions.

Let us now shift from '$(x)Fx \supset Fy$' to another obviously valid schema, '$Fy \supset (\exists x)Fx$'. From this we may proceed to:

(7) $Gyy \supset (\exists x)Gxy$

by the legitimate substitution of '$G①y$' for 'F'; but it would be illegitimate to substitute '$Gx①$' for 'F' and thus proceed to:

(8) $Gxy \supset (\exists x)Gxx.$ (invalid)

An example of (7) is 'If Herbert hates himself then someone hates Herbert', which is quite unexceptionable; but an example of (8) is 'If Amos is uncle of Herbert then someone is uncle of himself'. Note that though the same principles of substitution are operative here as before, the pair (7) and (8) is rather opposite in appearance to (6) and (5). The valid (6) had unlike variables in the consequent, but in the valid (7) the opposite is the case.

As far as substitution in our particular examples '$(x)Fx \supset Fy$' and '$Fy \supset (\exists x)Fx$' is concerned, note that the net effect of the two restrictions is just this: the respective sentence schemata S_x and S_y which come to supplant 'Fx' and 'Fy' must be alike except that S_y has free 'y' wherever S_x has free 'x'. (S_x and S_y may also have additional free occurrences of 'y', as seen in (6) and (7).) Any such S_x and S_y can be made to supplant 'Fx' and 'Fy', in '$(x)Fx \supset Fy$' and '$Fy \supset (\exists x)Fx$', by substituting for 'F' the predicate-schema which is like S_x except for having '①' in place of all free 'x'. So, insofar as we are concerned merely with substitution in '$(x)Fx \supset Fy$' and '$Fy \supset (\exists x)Fx$', we may omit all thought of predicate-schemata, instead directly supplanting 'Fx' as a whole by any sentence schema S_x containing free 'x', and 'Fy' by a schema S_y which is like S_x except for having free 'y' in place of all free 'x'.

Such, then, is the notational relation between sentence schemata that are suited to the respective roles of '$(x)Fx$' and 'Fy' in '$(x)Fx \supset Fy$', or of '$(\exists x)Fx$' and 'Fy' in '$Fy \supset (\exists x)Fx$'. It has a name: the one schema is called an *instance* of the other. 'Fy' is an instance of '$(x)Fx$' and '$(\exists x)Fx$'. The terminology applies also, of course, where letters other than 'x' and 'y' are used; thus 'Fw' is an instance of '$(y)Fy$' and '$(\exists y)Fy$'. Furthermore, 'Gww' is an instance of '$(y)Gwy$', of '$(\exists y)Gwy$', of '$(y)Gyy$', of '$(\exists y)Gyy$', of '$(y)Gyw$', and of '$(\exists y)Gyw$'. On the other hand 'Gwy' is not an instance of '$(y)Gyy$' or '$(\exists y)Gyy$'.

The general description is this: an instance of a quantification exactly matches the old open schema that followed the quantifier, except that it may show a different variable in place of the recurrences of the variable of that quantifier. If it does show a different variable, it must show it in all the places (at least) where the old variable had been free in the old open schema that followed the quantifier. Moreover, it must show it *free* in those places. The reader will recognize in these requirements the effects of the restrictions on substitution for predicate letters.

A universal quantification implies each of its instances, and an existential quantification is implied by each of its instances. Such are the implications that come of substitution in the valid schemata '$(x)Fx \supset Fy$' and '$Fy \supset (\exists x)Fx$'.

When we substitute for 'F' in the valid closed schemata:

(9) $(y)[(x)Fx \supset Fy]$,   (11) $(\exists y)[Fy \supset (x)Fx]$,

(10) $(y)[Fy \supset (\exists x)Fx]$,   (12) $(\exists y)[(\exists x)Fx \supset Fy]$

(of Chapter 24, Ex. 1), the effect of the two restrictions is more stringent: the sentence schemata S_x and S_y which supplant 'Fx' and 'Fy' here must be alike except that S_y has free occurrences of 'y' in all *and only* the places where S_x has free occurrences of 'x'. For, the second restriction requires that the predicate-schema substituted for 'F' be devoid of free occurrences of 'y', in view of the initial quantifiers in (9)–(12).

Thus, whereas it was allowable to substitute '$G①y$' for 'F' in '$(x)Fx \supset Fy$' and '$Fy \supset (\exists x)Fx$' so as to obtain (6) and (7), it is forbidden to make the same substitution in (9)–(12) so as to obtain:

(13) $(y)[(x)Gxy \supset Gyy]$,   (15) $(\exists y)[Gyy \supset (x)Gxy]$,   (invalid)

(14) $(y)[Gyy \supset (\exists x)Gxy]$,   (16) $(\exists y)[(\exists x)Gxy \supset Gyy]$.   (invalid)

(13) and (14) happen indeed to be valid anyway, but only because they are the universal closures of the valid open schemata (6) and (7). (15) is not valid, as may be seen by adopting a universe of two or more objects and interpreting 'G' as 'is identical with'. ('Gyy' thereupon becomes true and '$(x)Gxy$' false for every object y; hence '$Gyy \supset (x)Gxy$' becomes false for every object y; thus (15) comes out false.) Likewise (16) is not valid, as may be seen by interpreting 'G' as 'is distinct from'.

EXERCISES

1. List all the schemata whose validity can be shown by legitimate substitution of one or another of the following predicate-schemata for 'F' in '$(x)Fx \supset Fy$' or '$Fy \supset (\exists x)Fx$' or (2) or (11) or (12):

    $Gx① \lor G①y$, $Gx① \lor G①x$, $Gy① \lor G①y$, $(y)(Gy① \lor G①y)$.

    Taking the universe as the members of the council and interpreting '$G①②$' as '① denounced ②' and 'p' as 'steps must be taken', put the results into ordinary language.

2. Determine which of the following schemata are legitimately obtainable from '$(x)Fx \supset Fy$' or '$Fy \supset (\exists x)Fx$' or (2) or (11) or (12) by substitution. Identify the substituted predicate-schema in each case.

    $(x)Fxx \supset Fyy$, $Gyx \supset (\exists x)Gxy$,

    $(\exists x)[Gxx \supset (\exists y)Gyy]$, $(\exists y)[Gy . Hz . \supset . (x)Gx . Hz]$,

    $(x)(Gyx \supset Hxz) . \supset . Gyy \supset Hyz$, $Gxy . Hyz . \supset (\exists x)(Gxx . Hxz)$,

    $Gy . (z)(Gy \supset Gz) . \supset (\exists x)[Gx . (z)(Gx \supset Gz)]$,

    $(x)[(y)(Gxy \supset Gyy) \supset Gyy] \equiv . (\exists x)(y)(Gxy \supset Gyy) \supset Gyy$.

28
PURE EXISTENTIALS

In general quantification theory as elsewhere, implication is validity of the conditional. To justify an inference, then, such as the one in Chapter 25 about the philosopher, what we need to do is prove the validity of a conditional. In this example the appropriate conditional is:

(1) $(\exists y)[Fy \, . \, (x)(Fx \supset Gxy)] \supset (\exists x)(Fx \, . \, Gxx)$

(cf. Chapter 25, (4)). Converting it to prenex form, we get perhaps:

$$(y)(\exists x)(\exists z)(Fy \, . \, Fx \supset Gxy \, . \supset . \, Fz \, . \, Gzz).$$

Other prenex equivalents could be got (cf. Chapter 23), but this will do. In fact, since validity is our concern, we may as well drop the '(y)'; for we know that an initial universal quantifier is indifferent to validity. What we want to show, then, is the validity of this schema:

(2) $(\exists x)(\exists z)(Fy \, . \, Fx \supset Gxy \, . \supset . \, Fz \, . \, Gzz).$

Now try this experiment: substitute the free 'y' for the existential variables, dropping the quantifiers. The result:

(3) $Fy \, . \, Fy \supset Gyy \, . \supset . \, Fy \, . \, Gyy$

is truth-functionally valid. This outcome, properly viewed, establishes the validity of (2) and therewith of (1). For (3) is an instance of:

$$(\exists z)(Fy \, . \, Fy \supset Gyy \, . \supset . \, Fz \, . \, Gzz)$$

and accordingly implies it, which in turn implies (2).

The *matrix* of a prenex schema is what comes after the quantifiers. A *pure existential* is a prenex schema with none but existential quantifiers. Now what the example above teaches us is that if a pure existential has just one free variable, and substitution of that variable for the existential variables turns the matrix truth-functionally valid, then the pure existential was valid.

We can claim more: the pure existential is valid *only* if that substitution turns the matrix truth-functionally valid. The reason may best be seen through another example. Let us modify (2) just enough to spoil it.

(2') $(\exists x)(\exists z)(Fy \, . \, Fx \lor Gxy \, . \supset . \, Fz \, . \, Gzz).$

Substitution of 'y' for 'x' and 'z' in the matrix of (2') gives:

(3') $Fy \, . \, Fy \lor Gyy \, . \supset . \, Fy \, . \, Gyy,$

which, rather than being truth-functionally valid, is falsifiable by assign-
ing T to 'Fy' and $\bot$ to 'Gyy'. But (2') itself boils down to (3') in a universe
of just a single object y. So (2') comes out false in that universe if we interpret 'F' and 'G' so that Fy and $-Gyy$. So (2') is not valid: not true under
all interpretations of 'F' and 'G' in all nonempty universes.

We have arrived at a decision procedure for pure existentials in one
free variable. The schema is valid if and only if its matrix becomes truth-
functionally valid on substitution of the free variable for the existential
variables.

The test can be extended to pure existentials in more than one free
variable. In such a case there are a multiplicity of ways of substituting
the free variables for the existential ones; but then we take the alternation
of all such results and check it for truth-functional validity. Example:

(4) $(\exists z)(Fxz \supset Fzy).$

There are two ways of substituting the free variables for the existential
variable. They give '$Fxx \supset Fxy$' and '$Fxy \supset Fyy$'. The alternation:

(5) $Fxx \supset Fxy \, . \lor . \, Fxy \supset Fyy$

is truth-functionally valid. Each half of (5) implies (4); so any interpretation that makes either half true makes (4) true. In short, (5) implies (4).
So (4) is valid.

To see in general that the validity of the alternation is not only sufficient for the validity of the pure existential but also necessary, let us again
reason from an example. Let us modify (4) just enough to spoil it.

(4') $(\exists z)(Fxz \supset Fyz).$

The alternation:

(5') $Fxx \supset Fyx \, . \lor . \, Fxy \supset Fyy$

is falsifiable by assigning T to 'Fxx' and 'Fxy' and $\bot$ to 'Fyx' and 'Fyy'.
But (4') itself boils down to (5') if we take a universe of just x and y. So
(4') comes out false in that universe under such an interpretation of 'F'.

At this point the form of argument is evident for this general theorem:
*a pure existential is valid if and only if we get a truth-functionally valid schema
by taking the alternation of the results of substituting the free variables for the
existential ones in the matrix.*

In hopes of checking validity along these lines, we do well, when converting a schema to prenex form, to choose our steps so as to give priority to universal quantifiers where possible. If we can get them all in front, we can drop them and test the pure existential. If in converting (1) we had brought its final '$(\exists x)$' out first, this test would have been denied us.

Two fringe cases need notice. What if on conversion to prenex form all the quantifiers become universal, and thus are dropped? Then of course we test the schema as it stands for truth-functional validity, there being no quantifiers. And what if we end up rather with just existential quantifiers and no free variables? Then we just put the arbitrary letter 'x' for the variables in the matrix and test the resulting one-variable schema for truth-functional validity. E.g., the validity of:

$$(\exists x)(\exists y)(Fxy \supset Fyx)$$

comes down to that of '$Fxx \supset Fxx$'. The criterion is sufficient, since the one-variable schema is an instance (of an instance . . .) of the existential schema and so implies it. And it is necessary, since, in the universe of a single object x, the existential schema boils down to the one-variable schema.

Valid polyadic schemata may or may not be monadically valid (cf. Chapter 27). The validity of (1) and (4) is an irreducibly polyadic matter. The same is true of:

(6) $$(\exists x)(y)Fxy \supset (y)(\exists x)Fxy,$$

which tends to be the first genuinely polyadic example that one thinks of. Let us try our new method on it. Converting it to prenex form with priority on universal quantifiers, we get:

$$(x)(y)(\exists z)(\exists w)(Fxz \supset Fwy)$$

and so proceed to test this:

(7) $$(\exists z)(\exists w)(Fxz \supset Fwy).$$

One way of substituting the free variables of (7) for 'z' and 'w' in '$Fxz \supset Fwy$' gives '$Fxy \supset Fxy$'; and there are three others. The test of validity of (7), and hence of (6), would consist in forming the alternation of '$Fxy \supset Fxy$' with its three companions and examining the result for truth-functional validity. But of course there is no need of all this, since '$Fxy \supset Fxy$' is valid by itself; the alternation has to be valid.

It happens conveniently often, in testing pure existentials, that a single such result of substitution turns out thus to be valid by itself. Thus take the example in Chapter 25 about drawing circles. Here the conditional to test for validity is:

(8) $(x)(Fx \supset Gx) \supset (y)[(\exists x)(Fx \, . \, Hyx) \supset (\exists x)(Gx \, . \, Hyx)]$

(cf. Chapter 25, (1)). Converting it to prenex form with priority on universal quantifiers, and then dropping the omitted universal quantifiers, we get the pure existential:

(9) $(\exists z)(\exists w)(Fz \supset Gz \, . \supset : Fx \, . \, Hyx \, . \supset . \, Gw \, . \, Hyw).$

Now there are four ways of substituting 'x' and/or 'y' for 'z' and 'w' in the matrix of (9). One way gives:

(10) $Fx \supset Gx \, . \supset : Fx \, . \, Hyx \, . \supset . \, Gx \, . \, Hyx,$

and there are three others. The test of validity of (9), and hence of (8), would consist in forming the alternation of (10) with the other three and testing the long result for truth-functional validity. But again we do better to look before leaping; (10) itself is truth-functionally valid, so of course the alternation will be so likewise.

The reader will have the same experience again if he tries the second example in Chapter 25, the one about the paintings; again a single result of substitution turns out valid. Sometimes, however, we have to press on to the alternation of two or more such results of substitution. This was true already of the simple example (4); neither half of (5) is valid by itself.

So we have a decision procedure for validity of pure existentials. In view of the warning that there is no general decision procedure for validity of quantificational schemata, then, we may be sure that universal quantifiers cannot always be maneuvered into initial position. Here is a simple valid schema that resists such treatment:

(11) $(\exists y)(z)(Fxz \supset Fyz).$

To prove the validity of such schemata we shall have to resort to more general methods.

But it is good policy, when trying to prove the validity of a schema, to try first for a pure existential. This often succeeds, and when it does there are two advantages. One is that a direct test is available, assuring a conclusively negative answer or a proof. The other is that the process tends to be relatively swift, since it so often happens, as in all three of the examples that we have been examining from Chapter 25, that a single substitution of universal variables for the existential ones settles matters.

Incidentally we now have another general decision procedure for validity of monadic schemata, alternative to the methods in Part II. For we saw in Chapter 23 how any monadic schema can be purified; and we saw that, once purified, it will have no stacked quantifiers. But the rules of passage enable us to bring quantifiers into prenex position in any order we like if none of them are stacked. Thus any monadic schema can be tested for validity by the method of pure existentials.

By way of opening a field for further examples involving polyadic schemata, let us acquaint ourselves with *symmetry, transitivity, reflexivity,* and related concepts—these being worth noting also in their own right. A dyadic relative term is called symmetrical, asymmetrical, transitive, intransitive, totally reflexive, reflexive, or irreflexive according as it fulfills:

$$(x)(y)(Fxy \supset Fyx)$$ (symmetry)
$$(x)(y)(Fxy \supset -Fyx)$$ (asymmetry)
$$(x)(y)(z)(Fxy \,.\, Fyz \,.\supset Fxz)$$ (transitivity)
$$(x)(y)(z)(Fxy \,.\, Fyz \,.\supset -Fxz)$$ (intransitivity)
$$(x)Fxx$$ (total reflexivity)
$$(x)(y)(Fxy \supset.\, Fxx \,.\, Fyy)$$ (reflexivity)
$$(x) -Fxx$$ (irreflexivity)

The relative term 'compatriot' is symmetrical, in that if x is a compatriot of y then y is a compatriot of x. It is also transitive, if we disallow multiple nationality; for then if x is a compatriot of y and y of z, x will also be a compatriot of z. It is also reflexive, if we consider a person a compatriot of himself—as indeed we must if 'compatriot of' means 'having same nationality as'. But it is not totally reflexive, if we think of our universe as containing any things devoid of nationality. Examples of total reflexivity are rare and trivial; 'identical' and 'coexistent' are two such.

The relative term 'north' is again transitive, but it is asymmetrical and irreflexive; 'x is north of y' excludes 'y is north of x', and nothing is north of itself. The relative term 'mother' is intransitive, asymmetrical, and irreflexive.

The relative term 'loves' lacks all seven properties. Where x loves y, y may or may not love x; thus 'loves' is neither symmetrical nor asymmetrical. Where x loves y and y loves z, x may or may not love z; thus 'loves' is neither transitive nor intransitive. And, since some love themselves while others (even among those who love or are loved) do not love themselves, 'loves' is neither reflexive nor irreflexive.

The reader may wonder why, parallel to the distinction between reflexivity and total reflexivity, a distinction is not drawn between "irreflexivity" in the sense of:

$$(x)(y)(Fxy \supset.\, -Fxx \,.\, -Fyy)$$

and "total irreflexivity" in the sense of '$(x)-Fxx$'. The reason is that this latter distinction is illusory; the two schemata are equivalent. To show this we establish the validity of two conditionals, as follows:

(12) $$(x)(y)(Fxy \supset.\, -Fxx \,.\, -Fyy) \supset (x)-Fxx,$$

(13) $(x) - Fxx \supset (x)(y)(Fxy \supset . - Fxx . - Fyy)$.

Turning them into prenex form and dropping initial universal quantifiers, we get:

(14) $(\exists x)(\exists y)(Fxy \supset . - Fxx . - Fyy :\supset - Fzz)$,

(15) $(\exists z)(- Fzz \supset : Fxy \supset . - Fxx . - Fyy)$.

The one is shown valid by this truth-functionally valid result of substitution:

$$Fzz \supset . - Fzz . - Fzz :\supset - Fzz$$

and the other by this truth-functionally valid alternation of two:

$$- Fxx \supset : Fxy \supset . - Fxx . - Fyy .:\text{v}:. - Fyy \supset : Fxy \supset . - Fxx . - Fyy.$$

As another example it will be proved that symmetry and transitivity together imply reflexivity. This means proving the validity of this conditional:

(16) $(x)(y)(Fxy \supset Fyx) . (x)(y)(z)(Fxy . Fyz .\supset Fxz)$
                                    $.\supset (x)(y)(Fxy \supset . Fxx . Fyy)$.

Turning it into prenex form and dropping initial universal quantifiers, we get:

(17) $(\exists v)(\exists w)(\exists x)(\exists y)(\exists z)(Fvw \supset Fwv : Fxy . Fyz .\supset Fxz$
                                    $:\supset : Ftu \supset . Ftt . Fuu)$.

This is shown valid by the truth-functional validity of the alternation of two of the results of substituting 't' and 'u' for the existential variables.

(18) $Ftu \supset Fut : Ftu . Fut .\supset Ftt :\supset : Ftu \supset . Ftt . Fuu$
              $.:\text{v}:. Ftu \supset Fut : Fut . Ftu .\supset Fuu :\supset : Ftu \supset . Ftt . Fuu.$

The reader is urged to do a painstaking truth-value analysis before agreeing to the truth-functional validity of this alternation.

HISTORICAL NOTE: The existence of a validity test to this purpose seems to have been first noted by Bernays and Schönfinkel, 1928. In the present method there are echoes of Herbrand that will become clearer in Chapter 35.

EXERCISES

1. Delineate all the steps of passage, relettering, and deletion that carry (1) into (2); (6) into (7); (8) into (9); (12) into (14); (13) into (15); (16) into (17).

2. Check the validity of (18).

3. Do the example in Chapter 25 about the paintings.

4. Repeat the exercises of Chapter 24 by the new method.

5. Prove that asymmetry implies irreflexivity.

6. Prove that intransitivity implies irreflexivity.

7. Prove that transitivity and irreflexivity together imply asymmetry.

8. Supply the general argument for the foot of page 156.

29
THE MAIN METHOD

We turn now to a proof procedure that will be found to be complete: adequate to establishing the validity of any valid quantificational schema and hence also to establishing any implication and any inconsistency. In fact it will be oriented to inconsistency proofs. To prove a schema valid we shall prove its negation inconsistent; and to prove implication we shall prove that the one schema is inconsistent with the negation of the other.

In (11) of the preceding chapter we saw a candidate for a validity proof, inaccessible to the method of pure existentials. To prove it valid by the new method we negate it, assume the prenex form of the negation as premise, and proceed to generate instances from it as follows:

PREMISE: $(y)(\exists z) - (Fxz \supset Fyz)$.
INSTANCES: $(\exists z) - (Fxz \supset Fxz)$,
       $-(Fxu \supset Fxu)$.

Proofs of inconsistency in this system always end up with a truth-functionally inconsistent schema, as here, or a truth-functionally inconsistent

combination of schemata; and this melancholy exhibit is meant to show that
the premise was at fault and thus inconsistent. Each successive line is an
instance of an earlier line.

We seem to see here the pattern traditionally known as *reductio ad
absurdum:* disproof by derivation of a clear contradiction. But derivation
how? Do quantifications imply their instances?

Universal quantifications do indeed. The first line of the proof above
implies the second. The operation of *universal instantiation*—UI, as I shall
call it—which leads from the first line to the second is implicative.

But *existential* instantiation, EI, which leads from the second line to
the last, is not implicative. '$(\exists x)Fx$' does not imply 'Fy'. Consequently
it is not evident that the derivation of an inconsistency by progressive
instantiation, as in the proof above, suffices to show the premise inconsistent. It does suffice, but the point will take some proving.

Before proceeding to justify the method, let us get a firmer idea of
what the method is. For one thing, EI is to be hedged thus: The *instantial
variable*, which is substituted for the variable that was bound by the
dropped existential quantifier, must be *new*. More accurately: it must be
free in no line prior to this instantiation.

Another point, this time one of liberality rather than of hedging, is
that we can have more than one premise. For an example let us recur to
the old familiar implication that was proved in the preceding chapter by
proving the validity of (6). To prove it by the present method we would
assume as premises '$(\exists x)(y)Fxy$' and the prenex form of the negation of
'$(y)(\exists x)Fxy$', and proceed to instantiate to a truth-functional inconsistency:

PREMISES: $(\exists x)(y)Fxy,$
               $(\exists y)(x)-Fxy.$
INSTANCES: $(y)Fzy,$
               $(x)-Fxw,$
               $Fzw,$
               $-Fzw.$

Here, next, is a more substantial example. It will serve as a source of illustration when we get to justifying the method.

PREMISES: (1) $(\exists u)(y)Fuy,$
               (2) $(x)(\exists v)(y)-(Fvy \cdot Fyx),$
               (3) $(x)(y)(\exists w)(Fxy \supset : -Fxw \cdot Fwy \,.\text{v}.\, Fyw \cdot Fwx).$
INSTANCES: (4) $(y)Fzy$ [of (1)],
               (5) $(\exists v)(y)-(Fvy \cdot Fyz)$ [of (2)],
               (6) $(y)-(Fty \cdot Fyz)$ [of (5)],
               (7) Fzt [of (4)],
               (8) $(y)(\exists w)(Fzy \supset : -Fzw \cdot Fwy \,.\text{v}.\, Fyw \cdot Fwz)$ [of (3)],
               (9) $(\exists w)(Fzt \supset : -Fzw \cdot Fwt \,.\text{v}.\, Ftw \cdot Fwz)$ [of (8)],
               (10) $Fzt \supset : -Fzs \cdot Fst \,.\text{v}.\, Fts \cdot Fsz$ [of (9)],
               (11) Fzs [of (4)],
               (12) $-(Fts \cdot Fsz)$ [of (6)].

(7), (10), (11), and (12) are together inconsistent by truth-value analysis. We conclude that (1)–(3) are together inconsistent.

The proof procedure for inconsistency that I have now described will be called the *main method*, to distinguish it from alternatives in Chapters 28 and 34–37. Summed up, it is the following slight affair. Instantiation: apply UI and EI, always choosing new instantial variables for EI. Termination: a truth-functionally inconsistent assemblage of unquantified instances.

I have still to show that the method is sound—i.e., that it generates a truth-functional inconsistency only when the premises are inconsistent. In showing this I shall need some terminology. I shall use 'generic' as the correlative of 'instance'; thus a step of UI or EI derives an instance from its generic. I shall speak of U-instances and E-instances. Thus in the inconsistency proof (1)–(12) the E-instances are (4), (6), and (10), and their generics are (1), (5), and (9). By an EI-*conditional* I shall mean a conditional whose consequent and antecedent copy an E-instance and its generic. If for compactness I simply write the numerals themselves as abbreviations of the numbered lines, then the EI-conditionals of the inconsistency proof (1)–(12) are '1 ⊃ 4', '5 ⊃ 6', and '9 ⊃ 10'.

Now observe that each instance, in such a proof, is implied by previous lines plus EI-conditionals. For each U-instance is implied by its generic, and each E-instance is truth-functionally implied by its generic and its EI-conditional. (E.g., (4) is implied by (1) and '1 ⊃ 4'.) Ultimately, therefore, all the instances are implied by the premises and the EI-conditionals. So, since the instances are inconsistent, the conjunction of the premises and the EI-conditionals is inconsistent. In our example this conjunction is:

$$1 . 2 . 3 . 1 \supset 4 . 5 \supset 6 . 9 \supset 10.$$

As noted early in Chapter 24, it will remain inconsistent when an existential quantifier is prefixed. Let us prefix one containing the instantial variable of the last E-instance.

$$(\exists s)(1 . 2 . 3 . 1 \supset 4 . 5 \supset 6 . 9 \supset 10).$$

Now we use the fact that this instantial variable, having been new (i.e., free in no prior line), is free nowhere in our conjunction except in the last EI-conditional, and only in its consequent at that. We can confine the quantifier to that part by the rules of passage (1) and (5) of Chapter 22.

$$1 . 2 . 3 . 1 \supset 4 . 5 \supset 6 . 9 \supset (\exists s)10.$$

But (9) and '(∃s)10' are alike except for the alphabetical choice of the existential variable. So '9 ⊃ (∃s)10' is valid and can be dropped from the conjunction, leaving '1 . 2 . 3 . 1 ⊃ 4 . 5 ⊃ 6'. Then by a similar argument we get rid of '5 ⊃ 6' and finally of '1 ⊃ 4'. Thus the whole inconsistent conjunction has boiled down to the premises, which are therefore inconsistent, Q.E.D. In this argument I have leaned increasingly on the particular example, but still the general reasoning shines through.

We see thus that our main method is a sound one. It is rather a natural one, moreover, despite the austerity of the argument above. The pattern (1)–(12) could be verbalized, as a disproof of some conjunction of actual statements in lieu of (1)–(3), along the following line. According to (1), there is something that is F to everything. Very well, call it z. So we have (4). But (2) said that everything x is such that . . . . . Well then in particular z will be that way. So we have (5): that there is something such that . . . . . Call it t. Continuing thus, we get to the contradiction (7), (10)–(12). The premises (1)–(3) are thus disproved. One or two of them may be true, but not all three.

Premises must be put in readiness in two respects before the main method is applied to them. They must be converted to prenex form; this we know. The further point is that the letters used as bound variables in each premise should be so chosen as not to match a free variable of any premise. E.g., consider '$(\exists w)-Fyw$' and '$(x)(y)Fxy$'. They are inconsistent, but the reader can try in vain to show them inconsistent by the main method as they stand; whereas the proof goes smoothly through if the bound 'y' is rewritten as 'z'.

PREMISES:　　$(\exists w)-Fyw,$
　　　　　　　$(x)(z)Fxz.$
INSTANCES:　 $-Fyu,$
　　　　　　　$(z)Fyz,$
　　　　　　　$Fyu.$

We shall see in Chapter 31 that the main method, for all its slightness, is complete. We shall see that for every inconsistent conjunction of schemata, prepared in the two respects just now indicated, it affords an inconsistency proof.

HISTORICAL **NOTE:** Reductio ad absurdum, also called *indirect proof*, was known to the ancients under the name of *apagoge*. Its advantage over direct proof of validity turns only on a small point of technical convenience which will be noted in Chapter 35. The first proof procedure for quantification theory—Frege's of 1879—proceeded rather in the axiomatic style of Chapter 13; see Chapter 36 below. This style continued to prevail through the thirties. Already in 1928 and 1930, however, Skolem and Herbrand presented proof procedures more akin to what I am calling the main method; see Chapters 34 and 35. The main method figured in a 1955 appendix to earlier printings of the present book.

EXERCISES

1. Find fault with the following purported proofs of inconsistency.

PREMISES: $(\exists x)Fxy,$ $-(\exists x)Fxx,$ $(\exists x)Fxy,$
             $(x)-Fxx.$ $(y)Fyy.$ $(\exists x)-Fxy.$

INSTANCES: $Fyy,$ $-Fzz,$ $Fzy,$
              $-Fyy.$ $Fzz.$ $-Fzy.$

Is any of these pairs of premises really inconsistent? Which? Prove it so.

2. Repeat Exercises 3–7 of Chapter 28 by the main method.

3. Describe the obstacle to showing '$(\exists w)-Fyw$' and '$(x)(y)Fxy$' inconsistent by the main method as they stand.

30

APPLICATION

When our proof procedure is to be brought to bear upon statements couched in ordinary language, the task of suitably paraphrasing the statements and isolating their relevant structure becomes just as important as the proof for which that preliminary task prepares the way (cf. Chapter 8).

In Chapter 14 we noted a considerable variety of ways in which the categorical forms **A**, **E**, **I**, and **O** may appear in ordinary language; and in Chapter 21 we saw how to put those forms over into quantificational notation. These observations provide the beginning of a guide to the translation of words into quantificational symbols. But we saw also, from examples such as 'A lady is present', 'A Scout is reverent', 'John cannot outrun any man on the team', and 'Tai always eats with chopsticks' (Chapter 14), that it is a mistake to trust to a pat checklist of idioms. The safer way of paraphrasing words into symbols is the harder way: by a sympathetic re-thinking of the statement in context. If there are obvious ways of rectifying logically obscure phrases by rewording, it is well to do so before resorting to logical symbols at all.

A drastic departure from English is required in the matter of tense. The view to adopt is the Minkowskian one, which sees time as a fourth dimension on a par with the three dimensions of space. Quantifiers must be read as timeless. The values of 'x' may themselves be thing-events, four-dimensional denizens of space-time, and we can attribute dates and durations to them as we can attribute locations and lengths and breadths to them; but the quantifier itself attributes none of these things. '$(\exists x)$' says neither 'there was' nor 'there will be', but only, in a tenseless sense, 'there is'.

This four-dimensional view was needed, as everyone knows, to make sense of Einstein's relativity physics. But it also has long been a great help in clarifying ordinary talk on more humdrum matters. When we say how many presidents or popes there have been, we state the size of a class whose members have never all coexisted. When we compare Napoleon to Caesar or trace David's descent from Abraham, we relate persons who never coexisted. Puzzles both conceptual and verbal are minimized by seeing spatial and temporal associations as logically alike. Much as Boston and Birmingham are 3000 miles apart, Caesar and Napoleon are 1800 years apart; and the 'are' here had better be read as tenseless.

From long habituation we are proof against silly fallacies of this sort: George V married Queen Mary, Queen Mary is a widow, therefore George V married a widow. Clearly, however, a logic designed to control this sort of thing explicitly would be needlessly elaborate. We do better to make do with a simpler logical machine and then, when we want to apply it, to paraphrase our sentences to fit it. Already in Chapter 14 we had a glimpse of the varied ways in which temporal references might fare under such paraphrase. Not, of course, that the ubiquity of tense in English will require us to make explicit reference to time in all the paraphrases. As often as not the temporal matter is superfluous, and foisted on us only by English usage. Still more often, in practice, we can even leave the tensed verbs themselves undisturbed, as long as there is no danger of equivocation within the space of the proof. (Cf. Chapter 8.)

In paraphrasing more complex statements into quantificational form, a problem that obtrudes itself at every turn is that of determining the intended groupings. The cues to grouping which were noted at the truth-functional level in Chapter 4 continue to be useful here, but the most important single cue proves to be the additional one which was noted in connection with (22) of Chapter 21: *The scope of a quantifier must reach out far enough to take in any occurrence of a variable that is supposed to refer back to that quantifier.*

The technique of *paraphrasing inward* (Chapter 8), as a means of dividing the problem of interpretation into manageable parts and keeping the complexities of grouping under control, is as important here as at the truth-functional levels; more important, indeed, in proportion to the increasing complexity of the statements concerned. After each step of paraphrasing, moreover, it is well to check the whole against the original statement to make sure that the intended idea is still being reproduced.

By way of a serious venture in paraphrasing, let us try putting the following premises and conclusion over into quantificational form preparatory to setting up a deduction.

PREMISES: The guard searched all who entered the building except those who were accompanied by members of the firm,
Some of Fiorecchio's men entered the building unaccompanied by anyone else,
The guard searched none of Fiorecchio's men;
CONCLUSION: Some of Fiorecchio's men were members of the firm.

The first premise says in effect:

Every person that entered the building and was not searched by the guard was accompanied by some member(s) of the firm.

Setting about now to paraphrase this premise inward, we inspect it for its outermost structure, which obviously is '$(x)(\ldots \supset \ldots)$':

$(x)(x$ is a person that entered the building and was not searched by the guard $\supset x$ was accompanied by some members of the firm).

The virtue of thus paraphrasing inward a step at a time is that the unparaphrased internal segments can now be handled each as a small independent problem. The clause 'x was accompanied by some members of the firm', e.g., regardless of context, becomes:

$(\exists y)(x$ was accompanied by y . y was a member of the firm).

The other clause, 'x is a person that entered the building and was not searched by the guard', needs little more attention; we have merely to make it an explicit conjunction:

x is a person that entered the building . x was not searched by the guard.

So the whole becomes:

$(x)[x$ is a person that entered the building . x was not searched by the guard . $\supset (\exists y)(x$ was accompanied by y . y was a member of the firm)].

Care must be taken, as here, to insert dots or parentheses to indicate intended grouping.

Finally, writing 'Fx' for 'x is a person that entered the building', 'Gx' for 'x was searched by the guard', 'Hxy' for 'x was accompanied by y', and 'Jy' for 'y was a member of the firm', we have:

$$(x)[Fx . -Gx . \supset (\exists y)(Hxy . Jy)]$$

as the logical form of the first premise.

Instead of carrying the word 'person' explicitly through the above analysis, we might, as an alternative procedure, have limited the universe to persons. But in the present example this would have made no difference to the final symbolic form, since 'x is a person that entered the building' has all been fused as 'Fx'.

The reason for representing so long a clause as this simply as 'Fx', without further analysis, is that we know that no further analysis of it will be needed for the proposed deduction. We are assured of this by the fact that 'entered' never occurs in premises or conclusion except as applied to persons entering the building. Similarly we were able to leave 'x was searched by the guard' unanalyzed, because 'searched' never occurs except with 'by the guard'. On the other hand it behooved us to break up 'x was accompanied by some members of the firm', since accompaniment and membership in the firm are appealed to also outside this combination in the course of the premises and conclusion. In general, when we paraphrase words into logical notation and then introduce schematic letters as above, it is sound policy to *expose no more structure than promises to be needed for the proposed deduction.* This restraint not only minimizes the work of paraphrasing, but also minimizes the length and complexity of the schemata that are to be manipulated in the deduction.

Turning to the second premise, and writing 'Kx' for 'x was one of Fiorecchio's men', we get this as the obvious outward structure:

$$(\exists x)(Kx \,.\, Fx \,.\, x \text{ was unaccompanied by anyone else}).$$

It remains to paraphrase the component clause 'x was unaccompanied by anyone else'. Clearly the intended meaning is:

$$\text{Anyone accompanying } x \text{ was one of Fiorecchio's men,}$$

which becomes '$(y)(Hxy \supset Ky)$', so that the second premise as a whole becomes:

$$(\exists x)[Kx \,.\, Fx \,.\, (y)(Hxy \supset Ky)].$$

The third premise and conclusion immediately become:

$$(x)(Kx \supset -Gx), \qquad (\exists x)(Kx \,.\, Jx).$$

Taking then as our four premises these three premises and the negation of the conclusion, all converted to prenex form, we proceed with the main method.

PREMISES: $(x)(\exists y)(Fx \,.\, -Gx \,.\!\supset.\, Hxy \,.\, Jy),$
$(\exists x)(y)(Kx \,.\, Fx \,.\, Hxy \supset Ky),$
$(x)(Kx \supset -Gx),$
$(x)-(Kx \,.\, Jx).$

INSTANCES: $(y)(Kz . Fz . Hzy \supset Ky)$,
$(\exists y)(Fz . -Gz . \supset . Hzy . Jy)$,
$Fz . -Gz . \supset . Hzw . Jw$,
$Kz . Fz . Hzw \supset Kw$,
$Kz \supset -Gz$,
$-(Kw . Jw)$.

The reader can verify that the four unquantified instances are inconsistent.

When we undertake to inject logical rigor into inferences encountered in informal discourse, we are likely to confront a second problem of interpretation over and above that of paraphrasing verbal idioms into logical notation. This second problem is that of supplying suppressed premises; and it is occasioned by the popular practice of arguing in *enthymemes*. An enthymeme is a logical inference in which one or more of the premises are omitted from mention on the ground that their truth is common knowledge and goes without saying; thus we argue:

Some Greeks are wise; for, some Greeks are philosophers,

omitting mention of the additional premise 'All philosophers are wise' on the ground that this would naturally be understood by all concerned.[4]

In everyday discourse most logical inference is enthymematic. We are constantly sparing ourselves the reiteration of known facts, trusting the listener to supply them where needed for the logical completion of an argument. But when we want to analyze and appraise a logical inference which someone has propounded, we have to take such suppressed premises into account. At this point two problems demand solution simultaneously: the problem of filling in the details of a logical deduction leading from premises to desired conclusion, and the problem of eking out the premises so that such a deduction can be constructed. Solution of either problem presupposes solution of the other; we cannot set up the deduction without adequate premises, and we cannot know what added premises will be needed until we know how the deduction is to run.

Sometimes, as in the syllogistic example above, the form of logical inference intended by the speaker suggests itself to us immediately because of its naturalness and simplicity. In such a case there is no difficulty in identifying the tacit premise which the speaker had in mind. Sometimes, on the other hand, the form of inference itself may not be quite evident, but the relevant tacit premises are already somehow in the air because of recently shared experiences. Such a case differs in no practical way from the case where all premises are explicit.

---

[4] Traditionally 'enthymeme' meant, more specifically, a syllogism with suppressed premise—like the above example; but it is natural, now that logic has so far outstripped the syllogism, to refer to a logical inference of any form as an enthymeme when some premises are left tacit.

Sometimes, finally, neither the intended form of inference nor the intended tacit premises are initially evident; and in this case the best we can do is try to solve both problems concurrently. Thus we may start a tentative deduction on the basis of the explicit premises, and then, on coming to an impasse, we may invent a plausible tacit premise which would advance us toward the desired conclusion. Alternating thus between steps of deduction and supplementation of premises, we may, with luck, achieve our goal. Of course the tacit premises thus invoked must always be statements which can be presumed to be believed true by all parties at the outset; for it is only under such circumstances that a deduction using those tacit premises would give reason for belief in the conclusion. If we were to invoke as a tacit premise some statement which was (from the point of view of concerned parties) as much in need of proof as the conclusion itself, we should be guilty of what is known as *circular reasoning*, or *begging the question*, or *petitio principii;* any added conviction that might accrue to the conclusion through such argument would be deceptive. Deciding whether a statement is believed true by all parties at the outset is a task of applied psychology, but in most cases it offers no difficulty, there commonly being a wide gulf between the moot issues of an actual argument and the common fund of platitudes.

As an example of the kind of problem discussed in the foregoing paragraph, consider the explicit

PREMISES: All natives of Ajo have a cephalic index in excess of 96,
              All women who have a cephalic index in excess of 96
                have Pima blood

and the

CONCLUSION: Anyone whose mother is a native of Ajo has Pima blood.

Let us put these statements into logical notation, but for the present let us use obvious contractions instead of schematic letters 'F', 'G', etc., for we must keep the meanings of the words in mind in order to be able to think of relevant platitudes for use as tacit premises. The following, then, are the results of translation, supposing the universe to be comprised this time of persons:

PREMISES: $(x)(x$ is nat $\supset x$ has 96),
              $(x)(x$ is wom . x has 96 . $\supset x$ has P bl).
CONCLUSION: $(x)(y)(x$ is mo y . x is nat . $\supset y$ has P bl).

When we negate the conclusion and convert it to prenex form, we get:

$$(\exists x)(\exists y) - (x \text{ is mo } y . x \text{ is nat} . \supset y \text{ has P bl}).$$

But we can think about it better if we subject it immediately to the obvious truth-functional simplification, thus:

$$(\exists x)(\exists y)[x \text{ is mo } y \, . \, x \text{ is nat} \, . -(y \text{ has P bl})].$$

Then we start trying for an inconsistency proof, making the most natural instantiations.

PREMISES: $(x)(x \text{ is nat} \supset x \text{ has 96})$,
                 $(x)(x \text{ is wom} \, . \, x \text{ has 96} \, . \supset x \text{ has P bl})$,
                 $(\exists x)(\exists y)[x \text{ is mo } y \, . \, x \text{ is nat} \, . -(y \text{ has P bl})]$.
INSTANCES: $(\exists y)[z \text{ is mo } y \, . \, z \text{ is nat} \, . -(y \text{ has P bl})]$,
                 $z \text{ is mo } w \, . \, z \text{ is nat} \, . -(w \text{ has P bl})$,
                 $z \text{ is wom} \, . \, z \text{ has 96} \, . \supset z \text{ has P bl}$,
                 $z \text{ is nat} \supset z \text{ has 96}$.

For further stimulation of insights we make truth-functional simplifications of the accumulating unquantified instances. The three boil down to this information:

$$z \text{ is mo } w, \quad z \text{ is nat}, \quad z \text{ has 96},$$
$$z \text{ is wom} \supset z \text{ has P bl}, \quad -(w \text{ has P bl}).$$

What further information is there, of a platitudinous kind, that would build this out into an inconsistency? Being mother of w, z is a woman and so, by the above conditional, has Pima blood; but then so does w, her child. So the final negation above is contradicted.

Stated as generalities, the two saving platitudes are:

$$(x)(y)(x \text{ is mo } y \supset x \text{ is wom}),$$
$$(x)(y)(x \text{ is mo } y \, . \, x \text{ has P bl} \, . \supset y \text{ has P bl}).$$

Putting these with the original three premises to make five, and then deriving instances from the five in our by now familiar formal fashion until a truth-functionally inconsistent lot of unquantified instances is accumulated, will be for the reader a simple bit of bookkeeping.

EXERCISES

1.   Derive the inconsistent lot of instances as just now indicated.

2.   Paraphrasing inward step by step, put:

   Everyone who buys a ticket receives a prize

   into symbols using 'Fxy' for 'x buys y', 'Gy' for 'y is a ticket', 'Hz' for 'z is a prize', and 'Jxz' for 'x receives z'. Then show that this implies:

If there are no prizes then nobody buys a ticket.

3.   Paraphrasing inward step by step, put:

Every applicant who is admitted is examined beforehand

into symbols using 'Fx' for 'x is an applicant', 'Gxy' for 'x is admitted at time y', 'Hxz' for 'x is examined at time z', and 'Jzy' for 'z is before y'. Then show that this implies:

Every applicant who is admitted is examined sometime.

4.   Paraphrasing inward step by step, put:

There is a painting which is admired by every critic who admires any paintings at all

into symbols using 'F' for 'painting', 'G' for 'critic', and 'H' for 'admires'. Then add the further premise:

Every critic admires some painting or other

and show that these premises imply:

There is a painting which all critics admire.

5.   Assume that I like anyone who laughs at himself but detest anyone who laughs at all his friends. Show that these premises, and a platitudinous further one, together imply that if anyone laughs at all his friends then someone is no friend of himself. (Quimby)

⁵

31

COMPLETENESS

In proving the completeness of the main method we shall need what I call the *law of infinite conjunction*. It is substantially what has been known in topology as König's infinity lemma or Brouwer's fan theorem, and

---

⁵ All the rest of Part III is bracketed for omission for purposes of a short course.

elsewhere as the compactness theorem. In the form suited to our purposes, it says that *an infinite class of truth-functional schemata is consistent if each of its finite subclasses is.*

Figuratively speaking the law says that an infinite conjunction of truth-functional schemata is consistent if each finite conjunction of those schemata is separately consistent. This formulation gives the law its name, but is only figurative, since conjunctions are expressions, and expressions, literally speaking, are only finite strings of marks. The literal statement of the law speaks rather of an infinite class, as above. A class of truth-functional schemata is called consistent if there is an assignment of truth values to sentence letters that makes all the schemata in the class come out true.

To see why the law of infinite conjunction is true, assume some infinite class K of truth-functional schemata and assume that each K-conjunction (each finite conjunction of members of K) is consistent. Let us represent the sentence letters in these schemata as ‘p_1’, ‘p_2’, etc.

Definition. A given assignment of truth values to one or more sentence letters will be called *innocuous* (so far as K is concerned) if it conflicts with no K-conjunction, causing it to resolve to $\perp$ or to an inconsistency.

Definition. t_1 is $\top$ or $\perp$ according as assignment of $\top$ to ‘p_1’ is innocuous or not.

Lemma 1. Assignment of t_1 to ‘p_1’ is innocuous.

Proof. If assignment of $\top$ to ‘p_1’ conflicted with some K-conjunction and assignment of $\perp$ to ‘p_1’ conflicted with one too, then the conjunction of the two conjunctions would be an inconsistent K-conjunction outright, contrary to our hypothesis on K. So one or other of $\top$ and $\perp$ must be an innocuous assignment to ‘p_1’. Either way, t_1 is then innocuous by its definition.

Definition. t_2 is $\top$ or $\perp$ according as assignment of t_1 to ‘p_1’ and $\top$ to ‘p_2’ is innocuous or not.

Lemma 2. Assignment of t_1 to ‘p_1’ and t_2 to ‘p_2’ is innocuous.

Proof. If assignment of t_1 to ‘p_1’ and $\top$ to ‘p_2’ conflicted with some K-conjunction and assignment of t_1 to ‘p_1’ and $\perp$ to ‘p_2’ conflicted with one also, then mere assignment of t_1 to ‘p_1’ would conflict with the conjunction of the two conjunctions, contrary to Lemma 1. So either the assignment of t_1 to ‘p_1’ and $\top$ to ‘p_2’ or the assignment of t_1 to ‘p_1’ and $\perp$ to ‘p_2’ is innocuous. Either way, then, Lemma 2 holds, by virtue of the definition of t_2.

Definition. t_3 is $\top$ or $\perp$ according as assignment of t_1 to ‘p_1’, t_2 to ‘p_2’ and $\top$ to ‘p_3’ is innocuous or not.

Lemma 3. Assignment of t_1 to ‘p_1’, t_2 to ‘p_2’, and t_3 to ‘p_3’ is innocuous.

Proof from Lemma 2 like that of Lemma 2 from Lemma 1.

We have in the definitions the beginning of a series whose continuation is evident. Truth values t_1, t_2, t_3, t_4, ... are thereby defined which are designed for assignment to ‘p_1’, ‘p_2’, ‘p_3’, ‘p_4’, ... Continuing the lemmas to Lemma i, for any desired i, we show that assignment of t_1, t_2, ..., t_i to ‘p_1’, ‘p_2’, ..., ‘p_i’ is innocuous. Consider, then, any schema S in K, and take i large enough so that ‘p_1’, ‘p_2’, ..., ‘p_i’ exhaust the sentence letters in S. Then assignment of t_1, t_2, ..., t_i to those letters resolves S to $\top$ or $\perp$; but, by Lemma i, not to $\perp$; so to $\top$. But S was any member of K. So assignment of

t_1, t_2, ... to 'p_1', 'p_2', ... makes all members of K come out true. So K is consistent, Q.E.D.

I pause for a brief digression on constructiveness. Once the infinite class K has been specified, in whatever fashion, the truth values t_1, t_2, etc. are uniquely fixed by the definitions above. But this does not mean that, even knowing K, we can find out whether t_1 is T or $\bot$, nor whether t_2 is T or $\bot$, and so on. Even if we have a decision procedure for membership in K, we may have none for whether the assignment of T to 'p_1' would conflict with some or no conjunctions of members of K. On this account the proof of the law of infinite conjunction is not what is called a *constructive* proof. It proceeded by showing the existence of certain suitable objects (in this case t_1, t_2, etc.) without saying just which objects they are (e.g., whether t_1 is T or $\bot$). Much that is proved in mathematics is insusceptible to constructive proof; much else is proved constructively.

We turn now to the theorem of completeness of the main method. It says of any combination of (one or more) quantificational schemata that *either* they come out jointly true under some interpretation in a nonempty universe *or* some truth-functionally inconsistent combination of unquantified schemata can be derived from them by the familiar operations: convert to prenex form, reletter bound variables that match free ones, and then apply UI and EI, using only new instantial variables in EI.

Suppose then some premises, converted to prenex form and relettered as required. A rigid routine will be described for progressively instantiating them. It will be such as to assure that each existential line (each line beginning with an existential quantifier) gets instantiated once, and that each universal line gets instantiated with each free variable that ever turns up.

Begin with a great wave of EI: instantiate each existential line once, always using a new instantial variable. If new existential lines emerge in the process, instantiate them too. Then follow with a great wave of UI: instantiate each universal line, whether old or emergent, with each variable that is already free in the proof. (Some may be free in premises; others will have issued from EI.) Then another wave of EI, instantiating any further existential lines brought by the wave of UI. Then a double wave of UI: the old universal lines get instantiated with the newly added free variables, and any new universal lines get instantiated with all the variables now free in the proof. Then another wave of EI; then another double wave of UI; and so on.

In the special case where all premises are closed and universal, this pump-priming operation is necessary: perform UI using a new instantial variable.

Here is an example of the rigid routine. I shall prolong the alphabet of variables with help of accents: 'z''', 'z'''', etc.

PREMISES:	$(w)(\exists x)(Fz \vee Gwx)$	
	$(w)(\exists x)(y)(Gwx \, . \, -Fy)$	
INSTANCES:	$(\exists x)(Fz \vee Gzx)$	(2d wave; 1st was empty)
	$(\exists x)(y)(Gzx \, . \, -Fy)$	(2d wave)
	$Fz \vee Gzz'$	(3d wave)

$(y)(Gzz'' \,.\, -Fy)$ (3d wave)
$(\exists x)(Fz \lor Gz'x)$ (4th wave, 1st part)
$(\exists x)(Fz \lor Gz''x)$ (4th wave, 1st part)
$(\exists x)(y)(Gz'x \,.\, -Fy)$ (4th wave, 1st part)
$(\exists x)(y)(Gz''x \,.\, -Fy)$ (4th wave, 1st part)
$Gzz'' \,.\, -Fz$ (4th wave, 2d part)
$Gzz'' \,.\, -Fz'$ (4th wave, 2d part)
$Gzz'' \,.\, -Fz''$ (4th wave, 2d part)
$Fz \lor Gz'z'''$ (5th wave)
$Fz \lor Gz''z''''$ (5th wave)

and so on. The reader should examine this for conformity to the rigid routine.

Some examples terminate, with or without inconsistency, and some do not. In the unending cases, new free variables get introduced by EI without end; we may suppose them generated systematically by accentuation as above.

For each universal line, in any event, and each free variable that will ever turn up, we may be sure that that line will eventually be instantiated with that variable. For, each wave of EI, importing new variables, is followed by a wave of UI that uses them all. Moreover, each existential line is bound eventually to be instantiated once. For, under the above routine an existential line will be instantiated as soon as all unfinished business has been cleared up; and that business is limited.

Let $A_1, A_2, \ldots$ be, in an arbitrary order, all the schemata obtainable by applying predicate letters of the premises to variables that are free in the perhaps infinite suite of instances generated by the above routine. Thus in the above example $A_1, A_2, \ldots$ might be 'Fz', 'Gzz', 'Fz''', 'Gzz''', '$Gz'z$', '$Gz'z$', 'Fz'''', and so on. Whether there is an end to $A_1, A_2, \ldots$ will depend on whether there is an end to the instances; in some examples there is an end and in some not. In any event the unquantified instances will be truth functions of A_1, A_2, etc.

What was to be shown was that either the premises come out true under some interpretation in a nonempty universe or some finite set of unquantified instances is truth-functionally inconsistent. This will be shown to hold even when we consider only the instances generated under the rigid routine above.

I shall prove the theorem in this form: if each finite set of unquantified instances is truth-functionally consistent, then the premises are true under an interpretation in a nonempty universe—and a universe, in fact, of positive integers.

So suppose each finite set of unquantified instances is consistent. Then the whole set of unquantified instances is consistent, even if infinite—by the law of infinite conjunction (using A_1, A_2, etc. in place of 'p_1', 'p_2', etc. in that law). Therefore there is an assignment α of truth values $t_1, t_2, \ldots$ to $A_1, A_2, \ldots$ that makes all the unquantified instances true. Now let the universe consist of as many of the positive integers as there are free variables in the instances—all the positive integers if the variables are unending. Interpret the variables, say in order of first appearance, as naming 1, 2, etc. Then interpret each predicate letter as true of just the integers, or pairs, etc., that the assignment a declares it true of.

Thus consider again our example. An assignment a of truth values to 'Fz', 'Gzz', 'Fz'', 'Gzz'', etc., that makes all the infinitely many unquantified instances in that example come out true, is this: $\bot$ to all of 'Fz', 'Fz'', etc., and $\top$ to all of 'Gzz', 'Gzz'', '$Gz'z$', '$Gz'z'$', 'Gzz'''', '$Gz'z''$', '$Gz''z$', etc. So, taking z as 1, z' as 2, z'' as 3, etc., we proceed to interpret 'F' as true of no integers and 'G' as true of all pairs of integers. Thus this example turns out unusually trivial.

The plan is, in short, so to interpret the predicate letters as to grant A_1, A_2, etc. the respective truth values t_1, t_2, etc. In thus realizing the assignment a, the interpretation makes all the unquantified instances come out true.

But then any singly quantified instance comes out true too, if its quantifier is existential. For, we insured that each such line (indeed each existential line) gets instantiated; its instance will imply it, since '$\ldots z \ldots$' implies '$(\exists x)(\ldots x \ldots)$'; and its instance will be true, being unquantified.

Also any singly quantified instance comes out true if its quantifier is universal. For, call it '$(x)(\ldots x \ldots)$'. We insured that any such line gets instantiated with each free variable that ever turns up. But all these U-instances '$\ldots z \ldots$', '$\ldots z' \ldots$', etc. are true, being unquantified, and moreover the integers 1, 2, etc. that are the interpretations of these variables exhaust the universe; so '$\ldots x \ldots$' comes out true of everything in the universe, and thus '$(x)(\ldots x \ldots)$' comes out true.

From the truth of all unquantified instances we have been able to infer the truth of all singly quantified instances. From this result it follows similarly that all doubly quantified instances come out true. Repeating this reasoning as many times as a premise has quantifiers, we show finally that each premise comes out true.

The schemata are thus found to come out true under an interpretation in a nonempty universe. The universe was not empty thanks to the pump-priming operation, which assured at least one free variable and thus one integer.

HISTORICAL NOTE: The discovery and proof of the completeness of a proof procedure for the logic of quantification dates from work of Skolem, Herbrand, and Gödel, 1928–1930. It became explicit in Gödel. The proof procedures there concerned differ from ours, but this difference is of little moment; a completeness proof for one method of quantification theory can be adapted fairly easily to others. In the adaptation above I have depended partly on Gödel's original argument and partly on a variant due to Dreben.

EXERCISES

1. Continue the illustrative instantiations above, adding a dozen more.

2. Where the members of K are '$p_1 \supset \bar{p}_2$', '$p_2 \supset \bar{p}_3$', '$p_3 \supset \bar{p}_4$', and so on without end, determine t_1, t_2, t_3, etc.

3. The definition of t_i that was given, for each i, began: 't_i is T or ⊥ according as ...'. Try switching this to read 't_i is ⊥ or T according as ...'. Can Lemmas 1, 2, 3, etc. still be proved for these changed values? Check each step.

32
LÖWENHEIM'S THEOREM

The completeness proof serves at the same time to establish also an important older theorem due to Löwenheim (1915): *If a quantificational schema comes out true under an interpretation in a nonempty universe at all, it comes out true under an interpretation in the universe of positive integers.* The reasoning is as follows. The schema cannot engender an inconsistency under the main method, since that method is sound (Chapter 29). By the completeness proof above, then, the schema (if it is prenex) will come out true under some interpretation in a nonempty universe of positive integers. But then, by the argument in the middle of Chapter 18, it will come out true also under some interpretation in any containing universe—hence in the universe of all positive integers. Löwenheim's theorem thus holds for prenex schemata; and then it carries over to the others by virtue of their convertibility to prenex form.

There is no difference between affirming Löwenheim's theorem for single schemata and affirming it for finite classes of them, since finitely many schemata can be joined in conjunction. But its extension to infinite classes of schemata is a genuine extension, and was made by Skolem in 1920. It is the Löwenheim-Skolem theorem: *If all of a class of quantificational schemata come out true together under an interpretation in a nonempty universe, they come out true together under some interpretation in the universe of positive integers.*

The argument remains much the same as in the completeness proof. We suppose given, now, an infinite consistent class C of prenex schemata. Let C_1 be C plus all direct E-instances of its schemata, plus E-instances of those instances, and so on, with a new instantial variable for each. Let C_2 be C_1 plus instances of all its universal schemata, the instantial variables being all the free variables of C_1. Let C_3 be C_2 plus E-instances; and so on. It is just the rigid routine again, except that this ceases now to be a routine of performances and becomes rather a definition of an ascending series of infinite classes.

Finally consider all the unquantified instances that are reached in any of these classes C_1, C_2, ... If a finite lot of these were truth-functionally inconsistent, then the schemata in C that were their ultimate sources could be proved jointly inconsistent by the main method. But the whole original class C was consistent, by hypothesis. So we conclude that each finite lot of unquantified instances is truth-functionally consistent. So then are they all, by the law of infinite conjunction. From these unquantified instances, then, get A_1, A_2, . . . as in Chapter 31, and α, and the interpretation of the predicate letters in a universe of positive integers.

An importance of the Löwenheim-Skolem theorem, in its coverage of infinite classes of schemata, may be seen as follows. Consider any nonempty universe U and any assortment of predicates, all interpreted in that universe. Consider, further, the whole infinite totality of truths, known and unknown, that are expressible with help of those predicates together with the truth functions and quantification over U. Then the Löwenheim-Skolem theorem assures us that there is a reinterpretation of the predicates, in the universe of positive integers, that preserves the whole body of truths.

E.g., taking U as the universe of real numbers, we are told that the truths about real numbers can by a reinterpretation be carried over into truths about positive integers. This consequence has been viewed as paradoxical, in the light of Cantor's proof that the real numbers cannot be exhaustively correlated with integers. But the air of paradox may be dispelled by this reflection: whatever disparities between real numbers and integers may be guaranteed in those original truths about real numbers, the guarantees are themselves revised in the reinterpretation.

In a word and in general, the force of the Löwenheim-Skolem theorem is that the narrowly logical structure of a theory—the structure reflected in quantification and truth functions, in abstraction from any special predicates—is insufficient to distinguish its objects from the positive integers.

To say that a schema or class of schemata comes out true under some interpretation in the universe of positive integers is not to say that we can write out suitable interpretations of 'Fxy', 'Gx', etc. as formulas in arithmetical notation. Our proof of Löwenheim's theorem assured us that for any consistent schema there *is* a true interpretation in the universe of positive integers, but it gave us no way of finding and phrasing it. Our proof used the completeness theorem, the proof of which appealed, after all, to the nonconstructive t_1, t_2, etc. Nor does our proof assure us that the interpretation, even if it were found, could be phrased in a purely arithmetical vocabulary—the vocabulary of 'plus', 'times', 'power', 'equals', and the like.

There is, however, a constructive improvement on Löwenheim's theorem due to Hilbert and Bernays[6] that tells us all this: how to find and actually write out, for any consistent schema, a true interpretation in the universe of positive integers—and in purely arithmetical notation at that. In fact a vocabulary amounting to 'plus', 'times', 'equals', and the quantifiers and truth functions is sufficient—the vocabulary, as one says, of *elementary number theory*.

This result appears the more remarkable when we read, as we shall in the next section, that there can never be a fully general technique for establishing consistency. How then can Hilbert and Bernays give us a general rule for writing out a true interpretation of a consistent schema? What they give is a general rule for writing out, for *any* schema, an arithmetical interpretation which can be depended upon to come out true in case the schema does happen to be consistent. This strengthening cannot be managed for the Löwenheim-Skolem theorem, with its coverage of infinite classes of schemata, but it works for Löwenheim's.

The proof and even the statement of this Löwenheim-Hilbert-Bernays theorem are beyond the scope of this book. It will be worthwhile, however, to notice a certain bearing that it has on the very notion of interpretation.

In Chapters 18 and 25 there was no outright statement of what an interpretation of a predicate letter *is*, but only a statement of what it means to have given one: it means having settled what members of the universe, or what pairs, etc., the letter is to be counted as true of. One way of settling this is by supplying a predicate (Chapter 26), but there are other more discursive ways. Also there are degrees of settling, and, therewith, degrees of having interpreted; we interpret the predicate letter *insofar* as we settle what to take it as true of.

To face it, then: what is an interpretation? Is it an expression, namely the predicate that we are prepared to substitute for the predicate letter? Or is it a class, namely the class of the things that the predicate letter is taken to be true of? *Prima facie*, the choice between these two alternatives should make a material difference; for there is no assurance that each class of objects in our universe is specifiable as the extension of some predicate or open sentence in our language. It depends on our choice of universe and also on how rich a vocabulary we assume there to be at our disposal over and above our logical notations of truth functions and quantification. If the classes thus outrun the available expressions, then we may expect there to be a difference, e.g. in the concept of validity, according as we define it as truth under all interpretations in the class sense or as truth under all interpretations in the predicate sense. Moreover, it has been an accepted tenet of classical set theory from Cantor onward that the classes do outrun the expressions.

But now a remarkable thing about the Löwenheim-Hilbert-Bernays

---

[6] Volume 2, pp. 234–253. For a strengthened version, more simply proved, see Kleene, 1952, p. 394, Theorem 35.

theorem is that it cuts through all this. However extravagantly the classes may outrun the expressions, this theorem assures us that when we define validity and consistency it is indifferent whether we talk of all and some interpretations in the sense of classes or in the sense of predicates. The theorem assures us that all those extra classes will be indifferent to validity and consistency, in this sense: if a schema is fulfilled (or falsified) by some unspecifiable interpretation involving nameless classes, it is *also* fulfilled (or falsified) by some other interpretation that can be written in the notation of arithmetic.

The Löwenheim-Hilbert-Bernays theorem enables us, for that matter, simply to bypass the term 'interpretation' and talk directly of substitution. A schema is valid if all statements obtainable from it by substitution are true, and it is consistent if some of them are true. The theorem assures us that we can retreat to this homely formulation with impunity as long as the vocabulary which we suppose available for such substitutions is not so grotesquely impoverished as to be inadequate to elementary number theory.

There is philosophical comfort in the assurance that we can talk of logical validity and consistency without appealing to a limitless realm of abstract objects called classes. We feel that in talking of substitution of expressions we still keep our feet on the ground.

A related point could be made on the basis directly of the completeness theorem, even independently of Löwenheim, Hilbert, and Bernays. That theorem already furnishes formulations of validity and consistency that say nothing of classes—nor even of substitution of predicates, for that matter. A schema is valid if, from the prenex form of its negation, a truth-functional inconsistency is derivable by the main method.

33
DECISIONS AND THE UNDECIDABLE

It is indifferent to the main method whether we write our premises with or without initial existential quantifiers. This is not to be wondered at, for we noted early in Chapter 24 that initial existential quantifiers were indifferent to consistency. This indifference is reflected in the rigid routine of Chapter 31, since it provides that an existential quantifier, if not preceded by a universal, gets instantiated once for all; we never get back to it. The E-instance with its instantial variable could as well have been the premise to begin with.

It is the existential quantifiers preceded by universals that make proofs run long. Such a quantifier returns to the surface repeatedly as those universal quantifiers get repeatedly and variously instantiated. Each time it surfaces it gets instantiated again, since it initiates a line each time that is altered by having received different instantial variables through the new UI steps. Each of these EI steps, then, furnishes a new variable that is grist for further UI, and in this way we may go on grinding out instances without end. The unending example at the middle of Chapter 31 should be looked at with this in mind.

When all the premises are such that no existential quantifiers are preceded by universals, our rigid routine of Chapter 31 always grinds gratifyingly to a halt. There is just the fixed initial supply of what are in fact or in effect free variables, and these are all that get used in UI. The total number of instances allowed by the rigid routine, for each such premise, will be just the number of universal quantifiers in that premise times the number of free (or existential) variables in the premises altogether. Indeed, as already remarked, the existential quantifiers, being initial here, could have been dropped in the first place; our premises are nothing more than *pure universals*.

We can check the totality of unquantified instances for truth-functional consistency, confident of an affirmative or negative answer. We are not then in the position of just checking more and more unquantified instances for inconsistency with never a notion of when to give up; we have a decision procedure.

In Chapter 28 we saw a decision procedure for validity of pure existentials. This already, implicitly, was a decision procedure for consistency of pure universals. For a schema is inconsistent if and only if its negation is valid; and the negation of a pure universal becomes a pure existential under the rules of passage (9) and (10) of Chapter 22. What is interesting in the decision procedure for consistency that has just now emerged from the main method is only the particular form in which it has appeared, and its relation to the main method. It does suggest that in converting schemata to prenex form we should favor existential quantifiers if we expect to apply the main method, just as we did the opposite when trying for pure existentials. Actually we can effortlessly switch course when we see fit, thanks to the aforementioned rules of passage (9) and (10) of Chapter 22.

I have alluded twice to the impossibility of a decision procedure for quantificational schemata generally. The proof, due to Church and Turing in 1936, exceeds the scope of this book,[7] but some remarks are called for regarding its significance. It does not preclude mechanical proof procedures; the rigid routine of Chapter 31 is one. Any proof procedure can

---

[7] For a fairly readable rendering see my *Selected Logic Papers*, pp. 212–219.

in principle be got down to a mechanical routine in at least this silly way: just scan all the single typographical characters admissible in the proof procedure in question, then all possible pairs of them, then all strings of three, and so on until you get to the proof. The usual dependence on luck and strategy in finding proofs is merely a price paid for speed: for anticipating, by minutes or weeks, what a mechanical routine would eventually yield.

Where a complete proof procedure differs from a decision procedure, then, is not in being less mechanical. The difference is just that the proof procedure is not a yes-or-no affair; it does not deliver negative answers. Failure to reach an inconsistency proof after a large number of steps, however systematically and mechanically programmed, does not show consistency. A proof procedure is only half of a decision procedure.

When there is both a proof procedure and a disproof procedure (for validity or consistency or any other property), there is also a decision procedure.[8] The two halves can be joined as follows. First we would mechanize both the proof procedure and the disproof procedure, in the silly way if not otherwise. Then, to decide whether a formula had the property in question (validity or consistency or whatever), we would set one man or machine in quest of a proof and another in quest of a disproof and await the eventual answer from one of them.

In particular, then, knowing as we do from Chapter 31 that there is a complete procedure for disproving the consistency of a quantificational schema, and from Church and Turing that there is no decision procedure, we conclude that *there is no complete procedure for proving quantificational schemata consistent.* Commonly we prove a schema consistent by producing a true interpretation; and this is quite the right way, as long as we can find truths to the purpose and show them true. So what we have to recognize is that no sound proof procedure can be so strong as to afford proofs of statements illustrative of all consistent quantificational schemata.

Meanwhile there is an obvious procedure for deciding whether a schema comes out true under all or some or no interpretations in a universe of given finite size n. Just transcribe the universal and existential quantifications as n-fold conjunctions and alterations, as noted in Chapter 25, and then check for truth-functional validity and consistency. It follows that there is a complete procedure (no longer a decision procedure, but still a proof procedure) for showing that a schema is *finitely consistent*—i.e., that it comes out true under at least one interpretation in at least one nonempty finite universe. This proof procedure consists simply in alleging an adequate size n of universe, and leaving the reader to check it by the truth-functional method.

Thus an important contrast emerges between finite and infinite universes: there is a complete proof procedure for finite consistency, but none for consistency. The schemata that are consistent but not finitely so are the stubborn kind. They may be called *infinity schemata.* An easily recognizable example is:

---

[8] This observation is due to Kleene, 1943. Or see Kleene, 1952, p. 284, Theorem VIc.

(1) $(x)[-Fxx \, . \, (y)(z)(Fxy \, . \, Fyz \, . \supset \, Fxz) \, . \, (\exists w)Fxw]$.

It requires an infinite universe. For, take anything x_1. By the last part of (1) we have Fx_1x_2 for some x_2; also Fx_2x_3 for some x_3; and so on without end. Then, by the transitivity affirmed in the middle of (1), we get also Fx_1x_3, Fx_1x_4, Fx_2x_4, Fx_1x_5, and so on. Moreover, by the '$-Fxx$' in (1), these things x_1, x_2, x_3, ... are all distinct. Thus (1) is not finitely consistent. Yet it is consistent; it comes out true in the universe of integers when 'F' is interpreted as '$<$'.

Here is another infinity schema, briefer but less readily recognized:

$$(x)(\exists y)(z)(Fxy \, . \, -Fxx \, . \, Fyz \supset Fxz).$$

From a 1933 paper by Gödel it is known that this prefix '$(x)(\exists y)(z)$' is the simplest that a prenex infinity schema can have.

There is no complete proof procedure for showing schemata to be infinity schemata. For, if there were, we could add it to our complete proof procedure for finite consistency, and get a complete proof procedure for consistency.

The infinity schemata constitute a stubborn class which is the common part AB of two stubborn classes: A, the class of all consistent schemata, and B, the class of all finitely inconsistent schemata (schemata true under no interpretations in nonempty finite universes). We have observed that there is no complete proof procedure for membership either in A or in AB. The same can be said of B; this follows from a theorem of Trachtenbrot, according to which there is no complete proof procedure for finite validity.

Taken in combination with the Löwenheim-Hilbert-Bernays theorem (Chapter 32), the impossibility of a complete proof procedure for A has a startling further consequence: Gödel's theorem of the impossibility of a complete proof procedure for elementary number theory. If we could prove each true sentence of elementary number theory, then we could prove the consistency of each consistent quantificational schema by proving a truth of elementary number theory illustrative of that schema.

This is not the historical route to Gödel's theorem. I have appealed here to the impossibility of a complete proof procedure for consistency. This I inferred from the Church-Turing theorem that there is no decision procedure for quantificational validity. But the proof of the Church-Turing theorem, omitted here, uses the essential trick of Gödel's proof of his own theorem; and Gödel's came first, in 1931.

Gödel's way was to argue directly to the incompletability of elementary number theory, by showing how, for any given proof procedure P for elementary number theory, a statement S_P of elementary number theory can be constructed which will be true if and only if it is not provable by the procedure P. Either S_P is provable, in which case it is false and so the general proof procedure P is discredited, or else S_P is true and not provable, in which case the proof procedure P is incomplete.

In broadest outlines, Gödel's construction of S_P is as follows. It is easy to assign integers in a systematic way to all the finite strings, however long, of signs of a given alphabet. If the alphabet has just nine signs, we can assign them the integers from 1 to 9 and then we can get the integer for any string of signs by concatenating the corresponding digits into a long numeral. If the alphabet has more than nine signs, we can easily adapt this method or choose another. Suppose this done for the notation of elementary number theory. Thus each sentence in that notation has its so-called *Gödel number*. Gödel then shows that, given P, it is possible within the notation of elementary number theory to formulate an open sentence, '...x...' say, which is true of any number x if and only if x is the Gödel number of a statement provable by P. If we put for 'x' in '$-$(...x...)' the actual numeral designating some particular number n, clearly the resulting statement, schematically '$-$(...n...)', will be true if and only if that chosen n is not the Gödel number of a statement provable by P. But Gödel shows that n can be so chosen as to turn out to be the Gödel number of a statement equivalent to '$-$(...n...)' itself. The statement produced by that sly choice of n is the sought S_P, true if and only if not provable by P.[9]

When we are concerned with complete proof procedures and decision procedures for the truth of statements, as in elementary number theory, rather than for properties of schemata, the difference between the two disappears—at any rate if our vocabulary includes negation. For, a proof procedure for the truth of statements carries with it a disproof procedure: you disprove a statement by proving its negation. So, by the zigzag argument lately attributed to Kleene, a complete proof procedure for the truth of statements assures a decision procedure. Still a complete proof procedure for validity or consistency or inconsistency of schemata remains far short of a decision procedure, simply because a schema can be consistent without its negation's being inconsistent, and a schema can fail of validity without its negation's being valid.

Thus, though the impossibility of a complete proof procedure for elementary number theory comes as a shock, the impossibility of a decision procedure for elementary number theory says as much. This is a curious point, since the impossibility of a decision procedure seems less surprising than the other. Various unsolved problems of long standing, after all—notably the celebrated one of Fermat—can be formulated within the notation of elementary number theory, and a decision procedure for that domain would have made a clean sweep of them all.

Presburger and Skolem have shown that when elementary number theory is further limited to the extent of dropping multiplication and keeping just addition, or vice versa, the resulting theory does admit of a decision procedure. What is more surprising, Tarski has shown that the elementary algebra of real numbers likewise admits of a decision procedure. The notation of this elementary algebra is precisely the same as that de-

---

[9] Fuller details of Gödel's argument may be found not only in his 1931 paper but also in his 1934 English presentation, and in Carnap's *Logical Syntax* (esp. pp. 129–134), and in Chapter 7 of my *Mathematical Logic*.

scribed above for elementary number theory, including both addition and multiplication; the only difference is that the variables are construed now as referring to real numbers generally rather than just to whole ones. Despite the seemingly greater complexity of its subject matter, elementary algebra is completable and mechanically decidable while elementary number theory is not.

Now if in view of Gödel's result our knowledge about number is subject to unexpected limitations, the very opposite is true of our knowledge about such knowledge. One of the few things more surprising than the incompletability of elementary number theory is the fact that such incompletability can actually have become known to us. Gödel's result brings a new branch of mathematical theory to maturity, a branch known as "metamathematics" or proof theory, whose subject matter is mathematical theory itself.

Much remains to be discovered regarding the limits of completable theories, and the essential structural features which set such theories apart from those which are incompletable. But the reader who would acquire the key concepts and techniques of this crucial new field of study, metamathematics or the theory of proof, must look beyond the bounds of this logic book. See Tarski, *Undecidable Theories;* Hilbert and Bernays; Kleene; Smullyan; Davis; Rogers; Shoenfield.

EXERCISES

1. Can there be a complete disproof procedure for elementary number theory? Or a decision procedure adequate to all but a finite number of the statements in the notation of elementary number theory? Justify your answers.

2. From Trachtenbrot's theorem how does it follow that there can be no complete proof procedure for membership in *B*?

34
FUNCTIONAL NORMAL FORMS

Getting all existential quantifiers out in front has, we saw, two advantages under our main method: the minor advantage that we can just forget those quantifiers, and the major advantage that the proof procedure becomes a decision procedure. It also has a third advantage: the remaining quantifiers, being uniformly universal, can be instantiated simultaneously rather than in sequence.

Now there is a devious device that enables us to enjoy this third benefit even when existential quantifiers can not all be got to the front and a decision procedure is not to be hoped for. To see the fundamental idea, consider '$(x)(\exists y)Fxy$'. It says that for any object x there is an object y, possibly different for different choices of x, such that Fxy. Roughly speaking therefore it says there is a *function*—a way of picking, for each object x, a dependent object y_x—such that $(x)Fxy_x$. The gain in this rephrasing is that our new tacit existential quantifier—'there is a function'—comes before '(x)' instead of after it as '$(\exists y)$' did. Coming thus initially, it can be left tacit in inconsistency proofs.

Such is the thought behind what I call the *functional normal form* of a prenex quantificational schema. Delete all existential quantifiers and attach, to the recurrences of the variable of each such quantifier, subscripts listing the variables of all the universal quantifiers that preceded that existential quantifier. Thus the functional normal form of '$(x)(\exists y)Fxy$' is '$(x)Fxy_x$'. The functional normal form of:

$$(\exists x)(y)(z)(\exists w)(u)(\exists v)Fxyzwuv$$

is:

$$(y)(z)(u)Fxyzw_{yz}uv_{yzu}.$$

The account of this notation in terms of the existence of functions is not an account to rest with, as in any sense a proof of equivalence of a schema to its functional normal form. The account slurred over points of set theory that I shall not go into—the nature and existence of functions and, what is more serious, something known as the axiom of choice. None of this is needed to show the soundness or completeness of the proof procedure that I shall present in terms of functional normal forms; these things will be brought out rather by a direct collation of this proof procedure to the main method. The point of the talk of functions was just to give a feeling for the notation.

We turn now to illustration and closer examination of the method of proving inconsistency by functional normal forms. Justification will come afterward.

Let us go back to the premises (1)–(3) on page 162. A rule of the method of functional normal forms is that before converting premises to functional normal form we must reletter all existential quantifiers so that their variables are distinct from one another and from variables that are free in any premise. The premises (1)–(3) are already in order on this score. Putting them into functional normal form and deriving instances purely by UI, we get this new inconsistency proof:

PREMISES: $(y)Fuy,$

$(x)(y) - (Fv_xy . Fyx),$

$(x)(y)(Fxy \supset : - Fxw_{xy} . Fw_{xy}y .\lor. Fyw_{xy} . Fw_{xy}x).$

INSTANCES: $Fuv_u,$

$Fuv_u \supset : - Fuw_{uv_u} . Fw_{uv_u}v_u .\lor. Fv_uw_{uv_u} . Fw_{uv_u}u,$

$Fuw_{uv_u},$

$- (Fv_uw_{uv_u} . Fw_{uv_u}u).$

These four instances, like the four unquantified instances (7), (10), (11), and (12) in the rendering on page 162, are truth-functionally inconsistent. But it is characteristic of the method of functional normal forms that the only instances that appear at all are unquantified. The instances come directly from the premises by multiple UI, and it is important to note that the universal variables are instantiated in subscript positions as well as elsewhere. The expressions instantiating them are no longer just simple variables, but any expressions belonging to what I call the *lexicon* of the premises. To get the lexicon we look to the premises in functional normal form and pick out, first, the simple free variables—in this case just 'u'. They belong to the lexicon. Then we take also the function letters, i.e., the letters that carry subscripts; each function letter, taken together with any members of the lexicon in place of its subscripts, constitutes a member in turn of the lexicon. Thus the lexicon of the premises above comprises 'u', 'v_u', 'w_{uu}', 'v_{v_u}', 'w_{v_uu}', 'w_{uv_u}', '$w_{v_uv_u}$', '$v_{w_{uu}}$', and so on. In proving inconsistency there is never any need to instantiate with anything but lexicon.

This method of inconsistency proof is an extension of one that was presented by Skolem in 1928. Essentially the difference is just that his served only to prove the inconsistency of a single prenex premise rather than a combination of them.

The method is advantageous not merely in allowing us to perform several UI steps at once. A more important advantage is, in a mountaineering metaphor, that it eliminates the need of advance bases. Under the main method we would move perhaps from a premise '$(x)(\exists y)(z)Fxyz$' to '$(\exists y)(z)Fvyz$' to '$(z)Fvwz$' to '$Fvwv$', recording and saving the two intermediate lines, and then later we might recur to one of these intermediate lines, '$(z)Fvwz$', to get to '$Fvww$'. Under the method of functional normal forms, on the other hand, we pass from the premise direct to '$Fvwv$' and again direct to '$Fvww$' in two independent and uninterrupted sorties, with no need of the branching point '$(z)Fvwz$' as a way station. Under this method the premise has really become '$(x)(z)Fxy_xz$', of course, and the two end results '$Fvwv$' and '$Fvww$' have become, strictly speaking, 'Fvy_vv' and 'Fvy_vy_v'.

To relate this method to the main method, take the main method in the relaxed form in which it was last contemplated, viz., with initial existential quantifiers dropped from all premises. The only existential quantifiers in the premises are those buried under universal quantifiers. Now consider the route, according to the main method, from one of these premises—say again '$(x)(\exists y)(z)Fxyz$'—to each of its unquantified instances. Why can we not cover each such route in one leap? Simply because the choice of instantial variables for the EI step is not free. Whenever the '(x)' is instantiated anew, to yield a novel intermediate line, the ensuing EI step demands a fresh variable. When on the other hand the routes from the premises to two unquantified instances instantiate '(x)' identically but diverge ultimately on '(z)', we are free to instantiate '$(\exists y)$' identically; under the rigid routine of Chapter 31, indeed, we would be bound to. The main method handles these dependences by establishing an advance base or way station like '$(z)Fvwz$', we noted, from which to proceed now to '$Fvwv$' and now to '$Fvww$'. The alternative, instant instantiation, requires automatic bookkeeping, calculated to allow two unquantified instances of '$(x)(\exists y)(z)Fxyz$' to have any variables in place of 'x' and 'z', but to make them agree or disagree on the variable for 'y' according as they agree or disagree on that for 'x'. (I put the matter strongly because I am back on the rigid routine.) The functional normal form provides the bookkeeping device: a complex existential "variable", in effect, namely 'y_x', which will automatically instantiate identically under identical instantiations of the preceding quantifier '(x)' and differently under different instantiations of '(x)'.

Such, then, without talk of functions, is the role of the subscripts on the existential variables. It becomes clear, despite the specificity of the example above, that the method of functional normal forms is just a quick way of doing the work that is done by the main method under the rigid routine.

There is a variant method of functional normal forms, due to Dreben, that does not depend on prenex form. Schemata need little preparation. Conditionals and biconditionals need to be expanded into terms of alternation, conjunction, and negation if their components contain quantifiers, but not otherwise. Negation signs need to be driven inward by DeMorgan's laws and the rules of passage of negation ((9) and (10) of Chapter 22), but only until no quantifier appears in a negated schema. In short, what is required is that quantifiers be overlain only by conjunction, alternation, and quantifiers. Also, as in the previous method of functional normal forms, the existential quantifiers must be relettered so that their variables are distinct from the free variables and from one another.

Thus suppose we want to prove these premises inconsistent:

(1) $(\exists x)(y)Fxy,$

(2) $-(\exists x)(z)(\exists y)(Fzy \cdot Fyx),$

(3) $(x)(y)[Fxy \supset . (z)(Fzy \supset Fxz) \supset (\exists z)(Fyz \cdot Fzx)].$

We prepare (2) by using the rules of passage to drive the negation sign inward:

$$(x)(\exists z)(y) - (Fzy \cdot Fyx).$$

We prepare (3) by translating the outer two conditional signs and then driving a resulting negation sign inward.

$$(x)(y)[-Fxy \lor (\exists z)-(Fzy \supset Fxz) \lor (\exists z)(Fyz . Fzx)].$$

We prepare (1)–(3) further by relettering the existential quantifiers for diversity. For clarity I carry this relettering a little farther than is strictly necessary.

$$(\exists u)(y)Fuy,$$
$$(x)(\exists v)(y)-(Fvy . Fyx),$$
$$(x)(y)[-Fxy \lor (\exists w)-(Fwy \supset Fxw) \lor (\exists t)(Fyt . Ftx)].$$

The reader may have begun to recognize that these are equivalent to the premises (1)–(3) of page 162, which were used again in the present chapter to illustrate the first method of functional normal forms. But let us go ahead now with the new method. We form the functional normal forms again, just as before.

(4) $(y)Fuy,$
(5) $(x)(y)-(Fv_xy . Fyx),$
(6) $(x)(y)[-Fxy \lor -(Fw_{xy}y \supset Fxw_{xy}) \lor. Fyt_{xy} . Ft_{xy}x].$

This time the lexicon comprises 'u', 'v_u', 'w_{uu}', 't_{uu}', 'v_{v_u}', and so on. Inconsistent instances are forthcoming.

This bypassing of the prenex form has an effect on the rule for forming the functional normal form, though it did not happen to show itself in the above example. The subscripts on an existential variable should list just the variables of the universal quantifiers whose scopes contained that existential quantifier; and these need not be all the preceding universal quantifiers, when the schema is not prenex. E.g., the schema:

(7) $(x)(\exists y)Fxy . (z)(\exists w)Gzw$

has the functional normal form '$(x)Fxy_x . (z)Gzw_z$'; the occurrence of '(x)' off to the left does not impose a subscript 'x' on the 'w', because the scope of '(x)' stops short of there.

If we had begun by turning (7) into prenex form so as to subject it to the previous method of functional normal forms, we should have had to settle for one or other of:

$$(x)(\exists y)(z)(\exists w)(Fxy . Gzw), \qquad (z)(\exists w)(x)(\exists y)(Fxy . Gzw),$$

not to mention less prudent choices such as:

$$(x)(z)(\exists y)(\exists w)(Fxy . Gzw).$$

This would mean ending up with one or other of the functional normal forms:

$$(x)(z)(Fxy_x \cdot Gzw_{xz}), \qquad (z)(x)(Fxy_{zx} \cdot Gzw_z).$$

Either way we get a double subscript, as we did not when we proceeded directly from (7) in Dreben's way. This brings out an advantage of Dreben's method additional to the advantage of sparing us the excursion into prenex form: it sometimes issues in simpler subscripts, thereby simplifying the eventual search for inconsistent instances.

Justification of this method will be omitted here.

EXERCISES

1. Find inconsistent instances of (4)–(6).

2. By way of further exercises in generous number, repeat the examples and exercises of Chapters 28 and 30 by the methods of functional normal forms.

35

HERBRAND'S METHOD

The main method and the methods of functional normal forms were methods of proving inconsistency. Now validity is truth under all interpretations, as inconsistency is falsity under all interpretations. Validity and inconsistency are related as truth and falsity, hence by duality (Chapter 12). Alternation is similarly related to conjunction, and existential quantification to universal. Each of these inconsistency methods, then, can be converted to a validity method by duality. Thus take again the main method. The formal moves undergo little change. UI and EI switch their roles; however, since both were present and both remain present, this only means transferring to UI the requirement that the instantial variable be new. But the goal changes radically; what is wanted now of an accumulation of unquantified instances is not that their conjunction be truth-functionally inconsistent, but that their alternation be truth-functionally

valid. What we prove by achieving this goal, moreover, is not that the conjunction of the premises was inconsistent, but that their alternation was
valid.

Thus consider, to begin with, a trivial inconsistency proof by the main
method. The top two lines are premises and the succeeding four are
instances.

$$(\exists x)(y)Fxy,$$
$$(\exists y)(x) - Fxy,$$
$$(y)Fzy,$$
$$(x) - Fxw,$$
$$Fzw,$$
$$- Fzw.$$

This proves the inconsistency of the conjunction:

$$(\exists x)(y)Fxy \; . \; (\exists y)(x) - Fxy.$$

Now the validity of the alternation:

$$(x)(\exists y)Fxy \; \lor \; (y)(\exists x) - Fxy$$

has the following proof, the dual of the inconsistency proof above.

$$(x)(\exists y)Fxy,$$
$$(y)(\exists x) - Fxy,$$
$$(\exists y)Fzy,$$
$$(\exists x) - Fxw,$$
$$Fzw,$$
$$- Fzw.$$

It is the validity of the alternation '$Fzw \lor - Fzw$' of these last two instances,
not the inconsistency of their conjunction, that attests to the validity of
the alternation of the two top schemata.

This same latter proof might be thought to double as a proof of the
inconsistency of the conjunction of its top schemata by the main method.
This would be wrong; the final step of EI violates the inconsistency method
in using an old instantial variable 'z'. Moreover the top schemata are in
fact consistent; interpret 'Fxy' as '$x = y$' and they both become true.

From the point of view of implication, the inconsistency proofs and
the validity proofs face opposite ways. In the inconsistency proofs, implication tended downward. UI was implicative. EI was not, and that was
what complicated the soundness argument. In the validity proofs, implication tends upward. EI is what is implicative here, but upward. The reason
the last step of the validity proof above does no harm, despite the staleness
of the 'z', is simply that '$- Fzw$' implies '$(\exists x) - Fxw$'. If we were inde-

pendently to establish the soundness of this proof procedure for validity—
which we could do by precisely arguing the soundness proof in Chapter 29
of the main method, duality for duality—we would find that what complicates this argument is that the UI of this method is not implicative
upward. And now it is UI, not EI, that has to be hedged by the fresh-
variable requirement in order that the justification be made to go through.

For a more substantial example let us form the dual of the inconsistency
proof (1)–(12) of Chapter 29. As an aid to writing the dual we think of the
'⊃' in that proof as 'v' with the antecedent negated. The duals of the old
premises will be called "alternative theses," since they are now schemata
whose alternation is to be proved valid.

ALTERNATIVE	(1)	$(u)(\exists y)Fuy,$	
THESES:	(2)	$(\exists x)(v)(\exists y) - (Fvy \vee Fyx),$	
	(3)	$(\exists x)(\exists y)(w)(-Fxy . -Fxw \vee Fwy . Fyw \vee Fwx).$	
INSTANCES:	(4)	$(\exists y)Fzy$	[of (1)],
	(5)	$(v)(\exists y) - (Fvy \vee Fyz)$	[of (2)],
	(6)	$(\exists y) - (Fty \vee Fyz)$	[of (5)],
	(7)	Fzt	[of (4)],
	(8)	$(\exists y)(w)(-Fzy . -Fzw \vee Fwy . Fyw \vee Fwz)$	[of (3)],
	(9)	$(w)(-Fzt . -Fzw \vee Fwt . Ftw \vee Fwz)$	[of (8)],
	(10)	$-Fzt . -Fzs \vee Fst . Fts \vee Fsz$	[of (9)],
	(11)	Fzs	[of (4)],
	(12)	$-(Fts \vee Fsz)$	[of (6)].

The alternation of (7), (10), (11), and (12) is found by truth-value analysis
to be valid, and this is meant to prove that the alternation of (1), (2), and
(3) is valid.

Present methods aside, proofs of validity are intuitively preferable to
proofs of inconsistency. Truth is our game, and direct aim is more straightforward than snaring and trapping. However, we see from the examples
above that the proof of inconsistency proceeds more naturally under the
main method than that of validity under the present method. There are
two reasons for this. One is that a downward-trending implication, in
which the implying schema is given and the implied one is sought, comes
more easily than the opposite. The other reason is that we find it much
more natural to view an accumulating lot of instances conjunctively than
in alternation.

This difference in naturalness on the part of the two methods can be
partly offset by adjusting the notation. We can turn the validity proofs
upside down and render the alternations explicit, *dilemma* fashion.

$$Fzw \vee -Fzw,$$
$$(\exists y)Fzy \vee (\exists x) - Fxw,$$
$$(x)(\exists y)Fxy \vee (y)(\exists x) - Fxy.$$

This is indeed natural. We set down, to begin with, an unquantified schema
that is palpably truth-functionally valid. Then we derive further lines by

operating on the clauses of the alternation. Now that the proof is turned over, these operations are the inverses of UI and EI; hence UG and EG, which is to say *universal* and *existential generalization*. Instead of producing instances from their generics (Chapter 29), they lead from instances to their generics. More specifically they are *clausal* UG and EG, operating as they do on clauses of the new alternations and not just on the whole new lines.

Let us try a similar inversion and transformation of the proof (1)–(12). Our top line now will be the valid alternation of (7), (10), (11), and (12). The next line will be the corresponding alternation of the generics of (7), (10), (11), and (12), namely, (4), (9), (4), and (6). Now here we see a first irregularity to adjust: drop the duplicate clause (4) from the alternation, keeping just the alternation of (4), (9), and (6). The next line will be the alternation of (1), (8), and (5), these being the generics of (4), (9), and (6). The final line will be the alternation of (1) again (there being no higher to go), and (3) (as generic of (8)), and (2) (as generic of (5)). This is the alternation whose validity was to be proved. The reader is advised to write out the above proof explicitly in full schemata, using wide paper. (∗)

This procedure starts with a truth-functionally valid line and derives further valid lines progressively by clausal UG, clausal EG, and, we have seen, a trivial third operation: deletion of duplicate clauses. This third operation accomplishes what, before inversion, had been accomplished by using one line as source of more than one instance. The change in style is caused by our having joined up the instances in alternation.

The proof procedure to which we are led by these rearrangements is one that dates from Herbrand. It exhibits an axiomatic style comparable to what we saw in Chapter 13. Our axiom schemata now, unlike those others, are infinite in number: all the truth-functionally valid schemata qualify outright. This is all right; infinitude of axioms is manageable as long as we have a way of deciding whether a schema is an axiom, and this we have in truth-value analysis. Our rules of inference now are three in number; no longer modus ponens and substitution, but rather clausal UG, clausal EG, and deletion of duplicates.

The two proofs by which we have thus far illustrated the Herbrand method have been needlessly compact, what with the simultaneous generalization of coordinate clauses. The axiomatic structure of the procedure emerges better if we take the steps one at a time. The proof of:

$$(x)(\exists y)Fxy \lor (y)(\exists x)-Fxy,$$

which was represented in three lines above, would then appear rather thus:

$$Fzw \lor -Fzw,$$
$$(\exists y)Fzy \lor -Fzw,$$
$$(\exists y)Fzy \lor (\exists x)-Fxw,$$
$$(x)(\exists y)Fxy \lor (\exists x)-Fxw,$$
$$(x)(\exists y)Fxy \lor (y)(\exists x)-Fxy.$$

Each line proceeds from its predecessor by a step of clausal UG or EG. The reader would do well to write out the proof of the alternation of (1), (2), and (3) now in this style of one step at a time. There will be eleven long lines altogether, beginning with the truth-functionally valid axiom consisting of (7), (10), (11), and (12). Each succeeding line will proceed from its predecessor by UG or EG or—in one case—deletion of a duplicate. (†)

Let us formulate clausal UG explicitly. We look back to the UI which it inverts. That was UI in the form suited to the style of validity proof with which this chapter began. It was subject to the requirement that the instantial variable be new—i.e., free nowhere hitherto. Now that we have inverted the proof, this newness requirement gives way to an obsolescence requirement: the instantial variable must not still be free anywhere in the derived line.

Indeed, since we now join the old short lines into long ones by alternation, we must not let the instantial variable be free even in the other clauses of alternation within its own line. However, this requirement, that the variable not be free in a coordinate clause, turns out to be assured already by the requirement that it not be free in the derived line. (It is assured as long as we set out our proofs explicitly in the style of one step at a time.) For, if the variable were free in a coordinate clause, then it would be free in the next line too, since those clauses come down.

Clausal UG, then, formulated directly, is just this: *if a line is an alternation of one or more clauses, supplant any of them by a universal quantification whereof it is an instance, provided that the instantial variable is not free in the line thus derived.* It must be stressed that the clauses concerned are strictly clauses of alternation.

It may seem that, symmetrically with the original requirement that the instantial variable be new, we should now require that it be free nowhere in any future lines. In fact this precaution is idle, as long as the variable is not free in the immediately derived line. For our three rules of inference provide no way of introducing a free variable, or of freeing a variable.

Clausal EG is simpler: *if a line is an alternation of one or more clauses, supplant any of them by an existential quantification whereof it is an instance.* There is no restriction on the instantial variable here, as there was none on that of EI in the style of validity proof at the beginning of the chapter.

What is required of a rule of inference in an axiomatic system of valid schemata is not that it be implicative, but just that it transmit validity: that it lead from valid schemata to none but valid schemata. Implicativity is one way of meeting this requirement; schemata implied by valid schemata are indeed valid. But a rule of inference can transmit validity without being implicative. An example is substitution. It is not implicative; '$p \vee qr$' yields '$q \vee \bar{r}s$' by substitution, but does not imply it. What matters is just that when we start with a valid schema, e.g. '$p \vee \bar{p} \vee q$', substitution gives only valid schemata.

Now the systems in Chapter 13 had one rule of inference that was implicative, namely modus ponens, and one that was not, namely substitution. The axiom system newly arrived at has two rules of inference that are implicative and one that is not. Obviously the rule of deletion of duplicates is implicative. Also clausal EG is implicative. For, to begin with, the instance clause implies its generalization; '*Fy*' implies '$(\exists x)Fx$'. Further, if a clause *A* implies a clause *B* then the alternation of *A* with any further material *C* implies the alternation of *B* with *C*; this is evident on truth-functional grounds.

Clausal UG is not implicative, but it transmits validity. This is essentially just the fact, familiar from Chapter 24, that universal quantifications of valid schemata are valid. Further considerations are a relettering and a rule of passage, (4) of page 119. Let us sort out these considerations.

If to a valid schema we apply a universal quantifier governing the whole line, the result is again valid; that is the familiar fact from Chapter 24. Our present UG is only clausal, but it results in a line that is equivalent to the line that could be got by quantifying the whole; this we see from the rule of passage (4) of page 119. Thus look back to the five-line validity proof last displayed. The fourth line comes from the third by clausal UG. The reasoning behind the transmission of validity is that, having found the third line valid, we know that its quantification:

$$(z)[(\exists y)Fzy \vee (\exists x)-Fxw]$$

is valid; and this reduces, by the rule of passage, to:

$$(z)(\exists y)Fzy \vee (\exists x)-Fxw,$$

which is the same as the fourth line except for an inconsequential relettering. The step of clausal UG that leads from this fourth line to the last line admits of similar analysis.

The appeal to the rule of passage requires that the variable that we are generalizing not be free in other clauses of the alternation. But we saw that this assurance is provided indirectly by the proviso regarding instantial variables that was incorporated into the formulation of clausal UG.

What now of the inconsequential relettering noted above? Clausal UG allows it; but how does the formulation of clausal UG keep the lettering inconsequential? To reletter '*z*' in '$(z)Gzw$' as '*w*', e.g., would give '$(w)Gww$' and thus change not just the notation but the structure. It is prevented as follows. What in our present analysis of clausal UG we are picturing as a step first of generalization from '*Gzw*' to '$(z)Gzw$', and then of (faulty) relettering to '$(w)Gww$', would have been seen in terms of clausal UG rather as a single step changing the clause '*Gzw*' to '$(w)Gww$'; and this step violates clausal UG simply because '*Gzw*' is not an instance of '$(w)Gww$'. Granted, '*Gww*' is an instance of '$(z)Gzw$'; but not '*Gzw*' of '$(w)Gww$'.

Might we then use clausal UG to supplant '*Gww*' somewhere by '$(z)Gzw$'? No, not that either—for a different reason. The instantial variable, '*w*' here, would continue free in the '$(z)Gzw$' of the derived line, in violation of the proviso on instantial variables in the formulation of clausal UG.

First, in this chapter, we got a proof procedure for validity from our main method for inconsistency, by duality considerations. Its soundness was provable by an argument dual to that for the soundness of the main method. Then we gave this validity method an axiomatic form, indeed Herbrand's, by inverting it and writing in the alternation signs. Finally, for good measure, we have just seen a direct proof of the soundness of the method thus reformulated. Just as the main method was a method of proving the joint inconsistency of one or more prenex schemata, so this one is a method of proving the validity of an alternation of one or more prenex schemata.

To simplify the formulation and justification of this method I switched to the style, a few pages back, of one step at a time. This imposes the labor, needless in practice, of rewriting the whole long line for each change of a single clause. In practice we would retreat of course to our intermediate condensed style, that of operating on clauses side by side.

It seems, even so, that inconsistency proofs are swifter and easier still—despite the seeming perversity of orientation. There we can leave the premises short and numerous, and the instances likewise, and we can consider them in groups without straining the imagination, all because the relevance of the grouping is conjunctional rather than alternational.

EXERCISES

1. See (∗) and (†). Turn your paper so as to allow long lines.

2. Do examples and exercises from Chapter 28 by Herbrand's method. How is this method a direct extension of that of Chapter 28?

36
OTHER METHODS FOR VALIDITY

We saw how to move from the main method to a validity method by duality, and thence to Herbrand's by inverting the proofs and linking up its lines in alternation. Similar transformations can be performed on the method of functional normal forms (Chapter 34).

Let us begin by simply taking the dual of that method. Universal and existential quantification switch roles. Thus, in forming the functional normal form for validity proofs, we drop universal quantifiers rather than existential ones; and to the recurrences of their variables we attach sub-scripts recording the variables of prior existential quantifiers. In lieu of premises now we have alternative theses; and their alternation is proved valid by instantiating the existential quantifications by means of lexicon until instances have been accumulated whose alternation is truth-func-tionally valid.

We may illustrate this method by proving, again, the validity of the alternation of (1)–(3) of the preceding chapter. The proof is simply the dual of the inconsistency proof at the top of page 187, and begins with the new functional normal forms.

ALTERNATIVE	(1)	$(\exists y)Fuy$,
THESES:	(2)	$(\exists x)(\exists y)-(Fv_xy \lor Fyx)$,
	(3)	$(\exists x)(\exists y)(-Fxy \, . \, -Fxw_{xy} \lor Fw_{xy}y \, . \, Fyw_{xy} \lor Fw_{xy}x)$.
INSTANCES:	(4)	Fuv_u,
	(5)	$-Fuv_u \, . \, -Fuw_{uv_u}v_u \lor Fw_{uv_u}v_u \, . \, Fv_uw_{uv_u} \lor Fw_{uv_u}u$,
	(6)	Fuw_{uv_u},
	(7)	$-(Fv_uw_{uv_u} \lor Fw_{uv_u}u)$.

The alternation of (4)–(7) can be seen to be truth-functionally valid.

If we prefer to invert this validity proof and make the alternations explicit, we can make two long lines suffice. Our top line becomes the alternation of (4)–(7), generously spaced so as to facilitate our writing doubly generalized clauses underneath. Then our second line is the alterna-tion of (1), (3), (1) again, and (2); each of these clauses stands beneath the instance that it generalizes. Then we cross out the repetition of (1). What remains, the alternation of (1)–(3), amounts to a functional normal form of the alternation of quantificational schemata whose validity was to be proved (viz. that of (1)–(3) of Chapter 35). (∗)

Simultaneous multiple EG has enabled us to get this all at once. This advantage of functional normal forms in validity proofs corresponds to the advantage of them that we noted in inconsistency proofs (Chapter 34), viz. that we could plunge directly to unquantified instances by multiple UI.

Let us look next to Dreben's method of functional normal forms without prenexing. This time I shall go directly to the final method which comes of that one by dualizing, inverting, and marking alternations. We want, say, to prove the validity of:

$$(y)\{(x)[(\exists z)(Fxz \, . \, Fzx) \supset -Fxy] \supset (\exists x)[-Fxy \, . \, (w)(Fxw \supset -Fwx)]\}.$$

We prepare it by clearing it of the conditional signs that overlie the quantifiers.

$$(y)\{-(x)[-(\exists z)(Fxz \, . \, Fzx) \lor -Fxy] \lor (\exists x)[-Fxy \, . \, (w)(Fxw \supset -Fwx)]\}.$$

Also we drive in all such negation signs.

$$(y)\{(\exists x)[(\exists z)(Fxz \, . \, Fzx) \, . \, Fxy] \vee (\exists x)[-Fxy \, . \, (w)(Fxw \supset -Fwx)]\}.$$

We would reletter the universal quantifiers (no longer the existential) if they showed duplications; but they do not. So we move to the functional normal form.

(1) $(\exists x)[(\exists z)(Fxz \, . \, Fzx) \, . \, Fxy] \vee (\exists x)(-Fxy \, . \, Fxw_x \supset -Fw_x x).$

We proceed with the proof by writing down this truth-functionally valid formula.

$$Fyy \, . \, Fyy \, . \, Fyy \, .\text{v.} \, Fw_y y \, . \, Fyw_y \, . \, Fw_y y \, .\text{v.} - Fyy \, . \, Fyw_y \supset -Fw_y y.$$

Under this, finally, we perform five simultaneous steps of EG. Under the clause '$Fyy \, . \, Fyy \, . \, Fyy$' we write, as its generalization, the first half of (1); under the clause '$Fw_y y \, . \, Fyw_y \, . \, Fw_y y$' we write again the first half of (1); and under the final '$-Fyy \, . \, Fyw_y \supset -Fw_y y$' we write the second half of (1). The resulting line, with its duplicate clause crossed out, is (1) as desired. (†)

Before leaving the topic of proof procedures for validity, we should pause a moment over the axiomatic approach. The Herbrand method in the preceding chapter was seen to fall under this head, with its infinitude of axioms (the truth-functionally valid schemata) and its three rules of inference (clausal UG, clausal EG, and deletion of duplicates). But there are also axiomatizations more similar in character to the truth-functional systems of Chapter 13: systems with just a few axiom schemata and with modus ponens and substitution as rules of inference. This was once the accepted way of developing the subject. A typical axiomatization of the kind, covering both the truth functions and quantification, has as axioms the schemata (1)–(3) of Chapter 13 and, in addition, these:

(2) $(x)Fx \supset Fy, \qquad (x)(p \supset Fx) \supset . \, p \supset (x)Fx.$

Its rules of inference include again modus ponens and substitution, but substitution in the sense of Chapter 27. In addition there is a rule allowing the relettering of variables. Also there is simple, nonclausal UG: the attachment of a universal quantifier to a proved line. The system visibly treats only of negation, the conditional, and universal quantification; however, the coverage is extended as desired by translating the other truth-function signs and the existential quantifiers into this notation in the well-known ways.

I pause only for one small sample of a proof in this system. By substituting in the two axioms last stated, and relettering one bound variable, we have:

$$(z)(x)(Gz \supset Fx) \supset (x)(Gy \supset Fx),$$
$$(x)(Gy \supset Fx) \supset . Gy \supset (x)Fx.$$

By substituting in the axiom (1) of page 72, we have:

$$(z)(x)(Gz \supset Fx) \supset (x)(Gy \supset Fx) . \supset :. (x)(Gy \supset Fx) \supset . Gy \supset (x)Fx$$
$$: \supset : (z)(x)(Gz \supset Fx) \supset . Gy \supset (x)Fx.$$

From these three results, by two steps of modus ponens, we get:

$$(z)(x)(Gz \supset Fx) \supset . Gy \supset (x)Fx.$$

Proof of interesting schemata by this method is hardly worthwhile, though the system is known to be complete.

As urged in Chapter 13, derivation of theorems is unrewarding in domains admitting of a decision procedure. Hence the convenience of taking all truth-functionally valid schemata outright as axioms, as in Herbrand's method. We can carry this principle yet farther, since we have a decision procedure for monadic quantificational schemata: we can take all monadically valid quantificational schemata as axioms.

By this, as noted early in Chapter 27, I mean more than the valid monadic schemata. I mean also the polyadic schemata that can be got from valid monadic ones by substitution. There is a decision procedure not only for validity of monadic schemata but for monadic validity of polyadic schemata.

For, given any schema, make all possible monadic *superstitutions* on it; i.e., frame all the monadic schemata from which it can be got by substitution. They are soon exhausted, if we ignore purely arbitrary differences having to do with the alphabetical choice of schematic letters. E.g., the only possible superstitutions on '$Fyy \supset (\exists x)Fxy$', ignoring such differences, are '$Gy \supset (\exists x)Gx$', '$Gy \supset Hy$', '$Hy \supset (\exists x)Gx$', and further trivialities like '$p \supset (\exists x)Gx$', '$p \supset q$', 'p'. Then, in principle, we may test all these monadic schemata and see if one is valid. In practice of course one sees immediately which superstitution to make and test.

It can be shown that by taking all the monadically valid schemata as axioms, and just modus ponens and simple UG as rules of inference, we get a complete system of quantification theory.[10] Here is an example of a proof in it. The schemata:

$$Fxy \supset (\exists x)Fxy,$$
$$(y)[Fxy \supset (\exists x)Fxy] \supset . (y)Fxy \supset (y)(\exists x)Fxy,$$
$$(x)[(y)Fxy \supset (y)(\exists x)Fxy] \supset . (\exists x)(y)Fxy \supset (y)(\exists x)Fxy$$

all prove, by test, to be monadically valid and hence to qualify as axioms. (The reader would do well to elicit the relevant valid monadic schemata

---

[10] It is shown in my *Selected Logic Papers*, pp. 193 ff.

here by superstitution. The third one is '$(x)(Gx \supset p) \supset . (\exists x)Gx \supset p$'.)
Then, from the first of the three by UG, we have:

$$(y)[Fxy \supset (\exists x)Fxy].$$

From this and the second of the three we have by modus ponens:

$$(y)Fxy \supset (y)(\exists x)Fxy$$

and thence by UG:

$$(x)[(y)Fxy \supset (y)(\exists x)Fxy].$$

From this and the last of the three we have by modus ponens our favorite
little essentially polyadic theorem:

$$(\exists x)(y)Fxy \supset (y)(\exists x)Fxy.$$

In an adaptation of the condensed proof notation of Chapter 13 we may
write the whole proof thus:

[1] $Fxy \supset (\exists x)Fxy$,
[2] $[(y)1 \supset .](y)Fxy \supset (y)(\exists x)Fxy$,
      $[(x)2 \supset .](\exists x)(y)Fxy \supset (y)(\exists x)Fxy$.

The numeral '2' in the last line stands for line [2] *minus* its bracketed
matter '$[(y)1 \supset .]$'. The intention of the notation is that each line, with its
bracketed initial matter included, is monadically valid.

HISTORICAL **NOTE:** As remarked at the end of Chapter 29, the axiomatic style illustrated by (2) was Frege's. The particular axioms (2) were
Russell's, 1908, except that he used 'v' twice instead of '$\supset$'. His supporting
truth-functional axioms were less neat than the Łukasiewicz axioms chosen
above, viz. (1)–(3) of pages 72f.

EXERCISES

1.   Carry out (∗) and (†).

2.   As a basis for further exercises, the last method of the chapter is
     recommended: derivation from monadically valid schemata using the
     condensed proof notation. Do various of the examples and exercises
     of Chapters 28 and 30 again by this method.

37
DEDUCTION

Not only can the main method be inverted to give a direct proof procedure for validity (Chapter 35); it can also be split and partly inverted to give a direct proof procedure for implication. This plan may best be seen through an example. Consider again the example in Chapter 25 about paintings and critics. The reader proved it in Ex. 2 of Chapter 29 by proving that the premise:

(1) $\qquad\qquad (\exists y)(x)(Fy \cdot Gx \supset Hxy)$

was inconsistent with what the desired conclusion:

(2) $\qquad\qquad (x)(\exists y)(Gx \supset. Fy \cdot Hxy)$

became under negation, namely:

(3) $\qquad\qquad (\exists x)(y) - (Gx \supset. Fy \cdot Hxy).$

He proved the inconsistency of (1) and (3) by deriving '$Fz \cdot Gw \supset Hwz$' from (1) by EI and UI, and deriving '$-(Gw \supset. Fz \cdot Hwz)$' from (3) by similar steps, and then noting the truth-functional inconsistency of these two instances. Now the new plan, accentuating the positive, says to proceed not from (1) and (3) to absurdity but from (1) alone to (2). We proceed to the instance '$Fz \cdot Gw \supset Hwz$' of (1) as before. But this must truth-functionally imply '$Gw \supset. Fz \cdot Hwz$', if it was going to be truth-functionally inconsistent with '$-(Gw \supset. Fz \cdot Hwz)$'. So from '$Fz \cdot Gw \supset Hwz$' we simply infer '$Gw \supset. Fz \cdot Hwz$' by a new rule TF, *truth-functional inference;* and from this we climb to the desired (2) by steps of EG and UG, the reverse of the steps of EI and UI which in the old proof led from (3) to '$-(Gw \supset. Fz \cdot Hwz)$'.

In this way we get a *deduction* of (2) from (1). It runs as follows:

PREMISE:	$(\exists y)(x)(Fy \cdot Gx \supset Hxy).$	
DEDUCTION:	$(x)(Fz \cdot Gx \supset Hxz)$	(EI),
	$Fz \cdot Gw \supset Hwz$	(UI),
	$Gw \supset. Fz \cdot Hwz$	(TF),
	$(\exists y)(Gw \supset. Fy \cdot Hwy)$	(EG),
	$(x)(\exists y)(Gx \supset. Fy \cdot Hxy)$	(UG).

The procedure is essentially the same when, as in the following example, the premise is milked for more than one unquantified instance.

PREMISE: $(w)(x) - (Fxy \cdot Fxw \cdot Fwx)$.
DEDUCTION: $(x) - (Fxy \cdot Fxy \cdot Fyx)$ (UI),
              $- (Fyy \cdot Fyy \cdot Fyy)$ (UI),
              $- (Fzy \cdot Fzy \cdot Fyz)$ (UI),
              $- Fyy \cdot - Fyz \vee - Fzy$ (TF),
              $(w)(- Fyy \cdot - Fyw \vee - Fwy)$ (UG),
              $(\exists x)(w)(- Fxy \cdot - Fxw \vee - Fwx)$ (EG).

A difference between this deduction and the preceding one is that the line got by TF here is got from the two lines preceding it; it is implied by them jointly.

The same thing happens when there are two or more premises.

PREMISES: $(x)(Gx \supset. Fx \vee Hx)$,
              $(\exists x)(Gx \cdot - Hx)$.
DEDUCTION: $Gy \cdot - Hy$ (EI),
              $Gy \supset. Fy \vee Hy$ (UI),
              $Fy \cdot - Hy$ (TF),
              $(\exists x)(Fx \cdot - Hx)$ (EG).

But a complication arises when more than one unquantified instance of the conclusion is called for. Suppose we are given the premise:

(4) $(y)(\exists x)(Fyy \cdot Fyx .\vee Fxy)$

and want the conclusion '$(y)(\exists x)Fxy$'. Under the main method we would negate this conclusion, convert the result to '$(\exists y)(x) - Fxy$', and then show this to be inconsistent with (4) by deriving inconsistent instances from '$(\exists y)(x) - Fxy$' and (4) as follows:

              $(x) - Fxz$,
              $(\exists x)(Fzz \cdot Fzx .\vee Fxz)$,
              $Fzz \cdot Fzw .\vee Fwz$,
              $- Fzz$,
              $- Fwz$.

But when we try to turn this inconsistency proof into a deduction by our trick of partial inversion, we fail; for '$(\exists y)(x) - Fxy$' contributed not just one unquantified instance but two, '$- Fzz$' and '$- Fwz$'. The truth-functional inconsistency of these two with the instance '$Fzz \cdot Fzw .\vee Fwz$' of (4) does not entitle us to claim either 'Fzz' or 'Fwz' as a TF consequence of '$Fzz \cdot Fzw .\vee Fwz$'; the most we can claim is their alternation, '$Fzz \vee Fwz$'. From this alternation we can get to our desired conclusion '$(y)(\exists x)Fxy$'

only by strengthening our rules: two steps of *clausal* EG will yield the alternation of '$(\exists x)Fxz$' with itself, and then TF will get rid of the duplication and we can go on afterward by UG to '$(y)(\exists x)Fxy$'.

So our bolstered deductive procedure uses these rules: UI, EI, TF, clausal EG, and (for similar needs in other examples) clausal UG. Simple EG and UG are still there, being just the special cases of clausal EG and UG where the clause is taken to be the whole line.

Let us now assemble the deduction of '$(y)(\exists x)Fxy$' from (4).

PREMISE:	$(y)(\exists x)(Fyy \cdot Fyx \cdot \lor Fxy)$.	
DEDUCTION:	$(\exists x)(Fzz \cdot Fzx \cdot \lor Fxz)$	(UI),
	$Fzz \cdot Fzw \cdot \lor Fwz$	(EI),
	$Fzz \lor Fwz$	(TF),
	$(\exists x)Fxz \lor Fwz$	(cl. EG),
	$(\exists x)Fxz \lor (\exists x)Fxz$	(cl. EG),
	$(\exists x)Fxz$	(TF),
	$(y)(\exists x)Fxy$	(UG).

If the deductions seen thus far in this chapter are compared with the inconsistency proofs to which they are related by partial inversion, it will be seen that what the EI of the inconsistency proof gives way to under inversion is not EG, but UG. For instance the last step of the deduction above goes from '$(\exists x)Fxz$' to the desired conclusion '$(y)(\exists x)Fxy$' by UG; the corresponding step in the inconsistency proof went from the negation of that desired conclusion, viz. '$(\exists y)(x) - Fxy$', to '$(x) - Fxz$' by EI. Consequently, just as EI in the main method was hedged by requiring a new instantial variable, so both EI and UG must now be hedged in some corresponding way. Indeed, since deduction is a way of proving implication, and yet neither EI nor UG is implicative, some such restriction was bound to be needed.

But the nature of the appropriate restriction is no longer so simple and evident as it was in the main method. We cannot require that the instantial variable of UG be new, for UG does not introduce an instantial variable; it eliminates it. Nor would it be sufficient now to invert matters and require, as in the Herbrand method (Chapter 35), that the instantial variable of UG not reappear afterward; for our deductive procedure uses EI as well as UG, and their instantial variables can collide in pernicious ways that this requirement would not prevent. Thus observe this fallacy:

PREMISE:	$(\exists x)Fx$.		
DEDUCTION:	Fy	(EI),	
	$(x)Fx$	(UG)	(wrong).

Certainly '$(\exists x)Fx$' does not imply '$(x)Fx$'.

There are, however, two neat restrictions that prove sufficient: *the instantial variables of EI and UG must be different for each such step, and the instantial variable of each such step must be alphabetically later than all free variables of the generic line of that step.* The soundness proof is available elsewhere.[11] If clausal UG is retained, we must stipulate further that its instantial variable must be free in no other clause of that line; however, clausal UG and EG will be superseded presently.

The fallacious little deduction last exhibited is disqualified by the ban on using the same instantial variable 'y' for two steps of the sensitive kinds EI and UG. Actually the big deduction just previously exhibited is disqualified too, in its EI step; for the 'z' in the generic line is alphabetically later than the instantial variable 'w'. However, this violation can be rectified without loss; we can simply use a variable alphabetically later than 'z', say 'z''', instead of 'w' in the three lines where 'w' appeared. From the readiness of this adjustment we see that the alphabetical restriction is really tighter than necessary. Its virtue is that it is simpler than its more liberal alternatives, and moreover the cases that it needlessly excludes are easily adjusted.

A real fallacy that is excluded by the alphabetical restriction, and cannot be patched up by relettering, is this:

PREMISE:	$(x)(\exists y)Fxy.$	
DEDUCTION:	$(\exists y)Fwy$	(UI),
	Fwz	(EI),
	$(x)Fxz$	(UG) (wrong),
	$(\exists y)(x)Fxy$	(EG).

The free variable 'z' in the line got by UG is alphabetically later than the instantial variable 'w' of that UG step. And if we rectify this by using 'z''' instead of 'w', we thereupon violate the alphabetical restriction in the EI step.

In order to facilitate conformity to these restrictions, and also for a further purpose that will be noted presently, it is convenient to *flag* each step of EI and UG by recording the instantial variable off to the right of the line which that step yields. Also it is convenient, and increasingly so in complex deductions, to number the lines at the left and then refer back to them, as sources, at the right. Indeed the citation of rules (UI, TF, etc.) is less to the point; we recognize the rule easily enough, given the source. Also, in preparation for a certain later departure, let us signal the premise no longer by name but rather by starting a column of stars there and running the column down the length of the deduction. Each star means that the starred line is affirmed only conditionally on the premise.

Here, then, rewritten in the new style and rectified in the alphabetical detail, is the long deduction last previously exhibited.

---

[11] In Section 28 of the preceding edition of this book. In that edition the deductive method played a central role, and so was treated more fully than here.

$$*(1) \quad (y)(\exists x)(Fyy \,.\, Fyx \,.\lor Fxy)$$
$$*(2) \quad (\exists x)(Fzz \,.\, Fzx \,.\lor Fxz) \qquad (1)$$
$$*(3) \quad Fzz \,.\, Fzz' \,.\lor Fz'z \qquad\qquad (2) \quad z'$$
$$*(4) \quad Fzz \lor Fz'z \qquad\qquad\qquad (3)$$
$$*(5) \quad (\exists x)Fxz \lor Fz'z \qquad\qquad (4)$$
$$*(6) \quad (\exists x)Fxz \lor (\exists x)Fxz \qquad (5)$$
$$*(7) \quad (\exists x)Fxz \qquad\qquad\qquad\;\; (6)$$
$$*(8) \quad (y)(\exists x)Fxy \qquad\qquad\quad\; (7) \quad z$$

The earlier little deduction which used two premises would now appear as follows.

$$*(1) \quad (x)(Gx \supset .\, Fx \lor Hx)$$
$$**(2) \quad (\exists x)(Gx \,.\, -Hx)$$
$$**(3) \quad Gy \,.\, -Hy \qquad\qquad (2) \quad y$$
$$**(4) \quad Gy \supset .\, Fy \lor Hy \qquad (1)$$
$$**(5) \quad Fy \,.\, -Hy \qquad\qquad\;\; (3)(4)$$
$$**(6) \quad (\exists x)(Fx \,.\, -Hx) \qquad (5)$$

By reference to the flagging device, our restrictions on EI and UG can now be phrased more succinctly: no variable is to be flagged twice, and no free variable of a flagged line is to be alphabetically later than the flag.

The status claimed for the last line in a deduction, or indeed any line, is that it is implied by its premises. Reservations are needed, however, in connection with flagged variables. This implication claim is in order provided that no flagged variable is free in the line that is said to be implied, nor in its premises. Thus the last deduction above shows that (1) and (2) therein imply (6), but not that they imply (5). And the reader can satisfy himself that they in fact do not. Again, take the deduction before last and imagine line (2) thereof as its premise, with (1) dropped; this deduction would not claim to show that (2) implies (8), since 'z' is free in that premise (2). A deduction is called *finished* if no flagged variable is free in its last line nor in any premise on which that last line depends; and then the point of a finished deduction is that its last line is implied by its premises.

There is a device that has had some currency, in deduction, under the name of *conditional proof*. Its adoption has the effect of dispensing with the clausal forms of UG and EG after all. It has also the more important effect of dispensing wholly, in deductions, with the requirement of prenex form. Also a certain naturalness can be claimed for it. It consists in adopting, temporarily, an additional premise, and eventually discharging it by *conditionalization* (Cd): by incorporating it into the conclusion as antecedent of a conditional. The pattern is this: on the assumption that p, we show that q; so we conclude that $p \supset q$.

The procedure requires some bookkeeping, to keep track of what lines depend on the temporary premise. This is where our notation of stars, rather pointless thus far, comes into its own. We star the temporary premise and each line that depends on it. If yet another temporary premise is adopted while one such is already in force, we begin a further column of stars yet farther to the right.

As an example let us return once more to the deduction before last and see how it might have been managed with help of conditional proof.

*(1)	$(y)(\exists x)(Fyy \, . \, Fyx \, .\lor \, Fxy)$	
*(2)	$(\exists x)(Fzz \, . \, Fzx \, .\lor \, Fxz)$	(1)
*(3)	$Fzz \, . \, Fzz' \, .\lor \, Fz'z$	(2) z'
**(4)	Fzz	
**(5)	$(\exists x)Fxz$	(4)
*(6)	$Fzz \supset (\exists x)Fxz$	*(5)
**(7)	$Fz'z$	
**(8)	$(\exists x)Fxz$	(7)
*(9)	$Fz'z \supset (\exists x)Fxz$	*(8)
*(10)	$(\exists x)Fxz$	(3)(6)(9)
*(11)	$(y)(\exists x)Fxy$	(10) z

The column of stars belonging to a premise is finished for good when interrupted. The little right-hand column of two stars at (4) and (5) belongs to the temporary premise 'Fzz' and has nothing to do with the similar column at (7) and (8), which belongs to the temporary premise '$Fz'z$'.

The deduction above could be extended still by adding an unstarred line:

(12) $(y)(\exists x)(Fyy \, . \, Fyx \, .\lor \, Fxy) \supset (y)(\exists x)Fxy$ *(11)

thus absorbing the original premise itself into the conclusion. When the last line of a finished deduction is unstarred, it claims validity outright; it is no mere consequence of a premise.

A final example illustrates the utility of temporary premises and conditionalization in probing schemata that are not prenex. It is the one again about paintings and critics, which was done at the beginning of the present chapter. Now, however, we render the premise and conclusion directly in the forms that they received in Chapter 25. We neither put them into prenex form nor negate the conclusion.

*(1)	$(\exists y)[Fy \, . \, (x)(Gx \supset Hxy)]$	
*(2)	$Fz \, . \, (x)(Gx \supset Hxz)$	(1) z
*(3)	$(x)(Gx \supset Hxz)$	(2)
*(4)	$Gw \supset Hwz$	(3)
**(5)	Gw	
**(6)	$Fz \, . \, Hwz$	(2)(4)(5)
**(7)	$(\exists y)(Fy \, . \, Hwy)$	(6)
*(8)	$Gw \supset (\exists y)(Fy \, . \, Hwy)$	*(7)
*(9)	$(x)[Gx \supset (\exists y)(Fy \, . \, Hxy)]$	(8) w

HISTORICAL NOTE: The method set forth in the present pages is of a type known as *natural deduction,* and stems, in its broadest outlines, from Gentzen and Jaśkowski (1934). The rule of conditionalization, which is the crux of natural deduction, appeared as an explicit formal rule somewhat earlier, having been derived by Herbrand (1930) and also in effect by Tarski (1929) from systems of their own of a type other than natural deduction. The derivation consisted in showing that whenever one statement could be deduced from another in the concerned system, the conditional formed of the two statements could also be proved as a theorem by the original rules of that system. In this status of derived rule relative to one system or another, the rule of conditionalization has come to be known in the literature as the *theorem of deduction.*

Jaśkowski's system of natural deduction is conspicuously unlike that of the present pages; for Jaśkowski dispenses with EG and EI, and gets along with milder restrictions on UG, by the expedient of treating '$(\exists x)$', '$(\exists y)$', etc., as abbreviations of '$-(x)-$', '$-(y)-$', etc. This course is economical in rules, but greatly increases the difficulty and complexity of the deductions themselves. The crucial difference between Gentzen's system and that of the present pages is in EI; he had a more devious rule.

Because of the presence of EI, the present system differs from Gentzen's and Jaśkowski's considerably on the score of restrictions upon the rules. In particular the device of flagging is a novelty. Gentzen and Jaśkowski had restrictions too, but gave them different forms. Cooley, in pp. 126–140 of his *Primer of Formal Logic* (1942), made use of natural deduction in a form which included substantially EI, but without exact formulation of restrictions. Explicitly formulated rules and restrictions, resembling the present system except for varied restrictions, were set forth by Rosser and independently by me in mimeographed lecture notes from 1946 on..

EXERCISES

1. Check each of the following to see whether it is a correct deduction according to the rules, and a finished one.

*(1)	Fy		
*(2)	$(x)Fx$	(1)	y
(3)	$Fy \supset (x)Fx$	*(2)	

*(1)	$(x)(Fx \supset Gx)$		
*(2)	$Fy \supset Gy$	(1)	
*(3)	$(\exists x)(Fy \supset Gx)$	(2)	
*(4)	$(w)(\exists x)(Fw \supset Gx)$	(3)	y

*(1)	$(x)(Fx \vee Gy)$		
*(2)	$Fy \vee Gy$	(1)	
*(3)	$(x)(Fy \vee Gx)$	(2)	y

*(1)	$(x)(Fx \cdot Gx)$		
*(2)	$Fy \cdot Gy$	(1)	
*(3)	Fy	(2)	
*(4)	$(x)Fx$	(3)	y
*(5)	Gy	(2)	
*(6)	$(x)Gx$	(5)	y
*(7)	$(x)Fx \cdot (x)Gx$	(4)(6)	

*(1)	$Fx \vee Gy$		
*(2)	$(y)(Fx \vee Gy)$	(1)	y
*(3)	$(\exists x)(y)(Fx \vee Gy)$	(2)	

2. If any of the deductions above is correct but unfinished, append further lines so as to produce a finished deduction. If any is incorrect but can be revised into a correct deduction to the same effect, so revise it.

3. Do the examples and various exercises of Chapters 28 and 30 again by deduction.

IV
GLIMPSES BEYOND

38

EXISTENCE
AND SINGULAR
INFERENCE

The logic of truth functions and quantification is now under control. Some simple sorts of inference, however, still want discussion—notably those turning upon *singular terms* such as 'Socrates':

All men are mortal,   Socrates is a Greek,
Socrates is a man;   Socrates is wise;
∴ Socrates is mortal.   ∴ Some Greeks are wise.

Furthermore the theory of identity, including such evident laws as '$x = x$' and '$x = y . \equiv . y = x$', remains untouched. A few chapters will suffice to do justice to singular terms and identity. In conclusion we shall have a brief glimpse of set theory, or the theory of classes—a discipline which may be characterized both as higher logic and as the basic discipline of classical mathematics.

The logic of identity will be needed in the final treatment of the logic of singular terms, but meanwhile singular terms will be helpful in expounding the concept of identity. So let us begin with a preliminary study of singular terms.

It will be recalled that for purposes of the definition of validity in quantification theory (Chapter 24) we fixed the "interpretations" of sentence letters, predicate letters, and free variables respectively by assigning truth values, extensions, and single objects of the universe. Now the expressions that have truth values are statements, and the expressions that have extensions are predicates; and in completion of the picture the idea suggests itself that the expressions which similarly correspond to single objects are the singular terms that name them. Or to put the matter in another way: just as the sentence letters in a schema stand as dummy sentences and the predicate letters as dummy predicates, so the free variables stand as dummy singular terms. To represent the above inferences about Socrates schematically, therefore, we may simply use a free 'y' to represent 'Socrates'. The inferences are then justified directly by the two valid conditionals:

$$(x)(Fx \supset Gx) . Fy . \supset Gx,$$
$$Fy . Gy . \supset (\exists x)(Fx . Gx).$$

Another example:

PREMISES: Aldrich bribed every member of the committee,
                 Barr is a member of the committee;
CONCLUSION: Someone bribed Barr.

This is justified by the validity of the conditional:

$$(x)(Fx \supset Gzx) . Fw . \supset (\exists x)Gxw,$$

which goes into a pure existential and is quickly checked.

These valid conditionals show that the conclusions will come out true if the premises do, no matter what objects of the universe we choose in interpretation of 'y', 'z', and 'w'. In particular therefore we may choose Socrates, Aldrich, and Barr—provided merely that the universe contains such things.

But this last proviso is essential to the intended application of our deductive results. Singular terms do not, after all, stand to objects quite as statements and predicates stand to truth values and extensions; for whereas every statement has its truth value and every predicate its extension, empty or otherwise, a singular term may or may not name an object. A singular term always *purports* to name an object, but is powerless to guarantee that the alleged object be forthcoming; witness 'Cerberus'. The deductive techniques of quantification theory with free variables serve very well for inferences depending on singular terms when we are assured that *there are* objects such as those terms purport to name; so this question of existence then becomes the central question where singular terms are concerned.

I shall find no use for the narrow sense which some philosophers have given to 'existence', as against 'being'; viz., concreteness in space-time. If any such special connotation threatens in the present pages, imagine 'exists' replaced by 'is'. When the Parthenon and the number 7 are said to be, no distinction in the sense of 'be' need be intended. The Parthenon is indeed a placed and dated object in space-time while the number 7 (if such there be) is another sort of thing; but this is a difference between the objects concerned and not between senses of 'be'.

In contrast to 7 and the Parthenon, there is no such thing as Cerberus; and there is no such number as 0/0. Clearly these repudiations do not of themselves depend on any limitation of existence to space-time. The meaning of the particular word 'Cerberus' merely happens to be such that, if the word did name an object, that object would be a physical object in space and time. The word 'Cerberus' is like 'Parthenon' and 'Bucephalus' in this respect, and unlike '7' and '0/0'. But the word 'Cerberus' differs from 'Parthenon' and 'Bucephalus' in that whereas there is something in space-time such as the word 'Parthenon' purports to name (viz., at Athens for some dozens of centuries including part or all of the twentieth), and whereas there is (tenselessly) presumably something in space and time such as the word 'Bucephalus' purports to name (viz., at a succession of positions in the Near and Middle East in the fourth century B.C.), on the other hand there happens to be nothing such as the word 'Cerberus' purports to name, near or remote, past, present, or future.

It is surely a commonplace that some singular terms may, though purporting to name, flatly fail to name anything at all. 'Cerberus' is one example, and '0/0' is another. But, commonplace though this be, experience shows that recognition of it is beset with persistent confusions, to the detriment of a clear understanding of the logic of singular terms. Let us make it our business in the remainder of this chapter to dispel certain of these confusions.

There is a tendency to try to preserve some shadowy entity under the word 'Cerberus', for example, lest the word lose its meaning. If 'Cerberus' were meaningless, not only would poetry suffer, but even certain blunt statements of fact, such as that there is no such thing as Cerberus, would lapse into meaninglessness. Thus we may hear it said, e.g., that Cerberus exists as an idea in the mind. But this verbal maneuver conduces only to confusion. Of a tangible object such as the Parthenon, to change the subject for a moment, it would be wanton obscurantism to affirm a *double* existence: in Athens *and* in the mind. Far more straightforward to admit two (or many) objects: the tangible Parthenon in Athens, and the Parthenon-idea in the mind (or the Parthenon-ideas in many minds). 'Parthenon' names the Parthenon and only the Parthenon, whereas 'the Parthenon-idea' names the Parthenon-idea. Similarly not 'Cerberus', but 'the Cerberus-idea', names the Cerberus-idea; whereas 'Cerberus', as it happens, names nothing.

This is not the place to try to say what an idea is, or what existence in the mind means. Perhaps from the point of view of experimental psychology an idea should be explained somehow as a propensity to certain patterns of reaction to words or other stimuli of specified kinds; and perhaps "existing in the mind" then means simply "being an idea." But no matter; the idea of "idea" is entertained here only as a concession to the other party. The point is that though we be as liberal about countenancing ideas and other nonphysical objects as anyone may ask, still to identify the Parthenon with the Parthenon-idea is simply to confuse one thing with another; and to try to assure there being such a thing as Cerberus by identifying it with the Cerberus-idea is to make a similar confusion.

The effort to preserve meaning for 'Cerberus' by presenting some shadowy entity for 'Cerberus' to name is misdirected; 'Cerberus' remains meaningful despite not naming. Most words, like 'and' or 'sake', are quite meaningful without even purporting to be names at all. Even when a word is a name of something, its meaning would appear not to be identifiable with the thing named.[1] Mount Everest has been known, from opposite points of view, both as Everest and as Chomolungma;[2] here the named object was always one, yet the names can scarcely be viewed as having

---

[1] This much neglected point was well urged by Frege, "Über Sinn und Bedeutung."

[2] Erwin Schrödinger, *What is Life?*, last paragraph, nearly enough.

been alike in *meaning* or synonymous; for no insight into the combined minds of all users of 'Everest' and 'Chomolungma' could reveal that these named the same thing, pending a strenuous investigation of nature. Again there is Frege's example of 'Evening Star' and 'Morning Star'; the named planet is one, but it took astronomy and not mere analysis of meanings to establish the fact.

Precise and satisfactory formulation of the notion of meaning is an unsolved problem of semantics. Perhaps the meaning of a word is best construed as the associated idea, in some sense of 'idea' which needs to be made precise in turn; or perhaps as the system of implicit rules in conformity with which the word is used, supposing that a criterion of "implicit rule" can be devised which is selective enough to allow sameness of meaning on the part of distinct expressions. Perhaps, indeed, the best treatment of the matter will prove to consist in abandoning all notion of so-called meanings as entities; thus such phrases as 'having *meaning*' and 'same *in meaning*' might be dropped in favor of 'significant' and 'synonymous', in hopes eventually of devising adequate criteria of significance and synonymy involving no excursion through a realm of intermediary entities called meanings. Perhaps it will even be found that of these only significance admits of a satisfactory criterion, and that all effort to make sense of 'synonymy' must be abandoned along with the notion of meaning.[3] However all this may be, the important point for present purposes is that significance of a word, even of a word which (like 'Cerberus') purports to be a name, is in no way contingent upon its naming anything; and even if a word does name an object, and even if we countenance entities called meanings, there is still no call for the named object to be the meaning.

The mistaken view that the word 'Cerberus' must name something in order to mean anything turns, it has just now been suggested, on confusion of naming with meaning. But the view is encouraged also by another factor, viz., our habit of thinking in terms of the misleading word 'about'. If there is no such thing as Cerberus, then, it is asked, what are you talking *about* when you use the word 'Cerberus' (even to say that there is no such thing)? Actually this protest could be made with the same cogency (viz., none) in countless cases where no would-be name such as 'Cerberus' occurs at all: What are you talking about when you say that there are no Bolivian battleships? The remedy here is simply to give up the unwarranted notion that talking sense always necessitates there being things talked about. The notion springs, no doubt, from essentially the same confusion which was just previously railed against; then it was confusion between meanings and objects named, and now it is confusion between meanings and things talked about.

This mistaken view that 'Cerberus' must name something has been seen to evoke, as one lame effort to supply a named object, the notion that Cerberus is something in the mind. Other expedients to the same end are commonly encountered. There is, e.g., the relativistic doctrine

---

[3] See my *From a Logical Point of View*, Essays II and III.

according to which Cerberus exists in the world of Greek mythology and not in the world of modern science. This is a perverse way of saying merely that Greeks believed Cerberus to exist and that (if we may trust modern science thus far) they were wrong. Myths which affirm the existence of Cerberus have esthetic value and anthropological significance; moreover they have internal structures upon which our regular logical techniques can be brought to bear; but it does happen that the myths are literally false, and it is sheer obscurantism to phrase the matter otherwise. There is really only one world, and there is not, never was, and never will be any such thing as Cerberus.

Another such expedient which had best not detain us long, if only because of the mazes of metaphysical controversy in which it would involve us if we were to tarry, is the view that concrete individuals are of two kinds: those which are actualized and those which are possible but not actualized. Cerberus is of the latter kind, according to this view; so that there *is* such a thing as Cerberus, and the proper content of the vulgar denial of Cerberus is more correctly expressed in the fashion 'Cerberus is not actualized'. The universe in the broader sense becomes badly overpopulated under this view, but the comfort of it is supposed to be that there comes to *be* something Cerberus about which we may be said to be talking when we rightly say (in lieu of 'There is no such thing as Cerberus') 'Cerberus is not actualized'.

But this device depends on the possibility of Cerberus; it no longer applies when we shift our example from 'Cerberus' to some would-be name of complex form involving an out-and-out impossibility, e.g., 'the spherical pyramid of Copilco'. Having already cluttered the universe with an implausible lot of unactualized possibles, are we to go on and add a realm of unactualizable impossibles? The tendency at this point is to choose the other horn of the supposed dilemma, and rule that expressions involving impossibility are meaningless. Thence, perhaps, the not uncommon notion that a statement logically inconsistent in form must be reclassified as a nonstatement: not false but meaningless. This notion, besides being unnatural on the face of it, is impractical in that it rules out the possibility of tests of meaningfulness; for logical consistency admits of no general test, nor even of a complete proof procedure (cf. Chapter 33).

All this piling of expedients on expedients is, insofar as prompted by a notion that expressions must name to be meaningful, quite uncalled for. There need be no mystery about attributing nonexistence where there is nothing to attribute it to, and there need be no misgivings over the meaningfulness of words which purport to name and fail. To purport to name and fail is already proof of a full share of meaning.

If for *other* reasons the recognition of unactualized possibles is felt to be desirable, there is nothing in the ensuing logical theory that need conflict with it as long as essential distinctions are preserved. So-called mental ideas and so-called meanings were provisionally tolerated above; "ideas" of the Platonic stripe, including unactualized possibles, could be accommodated as well. What must be insisted on is merely that such shadowy entities, if admitted, be named in some distinguishing fashion: 'the Cerberus-possibility', or 'the Cerberus-idea', or 'the meaning of 'Cerberus' '. If we can get together on this much by way of convention, then everyone can be left to his favorite metaphysics so far as anything further is concerned. The essential message to be carried over from this chapter into succeeding ones is simply this: Some meaningful words which are proper names from a grammatical point of view, notably 'Cerberus', do not name anything.[4]

EXERCISES

1.   Show that the premises:

> Barr and Williams did not both contribute,
> If Blake contributed then so did everybody

imply the conclusion:

> Blake did not contribute,

allowing free variables to stand for the proper names.

2.   Show that the premises:

> Edith envies everyone more fortunate than she,
> Herbert is no more fortunate than any who envy him

imply the conclusion:

> Herbert is no more fortunate than Edith.

[4] For more on this theme see Russell, "On denoting," and my *From a Logical Point of View*, Essays I and VI.

39

SINGULAR TERMS VERSUS GENERAL TERMS

More remains to be said on the subject of singular inference than was covered by the simple considerations at the beginning of the preceding chapter. But as a tool for the further developments we shall need the theory of identity, which will be introduced in the next chapter. We must also render the scope and logical status of singular terms more explicit than has thus far been done; and this work will occupy the present chapter.

What were called "terms" in Chapters 14 and 25 and represented by '*F*', '*G*', etc., are *general terms*, as opposed to singular terms. But generality is not to be confused with ambiguity. The singular term 'Jones' is ambiguous in that it might be used in different contexts to name any of various persons, but it is still a singular term in that it purports in any particular context to name one and only one person. The same is true even of pronouns such as 'I' and 'thou'; these again are singular terms, but merely happen to be highly ambiguous pending determination through the context or other circumstances attending any given use of them. The same may be said of 'the man', or more clearly 'the President', 'the cellar'; these phrases (unlike 'man', 'president', and 'cellar' themselves) are singular terms, but the one and only one object to which they purport to refer in any given use depends on attendant circumstances for its determination.

Besides the classification of terms into singular and general, there is a cross classification into *concrete* and *abstract*. Concrete terms are those which purport to refer to individuals, physical objects, events; abstract terms are those which purport to refer to abstract objects, e.g., to numbers, classes, attributes. Thus some singular terms, e.g., 'Socrates', 'Cerberus', 'earth', 'the author of *Waverley*', are concrete, while other singular terms, e.g., '7', '3 + 4', 'piety', are abstract. Again some general terms, e.g., 'man', 'house', 'red house', are concrete (since each man or house is a concrete individual), while others, e.g., 'prime number', 'zoological species', 'virtue', are abstract (since each number is itself an abstract object, if anything, and similarly for each species and each virtue).

For attributes, as a realm of entities distinct from classes, I hold no brief; I mention them only as a concession to readers with preconceptions. If both sorts of entities are to be recognized, the one intelligible difference between them would seem to be that classes are considered identical with one another when they have the same members (e.g., the class of animals with kidneys and that of animals with hearts) while attributes may be viewed as distinct though applying to the same objects (e.g., heartedness and kidneyedness). Classes and attributes are equally abstract, but classes have the edge on attributes in point of clarity of identification and separation.

Those who draw a distinction between classes and attributes will see in 'humanity' a name of an attribute and in 'mankind' a name of a class, the class of all objects which partake of the attribute of humanity. But both terms are abstract singular terms, as opposed to the concrete general term 'man' or 'human'. This general term has the class mankind as its extension.

The correspondence exemplified between the abstract singular term 'mankind' or 'humanity' and the concrete general term 'man' is a systematic feature of our language. 'Piety' is an abstract singular term corresponding to the concrete general term 'pious person'; 'redness' is an abstract singular term corresponding to the concrete general term 'red thing'. In each such correspondence the abstract singular term purports to name an attribute (or perhaps a class) which is shared by (or embraces) all and only those individuals of which the corresponding general concrete term is true. Despite this correspondence the singular abstract term differs from the general concrete term in an important way: it purports to name one and only one object, abstract object though it be, while the general term does not purport to name at all. The general term may indeed "be true of" each of *many* things, viz., each red thing, or each man, but this kind of reference is not called naming; "naming," at least as I shall use the word, is limited to the case where the named object purports to be unique.

Occasionally, as language is ordinarily used, a word like 'man' which is normally a general concrete term may be used as a singular abstract term; e.g., 'Man is a zoölogical species'. But from a logical point of view it is well to think of such examples as rephrased using a distinctively singular abstract term (thus 'Mankind is a zoölogical species').

The division of terms into concrete and abstract is a distinction only in the kinds of objects referred to. The distinction between singular and general terms is more vital from a logical point of view. Thus far it has been drawn only in a very vague way: a term is singular if it purports to name an object (one and only one), and otherwise general. Note the key word 'purports'; it separates the question off from such questions of fact as the existence of Socrates and Cerberus. Whether a word purports to name one and only one object is a question of language, and is not contingent on facts of existence.

In terms of logical structure, what it means to say that the singular term "purports to name one and only one object" is just this: *The singular term belongs in positions of the kind in which it would also be coherent to use variables 'x', 'y', etc.* (or, in ordinary language, pronouns). Contexts like:

Socrates is wise,   Piety is a virtue,

Cerberus guards the gate, $7 = 3 + 4,$

etc., are parallel in form to open sentences:

$$x \text{ is wise,} \quad x \text{ guards the gate,} \quad x \text{ is a virtue,} \quad x = 3 + 4$$

such as may occur in closed statements having the form of quantifications: '$(\exists x)(x \text{ is wise})$', etc. The terms 'Socrates', 'Cerberus', 'piety', and '7' are, in short, substitutable for variables in open sentences without violence to grammar; and it is this that makes them singular terms. Whether there is in fact such an object as Socrates (which, tenselessly, there is) or Cerberus (which there is not) or piety or 7 (on which philosophers disagree) is of course a separate question.

General terms, in contrast to singular ones, do not occur in positions appropriate to variables. Typical positions of the general term 'man' are seen in 'Socrates is a man', 'All men are mortal'; it would not make sense to write:

(1)   Socrates is an x,   All x are mortal,

or to imbed such expressions in quantifications in the fashion:

(2) $(\exists x)$(Socrates is an x),
(3) (x)(all x are mortal $\supset$ Socrates is mortal).

The 'x' of an open sentence may refer to objects of any kind, but it is supposed to refer to them one at a time; and then application of '(x)' or '$(\exists x)$' means that what the open sentence says of x is true of all or some objects taken thus one at a time.

There are indeed legitimate open sentences somewhat resembling (1) but phrased in terms of class membership, thus:

(4)   Socrates is a member of x,   All members of x are mortal.

But these do not, like (1), show 'x' in place of a general term such as 'man'; rather they show 'x' in place of an abstract singular term, 'mankind' ('class of all men'), as in 'Socrates is a member of mankind', 'All members of mankind are mortal'. The open sentences (4) may quite properly appear in quantifications:

(5) $(\exists x)$(Socrates is a member of x),
(6) (x)(all members of x are mortal $\supset$ Socrates is mortal).

Incidentally (6) can be further analyzed:

(7) $(x)[(y)(y \text{ is a member of } x \supset y \text{ is mortal}) \supset \text{Socrates is mortal}]$.

As an alternative to (4) we might also appeal to attributes instead of classes, thus:

(8)   Socrates has x,   Everything that has x is mortal.

Here '*x*' appears in the position of an abstract singular term such as 'human-ity' which purports to name an attribute. Quantifications analogous to (5)–(7) can then be built on (8).

It may seem pedantic to reject (1)–(3) as meaningless while accepting (4)–(8). Why not accord (1) the meanings (4) or (8), and thus construe (2)–(3) as interchangeable with the quantifications (5)–(6) or with the analogous quantifications in terms of attributes? In short, why not simply rub out the distinction between general terms and abstract singular terms? The answer is as old as William of Ockham: "Entities are not to be multi-plied beyond necessity." Abstract singular terms purport to name abstract entities; and, as we saw early in the preceding section, singular inference commonly presupposes existence of the purportedly named object within the universe over which our variables of quantification range. The pre-supposition that our universe include abstract objects can be avoided, in much of our thinking, if we adhere to the point of view that words like 'man', in contexts like 'Socrates is a man' and 'All men are mortal', occupy positions which are inaccessible to variables—just as inaccessible as the positions occupied by '(' or 'and'. The positions occupied by general terms have indeed no status at all in a logical grammar, for we have found (Chap-ter 26) that for logical purposes the predicate recommends itself as the unit of analysis; thus 'Socrates is a man' comes to be viewed as compounded of 'Socrates' and '① is a man', the latter being an indissoluble unit in which 'man' stands merely as a constituent syllable comparable to the 'rat' in 'Socrates'.

If for any perverse reason we *should* want to rephrase 'Socrates is a man' or 'All men are mortal' in such a way as to make outright reference to abstract objects, the formulations:

Socrates is a member of mankind,   Socrates has humanity,
All members of mankind are mortal,   All having humanity are mortal,

are at our disposal. These versions do contain singular terms which purport to name abstract objects. But we keep the record straight by reserving recognizably singular terms like 'mankind' and 'humanity' for such naming of abstract objects. Then, so long as we are minded to proceed independ-ently of the question of the existence of abstract objects, we can eschew such idioms as the above in favor of 'Socrates is a man' and 'All men are mortal'. Eventually the question of abstract objects has to be faced any-way; more of this later. But it is sound policy to keep as much of our logic clear of the question as we can.

The distinction between general terms and abstract singular terms is a remnant of medieval logic which some modern logicians do not share my concern to preserve. Actually the significance of the distinction is clearer since the rise of quantification theory than it had traditionally been; sin-gular terms are accessible to positions appropriate to quantifiable variables, while general terms are not. In the foregoing paragraphs it has accordingly been urged that general terms have the virtue, as against abstract singular terms, of letting us avoid or at least postpone the recognition of abstract objects as values of our variables of quantification. Some logicians, however, attach little value to such avoidance or postponement. This attitude may be explained in some cases by a Platonic predilection for abstract objects; not so in other cases, however, notably Carnap's. His attitude is rather that quantification over abstract objects is a linguistic convention devoid of ontological commitment; see his "Empiricism, semantics, and ontology."

40
IDENTITY

Identity is such a simple and fundamental idea that it is hard to explain otherwise than through mere synonyms. To say that x and y are identical is to say that they are the same thing. Everything is identical with itself and with nothing else. But despite its simplicity, identity invites confusion. E.g., it may be asked: Of what use is the notion of identity if identifying an object with itself is trivial and identifying it with anything else is false?

This particular confusion is cleared up by reflecting that there are really not just two kinds of cases to consider, one trivial and the other false, but three:

$$\text{Cicero} = \text{Cicero}, \quad \text{Cicero} = \text{Catiline}, \quad \text{Cicero} = \text{Tully}.$$

The first of these is trivial and the second false, but the third is neither trivial nor false. The third is informative, because it joins two different terms; and at the same time it is true, because the two terms are names of the same object. For truth of a statement of identity it is necessary only that '=' appear between names of the same object; the names may, and in useful cases will, themselves be different. For it is not the names that are affirmed to be identical, it is the things named. Cicero is identical with Tully (same man), even though the name 'Cicero' is different from the name 'Tully'. To say anything about given objects we apply the appropriate verb or predicate to *names* of the objects; but there is no reason to expect that what is thereby said of the objects will be true also of the names themselves. The Nile, e.g., is longer than the Tuscaloosahatchie, but the names are oppositely related.

Still, since the useful statements of identity are those in which the named objects are the same and the names are different, it is only because of a peculiarity of language that the notion of identity is needed. If our language were so perfect a copy of its subject matter that each thing had but one name, then statements of identity would indeed be useless.[5] But such a language would be radically different from what we have. To rid language of redundant nomenclature of the simple type, e.g., 'Tully' and 'Cicero', would be no radical departure; but to eliminate redundancies among complex names, e.g., '7 × 5' and '27 + 8', or 'twenty-fifth President of U.S.' and 'first President of U.S. to be inaugurated at 42', or 'mean temperature at Tuxtla' and '93°F', would be to strike at the roots. The utility of language lies partly in its very failure to copy reality in any one-thing-one-name fashion. The notion of identity is then needed to take up the slack.

But to say that the need of identity derives from a peculiarity of language is not to say that identity is a relation of expressions in language. On the contrary, as lately emphasized, what are identical are the objects with themselves and not the names with one another; the names stand in the statement of identity, but it is the named objects that are identified. Moreover, no linguistic investigation of the names in a statement of identity will suffice, ordinarily, to determine whether the identity holds or fails. The identities:

Everest = Chomolungma (cf. Chapter 38),
Evening Star = Morning Star,
25th President of U.S. = first President of U.S. inaugurated at 42,
Mean temperature at Tuxtla = 93°F

all depend for their substantiation upon inquiry into extra-linguistic matters of fact.

A popular riddle, so commonly associated with identity that it should be touched on here, is this: How can a thing that changes its substance be said to remain identical with itself? How is it, e.g., that one's body may be spoken of as the same body over a period of years? The problem dates from Heraclitus, who said "You cannot step into the same river twice, for fresh waters are ever flowing in upon you." Actually the key to this difficulty is to be sought not in the idea of identity but in the ideas of thing and time. A physical thing—whether a river or a human body or a stone—is at any one moment a sum of simultaneous momentary states of spatially scattered atoms or other small physical constituents. Now just as the thing at a moment is a sum of these spatially small parts, so we may think of the thing over a period as a sum of the temporally small parts which are its successive momentary states. Combining these conceptions, we see the thing as extended in time and in space alike; the thing becomes a sum of momentary states of particles, or briefly particle-moments, scattered over a stretch of

---

[5] Thus it was that Hume had trouble accounting for the origin of the identity idea in experience. See *Treatise of Human Nature*, Bk. I, Pt. IV, Sec. II.

time as well as space. All this applies as well to the river or human body as to the stone. There is only a difference of detail in the two cases: in the case of the stone the constituent particle-moments pair off fairly completely from one date to another as momentary states of the same particles, whereas in the case of the river or human body there is more heterogeneity in this respect. The river or human body will regularly contain some momentary states of a particle and exclude other momentary states of the same particle, whereas with the stone, barring small peripheral changes or ultimate destruction, this is not the case. Here we have a distinction reminiscent of the distinction in traditional philosophy between "modes" and "substances". But things of both kinds are physical things in one and the same sense: sums of particle-moments. And each thing is identical with itself; we *can* step into the same river twice. What we cannot do is step into the same temporal part of the river twice, where the part is temporally shorter than a stepping-while. Diversity among the parts of a whole must not be allowed to obscure the identity of the whole, nor of each part, with itself.

Thus far we have been thinking of statements of identity composed of ' = ' flanked by singular terms. But ' = ' is an ordinary relative term, and so may be flanked as well by variables; e.g.:

$(x)(y)(x$ is a god . y is a god $. \supset . \ x = y),$
$(\exists x)[x$ is a god . $(y)(y$ is a god $\supset . \ x = y)],$
$(\exists x)(\exists y)(x$ is a god . y is a god . $x \neq y),$
$(x)(y)(z)(x$ is a god . y is a god . z is a god $. \supset : x = y$ .v. $x = z$ .v. $y = z).$

(The notation '$x \neq y$' is a convenient abbreviation for '$-(x = y)$'.) As the reader can verify on a little reflection, these four statements amount respectively to the following:

> There is one god at most,[6]
> There is exactly one god,
> There are at least two gods,
> There are two gods at most.

Statements of identity consisting of ' = ' flanked by singular terms are needed, we saw, because language includes a redundancy of names. But the need of ' = ' flanked by variables arises from a different peculiarity of language; viz., from its use of multiple variables of quantification (or their pronominal analogues in ordinary language). Two variables are allowed to refer to the same object, and they are also allowed to refer to different objects; and thus the sign of identity comes to be needed when, as in the above four examples, there arises the question of sameness or difference of reference on the part of the variables. From a logical point of view it is the use of

[6] This, according to a quip of the late Professor Whitehead's, is the creed of the Unitarians.

the identity sign between variables, rather than between singular terms, that is fundamental. We shall see, indeed (Chapter 42), that the whole category of singular terms is theoretically superfluous, and that there are logical advantages in thinking of it as theoretically cleared away.

The logic of identity is a branch not reducible to the logic of quantification. Its notation may be thought of as comprising that of the logic of quantification plus the one additional sign '$=$'. Thus the schemata of the logic of identity are the same as the quantificational schemata except that they may contain, along with the clauses 'p', 'q', 'Fx', 'Gxy', etc., additional clauses of the form of identities: '$x = y$', '$x = z$', etc. Validity may be defined for schemata of the logic of identity precisely as it was defined for quantificational schemata (Chapter 24). Thus there are valid schemata such as:

$$(\exists y)(x = y \cdot Fy) \supset (\exists y)(x = y)$$

which are like valid quantificational schemata except that '$x = x$', '$x = y$', etc., turn up instead of schematic clauses 'Gxx', 'Gxy', etc. These are valid still by virtue simply of their quantificational structure, and independently of any peculiarities of identity. But there are further valid schemata whose validity depends specifically on the meaning of identity; one such is:

(I) $\qquad\qquad\qquad Fx \cdot x = y \cdot \supset Fy.$

For, consider any choice of universe, any interpretation of 'F' therein, and any assignment of objects to the free variables 'x' and 'y'. If the object assigned to 'x' is the same as that assigned to 'y', and is an object of which 'F' is interpreted as true, then (I) comes out true through truth of its consequent 'Fy'; and in any other case (I) comes out true through falsity of its antecedent.

Through having added the identity sign to our logical notation we find ourselves able, for the first time, to write genuine sentences without straying from our logical notation. Hitherto, schemata were the best we could get; extralogical materials had to be imported from ordinary language when, for the sake of illustration, a genuine sentence was wanted. In '$x = x$' and '$(x)(x = x)$', however, we have sentences—the first open, the second closed and true.

Any schemata obtained by putting identities '$x = x$', '$x = y$', etc., in place of say 'Gxx', 'Gxy', etc., in valid quantificational schemata are, it has been explained, valid schemata of the logic of identity. But such putting of identities for schematic clauses can, when thorough, yield a sentence instead of a schema, e.g.:

$$x = x \cdot \supset (\exists y)(x = y).$$

It is convenient to allow the concept of validity to apply to such sentences along with schemata. The extension, indeed, is quite automatic. A schema has been explained as valid when it comes out true under every nonempty choice of universe and every interpretation therein of its schematic letters and free variables; and this characterization carries over unchanged to sentences such as the above, except that the provision for schematic letters becomes irrelevant. When furthermore the sentence has no free variables, the definition of validity reduces to 'true for every nonempty choice of universe'.

The example '$x = x . \supset (\exists y)(x = y)$' above is a sentence which is valid by virtue simply of its quantificational structure. Of those whose validity depends specifically on the meaning of identity, on the other hand, the simplest is:

(II) $x = x.$

Another, truth-functionally implied by the two foregoing sentences, is '$(\exists y)(x = y)$'.

Substitutions may be made for 'F' in (I) just as explained in Chapter 27, except that the substituted expressions may now contain identity signs instead of predicate letters. Reflection on the general mechanics of substitution (Chapter 27) reveals that, in (I) in particular, 'Fx' and 'Fy' may in effect be directly supplanted respectively by any schemata S_x and S_y which differ only in that S_x has free 'x' in some places where S_y has free 'y'. (For, the predicate or predicate-schema theoretically substituted for 'F' would then be simply S_x with '①' in the particular places where S_x and S_y are to differ.) Thus one result of substitution in (I) is:

$$w = x . x = y . \supset . w = y$$

—the law of transitivity of identity (cf. Chapter 28).

The universal closures of (I) and (II), viz:

$$(x)(y)(Fx . x = y . \supset Fy), \qquad (x)(x = x),$$

together with the universal closures of any results of substituting for 'F' in (I), will be called *axioms of identity*. Now the technique of proof in quantification theory carries over to the logic of identity; we simply treat the axioms as premises. E.g., the law '$x = y . \supset . y = x$' of the symmetry of identity follows truth-functionally from the case:

$$x = x . x = y . \supset . y = x$$

of (I) together with (II).

For further illustration let us show '$(y)(x = y . \supset Fy)$' equivalent to

'Fx', by establishing implication forward and backwards. An axiom of identity is inserted into the antecedent of each of the conditionals.

(1) $(y)(x = y . \supset Fy) . x = x . \supset Fx.$
(2) $Fx . (y)(Fx . x = y . \supset Fy) . \supset (y)(x = y . \supset Fy).$

Each of these conditionals is quickly checked for quantificational validity.

It must be remembered that in these proofs the identity sign behaves merely as an inert predicate letter, as if '$x = x$' and '$x = y$' were 'Gxx' and 'Gxy'. The peculiar properties of identity are invoked explicitly, when wanted, by inserting an axiom of identity into the antecedent of the conditional. It is convenient sometimes to insert the axiom along with its quantifier or quantifiers and sometimes without, as the above examples show.

HISTORICAL **NOTE:** Gödel showed in 1930 (Theorem VII) that the axioms of identity (I) and (II) are complete. That is, every valid schema or sentence of the logic of identity can be proved from them by the logic of quantification.

EXERCISES

1.   Writing 'y' for 'Barr', 'z' for 'the cashier', and 'F' for 'had a key', put the statement:

         None but Barr and the cashier had a key

into logical notation with help of identity. Show that this and:

         Someone who had a key took the briefcase

imply the conclusion:

         Barr or the cashier took the briefcase

with the help of an axiom of identity.

2.   Prove the equivalence of:

$$(\exists x)(Fx . x = y), \qquad Fy$$

by proving the two implications with help of axioms of identity.

41
DESCRIPTIONS

It is usual in logic to write '$(\imath x)$', with an inverted iota, to mean 'the object x such that'. Thus the complex singular terms 'the author of *Waverley*' and 'the prime number between 5 and 11' become:

$$(\imath x)(x \text{ wrote } Waverley), \qquad (\imath x)(x \text{ is prime } . \ 5 < x < 11).$$

Singular terms are called *descriptions* when written in this form. The singular terms of ordinary language which may be represented thus as descriptions begin typically with the singular 'the', but by no means necessarily so, as these examples show:

what he went after,	$(\imath x)$(he went after x);
where he was born,	$(\imath x)$(he was born at x);
John's mother,	$(\imath x)(x$ bore John);
Smith's house,	$(\imath x)(x$ is a house . x is Smith's).

In general a singular term purports to name one and only one object, and in particular a singular term of the form '$(\imath x)Fx$' purports to name the one and only object of which the predicate represented by 'F' is true. Thus, if y is the object $(\imath x)Fx$, then y must be such that

$$Fy \ . \ F \text{ nothing-but-}y.$$

This conjunction amounts to saying that, for each thing x, 'F' is true of x if $x = y$, and false of x otherwise. In short:

(1) $$(x)(Fx \equiv . \ x = y).$$

E.g., to say that Scott is $(\imath x)(x$ wrote *Waverley*) is to say that

$$(x)(x \text{ wrote } Waverley \equiv . \ x = \text{Scott}).$$

If 'F' is true of nothing or of many things, then there is no such thing as $(\imath x)Fx$. Actually the predicate appearing in the rôle of the 'F' of '$(\imath x)Fx$' in verbal examples from ordinary discourse very frequently needs supplementary clauses to narrow it down to the point of being true of only one object, but this situation can commonly be viewed merely as a case of the familiar practice of depending on context or situation to resolve ambiguities of ordinary language.

We saw in Chapter 38 that arguments involving a singular term can be carried through by straight quantification theory with a free variable, say 'y', for the singular term, but that the application of the results depends on construing y as the object named by the singular term, and hence is contingent on existence of such an object. This construing of y, and the existence assumption on which it rests, figured nowhere in the schematism of the proof, but only in the informal step of application. Now the beauty of descriptions is that here the construing of y as the named object can itself be schematized quite explicitly as an additional premise, of the form (1) above. So our technique for arguments involving descriptions is as follows: we use free variables for the descriptions as for any singular terms, but we also add a *descriptional premise* of the form (1) for each description. An axiom of identity is also usually called for, because of the '$=$' in the descriptional premise. Thus let us try this example:

PREMISE: The broker who hired John hired only honors graduates,

CONCLUSION: John was an honors graduate.

Here we have two singular terms, the simple one 'John' and the complex one 'the broker who hired John'. Let us represent them by free variables 'w' and 'y' respectively. Writing 'F' for 'broker' and 'G' for 'hired', we may also render the complex singular term as a description '$(\imath x)(Fx \; . \; Gxw)$'; so the corresponding descriptional premise is:

$$(x)(Fx \; . \; Gxw \; .\equiv. \; x = y).$$

So from this and the original premise, which is '$(x)(Gyx \supset Hx)$' where 'H' represents 'honors graduate', and perhaps an axiom of identity in addition, we want to show that 'Hw' follows. We do so by transforming the conditional:

$$(x)(Fx \; . \; Gxw \; .\equiv. \; x = y) \; . \; (x)(Gyx \supset Hx) \; . \; (x)(x = x) \; .\supset Hw$$

into a pure existential and quickly finding it valid.

    Whether a proposed deduction is to enjoy the benefits of a descriptional premise depends, evidently, on whether a given singular term can fairly be translated into the form of a description. Now fairness of translation is a vague matter, hinging as it does on the concept of synonymy which was so dimly regarded in Chapter 38. 'The author of *Waverley*' seems fairly translatable as '$(\imath x)(x$ wrote *Waverley*$)$', but 'Scott' and 'the author of *Ivanhoe*' do not, despite the fact that all of these name the same object; for it is felt that 'the author of *Waverley*' is connected with '$(\imath x)(x$ wrote *Waverley*$)$' by sheer meaning, whereas 'Scott' and 'the author of *Ivanhoe*' are connected with it through accidental matters of fact.

    At the same time it seems that singular terms can depart widely in form from the singular 'the' idiom and still be fairly deemed translatable into descriptions; witness 'John's mother'. Indeed, even so simple a term as 'Socrates', Russell has argued,[7] is for each of us synonymous with some description, perhaps '$(\imath x)(x$ was a philosopher $. \; x$ drank hemlock)' or perhaps another depending on how each of us first learned of Socrates. Are then all singular terms to be considered capable of fair translation into descriptions, except for those very few names which we may be supposed to have learned by direct confrontation with name and object? Must a separate category then be kept open for these few hypothetical exceptions?

Happily, we can isolate such epistemological considerations from the logic of singular terms by a very simple expedient: by insisting on the primacy of predicates. We may insist that what are learned by ostension, or direct confrontation, be never names but solely predicates. This we may insist on at the level strictly of logical grammar, without prejudice to epistemology or ontology. Without prejudice to ontology because the same things remain, whether as things which names name or as things which predicates are true of. Without prejudice to epistemology because we may grant the epistemologist any of the words which he traces to ostension; we merely parse them differently. Instead of treating the ostensively learned word as a *name of* the shown object to begin with, we treat it to begin with as a predicate *true* exclusively of the shown object; then we construe the name, as such, as amounting to '$(\imath x)Fx$' where 'F' represents that primitive predicate. No matter to epistemology, but much to the smoothness of logical theory.

So there is no longer an obstacle to treating all singular terms as descriptions. Given any singular term of ordinary language, moreover, say 'Socrates' or 'Cerberus' or 'the author of *Waverley*', the proper choice of 'F' for translation of the term into '$(\imath x)Fx$' need in practice never detain us. If a pat translation such as '$(\imath x)(x$ wrote *Waverley*)' lies ready to hand, very well; if not, we need not hesitate to admit a version of the type of '$(\imath x)(x$ is-Socrates)' or '$(\imath x)(x$ is-Cerberus)', since any less lame version would, if admissible as a translation at all, differ at most in expository value and not in meaning.

Proofs of the type of the broker example set forth above are in no way facilitated by thus trivially transforming simple singular terms into descriptions. Construing 'John' in the broker example as a description '$(\imath x)(x$ is-John)', or '$(\imath x)Jx$', would entitle us to a further descriptional premise '$(x)(Jx \equiv . \; x = w)$', but this is neither necessary nor useful for the progress of the deduction. The advantage of treating all singular terms as descriptions is of a more theoretical kind: that of sparing us having to admit into the framework of our technical theory a distinction between a category of descriptions and a category of nondescriptive singular terms. It is theoretically important not to have to admit this distinction because, as we have seen, the question of there being essentially nondescriptive singular terms at all, and if so what, was shrouded in the theory of knowledge and meaning.

---

[7] E.g., in "Knowledge by acquaintance."

We have segregated that issue from our concerns, by shifting it from the realm of singular terms into that of predicates. Every singular term can now, trivially if not otherwise, be handled as a description; what had been an issue over names learned ostensively versus names learned discursively now becomes an issue over predicates learned ostensively versus predicates learned discursively. In this form the issue ceases to cut across any of our schematism of logical forms and categories, and can be left to other minds.

There is a yet more striking benefit to be gained from treating all singular terms as descriptions, but it must await the next chapter.

EXERCISES

1. Express 'the tallest man in town' in the form '$(\imath x)(\ldots x \ldots)$', using 'taller than' but not 'tallest'.

2. Show that a descriptional premise, an axiom of identity, and the premise:

   The author of *Waverley* wrote *Ivanhoe*

together imply:

   Someone wrote both *Waverley* and *Ivanhoe*.

42

ELIMINATION OF SINGULAR TERMS

Let us next take up the problem, which has been looming for some time, of the truth value of such statements as 'Cerberus barks'. Falsity, as a sweeping answer covering all statements containing 'Cerberus', would be over-hasty: first, because the statement 'There is no such thing as Cerberus', at least, is true; and second, because whatever statements we adjudge false must admit of compounds, e.g., their negations, which will be true. Truth, as a sweeping answer, would encounter parallel difficulties.

Our deductive methods for singular terms throw no light on the question; for we already assume that the singular term names an object when we represent the singular term by a free variable, and we make the same assumption again when we adopt a descriptive premise for a description. Failing a named object, our methods show nothing, for what they purport to show rests then on a contrary-to-fact assumption. Common usage, moreover, likewise leaves us in the dark; for, excepting such contexts as 'There is no such thing as Cerberus', a singular term is ordinarily used only when the speaker believes or cares to pretend that the object exists.

Under ordinary usage, we saw (Chapter 3), truth values attach not to indicative conditionals as wholes but only to the consequents conditionally upon truth of the antecedents. Analogously, under ordinary usage truth values attach to contexts of singular terms for the most part only conditionally upon existence of the objects. But if we are to have a smooth logical theory we must fill such gaps, even though arbitrarily, in such a way that every statement comes to have a truth value. Thus it was that we conventionally extended the concept of the conditional, in Chapter 3, so as to allow truth values generally to conditionals as wholes. An extension in the same spirit is needed now on the score of singular terms that do not name.

We cannot, we have seen, accomplish this extension by any blanket decision that all contexts of a term such as 'Cerberus' are to be false, or all true. We can, however, decide the simple contexts and then let the truth values of the compounds follow from those decisions. Let us speak of a predicate as *simple*, for our purposes, when it does not explicitly have the form of a quantification, negation, conjunction, alternation, conditional, or biconditional of shorter components. When any such simple predicate is applied to a singular term which fails to name, let us classify the resulting sentence as false (for all values of any free variables it may have). Thus 'Cerberus barks', formed as it is by applying the simple predicate '① barks' to 'Cerberus', is adjudged false.

This rule is suited for use only upon sentences which are considered to be fully analyzed in point of logical structure. If the sentences are still to be subject to further paraphrasing of words into symbols, we must be wary of treating a predicate as "simple" in the sense above and then paraphrasing it into a complex one.

For illustration let us reexamine the statement:

(1)   The broker who hired John hired only honors graduates.

If we use '*F*' for 'broker' and '*G*' for 'hired', then 'the broker who hired John' may be rendered '$(\imath x)(Fx \, . \, G \, x \, \text{John})$'. To say that this alleged person hired *u* is then to say:

(2) $G \, (\imath x)(Fx \, . \, G \, x \, \text{John}) \, u,$

so that (1) becomes:

(3) $(u)[G\;(\imath x)(Fx\;.\;G\,x\;\text{John})\;u \supset Hu]$

where 'H' means 'honors graduate'. Now let us suppose that no broker
or several hired John, so that there is no such thing as *the* broker who hired
John. According to the decision which we have newly adopted to cover
such cases, the simple context (2) of '$(\imath x)(Fx\;.\;G\,x\;\text{John})$' is then to be
classified as false for all choices of u. Thereupon the conditional in (3)
becomes true for all choices of u through falsity of antecedent, so (3) becomes true. The outcome is therefore that (1) becomes true, independently
of any consideration of honors graduates, in case John was hired by no
broker or several. This particular outcome is the merest curiosity, neither
welcome nor unwelcome, since ordinary usage leaves cases such as this
undecided.

Even when a singular term fails to name, however, we do have very
proper preconceptions about the truth value of the special context 'There
is [or: is not] such a thing as ...'. But statements of this form call for a
separate analysis, along lines which are already pretty evident from these
past observations:

(a)   We may take '$(\imath x)Fx$' as the general form for singular terms.

(b)   '$(\imath x)Fx$' purports to name the one and only object of which 'F'
is true (supposing any particular predicate for 'F' here).

(c)   '$(x)(Fx \equiv .\; x = y)$' amounts to saying that y is the one and only
object of which 'F' is true.

To say that there is such a thing as $(\imath x)Fx$ is to say, in view of (b), that
there is one and only one object of which 'F' is true; and this may, in view
of (c), be said as follows:

(4) $(\exists y)(x)(Fx \equiv .\; x = y).$

Here, then, is an adequate formulation of 'There is such a thing as $(\imath x)Fx$';
and no more can be wanted, in view of (a), in formulation of the general
idiom 'There is such a thing as ...'.

Curiously enough, the translation (4) of 'There is such a thing as $(\imath x)Fx$'
is devoid of the singular term '$(\imath x)Fx$'. Now elimination of '$(\imath x)Fx$' from
other contexts can also be accomplished. For, think of 'G' as representing
any predicate which is "simple" in the recently defined sense. Then
'$G\;(\imath x)Fx$', which attributes 'G' to $(\imath x)Fx$, may be paraphrased as:

(5) $(\exists y)[Gy\;.\;(x)(Fx \equiv .\; x = y)].$

This is seen as follows. First suppose (Case 1) that there is such a thing
as $(\imath x)Fx$. Then the clause '$(x)(Fx \equiv .\; x = y)$' identifies y with $(\imath x)Fx$, and
accordingly (5) as a whole becomes true or false according as 'G' is true

or false of $(\imath x)Fx$. Next suppose (Case 2) that there is no such thing as $(\imath x)Fx$. Then '$(x)(Fx \equiv . x = y)$' becomes false for all choices of y; so (5) becomes false. But '$G (\imath x)Fx$' likewise is to be false in this case, according to our recent agreement about simple predicates in application to singular terms that do not name.

We are now in a position to eliminate singular terms everywhere. Given any sentence involving singular terms, we begin by paraphrasing the sentence into the explicit notation of quantification and truth functions as fully as we can, leaving the singular terms undisturbed as components but putting each in the form of a description. Then we supplant each simple context of each description by its equivalent of the form (5)—or by (4) if it happens to have the form 'there is such a thing as $(\imath x)Fx$'.

For simplicity we have been imagining always *closed* singular terms, as opposed to open ones such as '$x + 5$' or 'the eldest son of x' or '$(\imath x)(x$ wrote $z)$'. Clearly, however, the open ones admit of elimination by the same procedure; the fact that a free variable is being carried along alters nothing essential to the reasoning.

To see how the elimination of singular terms proceeds in practice, let us return to (1) and eliminate the singular terms 'John' and 'the broker who hired John'. As a first step we may eliminate the description from the simple context (2). The general method of doing this was seen in the translation of '$G (\imath x)Fx$' into (5); but what we have to deal with now in place of '$G (\imath x)Fx$' is (2), which is of the form of '$G (\imath x)Fx$' with '$F\text{①} . G\text{①}$ John' for 'F' and '$G\text{①}u$' for 'G'. These same substitutions in (5) give:

(6) $\qquad (\exists y)[Gyu . (x)(Fx . G x \text{ John} . \equiv . x = y)],$

then, as the translation of (2). But 'John' has yet to be dealt with. Writing 'J' for 'is-John', we render 'John' as a description '$(\imath z)Jz$', so that '$G x$ John' in (6) becomes '$Gx(\imath z)Jz$'. This clause is of the form '$G(\imath x)Fx$' with 'z' for 'x', 'J' for 'F', and '$Gx\text{①}$' for 'G'. Corresponding changes in (5) give:

(7) $\qquad (\exists w)[Gxw . (z)(Jz \equiv . z = w)],$

then, as translation of '$Gx(\imath z)Jz$'. Now we have eliminated both singular terms. It remains only to assemble the pieces, by putting (7) for '$G x$ John' in (6) and then putting the result for (2) in (3). We thus get:

$$(u)[(\exists y)(Gyu . (x)\{Fx . (\exists w)[Gxw . (z)(Jz \equiv . z = w)] . \equiv . x = y\}) \supset Hu]$$

as our final paraphrase of (1). But by now it begins to appear that the elimination of descriptions is of essentially theoretical interest, and that in practice the alternative handling of the broker problem which was noted in the preceding chapter recommends itself highly.

Nevertheless, the theoretical eliminability of singular terms—the dispensability of all names—is so startling that its importance scarcely needs dwelling upon, except in the negative fashion of pointing out what it does not mean. It does not mean that our language loses all means of talking about objects; on the contrary, the foregoing considerations show that the extrusion of singular terms is unaccompanied by any diminution in the power of the language. What the disappearance of singular terms does mean is that all reference to objects of any kind, concrete or abstract, is narrowed down now to one specific channel: variables of quantification. We can still say anything we like about any one object or all objects, but we say it always through the idioms of quantification: 'There is an object x such that ...' and 'Every object x is such that ...'. The objects whose existence is implied in our discourse are finally just the objects which must, for the truth of our assertions, be acknowledged as "values of variables"— i.e., be reckoned into the totality of objects over which our variables of quantification range. To be is to be a value of a variable. There are no ultimate philosophical problems concerning terms and their references, but only concerning variables and their values; and there are no ultimate philosophical problems concerning existence except insofar as existence is expressed by the quantifier '$(\exists x)$'. Except when we are concerned with philosophical issues of linguistic reference and existence, on the other hand, there is no point in depriving ourselves of the convenience of singular terms; and accordingly the techniques of inference hitherto developed for singular terms are not to be thought of as abandoned.

HISTORICAL NOTE: Frege had a notation for the description prefix in 1893. The present notation was adapted later from Peano by Russell. The important idea of eliminating descriptions by paraphrasing the context, substantially as above, was original with Russell, 1905; and it is in allusion to Russell's examples that the author of *Waverley* continues to be mentioned in subsequent writings on the subject. Russell did not take the further step of treating all names as descriptions and thus eliminating them too. He preferred to preserve an epistemological distinction between names that were short for descriptions and names that were irreducibly proper, learned by acquaintance.

EXERCISE

Put the statement:

The woman who lives above us is German and loves flowers

into symbols, using 'Fx' for 'x is a woman', 'Gx' for 'x lives above us', 'Hx', for 'x is German', and 'Jx' for 'x loves flowers'. Then transform the whole so as to eliminate use of description.

43
CLASSES

The evident analogy between variables '*x*', '*y*', etc., and schematic letters '*F*', '*G*', etc., tempts us to try using the latter in quantifiers, e.g., thus:

(1) $(F)[(x)Fx \supset (\exists x)Fx]$,
(2) $(\exists F)[(\exists x)Fx \,.\, -(x)Fx]$.

However, let us not be hasty in supposing that we understand (1) and (2). We have been reading the quantifiers '(x)' and '$(\exists x)$' in the fashion 'each thing *x* is such that' and 'something *x* is such that', but how are we to read '(F)' and '$(\exists F)$'? May we read '(F)' in the fashion 'each general term (or predicate) *F* is such that', and '$(\exists F)$' correspondingly? No, this is a confusion. '*F*' has never been thought of as referring to general terms (and thus as standing in place of *names of* general terms), but only as standing in place of general terms. If there were objects of a special sort, say gimmicks, of which general terms were names, then the proper readings of '(F)' and '$(\exists F)$' would be 'each gimmick *F* is such that' and 'some gimmick *F* is such that'. But the difficulty is that general terms are not names at all.

From time to time we have, however, associated certain abstract entities, called classes, or sets, with general terms. We have never treated general terms as names of classes, but we have spoken of general terms as having classes as their so-called extensions. So classes recommend themselves as objects for the newly quantified variable '*F*' to range over. We can read '(F)' and '$(\exists F)$' in (1) and (2) as 'each class *F* is such that' and 'some class *F* is such that', provided that we also reread '*Fx*' for present purposes as '*x* is a member of the class *F*'.

But we have now strained '*F*' away from its former usage in two important respects. The new reading of '*Fx*' involves use of '*F*' in positions appropriate no longer to general terms, but to abstract singular terms, viz. class names; and the use of '*F*' in quantifiers changes the status of '*F*' from schematic letter to variable. It is more conducive to clarity to renounce this altered usage of '*F*' and adopt instead a fresh notation for the new purposes: variables 'α', 'β', 'γ', ... for classes, and 'ε' for 'is a member of'. (1) and (2) then give way to:

(3) $(\alpha)[(x)(x \,\varepsilon\, \alpha) \supset (\exists x)(x \,\varepsilon\, \alpha)]$,
(4) $(\exists \alpha)[(\exists x)(x \,\varepsilon\, \alpha) \,.\, -(x)(x \,\varepsilon\, \alpha)]$.

Such sentences combine variables which range over two distinct universes. The variables '*x*', '*y*', etc., range over some unspecified universe *U*, while the variables 'α', 'β', etc., range over a distinct but related universe U_1 composed of the subclasses of U: the classes whose members belong to U. The simplest sentences of this class-theory notation consist of 'ε' with an ordinary variable on its left and a class variable on its right, in the manner '$x \varepsilon \alpha$'; and all further sentences are built up by quantification and truth functions from these simple ones.

Up to a point, despite its overt reference to a new realm of entities called classes, this new branch of logic can be created by definition in terms merely of the concepts of validity and consistency of quantificational schemata. To say that the schema '$(x)Fx \supset (\exists x)Fx$' is valid is, we know, to say that it comes out true under all choices of classes as extensions of 'F'; hence to affirm the statement (3) or (1) of class theory as true amounts merely to affirming the validity of the schema '$(x)Fx \supset (\exists x)Fx$'. Similarly to affirm (4) or (2) as true amounts to affirming the consistency of the quantificational schema '$(\exists x)Fx . - (x)Fx$'. Such an account of (3) and (4) is interesting in that, within its limits, it explains statements about classes without presupposing classes. Use is made merely of the concepts of quantificational validity and consistency. These concepts were themselves explained in turn in terms of classes at one stage, but in Chapter 32 we found that they could be specified also in terms of decision procedures or deductive rules, or again in terms of substitution, without dependence on the class concept.

A statement in our new class-theory notation can be explained in terms of validity or consistency, as was done for (3) and (4) above, as long as the statement is of the following sort: its class variables all refer back to prenex quantifiers, and furthermore all the quantifiers, through the last class quantifier, are uniformly universal or uniformly existential. If they are universal, truth of the statement amounts to validity of the corresponding quantificational schema; if they are existential, truth of the statement amounts to consistency of the schema. E.g., truth of the statements:

$$(x)(\alpha)[x \varepsilon \alpha . \supset (\exists y)(y \varepsilon \alpha)],$$
$$(\exists \alpha)(\exists \beta)(x)(x \varepsilon \alpha . \equiv . x \varepsilon \beta)$$

of class theory amounts to validity and consistency of the respective schemata:

$$Fx \supset (\exists y)Fy, \qquad (x)(Fx \equiv Gx)$$

of quantification theory.

This expedient can be pushed a bit. Quantifiers internal to a statement can be brought into prenex position in the usual way. Thus the statement:

$$(\exists \alpha)[(\beta)(x)(x \varepsilon \beta . \supset . x \varepsilon \alpha) \supset (\exists \gamma)(\exists x)(x \varepsilon \gamma . x \varepsilon \alpha)],$$

with buried class quantifiers '(β)' and '$(\exists \gamma)$', can be transformed through the stages:

$$(\exists \alpha)(\exists \beta)[(x)(x \, \varepsilon \, \beta \, . \supset . \, x \, \varepsilon \, \alpha) \supset (\exists \gamma)(\exists x)(x \, \varepsilon \, \gamma \, . \, x \, \varepsilon \, \alpha)],$$
$$(\exists \alpha)(\exists \beta)(\exists \gamma)[(x)(x \, \varepsilon \, \beta \, . \supset . \, x \, \varepsilon \, \alpha) \supset (\exists x)(x \, \varepsilon \, \gamma \, . \, x \, \varepsilon \, \alpha)],$$

and this last can be explained as merely affirming, in effect, the consistency of the quantificational schema:

$$(x)(Gx \supset Fx) \supset (\exists x)(Hx \, . \, Fx).$$

If all statements constructible in our class-theory notation could thus be equated to consistencies and validities of quantification theory, we could regard our theory of classes merely as a picturesquely transcribed account of quantification theory; classes would not need to be acknowledged as seriously presupposed entities. However, the situation is otherwise. Statements of class theory cannot be explained away in the above fashion when their prenex quantifiers are mixedly universal and existential as in the examples:

(5) $\qquad (\alpha)(\exists \beta)(x)(x \, \varepsilon \, \alpha \, . \equiv . \, x \, \varepsilon \, \beta),$
(6) $\qquad (x)(y)(\exists \alpha)(x \, \varepsilon \, \alpha \, . \equiv . \, y \, \varepsilon \, \alpha).$

It is in such statements that the irreducible substance of class theory is to be sought. Similarly for statements containing buried class quantifiers which, when brought into prenex position by the rules of passage, become mixedly universal and existential; e.g.:

(7) $\qquad (x)(y)[(\alpha)(x \, \varepsilon \, \alpha \, . \supset . \, y \, \varepsilon \, \alpha) \supset (\beta)(y \, \varepsilon \, \beta \, . \supset . \, x \, \varepsilon \, \beta)],$

which, transformed by (7) and (6) of Chapter 22, becomes:

$$(x)(y)(\exists \alpha)(\beta)(x \, \varepsilon \, \alpha \, . \supset . \, y \, \varepsilon \, \alpha \, : \supset : y \, \varepsilon \, \beta \, . \supset . \, x \, \varepsilon \, \beta).$$

That (5)–(7) are true is a point not expressible in terms merely of validity of quantificational schemata. Thus the general adoption of class variables of quantification ushers in a theory whose laws were not in general expressible in the antecedent levels of logic. The price paid for this increased power is ontological: objects of a special and abstract kind, viz., classes, are now presupposed. Formally it is precisely in allowing quantification irreducibly over class variables 'α', 'β', etc., that we assume a range of values for these variables to refer to. To be assumed as an entity is to be assumed as a value of a variable.

But this power of expressing irreducibly new laws would of itself justify little interest in class theory, were it not accompanied by a corresponding increase of power on the side of application. A good example of this effect may be seen in the definition of the predicate or relative term 'ancestor' on the basis of 'parent'. To simplify the situation let us understand 'ancestor' in a slightly broadened sense, thereby counting as a person's ancestors not only his parents, grandparents, and so on, but also the person himself. Let us represent 'parent' by 'F', so that 'Fxy' means 'x is a parent of y'. Now the problem is to write 'x is an ancestor of y' using only 'F' and our various logical symbols.

An important feature of the class of y's ancestors is that all parents of members of the class are members of it in turn. Another feature of it is that y himself belongs to it. But these two features do not yet fix the class of y's ancestors uniquely; there are larger classes which also contain y and contain all parents of members. One such class is the class of the ancestors of y's grandsons. Another such class is the combined class of y's ancestors and neckties; for, neckties being parentless, their inclusion does not disturb the fact that all parents of members are members. But clearly every class which contains y and all parents of members will have at least to contain all y's ancestors, no matter what extra things it may happen to contain. Moreover, *one* of these classes contains nothing but y's ancestors. Hence to be an ancestor of y it is necessary and sufficient to belong to every class which contains y and all parents of members. Therefore 'x is an ancestor of y' can be written thus:

x belongs to every class which contains y and all parents of members;

i.e.:

$(\alpha)(y \, \varepsilon \, \alpha$. all parents of members of α belong to α .$\supset$. $x \, \varepsilon \, \alpha)$;

i.e.:

(8) $(\alpha)[y \, \varepsilon \, \alpha$. $(z)(w)(w \, \varepsilon \, \alpha$. Fzw .$\supset$. $z \, \varepsilon \, \alpha)$.$\supset$. $x \, \varepsilon \, \alpha]$.

This ingenious construction admits of many applications besides this genealogical one. An application to number will be encountered in the next section. But what is significant about the construction for present purposes is that it makes essential use of quantification of a class variable 'α'.

A new example of the power gained by quantifying over classes has been proposed by Geach and perfected by David Kaplan, in private correspondence:

(9)   Some people admire one another and no one else.

Kaplan has proved that we cannot express this in terms of just the verb 'admires' and truth functions and quantification over persons. (9) does not imply that

$(\exists x)(\exists y)[x \neq y$. $(z)(x$ admires $z \equiv$. $z = y$: y admires $z \equiv$. $z = x)]$.

There might be no two such snobs as x and y here, but still (9) might hold by virtue of some group of say eleven mutual admirers. Invoking classes, we can do justice to (9):

$$(\exists \alpha)((\exists x)(\exists y)(x \, \varepsilon \, \alpha \, . \, y \, \varepsilon \, \alpha \, . \, x \neq y)$$
$$. \, (x)[x \, \varepsilon \, \alpha \, . \supset \, (y)(x \text{ admires } y \equiv . \, x \neq y \, . \, y \, \varepsilon \, \alpha)]).$$

A simpler illustration of our new access of power may be seen in the fact that the sign '$=$' of identity now becomes superfluous; for instead of writing '$x = y$' we may say that x and y belong to just the same classes, thus:

$$(\alpha)(x \, \varepsilon \, \alpha \, . \equiv . \, y \, \varepsilon \, \alpha).$$

Identity of classes, '$\alpha = \beta$', may be explained in a somewhat opposite way, as meaning that α and β have just the same members. So the convenient sign '$=$' may now be viewed as a mere abbreviation, according to these "definitions" or conventions of abbreviation:

'$x = y$'	for	'$(\alpha)(x \, \varepsilon \, \alpha \, . \equiv . \, y \, \varepsilon \, \alpha)$',
'$\alpha = \beta$'	for	'$(x)(x \, \varepsilon \, \alpha \, . \equiv . \, x \, \varepsilon \, \beta)$'.

So, while we may continue to use the sign '$=$' as a convenience, it is superfluous and may always be imagined eliminated as above.

Once the notation of identity is thus at hand, we can also allow ourselves the further luxury of the notation of *description* without having to reckon it into our inventory of basic notation. For we know from the preceding chapter how, with help of identity, to eliminate a description from any statement in which it occurs.

Occasion continually arises in class theory to speak of the class of all and only the objects fulfilling a given condition. Where 'Fx' represents any open sentence involving 'x', we write '$\{x : Fx\}$' for the class of all objects x such that Fx. Class names thus formed are called *abstracts*. Clearly we can define them as abbreviations of descriptions, thus:

$$\text{'}\{x : Fx\}\text{'} \quad \text{for} \quad \text{'}(\imath \alpha)(x)(x \, \varepsilon \, \alpha \, . \equiv Fx)\text{'}.$$

The special abbreviations '$\bar{\alpha}$', '$\alpha\beta$', and '$\alpha \vee \beta$', or others, are commonly adopted for the three abstracts:

$$\{x : -(x \, \varepsilon \, \alpha)\}, \quad \{x : x \, \varepsilon \, \alpha \, . \, x \, \varepsilon \, \beta\}, \quad \{x : x \, \varepsilon \, \alpha \, .\vee. \, x \, \varepsilon \, \beta\}.$$

This carries us back to the Boolean class algebra of Chapter 20. Once we are embarked on a general theory of classes, or set theory, naturally we take the Boolean class algebra as an integral part of it. Taken by itself, on the other hand, this algebra is in essential respects independent of the whole assumption of classes; cf. Chapter 20. The serious motive for assuming classes is to be found rather in constructions such as that of ancestor, or (9).

HISTORICAL NOTE: The construction illustrated in the definition of ancestor was introduced by Frege in 1879 for application to number. It was rediscovered independently a few years later by Peirce, and again by Dedekind, who propounded it in 1887 under the name of the method of *chains*. For other historical points see the end of Chapter 20.

EXERCISES

1. Using the above definitions, and the method of the preceding chapter for eliminating descriptions, expand '$y \, \varepsilon \, \{x : x \, \varepsilon \, \alpha\}$' step by step into unabbreviated class-theory notation.

2. If we were developing theorems for class theory, we should certainly want '$\alpha = \{x : x \, \varepsilon \, \alpha\}$' as one. Expand this into unabbreviated class-theory notation. Concerning the appropriate order of steps see fifth paragraph of Chapter 42.

44

NUMBER

We say the Apostles are twelve, but not in the sense in which we say they are pious; for we attribute piety, but not twelveness, to each. 'The Apostles are pious' has the form '$(x)(Fx \supset Gx)$', with 'F' for 'Apostle' and 'G' for 'pious'; but 'The Apostles are twelve' has no such form, and is more nearly comparable to the mere existential quantification '$(\exists x)Fx$'. This familiar quantification may be read 'The Apostles are at least one'; and we might analogously think of 'The Apostles are twelve' as written:

$$(\exists x)Fx,$$
$$12$$

using what is called a *numerically definite* quantifier.

Numerically definite quantifiers can be introduced on the basis purely of the theory of quantification and identity, as of Chapter 40; there is no need here of assuming classes as in Chapter 43. For, we can begin by explaining '$(\exists x)$' easily enough:

$$\text{`}(\exists x)Fx\text{'} \quad \text{for} \quad \text{`}-(\exists x)Fx\text{'}.$$
$$\quad {}_0 \qquad\qquad\qquad {}_0$$

Then we can explain each succeeding numerical quantifier in terms of its predecessor in a uniform way:

$$\text{`}(\exists x)Fx\text{'} \quad \text{for} \quad \text{`}(\exists x)[Fx . (\exists y)(Fy . y \neq x)]\text{'},$$
$$\quad {}_1 \qquad\qquad\qquad\qquad {}_0$$
$$\text{`}(\exists x)Fx\text{'} \quad \text{for} \quad \text{`}(\exists x)[Fx . (\exists y)(Fy . y \neq x)]\text{'},$$
$$\quad {}_2 \qquad\qquad\qquad\qquad {}_1$$
$$\text{`}(\exists x)Fx\text{'} \quad \text{for} \quad \text{`}(\exists x)[Fx . (\exists y)(Fy . y \neq x)]\text{'},$$
$$\quad {}_3 \qquad\qquad\qquad\qquad {}_2$$

and so on. The general pattern is this: for anything to be true of $n + 1$ things is for it to be true of something other than which it is true of n things. By a dozen steps of successive expansion according to these definitions, '$(\exists x)Fx$' goes over into a schema of pure identity theory as of Chapter 40.
${}_{12}$
Similarly for any other numerically definite quantification. However, we still have no expansion for '$(\exists x)Fx$' with variable 'n'. Thus, though we can
${}_n$
easily say there are twelve Apostles and twelve Muses, in the form:

$$(\exists x)Fx . (\exists x)Gx,$$
$$\;{}_{12} \qquad\quad {}_{12}$$

we find difficulty if we want to say simply 'There are just as many Apostles as Muses' without saying how many. The plan:

$$(\exists n)[(\exists x)Fx . (\exists x)Gx]$$
$$\qquad\quad {}_n \qquad\quad {}_n$$

is of no avail, for no definitions are at hand for expanding this expression into the notation of Chapter 40, nor even into that of Chapter 43.

All high-school students appreciate the persistence, and some the utility, of number variables in algebra. The example above and such related ones as 'There are twice as many eyes as faces' suggest that quantifiable number variables have a place also in the analysis of virtually unmathematical discourse.

If we are to have quantified variables for numbers we must find entities in our universe to view as numbers—or else expand our universe to include such entities. As a step toward a reasonable theory of numbers, consider the adjective 'twelvefold'. If we are to recognize such a predicate (and not merely a corresponding type of quantifier '$(\exists x)$'), we must recognize it as a
${}_{12}$
predicate which is true not of persons, e.g., Apostles, but rather of classes,

e.g., the class of Apostles. Thus we may define '12-fold α' as short for '$(\exists y)(y \, \varepsilon \, \alpha)$'; 'is twelvefold' means 'has twelve members'. Now the remaining step to the number 12 as an entity is a short one; for it is natural to construe 12 as the extension of 'twelvefold'. Thus 12 becomes identified with the class of all twelvefold classes.

Now we find ourselves exceeding the basis both of the theory of identity (Chapter 40) and of our present theory of classes. Variables ranging over numbers are going to have to be of a new category 'κ', 'λ', etc., taking as values classes of classes. The range U_2 of these new variables has as members the subclasses of U_1, just as U_1 has as members the subclasses of U. This supplementation of our theory of classes brings with it a new form of simple sentence, '$\alpha \, \varepsilon \, \kappa$'. Also we have now to add a third part to our definition of identity (see preceding chapter):

$$\text{'}\kappa = \lambda\text{'} \quad \text{for} \quad \text{'}(\alpha)(\alpha \, \varepsilon \, \kappa \, . \equiv . \, \alpha \, \varepsilon \, \lambda)\text{'}.$$

The notation of descriptions may likewise be extended now to include the form '$(\imath \kappa)F\kappa$'; for, now that identity and quantification are at hand for variables of the type 'κ', a procedure parallel to that in Chapter 42 enables us to eliminate '$(\imath \kappa)F\kappa$' at will from any statement in which it occurs. The abstraction notation '$\{\alpha: F\alpha\}$', for the class of all classes α such that $F\alpha$, is then forthcoming as well. (See end of preceding chapter.)

The singular terms '0', '1', '2', etc., as names of numbers, may be construed in the form of abstracts. 0, to begin with, is the class of all and only those classes α which have no members.

$$\text{'0'} \quad \text{for} \quad \text{'}\hat{\alpha} - (\exists x)(x \, \varepsilon \, \alpha)\text{'}.$$

In other words, 0 is the class whose sole member is Λ, the empty class. 1 is the class of all those classes α which have exactly one member y apiece:

$$\text{'1'} \quad \text{for} \quad \text{'}\{\alpha: (\exists y)(x)(x \, \varepsilon \, \alpha \, . \equiv . \, x = y)\}\text{'}.$$

'2', '3', etc. may be explained in turn as '1 + 1', '1 + 2', etc., once we get a definition of '+'.

Addition of numbers κ and λ is easily definable in the light of this circumstance: a class α has $\kappa + \lambda$ members if and only if α is breakable into two parts β and γ such that β has κ members and γ has λ members. Now to say that β has κ members, where κ is a number, is simply to say that $\beta \, \varepsilon \, \kappa$. So we can define $\kappa + \lambda$ as the class of all classes α such that α is breakable into two parts β and γ such that $\beta \, \varepsilon \, \kappa$ and $\gamma \, \varepsilon \, \lambda$.

$$\text{'}\kappa + \lambda\text{'} \quad \text{for} \quad \text{'}\{\alpha: (\exists \beta)(\exists \gamma)[\beta \, \varepsilon \, \kappa \, . \, \gamma \, \varepsilon \, \lambda \, . \, (x) - (x \, \varepsilon \, \beta \, . \, x \, \varepsilon \, \gamma) \\ . \, (x)(x \, \varepsilon \, \alpha \, . \equiv : x \, \varepsilon \, \beta \, . \text{v.} \, x \, \varepsilon \, \gamma)]\text{'}.$$

Numbers are classes of classes, but not all classes of classes are numbers. The class of all twelvefold classes is a number; on the other hand a class of classes that has some but not all twelvefold classes as members is not a number, nor is a class of classes which has both fivefold and twelvefold classes as members. So the problem is still before us of setting up a formal definition of what it means to say that a class of classes κ is a number.

It may seem from the expository references to number in the foregoing discussion of '$\kappa + \lambda$' that the notion of being a number was already presupposed in defining '$\kappa + \lambda$'; inspection of the formal definition shows, however, that there is no such presupposition. The definition of '$\kappa + \lambda$' is adopted regardless of whether κ and λ are numbers, though the definition is of interest only where κ and λ are numbers.

Numbers as spoken of in these pages are just 0, 1, 2, ...—that is, 0 and the positive integers. Negative numbers, fractions, irrationals, and imaginaries do not come in for present consideration, not being of the sort used in measuring class size. So our present problem is to define 'Nκ', 'κ is a number', in such a way that it will come out true when and only when κ is 0 or 1 or 2, etc. A means of accomplishing this is suggested by the treatment of 'ancestor' in the preceding chapter. Just as 'ancestor of y' means 'y or parent of y or parent of parent of y or ...', so 'number' means '0 or 1 + 0 or 1 + (1 + 0) or ...'. So 'Nκ' receives the following definition, in close analogy to (8) of the preceding chapter:

'Nκ'   for   '$(\phi)[0 \, \varepsilon \, \phi \, . \, (\lambda)(\lambda \, \varepsilon \, \phi \, . \supset . \, 1 + \lambda \, \varepsilon \, \phi) \, . \supset . \, \kappa \, \varepsilon \, \phi]$'.

In words: to be a number is to belong to every class to which 0 belongs and 1 + each member belongs.

This definition supports *mathematical induction*, a proof procedure central to number theory. We prove that $(\kappa)(N\kappa \supset F\kappa)$, where '$F\kappa$' stands for some condition on κ, by proving that $F0$ and $(\lambda)[F\lambda \supset F(1 + \lambda)]$; such is mathematical induction. The reader should observe how the definition of 'Nκ' justifies this inference.

A technical point to notice about this definition is that it exceeds our acknowledged notational equipment by quantifying over classes ϕ of classes of classes. It presupposes another supplementation of our logic, quite like the recent supplementation whereby the variables 'κ', 'λ', etc., were introduced.

Where α and β are the classes respectively of Apostles and Muses, we can now say that they have the same number of members:[8]

(1) $(\exists \kappa)(N\kappa \, . \, \alpha \, \varepsilon \, \kappa \, . \, \beta \, \varepsilon \, \kappa)$.

---

[8] Readers less gifted than yourself may feel at this point that the Muses are being treated more tolerantly than Cerberus (Chapter 38), thus failing to appreciate that our example is none the worse for being false.

But in order to say this we have had to exceed the logic of quantification and identity, and enter upon the theory of classes; moreover we have had to exceed the most basic theory of classes and enter upon that which quantifies over classes of classes; and we have had even to exceed that level and ascend to the level of quantification over classes of classes of classes, for the clause '$N\kappa$' occurring in (1) conceals within it a quantifier '(ϕ)'.

Our progressively accrued quasi-universes U, U_1, U_2, and U_3, and any others that might be added in the same spirit, are known as *types*. Each is the range of a special category of variables. Each succeeding type in the series is the class of all the subclasses of the preceding type; or, to say the same thing differently, the things of each succeeding type are the classes of the things of the preceding type.

We have not decided how many things there are to be in our basic type U, nor, therefore, how big a class of such things can be; but we may be sure that if there are just, say, 71 things in U, then this is the biggest class size we can hope for in U_1. Thereupon all of the numbers beyond 71, having as alleged members classes which are too big to exist, will turn out to be empty and thus identical with one another. So, though our definitions of '0', '1', '2', etc., and of '$N\kappa$' may be held to unconditionally, they will deliver the unending series of numbers of classical arithmetic only in case U is infinite. It is only through infinity of U that U_1 can supply classes in all of the finite sizes. Yet once all such sizes are at hand, there will also necessarily be odd sizes to burn; for, if U is infinite, then some of the classes in U_1 will themselves be infinite.

HISTORICAL NOTE: The definition of numerically definite quantification, in effect, is in Frege (1884). So is the interpretation of numbers as classes of classes of appropriate size, and so is the definition of number in the pattern of ancestor. The theory of types is due to Russell (1908). The observations regarding finitude or infinitude of U are due to Whitehead and Russell (1912).

EXERCISES

1. Translate the following three sentences into symbols, making use of '$+$' and any other symbols defined in the foregoing pages. Understand α here as finite.

    $\kappa > \lambda$, α has more members than β,
    α has twice as many members as β.

2. Spell out the justification of mathematical induction.

45
RELATIONS

In its unsupplemented state as of Chapter 43, class theory was conceived in a certain analogy to monadic quantification theory. The class variables 'α', 'β', etc. ranged over the extensions of the one-place predicates represented by monadic 'F', 'G', etc., in quantification theory. Now we might extend the analogy to polyadic quantification theory by adding a category of variables 'Q', 'R', etc., to range over the extensions of two-place predicates, and another category to range over the extensions of three-place predicates, and so on. Let us content ourselves with a brief consideration of the two-place supplementation, this being the most characteristic and important of the series.

Whereas the class variables 'α', 'β', etc., range over the type U_1 of subclasses of U, the variables 'Q', 'R', etc., are to range over $_1U_1$, whose members are classes of pairs of members of U; for such were conceived to be the extensions of two-place predicates. Such pair-classes are spoken of in modern logic as *dyadic relations* or briefly *relations*. To say that x *bears* the relation R to y, or in other words that the pair of x and y belongs to R, we write 'xRy'. So the simple sentences of our new theory are of two forms, '$x \, \varepsilon \, \alpha$' and '$xRy$'; and the rest of the sentences are built from these by truth functions and quantification.

Parallel to the definition of class identity in Chapter 43, we can define identity of relations thus:

$$\text{`}Q = R\text{'} \quad \text{for} \quad \text{`}(x)(y)(xQy \equiv xRy)\text{'}.$$

The form of description '$(\imath R)FR$' then becomes available, being eliminable along the usual lines. Now just as in class theory the main utility of the description notation '$(\imath \alpha)F\alpha$' was as a basis for the abstraction notation '$\{x: Gx\}$', so in relation theory the main utility of the description notation '$(\imath R)FR$' is as a basis for a notation of relational abstraction:

$$\text{`}\{xy: Gxy\}\text{'} \quad \text{for} \quad \text{`}(\imath R)(x)(y)(xRy \equiv Gxy)\text{'}.$$

The prefix '$\{xy$:' may be read 'the relation of anything x to anything y such that'; thus

$$\{xy: (\exists z)(x \text{ is brother of } z \, . \, z \text{ is parent of } y)\}$$

is the uncle relation.

Analogues of '$\bar{\alpha}$', '$\alpha\beta$', an '$\alpha \vee \beta$' can now be defined for relations in obvious fashion:

$$\text{'}\bar{R}\text{'} \quad \text{for} \quad \text{'}\{xy: -(xRy)\}\text{'}, \qquad \text{'}QR\text{'} \quad \text{for} \quad \text{'}\{xy: xQy \cdot xRy\}\text{'},$$
$$\text{'}Q \vee R\text{'} \quad \text{for} \quad \text{'}\{xy: xQy \vee xRy\}\text{'}.$$

But of more interest are the peculiarly relational notions which are now definable, notably the *converse* $\breve{R}$ of a relation R, the *relative product* $Q \mid R$ of a relation Q into a relation R, and the *image* $R``\alpha$ of a class α by a relation R. The definitions are these:

$$\text{'}\breve{R}\text{'} \quad \text{for} \quad \text{'}\{xy: yRx\}\text{'},$$
$$\text{'}Q \mid R\text{'} \quad \text{for} \quad \text{'}\{xy: (\exists z)(xQz \cdot zRy)\}\text{'},$$
$$\text{'}R``\alpha\text{'} \quad \text{for} \quad \text{'}\{x: (\exists y)(xRy \cdot y \,\varepsilon\, \alpha)\}\text{'}.$$

Examples: Where R is the relation of teacher to pupil, $\breve{R}$ is the relation of pupil to teacher. Where Q is the relation of father and R is the relation of mother, $Q \mid R$ is the relation of maternal grandfather and $R \mid Q$ is the relation of paternal grandmother. Where R is the relation of father and α is the class of honors students, $R``\alpha$ is the class of fathers of honors students.

We can also define the relation of identity:

$$\text{'}I\text{'} \quad \text{for} \quad \text{'}\{xy: x = y\}\text{'}.$$

'xIy' and '$x = y$' are equivalent, but 'I' and '$=$' figure differently in them. 'xIy' is a case of 'xRy', like 'Cicero R y' or 'Cicero I Tully'; 'I' is a singular term (ultimately a description) naming one of the objects over which the variable 'R' ranges. On the other hand '$x = y$' bears only a misleading notational resemblance to 'xRy'; the sign '$=$' is no name of a value of 'R', not having been introduced as a singular term at all. 'I' names a relation, viz. the extension of the predicate '① $=$ ②' (as applied to individuals), whereas '$=$' does not name. Note that there is no definable relation which corresponds to 'ε' as I does to '$=$'; we cannot write '$\{x\alpha: x \,\varepsilon\, \alpha\}$', for the mixed type of prefix '$x\alpha$' has been introduced by none of our definitions. There is indeed no such relation in $_1U_1$, for the relations in $_1U_1$ pair members of U only with members of U, not with members of U_1.

Readers acquainted with the branch of mathematics known as group theory will recognize in '$\breve{R}$', '$Q \mid R$', and 'I' the basic notions of that discipline. Some sample laws governing these and the other notions just now defined are:

$$\breve{\breve{R}} = R, \qquad\qquad (Q \vee R)``\alpha = (Q``\alpha) \vee (R``\alpha),$$
$$I``\alpha = \alpha, \qquad\qquad R``(\alpha \vee \beta) = (R``\alpha) \vee (R``\beta),$$
$$I \mid R = R \mid I = R, \qquad Q \mid (R \mid S) = (Q \mid R) \mid S,$$
$$\breve{(Q \mid R)} = \breve{R} \mid \breve{Q}, \qquad Q``(R``\alpha) = (Q \mid R)``\alpha.$$

These laws and concepts are typical of the old *algebra of relations*. Of itself this algebra, like the algebra of classes (Chapter 20), does no more than reproduce in another form the content of quantification theory—or, when I is included, quantification theory and identity theory. The theory of classes and relations has its special power in connection with problems and constructions which make crucial use of the added ontological assumptions; crucial use, in other words, of quantification over classes and relations. There is indeed use of such quantification in defining (or eliminating) the notation of description which underlies class abstraction and relational abstraction, and the notations of abstraction are used in turn in the above definitions of the notations '$\breve{R}$', '$Q \mid R$', etc., of the algebra of relations; but that substructure is still not essential to these notions, for we could, if we liked, import the same notions directly into the schematism of quantification theory as follows:

$$\text{`}\breve{F}xy\text{'} \quad \text{for} \quad \text{`}Fyx\text{'}, \qquad \text{`}(F \mid G)xy\text{'} \quad \text{for} \quad \text{`}(\exists z)(Fxz \,.\, Gzy)\text{'},$$
$$\text{`}(F\text{``}G)x\text{'} \quad \text{for} \quad \text{`}(\exists y)(Fxy \,.\, Gy)\text{'}.$$

But quantification theory is on the whole simpler to think with when not thus encumbered.

A construction stressed in recent chapters, in which crucial use was made of quantification over classes, was that of 'ancestor' from 'parent'. Incidentally, now that relations as objects are at hand, we can carry over that construction as a definition of the so-called *ancestral of* a relation R:

$$\text{`}^{*}R\text{'} \quad \text{for} \quad \text{`}\{xy: (\alpha)[y \,\varepsilon\, \alpha \,.\, (z)(w)(w \,\varepsilon\, \alpha \,.\, zRw \,.\, \supset\, .\, z \,\varepsilon\, \alpha) \,.\, \supset\, .\, x \,\varepsilon\, \alpha]\}\text{'}.$$

This construction could not be duplicated in the schematism of quantification theory. The nearest we can come is to define '$^{*}Fxy$' as an abbreviation of (8) of page 238; but there is no eliminating 'α' and 'ε' from (8) of page 238 by putting a schematic letter 'G' for 'α', because of the quantifier '(α)'.

The respect in which this construction goes essentially beyond quantification theory is, we see, in quantification over classes, not relations. Now an example making essential use of quantification over relations may be seen by recurring to the problem of defining what it means to say that α and β are alike in size. This problem was already solved in the preceding chapter (for finite sizes only) at the cost of ascending through type U_2 to U_3; but we shall see now that it can also be solved in a different way by quantification over relations, type $_1U_1$, without ascending even to U_2. We may explain likeness of size on the part of α and β as consisting in the possibility of *correlating* the members of α with those of β, in such a way that each member of α is correlated with exactly one of β and each member of β has exactly one of α correlated with it. So we first define a relation R to be a *correlation* if no two objects bear it to the same object and no one object bears it to two.

'Crln R'   for   '$(x)(y)(z)(xRz . yRz .\text{v.} zRx . zRy :\supset. x = y)$'.

Now '$\alpha \text{ sim } \beta$', meaning that α is like β in size, may be defined to mean that there is a correlation R which relates each member of α to some member of β, and to each member of β some member of α. I.e., in symbols:

$$(\exists R)(\text{Crln } R . (x)[x \, \varepsilon \, \alpha .\supset (\exists y)(y \, \varepsilon \, \beta . xRy)]$$
$$. (y)[y \, \varepsilon \, \beta .\supset (\exists x)(x \, \varepsilon \, \alpha . xRy)]).$$

Here the quantification over a relation variable 'R' is essential.

Note that there is nothing essential about the use of 'α' or 'β' in the above construction. We could write 'Fx' and 'Gy' in place of '$x \, \varepsilon \, \alpha$' and '$y \, \varepsilon \, \beta$', and reconstrue the whole performance in terms of schematic letters as an account not of '$\alpha \text{ sim } \beta$', but of the idiom:

$$Fx \text{ for exactly as many objects } x \text{ as } Gx.$$

But the work even when thus reconstrued ventures necessarily beyond schematic letters into relation variables, in view of the quantifier '$(\exists R)$'.

The positive integers and 0 are sometimes called the *natural numbers*. According to the preceding chapter, a natural number is the class of all the classes of some one finite size. Now a *cardinal number*, so-called in modern mathematics, is the class of all the classes of some one size, be that size finite or not. Having defined '$\alpha \text{ sim } \beta$', therefore, we are now in a position to define 'κ is a cardinal number':

$$\text{'NC}\kappa\text{'}   \text{for}   \text{'}(\exists\beta)(\kappa = \{\alpha : \alpha \text{ sim } \beta\})\text{'}.$$

One might suppose that the cardinal numbers, if they are not simply the natural numbers under another name, will differ from the latter only to the extent of there being one extra, an infinite cardinal number representing the size of all infinite classes. But to suppose this is to suppose that all infinite classes are alike in size; and this in turn is to suppose that the members of any two infinite classes can be correlated. But this, far from being obvious, can for generous universes be disproved.

Curiously enough, despite the fact that the cardinal numbers allow for these recondite infinites in addition to the familiar natural numbers, the above definition of '$\text{NC}\kappa$' does not demand as high types as did the definition of '$\text{N}\kappa$' in the preceding chapter. For '$\text{NC}\kappa$' we have to go beyond U_1 and $_1U_1$ into U_2, of course, simply because κ itself lies there; but the definition of '$\text{N}\kappa$' reached into U_3. On the other hand the definition of '$\text{NC}\kappa$' does make inroads on $_1U_1$ (through the definition of '$\alpha \text{ sim } \beta$'), while that of '$\text{N}\kappa$' did not.

Once we are prepared to ascend to U_3, however, the type $_1U_1$ is altogether dispensable for every purpose. The reasoning is as follows. We have been thinking of relations of type $_1U_1$ as somehow classes of pairs of objects of type U, though without making any precise sense of the notion of pair. Now any arbitrary notion of a pair of objects x and y will serve our purposes perfectly so long as these conditions are met: (i) for any objects x and y of U there is such a pair; (ii) as soon as a pair is given, its first object x is thereby uniquely determined, and so is its second object y. (Thus the pair of x and y is different from the pair of y and x, unless $x = y$.) It happens that these conditions are met when the pair of x and y, written '$\langle x, y \rangle$', is defined arbitrarily in the following way. First we explain $\{x\}$ as the class whose sole member is x, and $\{x, y\}$ as the class whose sole members are x and y, thus:

$$\text{'}\{x\}\text{'} \quad \text{for} \quad \text{'}\{z: z = x\}\text{'}, \qquad \text{'}\{x, y\}\text{'} \quad \text{for} \quad \text{'}\{z: z = x \,.\text{v.}\, z = y\}\text{'}.$$

Then we construe the so-called pair $\langle x, y \rangle$ as

$$\{\{x\}, \quad \{x, y\}\}$$

—hence as the class of classes which has as members just the class $\{x\}$ and the class $\{x, y\}$. So a pair $\langle x, y \rangle$ is of type U_2; accordingly relations, as classes of such pairs, become classes of type U_3. The once fundamental notation 'xRy' disappears now in favor of '$\langle x, y \rangle \,\varepsilon\, \phi$'.

Relations of type $_2U_2$, relating no longer objects of type U but classes of type U_1, could be reduced in parallel fashion to classes of type U_4; and so on up. We can consequently dismiss the complications of relation types, and countenance only the series U, U_1, U_2, ... of class types. This is seen to be an important simplification when we reflect that it does away not only with such relation types as $_1U_1$, $_2U_2$, etc., but also with a jungle of types of classes *of* relations, classes of classes of relations, classes of relations of classes, and so on. The whole logic of relations of any types reduces to the logic of classes, provided merely that the latter is carried into high enough types.

The theory of triadic relations can be reduced to the theory of classes by a fairly obvious extension of the above treatment of dyadic relations. Similarly for tetradic relations and higher.

HISTORICAL NOTE: The old algebra of relations stems from DeMorgan and Peirce, and in part from Cayley's group theory (1854). See above, end of Chapter 25. The theory of infinite cardinal numbers is due to Cantor (1890). It was he who equated sizes of classes by correlation of members, and proved, on certain reasonable assumptions in set theory, that there is no highest infinite. Wiener, in 1914, was the first to offer a general definition of the ordered pair. The version used above deviates from Wiener's and comes rather from Kuratowski.

EXERCISES

1. Where R is the relation that relates each man to each moment in which he lives, and α is the class of moments in the year 1930, specify the following four classes fairly naturally in words.

$$R``\alpha, \qquad R``\bar{\alpha}, \qquad -(R``\alpha), \qquad -(\bar{R}``\alpha).$$

2. Where Q is the relation of admiring, and R is *brother of*, specify the following seven relations fairly naturally in words.

$$-(Q\mid R), \quad \check{Q}\mid R, \quad Q\mid\check{R}, \quad \check{Q}\mid\check{R}, \quad {}^{\smile}(\check{Q}\mid R), \quad \check{Q}\mid R, \quad -(\check{Q}\mid\check{R}).$$

3. Find interpretations of 'Q', 'R', 'α', and 'β' such that

$$(QR)``\alpha \neq (Q``\alpha)(R``\alpha), \qquad R``(\alpha\beta) \neq (R``\alpha)(R``\beta).$$

Justify your answers.

46
SYSTEMS
OF SET THEORY

We have been seeing how various familiar expressions, mainly having to do with number, can be translated into the notation of the theory of classes. Our concern in the theory of classes has thus been with questions of definition and not of proof. Let us now turn briefly to the latter topic. The general method of proof in the theory of classes is as in identity theory: deduction of theorems from axioms by the deductive methods of quantification theory. In identity theory the axioms gave laws for the special predicate '='. In the theory of classes, correspondingly, the starting point consists of axioms giving laws for the special predicate 'ε'.

The most notable set of such axioms consists of results of substituting for 'F' (and universally quantifying any free variables) in:

(A) $$(\exists\alpha)(x)(x\,\varepsilon\,\alpha\,.\equiv Fx).$$

This is called the *principle of abstraction*. Its content, for cases without free variables, is simply that *every monadic predicate has a class as extension.*

For the sake of one sample proof in the theory of classes let us prove (I) of Chapter 40, viz., '$Fx\,.\,x=y\,.\supset Fy$', which was a schema for axioms of identity. We now construe '$x=y$' therein as '$(\alpha)(x\,\varepsilon\,\alpha\,.\equiv.\,y\,\varepsilon\,\alpha)$', in conformity with Chapter 43. We want to show that 'Fx' and '$x=y$' imply 'Fy'; so, invoking the main method, we take as premises 'Fx', '$x=y$' (expanded), and '$-Fy$', and from these and (A) we proceed to a contradiction.

PREMISES: $Fx,$
                  $(\alpha)(x\,\varepsilon\,\alpha\,.\equiv.\,y\,\varepsilon\,\alpha),$
                  $-Fy.$
AXIOM: $(\exists\alpha)(z)(z\,\varepsilon\,\alpha\,.\equiv Fz).$
INSTANCES: $(z)(z\,\varepsilon\,\beta\,.\equiv Fz),$
                  $x\,\varepsilon\,\beta\,.\equiv Fx,$
                  $y\,\varepsilon\,\beta\,.\equiv Fy,$
                  $x\,\varepsilon\,\beta\,.\equiv.\,y\,\varepsilon\,\beta.$

The two unquantified premises and the three unquantified instances are truth-functionally inconsistent.

We had to define '$x=y$' and '$\alpha=\beta$', in Chapter 43, in opposite ways:

$$(\alpha)(x\,\varepsilon\,\alpha\,.\equiv.\,y\,\varepsilon\,\alpha), \qquad (z)(z\,\varepsilon\,\alpha\,.\equiv.\,z\,\varepsilon\,\beta),$$

because 'x' and 'y' could not meaningfully follow 'ε', and 'α' and 'β' could not meaningfully precede 'ε'. But as soon as we ascend beyond the limits of Chapter 43 and into the type U_2, *both* ways of construing '$\alpha=\beta$' come to be meaningful; and consequently this *axiom of extensionality* then comes to be needed to connect the two:

(E) $$(z)(z\,\varepsilon\,\alpha\,.\equiv.\,z\,\varepsilon\,\beta)\,.\,\alpha\,\varepsilon\,\kappa\,.\supset.\,\beta\,\varepsilon\,\kappa.[9]$$

This says that any classes α and β which are alike in members are identical in the sense of belonging in turn to the same classes.

Ascent into U_2 also calls for a repetition of (A) with 'x' and 'α' changed to 'α' and 'κ'; and each continuation of the theory of classes into higher types—U_3, U_4, etc.—calls for a further repetition of both (A) and (E) with upward revision of the types of variables.

How such ascents of type may be called for has already been seen in

---

[9] The actual axiom is rather the universal closure of this, but the prenex universal quantifiers '$(\alpha)(\beta)(\kappa)$' are dropped for ease in reading. This way of stating axioms will be usual hereafter.

the course of constructing a few basic ideas of number theory. We were lured as far as U_3. If we were to go on to fractions, and then to the theory of real numbers generally (rational and irrational), and to the theory of functions of real numbers, and to the theory of functions of complex numbers (real and imaginary), we should find need of variables of quantification of higher and higher types.

It is a remarkable fact that the concepts of all such branches of pure mathematics can be defined within the meager notation of the theory of classes, just as strictly as has thus far been done for the simple arithmetical concepts '0', '1', '$\kappa + \lambda$', '$\alpha \operatorname{sim} \beta$', 'N$C\kappa$', and 'N$\kappa$'. But it is significant that the construction of these higher branches calls for the introduction of higher and higher types of variables of quantification. Even very elementary parts of arithmetic, we have seen, call for some quantification over abstract entities, and hence for abandonment of the ontological agnosticism that remained tenable until Chapter 43. It is sometimes said that classical mathematics reduces to logic, but in a different and more defensible sense of the word 'logic' it may be said that logic stopped and mathematics began with Chapter 43.

Be it logic or be it mathematics, the general theory of classes constitutes an impressive consolidation of the foundations of mathematics. Mathematical theorems come on translation to contain nothing but class-theory notation, and hence to be deducible from the basic laws of 'ε': the laws (A) and (E) and whatever further ones there may be. So the question of completeness of (A) and (E), or of completion of them, suddenly looms as a question of a general codification of mathematical truth. But the answer to this has confronted us since Chapter 33: no codification can cover even the limited sector that is elementary number theory.

So the fact is that (A) and (E) and their analogues for higher types are inadequate to the theory of classes, and can never be adequately eked out by adding even an infinity of further axioms. The only qualifications to which this sweepingly defeatist conclusion is subject are of a kind from which no comfort is to be drawn: it is assumed that the added axioms, if not actually listed, will at least be specified in such a way as to be recognizable by a mechanical process; and it is assumed that they will not be such as to enable us to deduce falsehoods.

So any effort toward a complete deductive theory of classes is doomed to failure. It is doomed as soon as it aspires to encompass even that well-behaved infinity of objects called positive integers. One can do no better, from that point forward, than add special axioms now and again to strengthen the system for specific purposes.

The practice of distinguishing the types U, U_1, U_2, etc. by the use of distinctive styles of variables is but one of various ways of fashioning the theory of classes, or set theory. A salient feature of the procedure is that forms like '$x \varepsilon x$', '$x \varepsilon y$', '$\alpha \varepsilon \alpha$', '$\alpha \varepsilon x$', etc. are rejected as meaningless; 'ε' is declared grammatically admissible only between variables of consecutive ascending types.

The obvious alternative to this procedure would be to pool the types and use the single style of variables '*x*', '*y*', etc., to represent entities of all sorts. Five considerations count in favor of this alternative.

(1) The notation is simpler.

(2) The application of quantification theory to class theory comes to be more direct: 'ε' comes to represent simply a particular interpretation of a two-place predicate letter of quantification theory. Supplementary adjustments of styles of variables cease to be called for.

(3) Principles such as (A) and (E) no longer need to be repeated for each type.

(4) A curious reduplication of constants is obviated. E.g., as long as we keep the logical types apart the number 12 to which the class α of Apostles belongs is not identifiable with the number 12 to which some class κ of a dozen classes belongs; for the one number 12 is of type U_2 while the other is of type U_3. Each succeeding type, correspondingly, demands a fresh number 12 of its own. When on the other hand we pool the types, this multiple mirroring ceases; all dozens, whatever their texture, come to be members of a single number 12.

(5) The distinct existence of the full quota of positive integers ceases to depend upon there being infinitely many individuals, or nonclasses (cf. end of Chapter 44). Once types are pooled, infinitely many entities are bound to be available for simultaneous membership in classes; for we then have at our disposal not only some few individuals but also classes of them, classes of such classes, and so on, all on an equal footing.

Despite these five considerations, however, Russell had a good reason for his type restrictions. As soon as we waive his type distinctions, and read (A) simply as:

$$(A') \qquad\qquad (\exists y)(x)(x \,\varepsilon\, y \,.\equiv Fx),$$

we find ourselves in trouble. For, substituting '$-(\text{\textcircled{1}} \,\varepsilon\, \text{\textcircled{1}})$' for '*F*', we can derive a palpable falsehood.

(1)   AXIOM: $(\exists y)(x)[x \,\varepsilon\, y \,.\equiv\, -(x \,\varepsilon\, x)]$.

    INSTANCES: $(x)[x \,\varepsilon\, z \,.\equiv\, -(x \,\varepsilon\, x)]$,

                       $z \,\varepsilon\, z \,.\equiv\, -(z \,\varepsilon\, z)$.

This difficulty is called *Russell's paradox*.

In addition to (1) there are an infinite variety of other cases of (A') which lead to contradiction just as surely, if less quickly. But it happens that all such cases, like (1), cease to be expressible once variables are distinguished as to type and 'ε' is held to positions between variables of consecutive ascending types.

However, there are also other ways of avoiding the contradictions. In the Zermelo tradition (A') is restricted not by complicating the notation of class theory so as to render such cases as (1) inexpressible, but more directly: by treating (A') as holding for some open sentences in the '*Fx*' position and failing for others. According to this theory some predicates have classes as extensions while others, notably the '$-(\text{①} \, \varepsilon \, \text{①})$' of (1), do not. The task of a foundation of class theory in the Zermelo line then comes to be the setting up of conditions under which a predicate is to be viewed as having an extension; in other words, the setting up of conditions on 'Fx' under which (A') is to be regarded as holding. Different sets of conditions to this end yield the different class theories in the Zermelo line. In Zermelo's own theory, (A') is assumed for the case where the sentence put for 'Fx' has the form of a conjunction '$x \, \varepsilon \, z \, . \, Gx$'; in other words, Zermelo adopts not (A') itself but:

$$(\exists y)(x)(x \, \varepsilon \, y \, . \equiv . \, x \, \varepsilon \, z \, . \, Gx).^{10}$$

Given any class z, this law furnishes other classes y all of which are subclasses of z; but of itself it furnishes no nonempty classes z to begin with. So Zermelo then goes on to assume various additional and still more special cases of (A') individually:

$$(\exists y)(x)(x \, \varepsilon \, y \, . \equiv : x = z \, . \text{v.} \, x = w),$$
$$(\exists y)(x)[x \, \varepsilon \, y \, . \equiv \, (\exists z)(x \, \varepsilon \, z \, . \, z \, \varepsilon \, w)],$$
$$(\exists y)(x)[x \, \varepsilon \, y \, . \equiv \, (z)(z \, \varepsilon \, x \, . \supset . \, z \, \varepsilon \, w)].$$

This combination of principles can be shown to guarantee the existence of any class whose existence would be guaranteed under the theory of types by assuming (A) for each type.

In class theories not involving types, the extensionality law (E) becomes:

(E') $(z)(z \, \varepsilon \, x \, . \equiv . \, z \, \varepsilon \, y) \, . \, x \, \varepsilon \, w \, . \supset . \, y \, \varepsilon \, w.$

This gives rise to a certain perplexity where x and y are not classes; for in this case '$z \, \varepsilon \, x$' and '$z \, \varepsilon \, y$' are felt to be trivially false for everything z, so that '$(z)(z \, \varepsilon \, x \, . \equiv . \, z \, \varepsilon \, y)$' comes true regardless of identity or diversity of x and y. An exception to (E') thus seems called for where x and y are not classes. This gives rise to a further problem of distinguishing between nonclasses and the empty class, which share the peculiarity of memberlessness. However, all these difficulties are conveniently resolved by treating so-called nonclasses not as memberless, but as having themselves as sole members. (E') can then be held to in its full generality. Moreover the notation '$x = y$' comes to be definable as an abbreviation for '$(z)(z \, \varepsilon \, x \, . \equiv . \, z \, \varepsilon \, y)$' without restriction to classes. (This definition has to be preferred to '$(z)(x \, \varepsilon \, z \, . \equiv . \, y \, \varepsilon \, z)$' when we come to systems in the von Neumann branch of the Zermelo line, touched on below.)

To the question of class existence—the question what cases of (A') to accept—the answer that fits the theory of types is that classes exist if they keep their level. The answer that fits Zermelo's system is rather that they

---

[10] See the preceding footnote.

exist unless they are too big. An effect is that Zermelo cannot accept the Fregean notion of number that we studied in Chapter 44. For, consider the number 1 as there defined. This number, for a given type, is the class of all one-member classes of next lower type. When we proceed to waive type distinctions and enjoy the advantages of Zermelo's system, the number 1 so construed becomes the class simply of all one-member classes. But this class is as big as all outdoors, since there is a one-member class for each single thing in the universe. 1 so construed is thus unavailable to Zermelo, and the same is true of 2, 3, and so on up.

However, Zermelo's system is saved by the availability of other versions of number. I shall explain one, due to von Neumann, which is available to Zermelo and at the same time is about as natural as Frege's. For von Neumann each number is the class of all the earlier numbers. Thus 0 is for him simply Λ (rather than $\{\Lambda\}$), and 1 is $\{0\}$, and 2 is $\{0, 1\}$, and so on. This version goes poorly with the theory of types, because of its persistent ascent of types; but it is all right for Zermelo. Its claim to naturalness is its connection with counting: the number 5, e.g., is simply the class of the first five numbers. What saves it from circularity is that we count 0; 5 is $\{0, 1, 2, 3, 4\}$. To say that a class x has 5 members is to say on the Frege version that $x \, \varepsilon \, 5$, and on the von Neumann version that x sim 5.

Von Neumann contributed also a set theory of his own. It departed from Zermelo's by admitting some additional classes, large ones, in a marginal status: they were declared incapable of being members of further classes. Here it is that a use was found for the superfluity of terms, 'set' and 'class': 'set' is reserved for classes that can be members. That x is a set can be rendered '$(\exists z)(x \, \varepsilon \, z)$'. It seems that the principle of abstraction (A') can be adopted for classes without restriction on 'F' as long as the members x are held to sets, thus:

$$(\text{A}'') \qquad\qquad (\exists y)(x)[x \, \varepsilon \, y . \equiv . (\exists z)(x \, \varepsilon \, z) . Fx].$$

Then the burden of further axioms comes in saying which classes are to qualify as sets. Von Neumann takes as sets Zermelo's classes.

Knowing as we do from Gödel's result that a complete system is not to be hoped for, we may reasonably incline to either of two attitudes in the adding of axioms: we may favor either strength or weakness. There is much to be said for a conveniently powerful set of axioms, incomplete though it be. But it is also illuminating to minimize the assumptions from which a given familiar body of theorems of classical mathematics can be derived. Weakness as an objective is principally attractive on account of the lingering risk, in strong systems, of undetected contradiction.

HISTORICAL NOTE: The reduction of the arithmetic of the positive integers and 0 to the theory of classes and relations is, as remarked, Frege's. The reduction of ratios is due to Peano, and that of reals is due chiefly to Dedekind (1872). The execution of the whole reduction program in detail

came with Whitehead and Russell's monumental *Principia Mathematica*
(1911–13), except for Wiener's step (1914) of reducing relation theory in
turn to that of classes.

Russell discovered his paradox in 1901. Zermelo's system is coeval with
Russell's theory of types: 1908. Von Neumann's version of number dates
from 1923, and his system of set theory from 1925. The reinterpretation of
nonclasses as self-membered, and the unrestricted rendering of (A″), are my
emendations (1937, 1940). For fuller exposition and comparison of these
systems and others see my *Set Theory and Its Logic.*

EXERCISES

1. The proof of '$Fx . x = y . \supset Fy$' at the beginning of the chapter can be
    done also, if somewhat clumsily, by the method of pure existentials.
    Do so.

2. Explain how (A) assures that

$$(\exists \alpha)(x)(x \, \varepsilon \, \alpha), \qquad (\exists \alpha)(x) \, -(x \, \varepsilon \, \alpha).$$

PARTIAL ANSWERS
TO EXERCISES

Chapter 1. *Ex. 2.*
The first three.

Ex. 4.
Yes, when 'p' and 'q' are both taken as false.

Chapter 2. *Ex. 1.*
The indicated routine gives:

$$-(pqr) -(\bar{p}\bar{q}r) -(\bar{p}q\bar{r}) -(p\bar{q}\bar{r}) -(\bar{p}\bar{q}\bar{r}).$$

But this is equivalent:

$$-(pqr) -(\bar{p}\bar{q}) -(\bar{q}\bar{r}) -(\bar{p}\bar{r}).$$

Chapter 3. *Ex. 2.*
$$-(-(p \vee \bar{q}) \vee -(\bar{p} \vee q)).$$

Chapter 4. *Ex. 1.*
John will play or sing and Mary will sing.
John will play or John and Mary will sing.

Ex. 3, second part.
$$-(p \vee q) \,.\, r \vee s \,.\supset\, -(p \vee q)s.$$

Ex. 5, last part.
ECpKAqrApKqsCAKNqNrKNpANqNsNp.

Chapter 5. *Ex. 2.*

$$\bot\bot \vee \top .\supset \top\bot$$
$$\bot \vee \top .\supset \bot$$
$$\top \supset \bot$$
$$\bot$$

Ex. 3, third part.

$$p \supset .\, p \supset q$$

$$\top \supset .\top \supset q \qquad \bot \supset .\bot \supset q$$

$$\boxed{\top \supset q} \qquad\qquad \top$$

$$q$$

$$\top \qquad \bot$$

Chapter 6.   *Ex. 1, second part.*

$$p \equiv q \, .\text{v.} \, p \equiv \bar{q}$$
$$\text{T} \equiv q \, .\text{v.} \, \text{T} \equiv \bar{q} \qquad \bot \equiv q \, .\text{v.} \, \bot \equiv \bar{q}$$
$$q \vee \bar{q} \qquad\qquad \bar{q} \vee q$$
$$\text{T} \qquad\qquad\qquad \text{T}$$

Ex. 2, first part.

$p \vee q \, . \supset q \, :\text{v}: q \supset . \, p \vee q.$

Ex. 4.
(a) No. (b) Yes, the negation of '$p \vee q$' is consistent.
(c) Yes, the negation of '$p \vee \bar{p}$' is inconsistent.

Chapter 7.   *Ex. 1.*

$$p \equiv . \, q \equiv r \, :\supset: r \equiv . \, q \supset p$$
$$\text{T} \equiv . \, q \equiv r \, :\supset: r \equiv . \, q \supset \text{T}$$
$$q \equiv r \, . \supset r$$
$$q \equiv \text{T} . \supset \text{T} \quad q \equiv \bot . \supset \bot$$
$$\text{T} \qquad\qquad q$$

$\qquad\qquad\qquad\quad$ T $\quad$ ⊥ $\qquad$ So '$p \equiv . \, q \equiv r$' does
$\qquad\qquad\qquad\qquad\qquad\qquad\qquad$ not imply '$r \equiv . \, q \supset p$'.

$$r \equiv . \, q \supset p \, :\supset: p \equiv . \, q \equiv r$$
$$r \equiv . \, q \supset \text{T} \, :\supset: \text{T} \equiv . \, q \equiv r$$
$$r \supset . \, q \equiv r$$
$$\text{T} \supset . \, q \equiv \text{T}$$
$$q$$
$$\text{T} \quad \bot \qquad\qquad\qquad \text{So not vice versa.}$$

Ex. 4.
Two fell swoops show that neither '$p \vee q \, . \supset r$' nor '$p \supset . q \vee r$' implies '$p \supset q$'.

$$
\begin{array}{ccc}
p \supset q & p \vee q \, . \supset r & p \supset . \, q \vee r \\
\text{T} \quad \bot & \text{T} \vee \bot . \supset r & \text{T} \supset . \, \bot \vee r \\
& r & r
\end{array}
$$

Two fell swoops show that '$p \supset q$' and '$p \vee q \, . \supset r$' each imply '$p \supset . \, q \vee r$'.

$$
\begin{array}{ccc}
p \supset . \, q \vee r & p \supset q & p \vee q \, . \supset r \\
\text{T} \quad \bot \quad \bot & \text{T} \supset \bot & \text{T} \vee \bot . \supset \bot \\
& \bot & \bot
\end{array}
$$

Truth-value analysis shows '$p \supset q \, . \supset: p \vee q \, . \supset r$' not valid. So '$p \supset q$' does not imply '$p \vee q \, . \supset r$'. But it would, by (ii), if '$p \supset . q \vee r$' did, since '$p \supset q$' implies '$p \supset . q \vee r$'; so '$p \supset . q \vee r$' does not imply '$p \vee q \, . \supset r$' either.

Ex. 7, partial answer.
The schemata are '$p \equiv qr$' and '$q \supset rp \, . \, \bar{q} \supset \bar{r}\bar{p}$'.

Chapter 8.   *Ex. 3.*

The 'then' clause extends through 'Barbuda', since the 'I'll' has to govern 'fly'. So the whole is a conditional:

> Either the Giants or the Bruins win and the Jackals take second place ⊃ I'll recover past losses and either buy a clavichord or fly to Barbuda.

The antecedent of this conditional is a conjunction and not an alternation, since 'the Giants' and 'the Bruins' are co-ordinated by the shared verb 'win'.

> The Giants or the Bruins win . the Jackals take second place . ⊃ I'll recover past losses and either buy a clavichord or fly to Barbuda.

The consequent is likewise a conjunction, since its 'either' stands after the 'and' rather than before the 'I'll'. Final result:

> The Giants win v the Bruins win . the Jackals take second place . ⊃ . I'll recover past losses . I'll buy a clavichord v I'll fly to Barbuda.

Chapter 9.   *Ex. 1.*

'$p \supset r . q \supset r$' is equivalent to '$p \lor q . \supset r$', and the other three are equivalent to '$pq \supset r$'. But the reader should produce the truth-value analyses.

Chapter 10.   *Ex. 1, first schema.*

$\bar{p} . q \lor -[r \lor -(q \lor p)]$,

$\bar{p} : q \lor . \bar{r} . q \lor p$,

$\bar{p}q \lor \bar{p}\bar{r}q \lor \bar{p}\bar{r}p$.

This simplifies to '$\bar{p}q \lor \bar{p}\bar{r}q$', and indeed to '$\bar{p}q$'. To see the advantage of working from the outside inward, try doing this exercise in the opposite way—first changing the innermost portion '$-(q \lor p)$' to '$\bar{q}\bar{p}$' and then working outward.

Ex. 1, last half.

The last three of the six schemata end up thus, after obvious simplifications:

$$pqr \lor \bar{p}\bar{q}\bar{r}, \qquad pqr \lor \bar{p}\bar{q}r \lor p\bar{q}\bar{r} \lor \bar{p}q\bar{r}, \qquad pqr \lor \bar{p}\bar{r} \lor \bar{q}\bar{r}.$$

But the reader should fill in all steps.

Ex. 2, last half.

Two of these last three have already gone into developed form, as seen above. The last one becomes:

$$pqr \lor \bar{p}q\bar{r} \lor \bar{p}\bar{q}\bar{r} \lor p\bar{q}\bar{r}$$

with omission of a repeated clause.

Ex. 3.
Yes. The reader should still justify it.

Ex. 4, last part (corresponding to Ex. 4 of Chapter 7).
The three schemata go into alternational normal form thus:

$$\bar{p} \lor q, \qquad \bar{p}\bar{q} \lor r, \qquad \bar{p} \lor q \lor r.$$

Developed, they eventually become respectively:

$$\bar{p}qr \lor \bar{p}\bar{q}r \lor \bar{p}q\bar{r} \lor \bar{p}\bar{q}\bar{r} \lor pqr \lor p\bar{q}\bar{r},$$
$$\bar{p}\bar{q}r \lor \bar{p}\bar{q}\bar{r} \lor pqr \lor \bar{p}qr \lor p\bar{q}r,$$
$$\bar{p}qr \lor \bar{p}\bar{q}r \lor \bar{p}q\bar{r} \lor \bar{p}\bar{q}\bar{r} \lor pqr \lor p\bar{q}r \lor p\bar{q}r.$$

Rearranged for matching, they appear thus:

$$pqr \lor \bar{p}qr \lor \qquad \bar{p}\bar{q}r \lor p\bar{q}r \lor \bar{p}q\bar{r} \lor \bar{p}\bar{q}\bar{r},$$
$$pqr \lor \bar{p}qr \lor p\bar{q}r \lor \bar{p}\bar{q}r \lor \qquad\qquad \bar{p}\bar{q}\bar{r},$$
$$pqr \lor \bar{p}qr \lor p\bar{q}r \lor \bar{p}\bar{q}r \lor pqr \lor p\bar{q}r \lor \bar{p}\bar{q}\bar{r}.$$

Containment then shows that the third schema is implied by the first and by the second, and that there are no other implications. Clearly the method is poor.

Chapter 11.   *Ex. 3, first part.*
We see by a fell swoop that '*qr*' implies the rest of the alternation and so is redundant. Dropping it, we have '*p$\bar{q}\bar{r}$* ∨ $\bar{p}q$ ∨ *pr*'. By a further fell swoop we see that this whole is implied by '*p$\bar{q}$*' and hence that the '$\bar{r}$' is still redundant.

Ex. 6, last half.
The last three schemata obtained in Ex. 1 of Chapter 10 yield no consensuses, since no two clauses are opposed in exactly one letter. So there are no further prime implicants.

Ex. 7, last half.
These three schemata have no shorter alternational normal equivalents, since all prime implicants are there and none is redundant.

Chapter 12.   *Ex. 1.*
The first is dual to each of the other three, these three being equivalent. For, by the second law of duality, '$p \equiv q$' is dual to '$-(\bar{p} \equiv \bar{q})$'.

Ex. 3, clausal part.
The clause is redundant if a fell swoop shows it to be implied by the rest of the schema.

Ex. 4, first schema.
$\bar{p} \cdot q \vee -[r \vee -(q \vee p)],$
$\bar{p} : q \vee . \bar{r} \cdot q \vee p,$
$\bar{p} \cdot q \vee \bar{r} \cdot q \vee q \vee p.$

Simplifying,

$\bar{p} \cdot q \vee \bar{r} \cdot q \vee p$
$\bar{p} \cdot q \vee \bar{r} \cdot q,$
$\bar{p}q.$

Chapter 13.   *Ex. 1.*
By (1), $[3 \supset :. 2 \supset :] \bar{p} \supset p . \supset . \bar{p} \supset q.$

Chapter 15.   *Ex. 2.*
Yes. There might be no F (and hence no G).

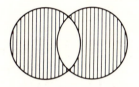

Chapter 17.   *Ex. 1, second inference.*
Write 'F', 'G', and 'H' for 'knows George', 'knows Mabel', and 'admires Mabel'.

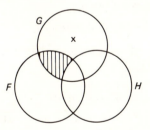

Ex. 3, second part.
Hint: extend the bar device of Diagram 11.

Chapter 18.   *Ex. 1, first example.*
$-\exists FG\bar{H}, \ -\exists F\bar{H}\bar{G}, \ \therefore \ -\exists F\bar{H}.$

Ex. 1, last example.
$-\exists -(G \vee H), \ -\exists FG, \ \therefore \ -\exists F\bar{H}.$

Ex. 2.
It does not. (Reader should still explain, or, if baffled, read on.)

Chapter 19. *Ex. 2.*

'*F*' is 'takes logic', '*G*' is 'takes Latin', and so on.

$$\exists FG\bar{H}\bar{J} \,.\, -\exists[(G \vee K) - (FJ)].$$

Negated:

$$-\{\exists FG\bar{H}\bar{J} \,.\, -\exists[(G \vee K) - (FJ)]\}.$$

Converted to conjunctional normal form:

$$-\exists FG\bar{H}\bar{J} \vee \exists[(G \vee K) - (FJ)].$$

Converted to an existential conditional:

$$\exists FG\bar{H}\bar{J} \supset \exists[(G \vee K) - (FJ)].$$

Fell swoop to test whether '$FG\bar{H}\bar{J}$' implies '$(G \vee K) - (FJ)$':

$$(G \vee K) - (FJ)$$
$$(\mathsf{T} \vee K) - (\mathsf{T}\!\perp)$$
$$\mathsf{T}$$

So the negation was valid. So the original was inconsistent.

Ex. 3, first part.

$$-\exists FG\bar{H} \,.\, -\exists F\bar{H}\bar{G} \,.\, \supset\, -\exists F\bar{H}.$$

Conjunctional normal form:

$$\exists FG\bar{H} \vee \exists F\bar{H}\bar{G} \vee -\exists F\bar{H}.$$

Existential conditional:

$$\exists F\bar{H} \supset \exists(FG\bar{H} \vee F\bar{H}\bar{G}).$$

Valid; for, fell swoop shows that '$F\bar{H}$' implies '$FG\bar{H} \vee F\bar{H}\bar{G}$'.

Chapter 20. *Ex. 1, second formula.*
$$\Lambda = (F \vee \bar{G})\bar{G} \vee -(F \vee \bar{G})G \,.\, \supset .\, \Lambda = F\bar{G} \vee \bar{F}G,$$
$$-\exists[F \vee \bar{G} \,.\, \bar{G} \,.\!\vee -(F \vee \bar{G})G] \supset -\exists(F\bar{G} \vee \bar{F}G),$$
$$\exists(F\bar{G} \vee \bar{F}G) \supset \exists[F \vee \bar{G} \,.\, \bar{G} \,.\!\vee -(F \vee \bar{G})G].$$

Verify by truth-value analysis that '$F\bar{G} \vee \bar{F}G$' implies:

$$F \vee \bar{G} \,.\, \bar{G} \,.\!\vee -(F \vee \bar{G})G.$$

Chapter 21. *Ex. 1, first example.*
(x)(x is a man on the team $\supset$ − John can outrun x).

Ex. 2, first example.
(x)(x is east of tracks $\supset$. x is slovenly $\vee$ x is poor),
−(x)(x is east of tracks $\supset$ x is poor),
∴ ($\exists x$)(x is slovenly . − x is poor).

Ex. 3, partial answer.
The two in the middle are not equivalent.

Chapter 22. *Ex. 2, partial answer.*
'$(x)(p \equiv Fx)$' and '$p \equiv (x)Fx$' resolve respectively to '$(x)-Fx$' and '$-(x)Fx$' when '$\bot$' is put for 'p', so they are not equivalent.

Ex. 3.
The first implies each and each implies the last. The reader should show this.

Chapter 23. *Ex. 1.*
Expanding '$\equiv$' and relettering, we have:

$$(x)Fx \supset. (y)Gy \supset (z)Hz . (v)Hv \supset (w)Gw.$$

Now we are free to choose the order of exportation of quantifiers. One of the final results is:

$$(\exists x)(\exists y)(\exists v)(z)(w)(Fx \supset. Gy \supset Hz . Hv \supset Gw).$$

Note also the following refinement. We might proceed as far as the intermediate stage:

$$(\exists x)\{Fx \supset. (z)[(y)Gy \supset Hz] . (w)[(v)Hv \supset Gw]\}$$

and then reletter thus:

$$(\exists x)\{Fx \supset. (z)[(y)Gy \supset Hz] . (z)[(v)Hv \supset Gz]\}$$

with a view to exploiting the distributivity law (21) of Chapter 21, thus:

$$(\exists x)\{Fx \supset (z)[(y)Gy \supset Hz . (v)Hv \supset Gz]\}.$$

The end result then has only four quantifiers.

$$(\exists x)(z)(\exists y)(\exists v)(Fx \supset. Gy \supset Hz . Hv \supset Gz).$$

Ex. 3.
$(\exists x)(y)(Fx \vee Gy \vee Hy . -Fx \vee -Gy \vee Hy)$,
$(\exists x)[(y)(Fx \vee Gy \vee Hy) . (y)(-Fx \vee -Gy \vee Hy)]$,
$(\exists x)[Fx \vee (y)(Gy \vee Hy) . -Fx \vee (y)(-Gy \vee Hy)]$,
$(\exists x)[Fx . (y)(-Gy \vee Hy) .v. -Fx . (y)(Gy \vee Hy)$
$\qquad\qquad$ .v. $(y)(Gy \vee Hy) . (y)(-Gy \vee Hy)]$,
$(\exists x)[Fx . (y)(-Gy \vee Hy) .v. -Fx . (y)(Gy \vee Hy)]$
$\qquad\qquad$ v. $(y)(Gy \vee Hy) . (y)(-Gy \vee Hy)$,
$(\exists x)[Fx . (y)(-Gy \vee Hy)] \vee (\exists x)[-Fx . (y)(Gy \vee Hy)]$
$\qquad\qquad$ v. $(y)(Gy \vee Hy) . (y)(-Gy \vee Hy)$,
$(\exists x)Fx . (y)(-Gy \vee Hy) .v. (\exists x)-Fx . (y)(Gy \vee Hy)$
$\qquad\qquad$ .v. $(y)(Gy \vee Hy) . (y)(-Gy \vee Hy)$.

Chapter 24.   *Ex. 4.*
Hint: represent the conclusion as:

$$(\exists x)(Fx \,.\, Gx) \supset (\exists x)(Hx \,.\, Jx).$$

Chapter 25.   *Ex. 4.*
$(x)[x$ was a finger of hers $\supset (\exists y)(y$ was a ring $.\ y$ was on $x)]$.

Ex. 5, last example.
Hint: as a first step put just the inside quantification into words, retaining 'x'.

Ex. 6, last example.
False. If x and z were as described, then by taking y as z we could conclude that x was between z and z.

Ex. 7, first example.
'$-(\exists x)-(\exists y)(x = y)$', or, equivalently, '$(x)-(y)-(x = y)$', or, equivalently, '$(x)(\exists y)(x = y)$'. True.

Chapter 26.   *Ex. 2.*
$②^x = ①y + ②$.

Ex. 3, left column.
The first two may be substituted; the third not. The results of the first two substitutions mean that y praised himself to someone and that y praised someone to his face.

Chapter 27.   *Ex. 1, partial answer.*
Only the third predicate-schema can be substituted in '$(x)Fx \supset Fy$' or in '$Fy \supset (\exists x)Fx$'; only the third and fourth in (2); none in (11) or (12).

Ex. 2, partial answer.
Four of the eight are thus obtainable. The second on the left and the three on the right are not, although two of these could be inferred in an additional step or two.

Chapter 28.   *Ex. 1, third part.*
Stages between (8) and (9):

$$(z)(Fz \supset Gz) \supset (y)[(\exists x)(Fx \,.\, Hyx) \supset (\exists w)(Gw \,.\, Hyw)],$$
$$(y)[(z)(Fz \supset Gz) \supset .\, (\exists x)(Fx \,.\, Hyx) \supset (\exists w)(Gw \,.\, Hyw)],$$
$$(y)\{(z)(Fz \supset Gz) \supset (x)[Fx \,.\, Hyx \,.\supset (\exists w)(Gw \,.\, Hyw)]\},$$
$$(y)(x)[(z)(Fz \supset Gz) \supset : Fx \,.\, Hyx \,.\supset (\exists w)(Gw \,.\, Hyw)],$$
$$(y)(x)(\exists z)[Fz \supset Gz \,.\supset : Fx \,.\, Hyx \,.\supset (\exists w)(Gw \,.\, Hyw)],$$
$$(y)(x)(\exists z)[Fz \supset Gz \,.\supset (\exists w)(Fx \,.\, Hyx \,.\supset .\, Gw \,.\, Hyw)],$$
$$(y)(x)(\exists z)(\exists w)(Fz \supset Gz \,.\supset : Fx \,.\, Hyx \,.\supset .\, Gw \,.\, Hyw).$$

Ex. 7.

$(x)(y)(z)(Fxy \cdot Fyz . \supset Fxz) . (x) - Fxx . \supset (x)(y)(Fxy$
$$\supset -Fyx),$$

$(x)(y)(z)(Fxy \cdot Fyz . \supset Fxz) . (w) - Fww . \supset (u)(v)(Fuv$
$$\supset -Fvu),$$

$(u)(v)(\exists x)(\exists y)(\exists z)(\exists w)(Fxy \cdot Fyz . \supset Fxz : -Fww$
$$: \supset . Fuv \supset -Fvu),$$

$(\exists x)(\exists y)(\exists z)(\exists w)(Fxy \cdot Fyz . \supset Fxz : -Fww$
$$: \supset . Fuv \supset -Fvu),$$

$Fuv \cdot Fvu . \supset Fuu : -Fuu : \supset . Fuv \supset -Fvu.$

Chapter 29. *Ex. 1.*

In 'Fyy' and '$-Fzy$' the instantial variable is not new. '$-(\exists x)Fxx$' is not prenex, but make it so and the proof goes through, with premises '$(x) - Fxx$' and '$(y)Fyy$' and instances as before.

Ex. 2, first part.
See beginning of Chapter 37.

Chapter 30. *Ex. 3, omitting some steps.*
$(x)(y)[Fx \cdot Gxy . \supset (\exists z)(Jzy \cdot Hxz)],$
$(x)[Fx \cdot (\exists y)Gxy . \supset (\exists y)Hxy].$

PRENEX PREMISES FOR INCONSISTENCY:
$(x)(y)(\exists z)(Fx \cdot Gxy . \supset . Jzy \cdot Hxz),$
$(\exists x)(\exists y)(z) - (Fx \cdot Gxy . \supset Hxz).$

INSTANCES:
$(z) - (Fu \cdot Guv . \supset Huz)$ (double step),
$(\exists z)(Fu \cdot Guv . \supset . Jzv \cdot Huz)$ (double step),
$Fu \cdot Guv . \supset . Jwv \cdot Huw,$
$-(Fu \cdot Guv . \supset Huw).$

Ex. 4.
For the results of paraphrasing, see answers to Chapter 34.

Ex. 5.
PREMISES:
$(x)(x$ laughs at $x \supset$ I like $x),$
$(x)[(y)(y$ is friend of $x \supset x$ laughs at $y) \supset$ I detest $x].$
PLATITUDE:
$(x)($ I detest $x \supset -$ I like $x).$
CONCLUSION:
$(\exists x)(y)(y$ is friend of $x \supset x$ laughs at $y)$
$$\supset (\exists x) - x \text{ is friend of } x.$$

PRENEX PREMISES FOR INCONSISTENCY:
$(x)(Gxx \supset Lx),$

$(x)(\exists y)(Fyx \supset Gxy . \supset Dx),$
$(x)(Dx \supset -Lx),$
$(\exists x)(y)(z) -(Fyx \supset Gxy . \supset -Fzz).$
INSTANCES:
$(y)(z) -(Fyw \supset Gwy . \supset -Fzz),$
$(\exists y)(Fyw \supset Gwy . \supset Dw),$
$Fvw \supset Gwv . \supset Dw,$
$Gww \supset Lw,$
$Dw \supset -Lw,$
$-(Fvw \supset Gwv . \supset -Fww)$ (double step),
$-(Fww \supset Gww . \supset -Fww)$ (double step).

Chapter 31.   *Ex. 2.*
The odd ones are ⊤ and the even ones ⊥.

Chapter 33.   *Ex. 1.*
There can be no complete disproof procedure here, since disproofs of negations afford proofs. There can be no decision procedure missing only finitely many of the truths, since that procedure together with a list of the omitted truths would afford a complete procedure.

Ex. 2.
Because otherwise you could always prove a schema to be finitely valid by proving that its negation was in *B*.

Chapter 34.   *Ex. 1.*
Make substitutions to match those that were made in the first proof in the chapter, except for using 't_{uv_u}' in (5).

Ex. 2.
Reworking Ex. 4 of Chapter 30 in Dreben's way:

PREMISES:
$(\exists x)\{Fx . (y)[Gy . (\exists z)(Fz . Hyz) . \supset Hyx]\},$
$(y)[Gy \supset (\exists z)(Fz . Hyz)],$
$-(\exists x)[Fx . (y)(Gy \supset Hyx)]$ (conclusion negated).
ADJUSTMENTS:
$(\exists x)\{Fx . (y)[-Gy \vee (z)-(Fz . Hyz) \vee Hyx]\},$
$(y)[-Gy \vee (\exists z)(Fz . Hyz)],$
$(x)[-Fx \vee (\exists y)-(Gy \supset Hyx)].$
FUNCTIONAL NORMAL FORMS:
$Fx . (y)[-Gy \vee (z)-(Fz . Hyz) \vee Hyx],$
$(y)(-Gy \vee . Fz_y . Hyz_y),$
$(x)[-Fx \vee -(Gy_x \supset Hy_x x)].$
INSTANCES:
$Fx . -Gy_x \vee -(Fz_{y_x} . Hy_x z_{y_x}) \vee Hy_x x,$
$-Gy_x \vee . Fz_{y_x} . Hy_x z_{y_x},$
$-Fx \vee -(Gy_x \supset Hy_x x).$

Chapter 35. *Ex. 2.*
Proof of (4) of Chapter 28:

$$Fxx \supset Fxy \text{ .v. } Fxy \supset Fyy,$$
$$(\exists z)(Fxz \supset Fzy) \text{ v } (\exists z)(Fxz \supset Fzy),$$
$$(\exists z)(Fxz \supset Fzy).$$

Chapter 36. *Ex. 2.*
Proof of (1) of Chapter 28 by last method of Chapter 36:

[1] $Fy . (x)(Fx \supset Gxy) \supset. Fy . Gyy,$
      $[(y)1 \supset.] (\exists y)[Fy . (x)(Fx \supset Gxy)] \supset (\exists x)(Fx . Gxx).$

What valid monadic schema covers [1]?

$$Fy . (x)(Fx \supset Hx) . \supset. Fy . Hy.$$

Proof of (4) of Chapter 28:

[1] $(z)Fxz \supset Fxy,$
      $[1 \supset] (\exists z)(Fxz \supset Fzy).$

The valid monadic schema that covers this last line is as follows. Test it for validity.

$$(z)Gz \supset Hx . \supset (\exists z)(Gz \supset Hz).$$

Proof of (8) of Chapter 28:

[1] $(x)(Fx \supset Gx) \supset. (\exists x)(Fx . Hyx) \supset (\exists x)(Gx . Hyx),$
      $[(y)1 \supset.] (x)(Fx \supset Gx) \supset (y)[(\exists x)(Fx . Hyx)$
      $\qquad\qquad\qquad\qquad\qquad\qquad \supset (\exists x)(Gx . Hyx)].$

Proof of (11) of Chapter 28:

[1] $(z)(Fxz \supset Fxz),$
      $[1 \supset] (\exists y)(z)(Fxz \supset Fyz).$

Chapter 37. *Ex. 1.*
The first and third on the left are correct but unfinished. The second on the left is incorrect (violating the alphabetical rule) and unfinished. The one at the upper right is correct and finished. The last one is finished but incorrect, '*y*' being flagged twice.

Ex. 2 in part.
Revise the last one by bringing in a new line '*Fz . Gz*'.

Ex. 3.
Reworking Ex. 5 of Chapter 30 (whereof see answer above):

*(1) $(x)(Gxx \supset Lx)$
**(2) $(x)[(y)(Fyx \supset Gxy) \supset Dx]$
***(3) $(x)(Dx \supset -Lx)$

****(4) $(\exists x)(y)(Fyx \supset Gxy)$
****(5) $(y)(Fyw \supset Gwy)$ (4) w
****(6) $Gww \supset Lw$ (1)
****(7) $(y)(Fyw \supset Gwy) \supset Dw$ (2)
****(8) $Dw \supset -Lw$ (3)
****(9) $Fww \supset Gww$ (5)
****(10) $-Fww$ (5)(6)(7)(8)(9)
****(11) $(\exists x) - Fxx$ (10)
***(12) $(\exists x)(y)(Fyx \supset Gxy) \supset (\exists x) - Fxx$ *(11)

Chapter 38.   *Ex. 1 by method of pure existentials.*
$-(Fy . Fz) . Fw \supset (x)Fx . \supset -Fw,$

$(\exists x)[-(Fy . Fz) . Fw \supset Fx . \supset -Fw],$

$-(Fy . Fz) . Fw \supset Fy . \supset -Fw$
$\qquad\qquad\qquad\qquad :v: -(Fy . Fz). Fw \supset Fz . \supset -Fw.$

Ex. 2.
$(x)(Fxy \supset Gyx) . (x)(Gxz \supset -Fzx) . \supset -Fzy,$
$(\exists x)(\exists w)(Fxy \supset Gyx . Gwz \supset -Fzw . \supset -Fzy),$
$Fzy \supset Gyz . Gyz \supset -Fzy . \supset -Fzy.$

Chapter 40.   *Ex. 1.*
Given that

$(x)(Fx \supset : x = y .v. x = z),$ $(\exists x)(Fx . Gx),$

and given '$(x)(w)(Gx . x = w . \supset Gw)$' as axiom of identity, to show that Gy v Gz. Main method:

PREMISES: $(x)(Fx \supset : x = y .v. x = z),$
$\qquad\qquad (\exists x)(Fx . Gx),$
$\qquad\qquad (x)(w)(Gx . x = w . \supset Gw),$
$\qquad\qquad -(Gy \text{ v } Gz).$
INSTANCES: $Fu . Gu,$
$\qquad\qquad Fu \supset : u = y .v. u = z,$
$\qquad\qquad Gu . u = y . \supset Gy,$
$\qquad\qquad Gu . u = z . \supset Gz.$

The last five lines are truth-functionally inconsistent. The reader might try repeating the exercise by the method of pure existentials.

Ex. 2.
The forward conditional is a variant of (I), by a rule of passage. The reverse implication, when buttressed with the case '$y = y$' of (II), holds by EG.

Chapter 41.   *Ex. 1.*
$(\imath x)[x$ is a man in town . $(y)(y$ is a man in town
$\qquad\qquad\qquad\qquad . x \neq y . \supset x$ is taller than $y)].$

Ex. 2 by method of pure existentials.

$(x)(x$ wrote W $\equiv. x = y) . y = y . y$ wrote I
$.\supset (\exists x)(x$ wrote W . x wrote I),

$(\exists x)(\exists z)(x$ wrote W $\equiv. x = y : y = y . y$ wrote I
$:\supset. z$ wrote W . z wrote I),

y wrote W $\equiv. y = y : y = y . y$ wrote I
$:\supset. y$ wrote W . y wrote I.

Chapter 42.

$H(\imath x)(Fx . Gx) . J(\imath x)(Fx . Gx),$
$(\exists y)[Hy . (x)(Fx . Gx .\equiv. x = y)]$
$. (\exists y)[Jy . (x)(Fx . Gx .\equiv. x = y)].$

Chapter 43.
Ex. 1.

$y \, \varepsilon \, (\imath\beta)(x)(x \, \varepsilon \, \beta .\equiv. x \, \varepsilon \, \alpha),$
$(\exists\gamma)(y \, \varepsilon \, \gamma . (\beta)[(x)(x \, \varepsilon \, \beta .\equiv. x \, \varepsilon \, \alpha) \equiv. \beta = \gamma]),$
$(\exists\gamma)(y \, \varepsilon \, \gamma . (\beta)[(x)(x \, \varepsilon \, \beta .\equiv. x \, \varepsilon \, \alpha) \equiv (x)(x \, \varepsilon \, \beta .\equiv. x \, \varepsilon \, \gamma)]).$

Ex. 2.
$(y)(y \, \varepsilon \, \alpha .\equiv. y \, \varepsilon \, \{x: x \, \varepsilon \, \alpha\})$. The further expansion of the part '$y \, \varepsilon \, \{x: x \, \varepsilon \, \alpha\}$' is in Ex. 1.

Chapter 44.
Ex. 1.
Hints: '$\kappa \geqq \lambda$' can be rendered '$(\exists\mu)(N\mu . \kappa = \lambda + \mu)$'.
Twice κ is $\kappa + \kappa$.

Chapter 45.
Ex. 1, last half.
$-(R``\alpha)$ comprises everything, human and otherwise, except the men who were alive in 1930. $-(\bar{R}``\alpha)$ consists of the men who were born before 1930 and survived that year.

Ex. 2, fourth relation.
The relation of x to y where x is admired by someone (male or female) who has y as a brother.

Ex. 3, second half.
Take R as the benefaction relation, α as the class of Armenians, and β as the class of orphans. Then $R``(\alpha\beta)$ comprises just the benefactors of Armenian orphans, whereas $(R``\alpha)(R``\beta)$ includes also anyone else who benefits both an Armenian and an orphan.

Chapter 46.
Ex. 2.
Take 'Fx' in (A) as '$x \, \varepsilon \, \beta .\supset. x \, \varepsilon \, \beta$' to get '$(\exists\alpha)(x)(x \, \varepsilon \, \alpha)$', and as '$x \, \varepsilon \, \beta . -(x \, \varepsilon \, \beta)$' to get '$(\exists\alpha)(x)-(x \, \varepsilon \, \alpha)$'.

BIBLIOGRAPHY

This list includes only such logical and nearly logical works as happen to have been alluded to, by title or otherwise, in the course of the book. For a comprehensive register of the literature of mathematical logic to the end of 1935 see Church's *Bibliography*. This work, which is helpfully annotated and thoroughly indexed by subjects, is invaluable to logicians. Subsequent literature is covered by the Reviews section of the *Journal of Symbolic Logic*, which is indexed by subjects every five years and by authors every two.

AIKEN, Howard H., and others. *Synthesis of Electronic Computing and Control Circuits*. Cambridge, Mass.: Harvard, 1951.

BEHMANN, Heinrich. "Beiträge zur Algebra der Logik, insbesondere zum Entscheidungsproblem." *Mathematische Annalen*, vol. 86 (1922), pp. 163–229.

BERNAYS. Paul, and Moses Schönfinkel. "Zum Entscheidungsproblem der mathematischen Logik." *Mathematische Annalen*, vol. 99 (1928), pp. 342–372.

BOOLE, George. *The Mathematical Analysis of Logic*. London: George Bell and Cambridge, England: Macmillan, 1847. Reprinted in *Collected Logical Works*, Oxford: Blackwell, and New York: Philosophical Library, 1948.

————. *An Investigation of the Laws of Thought*. London: Walton and Maberly, 1854. Reprinted New York: Dover, 1951.

CANTOR, Georg. "Über eine elementare Frage der Mannigfältigkeitslehre." *Jahresberichte* der deutschen Mathematiker-Vereinigungen, vol. 1 (1890–91), pp. 75–78. Reprinted in *Gesammelte Abhandlungen*, Berlin: Springer, 1932.

CARNAP, Rudolf. *The Logical Syntax of Language*. London and New York: Harcourt Brace, 1937.

————. *Meaning and Necessity*. Chicago: University, 1947, 1956.

————. "Empiricism, semantics, and ontology." *Revue Internationale de Philosophie*, vol. 4 (1950), pp. 20–40. Reprinted in *Meaning and Necessity*, 1956.

CARROLL, Lewis. *Symbolic Logic*. London: Macmillan, 1897.

CAYLEY, Arthur. "On the theory of groups as depending on the symbolical equation $\theta^n = 1$." *Philosophical Magazine*, vol. 7 (1854), pp. 40–47, 408–409. Reprinted in *Collected Mathematical Papers*, Cambridge, England: University, 1895.

CHURCH, Alonzo. *A Bibliography of Symbolic Logic.* Providence, R.I.: Association for Symbolic Logic, 1938. Reprinted from *Journal of Symbolic Logic* (1936, 1938).

————. "A note on the Entscheidungsproblem." *Journal of Symbolic Logic,* vol. 1 (1936), pp. 40–41. Correction on pp. 101–102.

COOLEY, John C. *A Primer of Formal Logic.* New York: Macmillan, 1942.

DAVIS, Martin. *Computability and Unsolvability.* New York: McGraw-Hill, 1958.

————, editor. *The Undecidable.* Hewlett, N.Y.: Raven Press, 1965.

DEDEKIND, Richard. *Stetigkeit und irrationale Zahlen.* Braunschweig: Vieweg, 1872. Later editions 1892, 1905, 1912.

————. *Was sind und was sollen die Zahlen?* Braunschweig: Vieweg, 1887.

DeMORGAN, Augustus. *Formal Logic.* London: Taylor, 1847.

————. "On the syllogism." *Transactions* of the Cambridge Philosophical Society, vol. 8 (1849), pp. 379–408; vol. 9 (1856), pp. 79–127; vol. 10 (1864), pp. 173–230, 331–358, 428–487. These had been read at earlier meetings: 1846, 1850, 1860, 1863.

DREBEN, Burton. "On the completeness of quantification theory." *Proceedings* of the National Academy of Sciences, vol. 38 (1952), pp. 1047–1052.

FEIGL, Herbert, and Wilfrid Sellars, editors. *Readings in Philosophical Analysis.* New York: Appleton-Century-Crofts, 1949.

FREGE, Gottlob. *Begriffsschrift.* Halle: Nebert, 1879. Translated in van Heijenoort.

————. *Die Grundlagen der Arithmetik.* Breslau: Marcus 1884. Reprinted with English translation, Oxford: Blackwell, and New York: Philosophical Library, 1950.

————. *Grundgesetze der Arithmetik.* Vol. 1, 1893; vol. 2, 1903. Jena: Pohle.

————. "Über Sinn und Bedeutung." *Zeitschrift für Philosophie und philosophische Kritik,* vol. 100 (1892), pp. 25–50. Translated in Feigl and Sellars.

FRIDSHAL, R. Abstract in *Summaries of Talks at the Summer Institute of Symbolic Logic.* Mimeographed. Ithaca, N.Y.: Cornell, 1957, pp. 211–212.

GENTZEN, Gerhard. "Untersuchungen über das logische Schliessen." *Mathematische Zeitschrift,* vol. 39 (1934–35), pp. 176–210, 405–431.

GERGONNE, J. D. "Essai de dialectique rationelle." *Annales de mathématiques pures et appliquées,* vol. 7 (1816–17), pp. 189–228.

GHAZALA, M. J. "Irredundant disjunctive and conjunctive forms of a Boolean function." *I.B.M. Journal of Research and Development,* vol. 1 (1957), pp. 171–176.

GÖDEL, Kurt. "Die Vollständigkeit der Axiome des logischen Funktionenkalküls." *Monatshefte für Mathematik und Physik,* vol. 37 (1930), pp. 349–360. Translated in van Heijenoort.

————. "Über formal unentscheidbare Sätze der Principia Mathematica und verwandter Systeme." *Ibid.,* vol. 38 (1931), pp. 173–198. Translated in van Heijenoort.

————. "Zum Entscheidungsproblem des logischen Funktionenkalküls." *Ibid.*, vol. 40 (1933), pp. 433–443.

————. "On undecidable propositions of formal mathematical systems." Mimeographed. Princeton, 1934. Printed in Davis, *The Undecidable*.

GOODMAN, Nelson. "The problem of counterfactual conditionals." *Journal of Philosophy*, vol. 44 (1947), pp. 113–128. Reprinted in *Fact, Fiction, and Forecast*, Indianapolis: Bobbs-Merrill, 1965.

HERBRAND, Jacques. *Recherches sur la théorie de la démonstration.* Warsaw: Société des Sciences et des Lettres, 1930. Translated in Herbrand, *Logical Writings*, Cambridge, Mass.: Harvard, 1971.

HILBERT, David, and W. Ackermann. *Grundzüge der theoretischen Logik.* Berlin: Springer, 1928. 2d edition, 1938. 3d edition, 1949.

———— and P. Bernays. *Grundlagen der Mathematik.* Vol. 1, 1934; vol. 2, 1939. Berlin: Springer.

JAŚKOWSKI, Stanisław. "On the rules of suppositions in formal logic." *Studia Logica*, no. 1 (Warsaw, 1934).

JEVONS, W. Stanley. *Pure Logic.* London: Stanford, 1864.

KLEENE, S. C. *Introduction to Metamathematics.* Amsterdam and New York: Van Nostrand Reinhold, 1952.

————. "Recursive predicates and quantifiers." *Transactions of the American Mathematical Society*, vol. 53 (1943), pp. 41–73.

KURATOWSKI, Casimir. "Sur la notion de l'ordre dans la théorie des ensembles." *Fundamenta Mathematicae*, vol. 2 (1921), pp. 161–171.

LEWIS, C. I. *A Survey of Symbolic Logic.* Berkeley: University of California, 1918.

LÖWENHEIM, Leopold. "Über Möglichkeiten im Relativkalkül." *Mathematische Annalen*, vol. 76 (1915), pp. 447–470. Translation in van Heijenoort.

ŁUKASIEWICZ, Jan. "O logice trójwartościowej" (On three-valued logic). *Ruch Filozoficzny*, vol. 5 (1920), pp. 169–171.

————. "Uwagi o aksyomacie Nicod'a i o dedukcyi uogólniajacej" (Remarks on Nicod's axiom and on generalizing by deduction). *Ksiega Pamiatkowa Polskiego Towarzystwa Filozoficznego we Lwowie*, Lwów, 1931.

————. "Zur Geschichte der Aussagenlogik." *Erkenntnis*, vol. 5 (1935–6), pp. 111–131.

NEUMANN, J. von. "Eine Axiomatisierung der Mengenlehre." *Journal für reine und angewandte Mathematik*, vol. 154 (1925), pp. 219–240. Correction in vol. 155, p. 128.

NICOD, Jean. "A reduction in the number of primitive propositions of logic." *Proceedings* of the Cambridge Philosophical Society, vol. 19 (1917–20), pp. 32–44.

PEANO, Giuseppe. *Arithmetices Principia.* Turin, 1889.

————. *Formulaire de Mathématiques.* Introduction, 1894; vol. 1, 1895; vol. 2, 1897–99. Turin. Vol. 3, 1901, Paris. Vol. 4, 1902–3; vol. 5 (s.v. *Formulario Matematico*), 1905–8. Turin: Bocca.

PEIRCE, C. S. *Collected Papers.* 6 vols. Cambridge, Mass.: Harvard, 1931–35.

POST, E. L. "Introduction to a general theory of elementary propositions."

American Journal of Mathematics, vol. 43 (1921), pp. 163–185. Reprinted in van Heijenoort.

PRESBURGER, M. "Über die Vollständigkeit eines gewissen Systems der Arithmetik." *Sprawozdanie* z I Kongresu Matematyków Krajów Slowánskych (Warsaw, 1930), pp. 92–101, 395.

QUINE, W. V. *Mathematical Logic*. New York, 1940. 2d printing, Cambridge, Mass.: Harvard, 1947. Revised edition, 1951.

——. *Elementary Logic*. Boston, 1941. Revised edition, Cambridge: Harvard, 1966.

——. *From a Logical Point of View*. Cambridge: Harvard, 1953.

——. *Set Theory and Its Logic*. Cambridge: Harvard, 1963, 1969.

——. *Selected Logic Papers*. New York: Random House, 1966.

——. "New foundations for mathematical logic." *American Mathematical Monthly*, vol. 44 (1937), pp. 70–80. Reprinted in *From a Logical Point of View*.

ROGERS, Hartley, Jr. *Theory of Recursive Functions and Effective Computability*. New York: McGraw-Hill, 1967.

RUSSELL, Bertrand. *The Principles of Mathematics*. Cambridge, England, 1903. 2d edition, New York, 1938.

——. "On denoting." *Mind*, vol. 14 (1905), pp. 479–493. Reprinted in Feigl and Sellars.

——. "Mathematical logic as based on the theory of types." *American Journal of Mathematics*, vol. 30 (1908), pp. 222–262.

——. "Knowledge by acquaintance and knowledge by description." *Proceedings* of the Aristotelian Society, vol. 11 (1911), pp. 108–128. Reprinted in *The Problems of Philosophy*, London: Williams and Norgate, and New York: Holt, 1912 and in *Mysticism and Logic*, New York: Longmans, 1918.

SAMSON, E. W., and B. E. Mills. "Circuit minimization: algebra and algorithms for new Boolean canonical expressions." *ARCRC Technical Report* 21, 1954.

SCHRÖDER, Ernst. *Der Operationskreis des Logikkalküls*. Leipzig: Teubner, 1877 (37 pp.).

——. *Vorlesungen über die Algebra der Logik*. Vol. 1, 1890; vol. 2, 1891–1905; vol. 3, 1895. Leipzig: Teubner.

SHANNON, Claude E. "A symbolic analysis of relay and switching circuits." *Transactions* of the American Institute of Electrical Engineers, vol. 57 (1938), pp. 713–723.

SHEFFER, H. M. "A set of five independent postulates for Boolean algebras." *Transactions* of the American Mathematical Society, vol. 14 (1913), pp. 481–488.

SHOENFIELD, Joseph R. *Mathematical Logic*. Reading, Mass.: Addison-Wesley, 1967.

SKOLEM, Thoralf. "Logisch-kombinatorische Untersuchungen über die Erfüllbarkeit oder Beweisbarkeit mathematischer Sätze." *Skrifter* utgitt av Det Norske Videnskaps-Akademi i Oslo, I. Mat.-naturv. Kl. 1920, no. 4. Translation in van Heijenoort.

————. "Über die mathematische Logik." *Norsk Matematisk Tidsskrift*, vol. 10 (1928), pp. 125–142. Translation in van Heijenoort.

————. "Über einige Satzfunktionen in der Arithmetik." *Skrifter* utgitt av Det Norske Videnskaps-Akademi i Oslo, I. Mat.-naturv. Kl. 1930, no. 7.

SMULLYAN, Raymond M. *Theory of Formal Systems*. Princeton: University, 1961.

TARSKI, Alfred. *Introduction to Logic*. New York: Oxford, 1941.

————. *A Decision Method for Elementary Algebra and Geometry*. Santa Monica: Rand, 1948. Revised edition, Berkeley: University of California, 1951.

————. *Logic, Semantics, Metamathematics*. Oxford: Clarendon Press, 1956.

————. "Remarques sur les notions fondamentales de la méthodologie des mathématiques." *Rocznik* Polskiego Towarzystwa Matematycznego, vol. 7 (1929), pp. 270–272.

————, A. Mostowski, and R. M. Robinson. *Undecidable Theories*. Amsterdam: North-Holland, 1953.

TRACHTENBROT, B. A. "Impossibility of an algorithm for the decision problem in finite classes" (Russian). *Doklady* Akademii Nauk SSSR, vol. 70 (1950), pp. 569–572. Reviewed in *Journal of Symbolic Logic*, vol. 15 (1950), p. 229.

TURING, Alan M. "On computable numbers, with an application to the Entscheidungsproblem." *Journal* of the London Mathematical Society, vol. 42 (1936–37), pp. 230–265. Correction in vol. 43, pp. 544–546.

VAN HEIJENOORT, Jean, editor. *From Frege to Gödel: a Source Book in Mathematical Logic*. Cambridge: Harvard, 1967.

VENN, John. *Symbolic Logic*. London: Macmillan, 1881. 2d edition, 1894.

————. "On the diagrammatic and mechanical representations of propositions and reasoning." *The London, Edinburgh, and Dublin Philosophical Magazine and Journal of Science*, vol. 10 (1880), pp. 1–18.

VON NEUMANN, see Neumann.

WHITEHEAD, A. N., and B. Russell. *Principia Mathematica*, vol. 1, 1910; vol. 2, 1912; vol. 3, 1913. Cambridge: University. 2d edition, 1925–27.

WIENER, Norbert. "A simplification of the logic of relations." *Proceedings* of the Cambridge Philosophical Society, vol. 17 (1912–14), pp. 387–390. Reprinted in van Heijenoort.

WITTGENSTEIN, Ludwig. *Tractatus Logico-Philosophicus*. London: Kegan Paul, 1922. Reprint of "Logisch-philosophische Abhandlung" (*Annalen der Naturphilosophie*, 1921) with English translation in parallel.

ZERMELO, Ernst. "Untersuchungen über die Grundlagen der Mengenlehre." *Mathematische Annalen*, vol. 65 (1908), pp. 261–281. Translated in van Heijenoort.

INDEX